P9-EDM-156

Visions *of* Service

Visions *of* Service

An introduction to five of the world's great religions,
with excerpts from the sacred writings
and questions for study and reflection
for those engaged in service

CONTRIBUTORS

John Butt
Elliot N. Dorff
Carool Kersten
Kalyan Ray
David Kwang-sun Suh

EDITOR

Linda A. Chisholm

The International Partnership for Service-Learning and Leadership
New York

The International Partnership for Service-Learning
and Leadership
815 Second Avenue, Suite 315
New York, NY 10017 U.S.A.

© 2004 by The International Partnership
for Service-Learning and Leadership
All rights reserved. Published 2004
Printed in the United States of America

ISBN 0-9701984-5-0
Library of Congress Control Number: 2004109904

This book is printed on acid-free paper.

HOWARD A. BERRY

1932–2002

sometimes skeptic, sometimes believer,
ever attentive to the needs of others

Contents

Preface

The shelves of libraries and bookstores around the globe hold hundreds — indeed, thousands — of books about religion. Many are written by world-renowned scholars of religion, theology, philosophy, history, and — especially today — political science. Why another?

Visions of Service focuses exclusively on the way five great religions of the world — Hinduism, Buddhism, Judaism, Christianity, and Islam — understand and promote the concept of serving others, especially those in need. It addresses specifically what these religions have to say to their adherents and to us all about social responsibility, about organizing to meet needs, about the treatment of strangers, and about the motivations and rewards of caring and then acting to alleviate suffering and tackle social problems.

Moreover, *Visions of Service* is designed for those who are not only studying religion from the standpoint of service, but are simultaneously actively engaged in serving. In education, we call this "service-learning." The pedagogy of service-learning unites formal academic study (usually for academic credit) with volunteer community service in such a way that the one reinforces the other. The mission statement of the International Partnership for Service-Learning and Leadership puts it this way: "The service makes the study immediate, applicable, and relevant; the study, in turn, informs the service."

All over the world, colleges and universities are adopting this form of education. Students and teachers are finding that when learning is connected to a service experience in which the students are actively involved and about which they care, the learning is deeper and lasts longer. In service-learning, they test classroom-learned theory against practice, and do so in a specific cultural context. Whether the service takes place in the local community or in a nation other than the students' own, they are learning to work with people usually very different from themselves. When young and healthy students assist the elderly or the ill; when they teach literacy; when they help set up microbusinesses with those who are impoverished and jobless, they are entering a new culture and learning to work cooperatively with its people.

Students have found that as they apply their intelligence, knowledge, energy, talent, and goodwill to address social and human needs, and as they learn not just from the classroom but from those with whom they work and serve, they must reexamine their own values and beliefs. The combination of service and learning stimulates them to think about the age-old questions of the student: What is the meaning of life, and the purpose of my life in particular? What am I called to do? Wherein will lie my satisfaction?

Of the many academic disciplines that are being linked to service, none raises these issues more profoundly than does religion.

Visions of Service, then, is not only a book about religions and their call to serve, but also a guide for applying the questions, tenets, and beliefs of religion to the experience of service in which a student is engaged.

The book begins with introductory essays by scholars of religion. Each writer has taught religion at an institution of higher education. These essays, focused as they are on the call to serve, may be supplemented by lectures and additional readings. (A list of suggested readings concludes the book.)

After the initial essays, there is a selection of what we have called the "sacred writings" from that religion — passages from

scripture, beloved stories and sayings, poetry, and speeches —
that focus on the call to serve others.

Following these sacred writings are questions for the
student to consider. You will note that these questions point
in two directions, one to the academic study of the religion,
the other to the experience of service.

The book arose from a service-learning program sponsored by the Henry Luce Foundation and designed and
managed by the International Partnership for Service-Learning
and Leadership. Bringing together students from across Asia
and the United States, the program is hosted by Trinity College
of Quezon City in the Philippines. Each student is assigned to
a not-for-profit service agency and spends twenty hours a week
for the duration of the program rendering service to those in
need in Manila. During their time together, the students take
two academic courses. The first is "Contemporary Social Issues
of the Philippines," which helps them understand the problems
that their service agency seeks to address. The second course
is "Major Asian Religions: Theologies of Service."

Over the years, we have found that for these students from
China (including Hong Kong and Tibet), East Timor, India,
Indonesia, Japan, Korea, the Philippines, Taiwan, Thailand,
Vietnam, and the United States, the course on religion is eye-
opening. They come not only from different religions and
nations, but from diverse socioeconomic backgrounds and
from both highly-selective and open-admissions colleges and
universities. But most of them, regardless of background, know
little about the religious beliefs and traditions of their own
countries and much less about others. Many puzzle about why
religion has been such a powerful force in history, and why it
is the cause of division and strife today.

Through the combination of service and learning, and in the hands of skilled teachers of Hinduism, Islam, Christianity, and Buddhism, they learn that, for adherents, religion is active and living, the ideal expression of a particular social and political philosophy and practice. Through service-learning, they learn about these religions not only in an abstract, theoretical, and intellectual way, but also on a personal and emotional level as they experience a transformation in themselves as a result of their service. They discover why serving others is a crucial element of these five religions.

The now almost two hundred students who have participated in this program have expressed gratitude and wonder at what they have learned. They declare that this course on religion, combined as it is with a substantive experience of volunteer service, has been one of the most enlightening educational experiences of their lives.

Wishing to extend the benefits to other students in colleges and universities around the world, The International Partnership for Service-Learning and Leadership offers *Visions of Service* as a means for learning about these five great religions of the world. When combined with service, students will discover the demands, challenges, joys, and satisfaction of service—and of learning through service.

Our world knows only too well that religion can be divisive. Religious differences are real. Still, there are commonalities, and service is primary among them. While we may not agree on issues of theology, we can recognize, appreciate, and celebrate this common calling. We can serve side by side with those whose religious loyalty and convictions differ from our own. Service can be a source of connection and understanding in a divided and angry world. May this book, and the study and service that accompany it, be so for you and your students, and may they, through their informed service, extend the benefits to others.

LINDA A. CHISHOLM
Editor

The International Partnership for Service-Learning and Leadership

Acknowledgments

We, of The International Partnership for Service-Learning and Leadership, are grateful to:

- the Henry Luce Foundation, Inc., for supporting the service-learning program which inspired this book, and then for supporting its writing, production and distribution.

- the scholars and writers John Butt, Elliot Dorff, Carool Kersten, Kalyan Ray, and David Kwang-sun Suh. Special note should be made of Kalyan Ray, the director of the India program of The International Partnership for Service-Learning and Leadership, who is a master of the pedagogy of service-learning. Each semester for a decade and more, he has mesmerized and enlightened his students by weaving the finest of scholarship in the origins, evolution, and beliefs of Hinduism with the students' reflections on their service experience, thereby demonstrating to and for them the Hindu process of self-realization.

- the president, teachers, and staff of Trinity College of Quezon City, Philippines, especially Dr. Deana Aquino and Dr. Cesar Orsal, the directors of the service-learning program that gave rise to this book; and to the staff and people of the service agencies of Manila who so hospitably receive and effectively guide the students in service.

🙢 Elizabeth Koenig, a professor at the General Theo-
logical Seminary in New York; Rabbi Leonard
Schoolman of the Center for Religious Inquiry at St.
Bartholomew's Church in New York; and the Rev. Dr.
Richard Wood, the president of the United Board for
Christian Higher Education in Asia for initial advice.

🙢 the director of publications, Kate Chisholm, for the
book and cover design, her careful editing, and for
managing the production of the book; also, to Kate
Egan Norris for copyediting, and to Barbara Wanasek,
who ensures distribution of books from the IPSL Press.

HINDUISM

Kalyan Ray

HINDUISM IN INDIA: ARYAN AND DRAVIDIAN

Like all religions and cultures, Hinduism evolved amid cultural and historical forces and continues to evolve today. It is important to emphasize the evolutionary nature of Hinduism at the very outset.

The history of Hinduism begins with the Aryans, a nomadic people from Central Asia whose life was dependent on the forces and vagaries of nature and whose prayers were often directed at the forces of nature.[1]

There is a generally accepted hypothesis that there were several waves of migration by the Aryans in different directions starting around the beginning of the second millennium B.C.E. The paleo-historian D. D. Kosambi speculates that the migrations could have been the result of prolonged droughts.[2]

No matter what caused the migrations, the Aryans reached India through the Himalayan mountain passes and came to the great western riverine stretches since named the Indus Valley. They found an older and declining civilization at the center of which lay vast and beautifully ordered cities such as Mohenjo Daro and Harappa, which were the demesne of the ancient Dravidian people. There are early Vedic hymns about the god Indra destroying the demon Vritra and releasing the waters. Scholars have speculated that these hymns may have originated in actual events during which roving Aryans captured and destroyed dams constructed by the Dravidians.

It is important to note that the Dravidian civilization in the Indus Valley was quite advanced. The numerous and beautifully crafted seals found there clearly have great significance, but they have not yet been deciphered by scholars. Nonetheless, the Bronze Age archaeological sites of these cities, with their geometric grid of wide streets laid out to facilitate ventilation as well as the elaborate water-supply system, suggest an advanced civilization. Their social and economic organization must have been quite complex to support what had clearly been impressive urban population centers. The architecture was calculated to produce comfort; some of the houses of the affluent "have walls seven feet thick, of well-burnt brick, which means that the houses rose to several stories."[3] It is also a curious archaeological find that the weaponry was inexplicably undeveloped. "The weapons found at Mohenjo-daro are weak as compared with the excellent tools. The spears are thin, without a rib; the spearhead would have crumpled at the first good thrust. There are no swords at all. The sturdy knives and celts are tools, not weapons."[4] The Aryans, it seems, came, saw, and conquered what was left of the Indus Valley civilization which, according to historians, was already in decline.

HOW ARYAN IS HINDUISM?

It has been the assumption of most Indians that the main elements of Hinduism as it is practiced today come from the Aryan heritage. They are about half right, at best. The influence of the ancient Dravidians upon what evolved into the recognizable aspects of Hinduism has been studied from a primarily linguistic point of view by one of India's most respected scholars, Professor Suniti Kumar Chatterii. His conclusions are startling: "The syntax of the later Indo-Aryan dialects agrees more with that of the Dravidian languages than with that of Vedic and of the extra-Indian Indo-European languages."[5]

The method of counting in ancient India is also not Aryan, but distinctly Dravidian. Many socioreligious practices such as the use of betelnut and coconut in Hindu religious ceremonies are also distinctly Dravidian. Even the Aryan form of ritual worship, the *homa*, is a rare occurrence today, for it calls for enormous and elaborate preparation and is essentially

4

a fire sacrifice with burnt offerings, the pouring of libation, and ritual hymnal chants. On the other hand, the most common form of worship in everyday Hinduism is derived from Dravidian tradition. It is the daily practice of most Hindus to sit at home in front of their private shrines, which include pictures of one or various favorite deities, a stone lingam of Shiva, and perhaps some pictures or mementos of dead ancestors off on one side. (The ancestors, though treated with affectionate respect, are never regarded as divine.) The rituals involve whispered prayers, offerings of water (usually Ganges water) in minute quantities (which become, in the process, holy water drunk or daubed on the head or forehead), and offerings of flowers and petals or sacred leaves such as those of the wood apple tree, wild basil, or tender grass stalks. Occasionally, sweets or small breads are also offered to the gods. When the worship is over, these sweets are distributed to children and other members of the household and also given to wild birds and other creatures. The rituals at most temples also follow this basic pattern. Often oil lights in decorative holders are held and waved gently before the deities in the shrine in a ritual of adoration. This practice, called *puja*, which is so commonly observed in most traditional Hindu households, is not an Aryan practice at all, Suniti Kumar Chatterii points out, but pre-Aryan. Scholars have pointed out that even the word "*puja*" is Dravidian, not Aryan, in origin.

According to anthropologists, the Indian population is a mixture of different peoples, among whom are the Negritos; the Proto-Australoid; the Paleo and Tibeto-Mongoloid; the Mediterranean; the western Brachycephals, consisting of the Alpinoid, the Dinaric, and the Armenoid; and others. Of all these, the Negritos survive today in India in very small tribal populations only in the Andaman Islands, near Travancore, in South India, and near the Rajmahal Hills in the northeast.[6]

All of these pre-Aryan groups have left their mark on the prevalent religion, which came to be called Hinduism as it evolved in India, and on Indian life in general. Scholars of linguistics trace a wealth of word roots (and therefore concepts) to all these different population groups. For instance, Sylvain Levi has pointed out that the word "*tabuva*," which occurs in the *Atharva Veda*, was related to the Polynesian "*tabu*."[7] Such Proto-Australoid derivatives through their migratory history are quite numerous. There are, for instance, remarkable similarities between the cosmogony of the Polynesians and the striking *Nasadiya* hymn in the *Rig Veda*, which will be discussed later. The Austric names for the phases of the moon may be seen in Sanskrit; these names have played an important role in the timing of important Hindu religious rituals as they evolved after the Aryans came to India. One constellation, the "*Matrika*" in Sanskrit—the Pleiades—is called *Matariki* in contemporary Polynesia; the configuration of constellations by which directions could be told were important to the pre-Aryan peoples who were formidable nomads over the ocean and have left their mark on Hindu theogony.

But that is not all: the very important Hindu idea of rebirth and re-death, from which comes the fundamental philosophical concern with karma in Hindu theology, seems to have come from the pre-Aryan Austric Proto-Australoid tribals of India. The idea of *avataras* is one without which the basis of the Hindu sacred Puranas could not have been formed. The idea of the universe born of an egg (the *Brahmanda*), the divine incarnation as tortoise, or the mythic ancestral princess who smells of fish are only a few of the important aspects of theological and cultural osmosis through which Hinduism was nourished by just one of the constituent pre-Aryan population groups that coexist now as part of the Hindu population of India. Hinduism drew upon many such early mytho-cultural sources. Even the use of the block of stone as a symbol of divinity is Austric in origin. Everywhere in India, in busy city streets, or in the remote villages, one may see such stones daubed with vermilion and sandalwood paste under ficus trees. Indeed, even the commonplace reverence for the flourishing tropical ficus tree is an Austric pre-Aryan tribal gift to the Hindu religious heritage.

It is important to understand how much of the supposedly Aryan heritage is really non-Aryan or, more accurately, pre-Aryan, and how important a position this has in the Hindu theological hinterland. The very word "Ganga" (Ganges is the hellenized version), the name of the holiest river of Hindu India, is of pre-Aryan tribal origin, and it appears to have simply meant "river," as in its modern Bengali equivalent "*gang*," meaning "river, channel." Original Austric speakers form the substratum in Burma, Indo-China, and South China also, and the Indian "Ganga" and "*gang*," the Indo-Chinese *Khong* (as in *Me-Khong*) and the South Chinese *Kiang* <*Kang*<*Ghang* (as in Yang-tsze-Kiang and a dozen other river names) are derived from the same ancient Austric root word.

In short, all the different constituent population groups enriched the religious content of what came to be Hinduism. Like all vital religions, it is hybrid, and continues to grow even today. Indeed, it could be said that Hinduism has undergone some very major changes in the last five centuries, as will be explained in the later segments of this chapter.

THE ANCIENT TEXTS: VEDAS AND UPANISHADS

The earliest of the Hindu theological texts, the Vedas and later the Upanishads, were not written down. That activity came many centuries later. There are over ten thousand verses in the *Rig Veda*. Though they are full of a dazzling array of metaphors and imagery of life such as farming, traveling through varied landscapes, and hymns celebrating *Vac* (Speech) and human understanding, there is no mention of the activity of writing. The Vedas, the oldest of the theological texts, are called *sruti*, which means "that which has been heard." It is tantalizingly left unclear whether the significance of the word *sruti* lies in the fact that it was "heard" as part of the first oral tradition or whether, connotatively, it is something heard within us when, seeking wisdom, we reach inner enlightenment and eternal truths are revealed within us. These truths are not the personal provenance or discovery of any particular seer or seers but the common heritage of humankind that is at once contemporary and everlasting.

Later sacred texts such as the epics *Ramayana* and *Mahabharata*, the early Puranas, certain verses dealing with law and society such as the *Dharma Sutra*, came to be known as *Smriti* or the "Remembered" texts. The sacred texts of the Vedas were transmitted from generation to generation with meticulous care in matters of pronunciation, down to the last careful inflection. The integrity of the complete texts was of paramount importance.

The Vedas are liturgical and filled with theological significance. They were not meant simply to be read — certainly not to be pored over in silent libraries. The Vedas were meant to be chanted or sung. The musical structure is lost to us. We do not know what instruments were used for accompaniment. We have only the literary text, much of which is metaphoric and poetic. It is as if we were groping to understand the beauty, the suggestive reach, the imaginative impact of opera from the libretti alone or the grandeur of Gregorian chant from merely the text. The poetic form, the liturgical purpose, and the elaborately ritualistic aspects of its language are keys to understanding the grand purpose of the Vedas. In its aural unfolding, the Vedic intent was to replicate divine revelation to the human mind. But it is also important to note that the point of view is, for the most part, human: questioning, awestruck, respectful, but unmistakably human, whether it praises Speech or wonders about Creation. It is not simply a detached, narrative voice. Nor is it the imperative voice of God. It is a human voice that dares to speculate about the possibility of a Creator of the present creator, or pleads with Death to go away, or prays for safe birth or clement weather. Even the chorus of frogs that signal the coming of the life-giving monsoons finds a place among the verses of the *Rig Veda*. The sweet joys of life and human companionship are celebrated. Some of these hymns have a simplicity and directness that touch us all:

> Let me not go to the house of clay... not yet. Have mercy, great ruler; be merciful.

> If I seem to stumble... O master of stones, have mercy; great ruler, be merciful.

> If through weakness of willpower I have somehow gone against the true current, O pure one, have mercy; great ruler, be merciful.[8]

Sruti, the most ancient of the Hindu scriptures, are the four Vedas. They are *Samhitas*, i.e., anthologies of constituent works. The most important Veda is the *Samhita* known as the *Rig Veda*, a compendium of 1,028 hymns and poems. A second Veda, the *Sama*, has little separate status; except for about one hundred stanzas, this Veda is a virtual repetition of works that appear first in the *Rig*. These are works that were meant to be chanted, and thus the *Sama Veda* has also been called the Book of Chants. The *Yajur Veda*, too, derives a large portion of its text from the

Rig Veda, but also has numerous original prose sections. The texts of the *Sama Veda* and those of the *Yajur Veda* were largely used for inclusion and recital, respectively, in the Soma libation rituals and in sacrificial rites to various deities. The *Atharva Veda*, the last of the four Vedic *Samhitas*, does not generally address itself to what may be called the higher gods, as the *Rig Veda* does, but is primarily concerned with incantations, magic, and preternatural areas, drawing on substrata of folk culture and superstition. Nonetheless, there are some poems of great beauty in the *Atharva Veda*, which does not otherwise have the religious gravitas of the first three Vedic *Samhitas*.

Some parts of the Vedic literature are appendages to the four Vedic *Samhitas*. They are the *Brahmanas* and the *Aranyakas*. As opposed to the Vedas, which are primarily written in verse, the *Brahmanas* are works of prose and focus on the intricate details of the rituals surrounding the sacrificial act. These rituals in the *Brahmanas* are complex and elaborate, and had apparently become a primary focus of Indo-Aryan society at the time. The tone in the *Brahmana* texts is dogmatic. The rituals, though described with vivid symbolism, are so complicated that historians have speculated that these may indicate the period when a specialized and distinct class of priestly Brahmins was beginning to form. These Brahmins are not to be confused with *Brahman* (God) or the *Brahmanas* (a constituent text of the Vedas). There is little by way of philosophic contemplation or speculation here, only a plenitude of rituals.

It is in the *Aranyakas,* or the Forest Treatises, however, that we note a flowering of the philosophic mind. The word "Áranyaka" comes from the ancient word "*aranya,*" or forest. The elders in society apparently withdrew into the forest to spend their last years in simple rusticity and contemplation; this was a move away from elaborate rituals, which are the staple of the *Brahmanas*. Instead of the horse sacrifice, for example, there was meditation centered upon the idea of dawn as a horse whose eye is the sun and whose life force is the air. It can safely be suggested that the *Aranyakas* lead directly to the philosophic path of the Upanishads.

Some religions claim to have immemorial pasts; there are those which are founded by historical figures like Gautama Buddha, Mahavira, or Muhammad, who can be placed in a specific period of history. Hinduism is a notable exception. For one thing, Hindu mythology claims that there are four ages, or "*Yugas*": the *Satya*, the *Treta*, the *Dwapar*, and the present one, the *Kali Yuga*. In each, there is a divine incarnation born in what corresponds loosely to the Golden Age and the gradual deterioration of humankind to the present age.

Many religions start with the narration of creation. The *Rig Veda* speculates about creation but it does not narrate. In this earliest of the Hindu texts, there is an unmistakable human voice questioning the ontology of the universe. This text, the *Nasadiya Sutra* in the *Rig Veda*, is very moving, for the voice is not divine or imperially declarative. It is a human voice, which marvels in the fact of creation, and dares to speculate even about the Creator. But sonorous poetry apart, this is a keen and skeptical mind, which considers possibilities ("perhaps it formed itself, or perhaps it did not") and ends fittingly in a speculation that is firmly based on the human art of enquiry:

> There was neither non-existence nor existence then; there was neither the realm of space nor the sky which is beyond. What stirred? Where? In whose protection? Was there water, bottomlessly deep?...

> There was neither death nor immortality. No boundaries lay between night or day...Darkness was hidden by darkness in the beginning...

Sages, seeking within, with wisdom found the bond
of existence in non-existence...

Who really knows? Who will here proclaim it?
Whence was it produced? Whence is this creation?
The gods came afterwards, with the creation of this
universe. Who then knows whence it has arisen?

Whence this creation has arisen—perhaps it formed
itself, or perhaps it did not—the one who looks down
on it, in the highest heaven, only He knows—or
perhaps He does not know.[9]

Is Hinduism, then, a religion that shuns philosophical
closure? It may be countered that philosophy itself discourages
closure. The Hindu philosophers end up emphasizing the
multiplicity, the inevitable plurality of views. At its best,
Hinduism emerges more as a way of seeing than as a set of
tenets, more a temper of mind than orthopraxy.

The Upanishads are the last part, the conclusion of the
Vedas, the most ancient of the Hindu religious texts. They are
thus called "Vedanta" ("*anta*" means "end"). Max Müller, the
eminent German indologist, has suggested that the word
"Upanishad" is derived from the constituent words "*upa*"
("near"), "*ni*" ("down") and "*sad*" ("to sit"); the scene evoked
is that of a disciple sitting down at the foot of the teacher,
perhaps in a hermitage (a *tapovan*, the woods of contemplation)
where he, or she, as in the case of several Upanishads, learns
sacred wisdom from the masters. From the constituent word
"*shad*" in "Upanishad," a number of Sanskrit scholars have
suggested a derivation which means "secret knowledge."

There is one important difference in direction between the
Rig Veda, the earliest of the ancient Hindu texts, and the
Upanishads. There is no insistence on the elaborate ritual and
ceremonies which are held to be so important in the earlier

Vedas. For instance, as previously noted, there are certain significant changes in the attitude toward ritual horse sacrifice that may be seen between *Rig Veda* and the *Brihadaranyaka Upanishad*. Instead of the actual sacrifice insisted upon by the *Rig Veda*, the *Brihadaranyaka* pictures the visible universe as a cosmic horse; we observe the move from the denotative and ritualistic to the symbolic and imaginative. From actual ritual sacrifice, there is a shift to the contemplation of the universe as a symbolic sacrificial horse:

> Dawn verily is the head of the sacrificial horse. The sun is his eye, the wind, his breath; the universal sacrificial fire, his open mouth; the year is the body of the sacrificial horse. The sky is his back; the atmosphere, his belly; the earth, his underbelly; the directions, his flanks.[10]

It is not that the *Rig Veda* does not see the implications of the ritual connectiveness of the horse sacrifice and the *rta* (the order) of the cosmos. The significance in the Upanishads is that the thought of the connection has become more important than the enactment of the connective ritual. The Upanishads, to put it in literary terms, achieve the metaphor. The activity of meditative thought replaces ritual action; the direction of religion at this stage of growth in Hinduism is interior.

Some of the most important ideas of Hinduism were developing when the earliest Upanishads were composed. It was a philosophical and theological watershed.

An important idea which was emerging, not from an external influence but from within the emerging Upanishadic texts of this early period, was that there is a perpetual, unchanging, and connective reality that underlies all of the cosmos. This connects the *Atman*, which is the quintessence of the human mind, to all of perceived and apprehended reality

13

and reaches in an unbroken connection to the idea of God, which is called *Brahman*.

In the *Rig Veda*, as in Parmenides or Plato in later Greece, there had been an apprehension of a single glorious deity. In the Vedas, there had been attempts to understand and name that deity: *Prajapati, Purusa, Visvakarman,* and *Brahman*. In the Upanishads we find dialogues and anecdotes that have a simplicity of narrative akin to folktales, which set forth without unnecessary obfuscation the nature of *Brahman* and the nature of *Atman*, the individual soul, and what connects them.

The *Brahman* is far beyond the simple conception of a nature god. *Brahman* is immeasurably beyond any such god or even Indra, who is the Zeus-like presiding deity over the gods, representing fire, water, or wind. The *Kena Upanishad* states simply and directly that *Agni* (fire) burns, *Vayu* (wind) blows, and so on, simply because all the gods and human apprehension depend entirely upon and merely work through *Brahman*:

> Who is the Spirit behind the eye and the ear? It is the ear of the ear, the eye of the eye, and the Word of words, the mind of minds, and the life of life. Those who follow wisdom pass beyond and, on leaving this world, become immortal.
>
> There the eye goes not, nor words, nor mind. We know not, we cannot understand, how He can be explained: He is above the known and He is above the unknown. Thus have we heard from the ancient sages who explained this truth to us.
>
> What cannot be spoken with words, but that whereby words are spoken: Know that alone to be Brahman, the Spirit; and not what people here adore.[11]

The *Brihadaranyaka Upanishad* goes further along these lines to emphasize the real source of our own senses (eyes, actions, apprehension) to *Atman*, which is held within and is a part of *Brahman*:

> This universe is a trinity and this is made of name, form, and action.
>
> The source of all names is the word, for it is by the word that all names are spoken. The word is behind all names, even as Brahman is behind the word.
>
> The source of all forms is the eye, for it is by the eye that all forms are seen. The eye is behind all forms, even as Brahman is behind the eye.
>
> The source of all actions is the body, for it is by the body that all actions are done. The body is behind all actions, even as Brahman is behind the body.
>
> Those three are one, Atman, the Spirit of life; and Atman, although one, is those three.
>
> The immortal is veiled by the real. The Spirit of life is the immortal. Name and form are the real, and by them the Spirit is veiled.[12]

How then may we lift the veil, given the problem that the *Brahman* lies beyond the possible reach of human description? In the same Upanishad we come across a prayer for just such an internal journey:

> From delusion lead me into Truth
> From darkness lead me into Light
> From death lead me towards immortality.[13]

The problem of understanding, let alone defining, the *Brahman* remains formidable. The sage Yajnavalkya uses the *neti neti* method: "He is not this, nor is He that. He is inconceivable for He cannot be conceived; unchangeable, for he does not change; untouched, for nothing touches Him."[14] In the same negative *neti neti* method, He is also described as *asat*—nonbeing—for He is not to be apprehended in the manner in which beings are understood and realized. Yet He alone is supremely real, because the universe is sustained through and by Him. It is from these seeds that Hindu ideas of *maya* and *samsara* were to grow.

What, then, can be the relationship between Him, the supremely real, and us who are mortal, limited, and seem apparently unconnected and unconnectable to the Supreme? In his *History of Indian Philosophy*, S. N. Dasgupta puts it simply: "We ourselves are but he, and yet we know not what he is. Whatever we can experience, whatever we can express is limited but he is the unlimited, the basis of all."[15] *Katha Upanishad* says that He is "that which is inaudible, intangible, invisible, indestructible, which cannot be tasted, nor smelt eternal, without beginning or end, greater than the great, the fixed."[16]

Because space, time, and causality emanate from Him, He cannot be explained by empiricism. He is infinite and is also in the smallest of matter, and therefore no description of him is possible except (*neti neti* again) by the denial of all attributes in the empirical cosmos. When Bahva, the great teacher, was asked by a disciple to explain the nature of *Brahman*, he kept silent. Urged to answer several times, he finally spoke, "I teach you indeed, but you do not understand: He is silence."[17]

The *Isa Upanishad*, one of the pithiest of the early Upanishads and one of Gandhi's favorites, thus describes the relationship between the individual human seeking knowledge of the *Brahman* and the path of proper action:

> Behold the Universe in the glory of God: and all that lives and moves on earth. Leaving the transient, find joy in the Eternal: set not your heart on another's possession...
>
> He moves and he moves not. He is far, and He is near. He is within all and He is outside all.
>
> The person who sees all beings in his own Self and his own Self in all beings loses all dread.
>
> When a wise man perceives this Unity and his Self has become all things, what mistake or misery can ever trouble him?
>
> Into deep darkness fall those who follow action. Into deeper darkness fall those who follow knowledge...
>
> One is the outcome of knowledge and the other is the outcome of action...
>
> Who knows *both knowledge and action*, with action overcomes death and with knowledge reaches immortality.[18] [Italics added.]

It is important to note the emphasis on *knowledge and action,* the combination of action and contemplation, of active service and contemplative learning. One without the other is meaningless, as the *Isa Upanishad* makes clear. The medieval Indian poet Devara Dasimayya put it succinctly in one of his *vacanas,* which lies directly within the Upanishadic tradition of wisdom:

Fire can burn
but cannot move.

Wind can move
but cannot burn.

Till fire joins wind
it cannot take a step.

Do men know
it's like that
with knowing and doing?[19]

The relationship between the *Brahman* and the *Atman*, between knowing and doing, between the Absolute and the mortal, provides the foundation upon which some of the most important discussions of Hindu philosophy are based. What indeed is the relationship between the Brahman and the Atman? The explanation in the *Chandogya Upanishad* has all the apparent simplicity of a folk story. It is the story of Svetaketu and his father Uddalaka, who, though a renowned teacher himself, has sent his twelve-year-old son away for twelve years to be educated away from home. The young man returned with a very high opinion of himself and his own learning. He father, seeing the pride in his son, asked him a question: "Have you asked for that knowledge whereby what is not heard is heard, what is not thought is thought, and what is not known is known?" It is interesting to note that the student himself was expected to elicit knowledge, initiating the process.

When Svetaketu asks his father the nature of that knowledge, Uddalaka tells him:

Bring me a fruit from this banyan tree.
Here it is father.
Break it.

It is broken, Sir.
What do you see in it?
Very small seeds, Sir.
Break one of them, my son.
It is broken, Sir.
What do you see in it?
Nothing at all, Sir.
Then his father spoke to him:
My son, from the very essence in
the seed which you cannot see comes
in truth this vast banyan tree.
Believe me my son, an invisible
and subtle essence is the Spirit of the
whole universe. That is Reality.
That is Atman. Thou art That.[20]

"*Tat Tvam Asi*"—"Thou (the individual soul, *Atman*) art That" (the divine *Brahman*). *Atman* is the soul, the essence of one's self. These words, repeated thrice by the father/teacher to his son/student in the *Chandogya* hold the essence of all the Upanishads. We are all connected to each other and to God. We are in essence related, intrinsically together, and what we do to others is what we, therefore, do unto ourselves and to God. Existence is Unity. Thou art That. This is the splendidly simple basis of *Advaita*—which means non-dualism in Hindu philosophy. The philosophic and social effect of this idea reverberates, as we will see later, throughout the later history of Hinduism and its reform movements.

The language that the *Chandogya Upanishad* uses should be particularly noted for its literary appropriateness and beauty. The explanatory images used elsewhere in the same Upanishad by Uddalaka are all organic and manifest around them in the sylvan surrounding of the *tapovan* the words of contemplation. As he continues to explain to his son the underlying unity and connectedness of *Atman* and *Brahman,* Uddalaka mentions how bees gather the various nectars into the one honey of the hive; all the rivers pour their waters into the one great ocean; all the parts of a great tree are unified within the life of that tree; thus all creatures in this organic metaphor are held by and within *Brahman*, the basis and lord of all existence.

> There is a light that shines beyond all things on earth, beyond us all, beyond the heavens, beyond the highest, the very highest heavens. This is the Light that shines in our heart.

> This is the Spirit that is in my heart, smaller than a grain of rice, or a grain of barley, or a grain of mustard-seed, or a grain of canary-seed, or the very kernel of a grain of canary-seed. This is the Spirit that is in my heart, greater than the earth, greater than the sky, greater than heaven itself, greater than all these worlds.

> He contains all works and desires and perfumes and all tastes. He enfolds the whole universe and in silence is loving to all. This is the Spirit that is in my heart, this is Brahman.[21]

This thread that runs through *Chandogya Upanishad* is also simply expressed in the *Katha Upanishad*, and indeed in all the important Upanishadic texts:

> There is one Ruler, the Spirit that is in all things, who transforms his own form into many. Only the wise who see him in their souls attain the joy eternal.

> He is the Eternal among things that pass away, pure Consciousness of conscious beings, the One who fulfills the prayers of many. Only the wise who see him in their souls attain the peace eternal.

"This is That" — thus they realize the ineffable joy supreme. How can "This" be known? Does He give light or does He reflect light?

There the sun shines not, nor the moon, nor the stars; lightnings shine not there and much less earthly fire. From His light all these give light, and His radiance illumines all creation...

The whole universe comes from Him and His life burns through the whole universe. In His power is the majesty of thunder. Those who know Him have found immortality...

Within the senses is the mind, and within mind is reason, its essence. Within reason is the Spirit in man, and within this is the Spirit of the universe, the evolver of all...[22]

A later Upanishad, the *Svetasvatara*, explains the pervasive divine presence even in the mundane world.

All this universe is in the glory of God, of Siva the god of love. The heads and faces of men are His own and He is in the hearts of all.[23]

From here, it is a short step to the assertion of Krishna in his theophany to Arjuna in the *Bhagavad Gita*, which is like an Upanishad interpolated into the epic *Mahabarata* and is a central text of later Hinduism—"*Jnani tva Atma eva me matam*" —"The Wise Man and I are One: I am the silence of mysteries, what men of knowledge know."[24]

SOME IMPORTANT CONCEPTS IN HINDU THEOLOGY

From the earliest Vedas through the Upanishads, the idea of free will in humans is implicit. As we have seen, the Vedas incorporate and encourage human inquiry. This places the responsibility squarely on the human, and the consequentiality of human thought and action forms one of the most important concepts of Hindu theology: karma. We are responsible not only for our actions but also for the thoughts that precede and follow them. These lead to our future actions and thoughts, and such a continuous braid forms our *jivan,* our life. The way we spend our days is the way we will have spent our lives. Our karma determines and consequentially forms us. It also affects our dharma.

The word "dharma" generally denotes religion. Hindus refer to their religion as the *"sanatan dharma,"* the ancient or traditional religion. But the significance of dharma is considerably more connotative than its most commonly interpreted meaning. The word "dharma" is derived from the Sanskrit root *"dhr,"* which means "that which holds together." Dharma holds society together; however, another important significance of the word "dharma" is "nature," as in "the nature of things," or "the nature of Man or individuals." For example, it may be said that the nature of wood is to float on water; about an individual it might be said that an individual has a generous or an angry nature. It is that which "holds" (*dhr*) a personality.

Yet a person's dharma is never as fixed as such a description might suggest. It describes the general personality, but a person's dharma is constantly affected by his karma. The two consistently interact and influence each other. A person who is by nature generous may do something mean (as which of us has not?), and that has an effect on her dharma. If that

22

person continues to act angrily or meanly, or deceitfully, it will likewise continue to affect her nature, and vice versa.

> According as a man acts and walks in the path of life, so he becomes. He that does good becomes good; he that does evil becomes evil. By pure actions he becomes pure; by evil actions he becomes evil.

> And they say in truth that a man is made of desire. As his desire is, so is his faith. As his faith is, so are his works. As his works are, so he becomes.[25]

So nothing is fixed: our karma continues to affect our essential dharma to the end of our days and, according to Hindus, beyond the limit of our lives.

The existence of our *Atman* does not, according to the Upanishads, cease with the end of our lives. The doctrine of rebirth, or reincarnation, is set forth in the same texts.

> Even as a heavy-laden cart moves on groaning, even so the cart of the human body, wherein lives the Spirit, moves on groaning when a man is giving up the breath of life.

> When the body falls into weakness on account of old age or disease, even as a mango-fruit, or the fruit of the holy fig-tree, is loosened from its stem, so the Spirit of man is loosened from the human body...

> And as when a king is going to depart, the nobles and officers, the charioteers and the heads of the village assemble around him, even so all the powers of life gather about the soul when a man is giving up the breath of life.

When the human soul falls into weakness and into seeming unconsciousness all the powers of life assemble around. The soul gathers these elements of life-fire and enters into the heart. And when the Spirit that lives in the eye has returned to his own source, then the soul knows no more forms...

Then at the point of the heart a light shines, and this light illumines the soul on its way afar. When departing, by the head, or by the eye or other parts of the body, life arises and follows the soul, and the powers of life follow life. The soul becomes conscious and enters into Consciousness. His wisdom and works take him by the hand, and the knowledge known of old.

Even as a caterpillar, when coming to the end of a blade of grass, reaches out to another blade of grass and draws itself over to it, in the same way the Soul, leaving the body... reaches out to another body and draws itself over to it.

And even as a worker in gold, taking an old ornament, moulds it...even so the Soul leaving the body...The Soul is Brahman, the Eternal.[26]

The Upanishads confront and deal with the poignant human question: "Why do we see in life that the wicked sometimes prosper without apparent retribution, and why do good people not seem to get their just reward in life?" The consequentiality and braiding of human action, thought, and nature, the interaction and interplay of individual dharma and karma determine the plight of the individual at the end of each incarnation and determine the new life into which it is born. No last-minute ritual act of contrition takes away from the entire sum of thought and act which the individual life has accrued.

According to the *Katha Upanishad*, the ones who have led truly virtuous lives are absorbed into the *Brahman*:

> He who has understanding, is careful and ever pure reaches the End of the journey from which he never returns. The one whose chariot is driven by reason, who watches and holds the views of his mind, reaches the End of the journey, the supreme everlasting spirit...
>
> As pure water raining on pure water becomes one and the same, so becomes, O Nachiketas, the soul of the sage who knows.[27]

The impure are born again, their individual "nature" predicated by the *karma-phal* (literally, the fruits of karma) into this imperfect world, called *samsara*, because they have followed the path of pleasure and not the path of joy. They have to pay, in this measure, for having been beguiled by falsity and illusion, known as *maya*.

There is an implicit point here: we have inherited our individual dharma at nativity from the karma of our previous births. Our own doing is our personal inheritance, so to speak. That is why twins may have different natures. At the same time, our circumstance and environment and, most important, our subsequent karma will continue to shape our dharma; any discussion of nature versus nurture in the context of Hindu theology must take that into account.

It is from this foundation that many of the other important ideas of Hinduism have evolved. The simple but revolutionary idea to emerge out of the Upanishads was that the human souls (*Atman*) are all connected to each other and ultimately to the divine (*Brahman*). The sociopolitical implications are profound. If we are all interconnected and ultimately linked to the divine, then there can be no cause for injustice or cruelty (in Sanskrit called *himsa*). It was this idea that produced the notion of *ahimsa* or nonviolence. In social terms, it lay at the root of vegetarianism. In religious derivatives of Hinduism, such as Jainism or monastic modes of non-violence, the principle of nonviolence is extended to all living creatures, including even insects.

The idea of *ahimsa* goes back to early periods of Hinduism and is perhaps contemporary with the transformation of the conquering nomadic tribes to the settled agricultural civilization it was to remain for many centuries. *Ahimsa* was preached by many teachers over these centuries, specifically focusing on compassion for one's kind in general and one's neighbor in particular.

The full sociopolitical impact of the idea of *ahimsa* could be seen in Gandhi's *satyagraha* movement, in which he united two apparently disparate ideas: political activism and nonviolence. In seeking the political dignity and independence of the Indians, Gandhi pointed out the Upanishadic connec-tiveness even to the alien British, and in refusing to use violence, taught respect for the divine in the persons of his political adversaries. In short, underneath the political differences lay human connectiveness. Such political confrontation he called *satyagraha* — "truth seeking" — to point to the adversary that all men are equal and thus deserving of independence and dignity.

In this nonviolent battle, Gandhi succeeded spectacularly. But the other side of *satyagraha* and nonviolent struggles was the evil within: the caste system. In this, Gandhi did not fail entirely. As India moves onward into the twenty-first century, the evils of the caste system are being systematically dismantled. The successes are largely in the urban industrial belt, but one hears of distressing news in the rural agricultural belt. There is much left to be reformed.

The medieval philosopher-saint Sankara's famous saying has entered the common parlance of Hindu discourse, even in contemporary India:

Brahma satya jaganmittya
Jibobraho naparhya

The Only Truth is Brahman
And the world is an illusion.
The Self is none other than Brahman itself.

It follows simply, therefore, that to show disrespect for other human beings is to show disrespect for *Brahman*, the Godhead. Likewise, any service to fellow humans is a service to *Brahman*. Gandhi's insistence was exactly on this interpretation of Hindu sacred texts.

MONOTHEISM/POLYTHEISM

In the *Rig Veda*, there are speculations of a monotheistic deity, but there are also mentions of other gods whose powers are subsidiary. The Upanishads are clearly monotheistic, but in later Hinduism many other gods began to be worshipped. Yet the Hindu will often invoke *Bhagavan*—God in the abstract—for whom there is no representation. It is said that Hindus have three hundred and thirty million gods. The impact is deliberately metaphoric. We humans would need advanced computers to name so many people, places, things, and would still find ourselves running short of that staggering number. The metaphor of the plentitude of gods is simply that we can choose whatever we want as a representative of the divine and worship it, if it satisfies the need for worship in us.

As humans, we know well some varieties of love: love for parent, child, friend, lover. In Hinduism, worship through each of these paradigms is possible. For example, to take only the instance of Lord Krishna, he may be worshipped as a child, as a lover (such as Radha does), as a friend (such as Sudama or Arjuna does), and so forth.

The Hindu trinity is perhaps the world's oldest theological trinitarian idea: Brahma, the creator god, is not to be confused with *Brahman* (supreme and sole Godhead) of the Upanishads; Vishnu, the preserver, who appears through the various ages or *yuga*s as incarnations or *avataras*; Shiva, the destroyer, who seems to have been derived from the conflation of the Rig Vedic deity Rudra and perhaps an earlier, pre-Aryan Dravidian deity. Yet Shiva is not merely a destroyer: he makes new creation possible, and during the tenure of the age he holds harmony over the elemental universe through his dance, and is thus known as Nataraja, the Lord of the Dance.

Throughout the subcontinent, one will find temples to Shiva and his consorts and the various incarnations of Vishnu, such as Krishna, Rama, and others. Oddly enough, there are few temples to Brahma. There are lesser gods also who have temples; some of them may have had a history of a pre-Aryan Dravidian or tribal past, such as Karthikeya, the benevolent elephant-headed god Ganesha, and others. Ganesha is worshipped as the god of auspicious beginnings and, in some parts of India, as the god of good handwriting! That is because Ganesha served as the amanuensis for the poet Vyasa, who dictated the epic *Mahabharata* to him. Many of these later gods were incorporated in the Hindu pantheon by the ingenious method of divine marriages: Ganesha and Karthikeya are simply described as the sons of Shiva in his union with Durga, the mother goddess.

In post-Upanishadic Hinduism, one of the theological doctrines that gained credence was that the High God was inactive and transcendent and the creative energy was personified in the feminine energy of Shakti, a new divinity that gave rise to the various forms of the Mother Goddess. The attendant literature (and the practices of some esoteric sects) has a sexual character. The Mother Goddess and the form of devotion and its attendant rites and literature are called *Shakta*.

There are various forms of Shakti who are all consorts of Shiva. Durga is a name derived from "*durg*," which in Sanskrit means, denotatively, "fort" and connotatively, "that which is well protected." Durga is the active goddess-principle, armed by ten gods (in essence, the equal of ten gods, a metaphor again!) who, accompanied by her four children (Ganesha; Karthikeya; Saraswati, the goddess of learning; and Lakshmi, the goddess of prosperity) destroy Mahish-asura, the demon of ignorance. It is worth noting that Saraswati's name also means "river," she who flows; stagnancy is ignorance.

Uma is another form of Shakti, and she is a gloriously meditative consort of Shiva, without whom Shiva would be distressed. She is the calm and beautiful peacegiver.

But there is one aspect of Shakti that is the most misunderstood in the West. She is Kali. It helps to realize that one aspect of Shiva is "*kal*," which is Time, and "Kali" is the feminine aspect of Time. Just as all things are born and destroyed in time, so do all beings exist through Kali and end within her — hence her dark and mysterious aspect, her swollen body that resembles pregnancy and lacks the lithe grace of the other goddesses. She is a terrifying goddess, but her arm is raised in a token of calm. Time devours, and yet without Time we would never be born or exist. Kali's significance is symbolic and interestingly enough, she is usually addressed (unlike any other deity) in the familiar "*tu*," and not in the formal mode. She is the familiar mother who can sometimes frighten and is inscrutable, but to whom one turns for familiar attention with all the problems of life and death. There are more numerous beautiful poems of adoration to this apparently grim deity than to any other god or goddess in rural folk poetry, except perhaps for Krishna. Nothing in life is excluded in the interactive relationship between the goddess and the devotees. There is, for example, one aspect of the Mother Goddess worship that is worth a mention. In most parts of the world, menstruating females are held to be unclean, but in Kamarupa, there is a festival called *Ambubachi*, during which for several days the menstruation of the Mother Goddess is celebrated, for it promises future fruition and growth.

There are lesser gods, too, who are worshipped locally, probably derived from pre-Aryan village worship. One of them is Sitala, who is the goddess of the pox. Mothers of small children were, understandably, the most assiduous offerers of prayer. Now, with the eradication of smallpox, it has to be the fear of chicken pox that keeps her worship alive.

There is a distinct hierarchy in the worship. Deities like Shiva, goddesses like Kali and Durga, or incarnations of Vishnu such as Krishna are held in the highest regard. At this juncture, it would be important to remember some lines from the *Bhagavad Gita*, which every Hindu knows by heart: "I am the enjoyer and the Lord of all sacrifices."[28]

A medieval religious chant for Shiva is as follows:

No matter what godhead you pray to,
Shiva is that God...
He will take note and grant your prayer.

Indeed, one of the ways in which the apparently polytheistic (and to many foreigners, chaotic) worship works is that, no matter which god is being worshipped, it is the act of worship that is important, not the god as such, for all worship is ultimately directed to the Godhead. Max Müller, the German Indologist, called this henotheism or kathenotheism.[29]

TEACHERS AND REFORMERS: CASTE, SOCIETY, AND SERVICE

In Hinduism, which does not have a historical founder such as Jesus, Muhammad, or the Buddha, the importance of sages and teachers is paramount. Theoretically, an Upanishad can be written even today. In this oldest of religions, the space for correction and change exists side by side with carefully preserved ancient traditions. Like all living religions, such changes are vital to the continuing life of Hinduism.

The great teachers in the Upanishads have insisted on the connection between all humans and the divine. It implies the equality of all humans; yet the tragic and glaring flaw that developed gradually with time was the canker of the caste system. In the "real world," as some people like to phrase it, the theory of religious equality and the sociopolitical reality of society have always been at variance. Such perceptions are reflected in ironic social parlance, in which the privileged are referred to as "Brahmins." Yet the grim truth is that once the Aryans had settled down and adapted from their peripatetic lifestyle to the agricultural economy of India, with control over the conquered tribes of darker people, the concept of division became more pronounced and apparently immutable. In an agricultural civilization that offered little possibility of geographic and economic mobility, the social accident of birth became destiny. With little technological advance in the centuries before the coming of the Industrial Revolution to India via western Europe, there was little to upset such a status quo.

The important thing to remember is that no matter how hard the Brahmins and the Kshatriyas (the priests and the warriors) tried to perpetuate the system of caste, called in India *varna*, a Sanskrit word that also means skin color, there were rebellious voices that challenged and negated the system that degraded other humans simply because of their birth. These were teachers in the same Upanishadic tradition who questioned the pieties of the orthodox, the justice of the oppressive system, and the very basis of such social division between humans who are all, as the Upanishads point out, connected to each other and to God. These teachers scoffed at the idea of brahminical ascendancy and turned their teachings and often their verses (for many of them were poets) against the evil of the caste system and the claims of the Brahmins. Social reform started again and again with the establishment of this claim of equality before God. The implication of service to God became synonymous with service to one's fellow humans. Religious service was subsumed by the idea of social service. The problems of society became the arena for those who sought God. By the end of the nineteenth century, Swami Vivekananda proclaimed:

Jeeb'e daya kore jei jon
Shei jon shebichhe Ishwar

The one who gives his compassionate action to
one's fellow human beings, is the one who
truly serves God.[30]

It is in this context that we need to understand the ideas and influences of the Virasaiva poets in the tenth and eleventh centuries, Kabir in the fifteenth century, followed by Caitanya and Tukaram in the succeeding centuries, and later Ramakrishna and Vivekananda in the nineteenth century. (It is important to remember that these are only some of the most important figures, and there are many others who, for a lack of space, could not be mentioned.)

Devara Dasimayya, the poet-saint of the tenth century, derided the idea of orthopraxic ritual prayers and pilgrimages in his *vacanas*, which are brief folk poems:

To the utterly at-one with Siva…
His front yard
is the true Benares…[31]

This strain is repeated in many of his other poems:

What does it matter
If the fox wanders
All over the sacred Jambu island?
Will he ever stand still
In true communion of the Lord?
What use is its incessant travels
Throughout the world
And his ablutions in a myriad holy rivers?
A pilgrim whose soul is not at one with you,
My Lord,
Wanders through the great world
Like a clown at a fair.[32]

By the time Kabir, another poet-saint, was teaching in the fifteenth century, the Islamic kings had firmly entrenched themselves in northern India. Many local people, especially from the erstwhile lower castes, had converted to Islam. Conflicts between the followers of the two religions had become common. Kabir asked all people to look beneath the surface of religions into their own hearts and see the commonality in humanity itself. It has been suggested that Kabir was sweeping away the encrusted layers of Hindu orthodoxy which had accumulated upon Upanishadic simplicity to the knowledge that we are all one and interrelated, and also beyond the orthodox Islamic divisions between Believer and infidel. His insistence was that each individual, regardless of his allegiance to any religion, look within himself and discover how his individual humanity is connected to the immanent Divinity.

Here are some selections from Kabir's poems, which are part of the common cultural knowledge in India:

> Where do you search for me, Devotee?
> Look and you will find me beside you—
> Neither in mosque nor temple,
> Not in the Kaaba or Kailasha,
> I am not in the rites of the orthodox
> Nor in ascetic penance:
> If you seek me truly, you will find me
> In a trice,
> For God is the breath of all breath—
> Sings Kabir.

> *   *   *

> I know that bathing in all the sacred places
> Is fruitless. I have bathed everywhere.
> There is nothing but water there.
> All the idols are clay. They do not speak.
> I have called out in prayer to them all.
> Mere words are the Puranas and the Koran:
> I have lifted their veils and looked within.
> Kabir sings: Look within your life's experience
> And know nothing else is the truth.

> *   *   *

> Do they assert that the fish in the water is thirsty?
> I laugh aloud.
> You who wander, seeking from wilderness to
>   wilderness,
> Do you not see that Reality resides in your own home.
> Hear the truth then: Make pilgrimages
> To distant Benares and Mathura or where you will,
> But without finding your Atman within yourself
> the world will be mere illusion.

> *   *   *

If God's address is the mosque,
Then who has ownership of this world?
If at the end of your arduous pilgrimage
You find Rama within the idol,
Who then knows what is happening
In the wide world outside?
To the east is Hari: To the west is Allah:
Look inside your soul.
You will find both Rama and Karim.

  ✱ ✱ ✱

In all the women and men in this world
You will see His living form.
Kabir sings: I am the child of Allah and of Rama:
He is my Guru, my very own Seer.[33]

At around the same time, in the southern part of India, Vemana, a Telugu poet, wrote poems about the conflict between the castes:

Why do we, everyday
Despise the low caste neighbor?
Do we differ in flesh and blood?
What is that Spirit, and what its caste,
That gives life to him and us?[34]

Likewise, the poetry of Tukaram, from north India, soothes and instructs, and he sees all humans as family:

You lead me everywhere, my Lord
I lean on You and You bear my load.
If in weary toil I speak rash words,
You wipe away my shame…
You bring me hope, a new world to be
Where everyone I meet is kin
So happily here like a child I play,

For here your grace and joy are spread.
Thus speaks and sings your Tukaram.[35]

In the last two hundred years of Hindu reform, two towering figures are Sri Ramakrishna and his disciple Swami Vivekananda, who spread his gospel and message throughout the West. Ramakrishna held the idea of service to be of seminal importance.

He belonged very much to the ancient tradition of the *Rig Veda* and the Upanishadic *Samhita*. He often pointed out that the *Rig Veda* has clearly stated:

> The foolish man who does not share with others obtains food to no purpose. I say the truth that it is really his destruction.[36]
>
> (*Rig Veda* X.117.6)

Ramakrishna took the essence of this teaching and focused on who one should serve. He invoked the idea *Vasudhaiva Kutumbakam*, "The world is one family." (literally: "The world is full of your close relatives").[37] The term used in Sanskrit is one that would be used for what we call "immediate and extended family." He merges the individual's self-interest and that of society at large. In a sense, he confronts the question "Why should I treat my neighbor as myself?" Ramakrishna would explain, in the homely language of ordinary folk, the lesson from the Upanishads: "You shall serve others because they and you are one."

There are many instances in the life of Ramakrishna that are illuminating. Once, in 1884, he sat during a learned explication by a Hindu teacher of the Vaishnava method of devotion, which delights in three things: ecstatically singing the name of God, kindness to all living creatures, and service to Vaishnavas. In the midst of this discussion, Ramakrishna fell into silence and then sank into a trance-like state in which he declared, "Kindness to living beings! Fool! Who are you, an insignificant creature, to show kindness to them? No, no, not kindness, but service to them, looking upon them as God Himself!"[38]

Swami Vivekananda (at this stage, before ordination, his name was Naren Datta) was present at this gathering, and this pronouncement had a profound effect upon him. He realized and continued to teach that Hinduism does not depend on the miracles of holy men who restore the dead to life, lepers to perfect health, and the blind to sight. The miracle which Hinduism insists on is the transformation within so that a person can be at one with others and learn to serve.

Religious orthodoxy or religious customs are no substitute for service. Once Ramakrishna had set out for a pilgrimage to the sacred city of Varanasi when he came upon a group of famine-stricken tribal Santhals near Deoghar. He refused to continue on his pilgrimage and stayed and served them until relief came. He called the poor *"daridra narayan,"* which means "the poverty-stricken God," and served the least of these tribals. Such instances can be found throughout the life of this sage. There are mystical anecdotes about his life that are recalled by well-respected contemporaries. One day, as he sat discussing religious doctrine with his followers, he cried out in pain; it was found that in a nearby temple, a warder was beating a beggar who had asked for food. Ramakrishna miraculously felt the pain, felt at one with the poor and dispossessed.

Early in his discipleship, Vivekananda asked for the perfect religious meditation—*nirvikalpa samadhi* and personal transcendence. His master Ramakrishna rebuked him sharply and guided him toward a life of service and contemplation. The great organization which Swami Vivekananda set up before his untimely death was called Ramakrishna Mission. The monks there renounce caste and spend their lives in service.

How is one to perform service? Ramakrishna and Vivekananda referred again and again to the text of the *Bhagavad Gita*. All service — indeed, all meaningful work — must be done with a kind of detachment that can come only to the individual who is not looking for personal gratification or profit. The *Gita* is clear about this, and in this theophanic text the incarnate God Krishna explains to his friend and disciple Arjuna that the service must be done in a disinterested manner — that one must seek to do good but be detached entirely from the idea of benefiting from the actions. Krishna admonishes Arjuna: *"Ma phaleshu kadachana."* ("You shall not seek the fruits of your labor.")

Ramakrishna thought all religions valid and worthy of respect, and said so repeatedly throughout his life. "All these religions are paths leading by different paths to the same body of water," he reiterated. He added further, "Where do you go to seek God? Are not all the poor, the miserable, the weak, gods? Why not worship and serve them first? Why do you dig a well right by the bank of the Ganges?"

From these teachings, Vivekananda put the ideal of service as foremost in the Hindu mind: "He who serves all creatures without bar is indeed best worshipping his deity."[39]

This labor of service became subsumed in the notion of "work is worship" and came under the rubric of karma yoga, but service was a direct result of the Upanishadic insight of *Advaita* (non-dualism), which says that all humans are interconnected and in a divine unity with God. The intentionality of service is important: "No activity is secular or sacred unless the mind of the doer paints it so."[40]

Swami Prabhananda, one of the monks of the Ramakrishna Mission who has written extensively on Vivekananda, points out:

> To spiritualize one's mundane activities, a practitioner of this discipline has to pass through two stages of development. In the first stage he finds service and worship, secular and sacred, incompatible; he thinks that an act of service is doing good to others but worship is doing good to oneself. In the next phase of development, he learns to practice service as worship; he keeps close watch on his motives, he guards against intrusion of his self-interest. And ultimately he comes to understand that service is but worship, "to labour is to pray." His inner spirit finds expression in the outward life of action in the form of service.[41]

The motto of the Ramakrishna Mission is revelatory: "*Atmano moksartham jagaddhitaya ca*": We must aspire not only for spiritual salvation (*moksa*), but do it through service and benefit to the world (*jagaddhitaya ca*). "There should be no schism between service and meditation; they must be in harmony," Vivekananda insisted.

Ramakrishna has dealt with the idea of humility in service very well. He rebuked the famous Indian novelist Bankim Chattopadhyay: "Charity! Doing Good! How dare you say you can do good to others? Man struts about so much...It is God alone that he serves—God who dwells in all things."[42]

Neither Ramakrishna nor Vivekananda deified poverty and suffering, and they refused to exalt them philosophically. The poor, however, must be treated with dignity. In doing this, Ramakrishna was in a direct line from the earlier teachers of Hinduism, such as Kapila: "*Arhaet danamanabhyam maitrya vinnena caksusa...*," i.e., one has to worship God in man with four elements. One has to offer something to meet the felt need of the person, and while offering it, one must give due respect to him. This is not enough, however; one also needs to give him love and friendship. And to fulfill all these conditions, one must have the faith that the same *paramatman* (Divinity) exists in the beneficiary as in oneself.[43]

Only on fulfilling these conditions will such service benefit its practitioner as well as the recipient. As Swami Prabhananda felicitously put it, "The concept of worship of man as God in the form of ameliorating services is the social expression of religion."[44] This is hardly a cakewalk; the eminent student of human history Arnold Toynbee reminds us, "Man is relatively good at dealing with non-human nature. What he is bad at is his dealing with human nature in himself and in his fellow beings."[45]

SELF, SOCIETY, AND SERVICE

> The riches of the man who gives fully do not run out, but the miser finds no one with sympathy...
>
> That man is no friend who does not give of his own nourishment to his friend, the companion at his side. Let the friend turn away from him; this is not his dwelling place. Let him find another man who gives freely, even if he be a stranger... The man who eats alone brings troubles upon himself.[46]

Such repeated Rig Vedic emphasis is on generosity of spirit and willingness to share in a commonwealth. In the Upanishads, too, such messages are reiterated. In the *Bhagavad Gita*, three types of giving are described. That which is given without any expectation of appreciation or reward benefits both the giver and the receiver; that which is given without any concern for the dignity of the recipient, and what is given at an inappropriate time, causing embarrassment, is detrimental both to the giver and the receiver.

This attitude toward giving, explained by Krishna in the *Bhagavad Gita*, which has its origin in the earlier *Isa Upanishad*, declares simply that the virtuous man does not seek the fruits of his labor. He does the right action because it is right, not merely for the rewards. The attitude which the *Gita* commands may best be described as "disinterested" (a term used in the West by Mathew Arnold).

> Be intent on action
> Not on the fruits of action;
> Avoid attraction to the fruits
> And attachment to inaction!
>
> Perform actions, firm in discipline,
> Relinquishing attachment;
> Be impartial to failure and success —
> This equanimity is called discipline...
>
> As the mountainous depths
> Of the ocean
> Are unmoved when waters
> Rush into it,
> So the man unmoved
>
> When desires enter him
> Attains a peace that eludes
> The man of many desires.
>
> When he renounces all desires
> And acts without craving,
> Possessiveness
> Or Individuality, he finds peace.[47]

This insistence on a life of righteous action, which is based on a foundation of detachment and contemplation, may be seen in ancient text after ancient text in Hinduism. The *Isa Upanishad* states:

> Into deep darkness fall those who follow action.
> Into deeper darkness fall those who follow
>   knowledge...
> He who knows both knowledge and action within
>   action
> Overcomes death and with knowledge reaches
>   immortality.[48]

Through the millennia of growth and evolution of Hindu theology, these ideas have been expounded, resisted, and re-affirmed. It has never been a smooth and linear path. By the age of Vivekananda, the idea of *su-karma* (good karma) and social amelioration had had centuries of affirmation. Vivekananda founded his theological vision of service on an Upanishadic axiom:

> This is the gist of all worship: to be good and to do good to others. He who sees Siva in the poor, in the weak, and in the diseased really worships Siva. If he sees Siva only in the image, his worship is but preliminary. He who has helped one poor man, seeing Siva in him, without thinking of his caste or creed or race or anything, with him Siva is more pleased than He is with the man who sees Him only in temples.[49]

Vivekananda, who was tireless in his efforts of social service, put his ideas forward simply, adding even a touch of local humor used earlier by Ramakrishna:

Do you love your fellow men? Where should you go to seek God? Are not all the poor, the miserable, the weak, Gods? Why not worship them first? Why go dig a well on the bank of the Ganges?[50]

Vivekananda reminded people of their connection to each other and to God, an Upanishadic precept:

Where is the eternal sanction of ethics to be found except in the only Infinite Reality that exists in you and in me and in all, in the self, in the soul? The infinite oneness of the soul is the eternal sanction of all morality, that you and I are not only brothers — every literature voicing man's struggle towards freedom has preached that for you — but that you and I are really one. This is the dictate of Indian philosophy. This oneness is the rationale of all ethics and spirituality.[51]

In doing so, he elevated the position of service to that of worship, taking care to explicate the true nature of service and its nexus with the principle of love. Here are his words in Sanskrit:

...*ayameva visesah-jive jirabuddya ya seva samarpita sa daya, na prema. Yadatmavuddhya jiva sevyate, tat prema... Tadasmakam prema eva saranam, na daya.*

In particular, service to beings by regarding them as beings is mere compassion, not love. And service to beings by regarding them as souls, is love proper... Therefore, we must rely on love, not mere compassion.[52]

The idea of love of God and love for one's fellow human beings comes together in the teachings of Vivekananda:

> You may invent an image through which to worship God; But a better image already exists — the living man. You may build a temple in which to worship God, and that may be good; but a better one, a much higher already exists — the human...[53]

The twelfth century South Indian mystic Basavanna had earlier pointed this out, placing as counterpoint the temple made by humans and the humans made by God:

> The rich will build temples
> For Siva.
> What shall I, the poor man,
> Do?
> My legs are pillars
> My body is the shrine
> My head is a cupola of gold.
> O Lord,
> Their buildings will fall one day,
> But the moving ones will always be here.[54]

Swami Vivekananda had, in his early youth, practiced the usual asceticism but came soon to the realization that service could transform him and society:

> People who have lost faith in a system of political wire-pulling find in the doctrine of Service to Jiva-Shiva, an alternative model for realising a new social order.[55]

To the end of his days, Vivekananda, like his teacher, referred to all the people he served as *daridra narayan*, or "The Lord in poverty." It is only natural that when he established the Ramakrishna Mission, named after his teacher, Vivekananda chose the motto meaning "For one's personal salvation and for the service of all."

Service is theology in action. Religious reflection leads toward service.

OTHER SACRED BOOKS

Since the earliest of the sacred texts were deliberately remembered and transmitted orally as part of the *sruti* tradition, it is awkward to call these "books" in the traditional sense. Indeed, all of the earlier texts were part of an immemorial oral tradition; the historian A. L. Basham notes that the word for "writing" does not occur even once in the early texts,[56] yet Western scholars were amazed to find in the nineteenth century that the recitals of the Vedic texts did not vary in word or inflection from the Himalayan Kashmir to the southernmost regions of the subcontinent. The oral transmission down through the generations was done reverentially, with not an iota of regional variation because each syllable of the text was considered sacred, and even the slightest mispronunciation regarded as nothing less than sacrilegious.

The texts of the Sanskrit epics *Ramayana* and *Mahabharata* are many—and there are major variations and versions that were available in manuscript and, later, in print. The tradition of writing had entered Hindu society by the ninth century C.E. and the epics were considered, at least in part, secular.

The *Ramayana*, as the title suggests, is the story of the north Indian prince Rama, who, after palace intrigues, leaves his kingdom for a prolonged exile, accompanied by his spectacularly faithful wife Sita and his obedient brother Lakshman. He winds his way south to Lanka, which many, but not all, scholars believe is the modern Sri Lanka, where Sita is abducted by the demon-king Ravana. Rama makes alliance with the monkey-king Sugriva after helping him in a dubious succession. The army includes the great simian warrior Hanuman, who, like Bhima of the later epic *Mahabharata*, is the son of Pavana, the wind god; Hanuman, naturally, has supernatural powers and can increase or decrease his size; his allegiance to Rama and his generosity are legendary.

Many scholars have suggested that the monkey army simply signified tribes whose totem was the monkey, and that Rama's conquest is a shadow narrative of Aryan incursion into the Deccan, just as in later Mediterranean myth, the Achaian conquest of Troy to retrieve the reluctantly rescued Helen was a mythologized story of Greek hegemony over the geopolitical area.

After the usual battles, and not a few episodes of questionable chivalry, Ravana is defeated and Lanka reduced to vassalage under Bibhishana, Ravana's turncoat brother who had become Rama's devotee. After this, Rama asks Sita to be tested by fire to judge her constancy. Throughout the epic, Sita is a dignified presence. She proves herself reluctantly, but makes the significant point that her word should have been enough.

Rama returns to claim his kingdom since the period of his exile is over, but his troubles are not. His subjects, skeptical of Sita's virtue, insist on her banishment, and she is sent away by Rama to live in the rural hermitage of sages where she gives birth to twin sons who grow up to defeat the aging king in battle.

Despite the authorial diktat in some of the later retellings that Rama is divine, there are many episodes in which he is seen in a less than favorable light. To the modern reader, he often comes across as a tragic figure, doomed to personal loss and grief in trying to live up to the ideal of a king in the eyes his fickle people. To the end of his days he remains monoga-mous in an age when kings acquired queens at the drop of an arrow. He also has an unusual humility and seems forever eager to provide peace and comfort to his subjects. Perhaps it was this, rather than his martial quality, that prompted Gandhi to call the ideal nation a *Ram Rajya*. In modern India, the ramifications of such a nomenclature have given rise to a species of Hindu fundamentalism which Gandhi would hardly countenance or recognize. It was a fanatic from that seedling political party who assassinated him.

But there are many *Ramayana*s. Apart from Valmiki's Sanskrit epic, the story is retold in numerous variations, not the least of which is the women's *Ramayana*, in which all the male-driven battles are omitted. The focus is on the life of Sita — her girlhood, her learning of the household arts, her fear of leaving her paternal home at marriage, her fear before child-birth; in short, a tender story of various aspects of domestic life, sorrows, and joy.

The many versions of the *Ramayana* emphasize qualities such as patience, respect for elders, filial piety, and stability of society. In these aspects, the *Ramayana* has been, in spite of being a less rich narrative than the *Mahabharata* (or perhaps because of it), a profound influence on the socioreligious aspects of the Hindu mind.

The *Mahabharata* had an earlier version, the *Jaya Kavya*, but the many-layered later epic is the one that has triumphed as a national treasure. It has a psychological complexity that is as relevant today as any modern work of world literature. There is no attempt to whitewash any character, and Krishna, the god incarnate, is not central to the narrative. In the interpolated *Bhagavad Gita*, which includes the divine teaching and the breathtaking sequence of the theophany, Krishna is undeniably divine. In the main body of the epic, he is a worldly-wise prince, a relative of both the families of warrior princes.

The story hinges on the succession of a kingdom, with an interesting take on primogeniture: Is the kingdom to be inherited by Prince Duryodhana, who was conceived earlier, or Prince Yudhistir, who was born first? The regent, Dhritarashtra, the father of Duryodhana, cannot be king in his own right for he was born blind, and his brother Pandu, Yudhistir's father, has died young because of a curse.

The story, then, is about internecine warfare, with Yudhistir and his four brothers (all born through divine intervention from several gods) pitted against Duryodhana and his ninety-nine brothers. Scholars believe it is probably based on a seed of actual history from when the Aryans, having consolidated their power, were working out which branch would have supremacy. But the narrative presents many situations that are cited everyday in the modern Indian political and social arena as ethical or dramatic models to be emulated or condemned.

However, the part of the *Mahabharata* that has had a profound and abiding influence on the Hindu mind is the *Bhagavad Gita*. In the narrative of the epic, the teaching of Arjuna by Krishna takes place on the battlefield itself as the two armies stand poised to engage. Looking at the two opposed armies, Arjuna is struck by dismay and misgiving. He relinquishes his arms and turns to his friend and mentor, Krishna, and asks him why he should join battle. If he wins, he will have killed many respected elders and his teacher, Drona, who have all joined his enemies for a variety of reasons, not the least of which is feudal loyalty. If he is killed, what he feels faces him is a lonely mortality. He is filled with pity and horror. What is a man's duty in the world? he asks. Among Krishna's words of instruction are these words:

The self is the friend of a man
Who masters himself through the self,
But for a man without self-mastery,
The self is like an enemy at war.[57]

The external battle is clearly a metaphor for the conflict of the soul with the body. Krishna, in his role as Vishnu incarnate, teaches him as so many seekers in the earlier Upanishads had been instructed. The difference here is that the instructor is no mere sage, and the teaching does not involve only hearing but also seeing. At one point in his lesson, Krishna, at Arjuna's request, grants him blessed vision so that he may behold Krishna in his divine and cosmic glory, a theophany the likes of which does not exist elsewhere in the high literature of Hinduism.

Krishna points out that disciplined action within the context of devotion is beneficial; however, there must be no hankering for the fruits of action. The disciplined soul follows his dharma and acts out his karma disinterestedly and with discipline and understanding. He does so because the actions are appropriate, not because they are lucrative. In doing this, he reaches peace:

Wise men are disciplined by understanding
Relinquish the fruit born of action
Freed from these bonds of rebirth,
They reach a place beyond decay.

When your understanding passes beyond
The swamp of delusion,
You will be indifferent to all
That is heard in sacred love.

When your understanding turns
From sacred love to stand fixed,
Immovable in contemplation,
then you will reach discipline...

In serenity, all his sorrows
Dissolve;
His reason becomes serene,
His understanding sure.

Without discipline,
He has no understanding or inner power.
Without inner power, he has no peace;
And without peace, where is joy?[58]

It has to be clearly understood that to reach the goal of peace, man's disinterestedness must be complete. He must also understand that he is connected to all other beings, uniting himself "with the self of all creatures."

Armed with discipline, he purifies
And subdues the self, masters his senses,
Unites himself with the self of all creatures;
Even when he acts, he is not defiled...

A man who relinquishes attachment
And dedicates actions to the infinite spirit
Is not stained by evil,
Like a lotus leaf sustained by water...

Truly free is the sage who controls
His senses, mind, and understanding,
Who focuses on freedom
And dispels desire, fear, and anger.[59]

These are words spoken on a battlefield where the dharma of the warrior is to fight; it is not an easy lesson. Paradoxically, it is an explication of the idea of Peace in moments before a great battle.

Krishna's theophany, which takes place to explain the cosmic design to Arjuna, is remarkable for its poetic force...

> If the light of a thousand suns
> Were to rise in the sky at once,
> It would be like the light
> Arjuna saw — all the universe
> In its many ways and parts
> Standing as one in the body
> Of the God of gods...[60]

In the thirteenth *adhyaya* (section) of the *Bhagavad Gita*, the Lord Krishna makes the metaphoric connection between the battlefield in which Arjuna stands and the symbolic field:

> The field denotes
> This body, and wise men
> Call one who knows it
> The field-knower.
>
> Know me as the field-knower
> In all fields...
>
> The field contains the great elements,
> Individuality, understanding,
> Unmanifest nature, the eleven senses,
> And the five sense realms.
>
> Longing, hatred, happiness, suffering,
> Bodily form, consciousness, resolve,
> Thus is this field with its changes
> Defined in summary.
>
> Knowledge means humility,
> Sincerity, non-violence, patience,

Honesty, reverence for one's teacher,
Purity, stability, self-restraint.[61]

It is with this knowledge that the mind progresses, seeing the unity in the diversity of existence, perceiving the same divine essence in all the living:

Undivided, it seems divided
Among creatures;
Understood as their sustainer...

By meditating on the self, some men
See the self through the self;
Others see by philosophical discipline;
Others by the discipline of action.[62]

This particular segment of the *Gita* expounds the relationship between the Creator and the creatures, and makes again the Upanishadic point that we are all connected because we are connected to God.

When he perceives the unity
Existing in separate creatures
And how they expand from unity,
He attains the infinite spirit...

Just as one sun
Illumines this entire world,
So the master of the field
Illumines the entire field.[63]

Apart from the Upanishadic idea of the divine connection between all human beings, the *Gita* emphasizes the importance of rejecting egotism in virtuous action.

When we consider the idea of service from the perspective of *Bhagavad Gita*, the insistence on the rejection of ego is very important. Do we undertake an action because it is praise-worthy (and a possible photo opportunity), because it is gratifying to feel patronizing, or because it is simply a good thing to do? This is an austere vision of virtuous action. The action is done well, dispassionately, and without any expectation of reward. There is no rejection of reward; there is no hankering for it. That is the difference.

> Action known for its lucidity
> Is necessary, free of attachment,
> Performed without attraction or hatred
> By one who seeks no fruit.[64]

Action must come from the well spring of one's personality, one's nature: One's karma should arise out of one's dharma. The importance of living one's own dharma instead of imitating another's is paramount:

> Better to fulfill one's own dharma imperfectly
> Than to follow another man's;
> By performing karma intrinsic to his dharma,
> A man avoids grave error.[65]

THEOLOGY, SERVICE, AND SERVICE-LEARNING

Let us return momentarily to the basic idea of the *Chandogya* and the other Upanishads, an idea repeated and reiterated throughout the Upanishadic collection: God is not apart from us; we are in Him as He is in us, and we humans are therefore intimately and divinely interconnected in essence and therefore in deed, in thought and in action, in service and in contemplation, in imagining and in execution, now and forever. How are we to act in this world in which the wise can see that it is permeated by *Brahman*?

It is instructive to look at the *Brihadaranyaka Upanishad*, which means the "Upanishad of the Great Forest." (The western poet T. S. Eliot used it in his poem "The Waste Land.") The gods, humans, and demons asked to be instructed by the Deity. The gods asked first for divine instruction. The Deity uttered the syllable "da" and asked them if they had understood. "We understood," they replied. "You commanded us *Damyata*" (control your natures). "Yes," agreed the Deity, "you have understood me."

When the humans came to Him with the same prayer, He uttered the same syllable "da" and asked them if they had comprehended Him. "We do," they answered. "You commanded us *Datta*" (give). "Yes," He said, "you have understood me."

When the demons came, He uttered the same syllable "da" and asked them if they had understood. "You told us *Dayadhvam*" (be merciful). "Yes," said He, "you have understood.

Thus it is that the voice of thunder repeats that lesson "da, da, da": be controlled, give, be merciful. It is significant that the gods and demons are asked to curb their natures, but the commandment to humans is "to give." Such giving is the gift of the essence of humanity, from our *Atman*, the innermost gift, which is quintessentially divine according to the teachings of the Upanishads. From within our mundane world, it is the gift of the infinite.

That gift, which comes from God, is what God demands we give each other; such is the essence of service. Without love, there can be no gift, no service. Any true giving, in the Upanishadic sense, must come from one's very essence—and that essence is at one with God, with goodness, and it is that which connects us at once to each other and to God. All gifts of service are therefore essentially divine and are virtuous karma.

By giving we are reminded of the intrinsic humility with which we must give that gift, for the *Brahman* has given us our divine and connective essence in the first place. Who denies God, denies himself. Who affirms God, affirms himself. Truly, no man is an island.

But how, according to Hindu theology, is the human constituted? If one were to ask this question in modern Western civilization, one would perhaps invoke the Freudian tripartite division of ego, superego, and id. It would probably be differently perceived in the Islamic world. The Hindu view, found in the *Taittiriya Upanishad,* divides the individual into several parts. First, there is our physical entity, which needs and lives upon food, and is called the *"annamaya"* (*"anna"* meaning "rice/food"; *"maya"* is a Sanskrit suffix, in this instance signifying "composition" and not to be confused with the homonym *"maya,"* which is illusion).

Within the *annamaya* is the *pranamaya* (*"prana"* meaning "vital breath") which in turn holds the *manomaya* (*"mano"* meaning "will"), which contains the *vijnanamaya* (*"vijnana"* meaning "intelligence"). But the innermost essence that lies within the *vijnanamaya* is the *anadamaya* (*"ananda"* meaning "joy or bliss").

This view of the interior structure of our being is of great import. Some commentators point out that the five-part division seems to echo our five senses. But the senses work simultaneously, in tandem. Here each part, or *kosa* (the word is significant: it means "sheath," as in the sheath of a sword, for instance), contains the next, which contains the next, and so on. The *annamaya kosa* contains the *pranamaya kosa*, within which lies the *manomaya kosa*, and so on, until we get to the very heart, the *anandamaya kosa*. Of course, such successive interiority reminds us of the *Chandogya Upanishad*, in which Uddalaka urges his son Svetaketu to bring the tiny fruit of the vast banyan tree, break it and look at the kernel, and then to examine the minute particles that lie within the kernel.

There is a method of reaching the interiority of knowledge in Hindu theology. Each step in knowledge leads further into the interior, so to speak, of the previous concept, until step by step one comes to the heart of the matter. Indeed, temple architecture imitates that concept in stone. The seeker enters deeper and deeper into the Hindu temple until finally confronted with the central residing deity in the tiny *garbhagrha* (the womb) room.

We are led thus, deeper and deeper, into the layers of the *Atman*, into the very heart of the ontological journey. The emphasis is on the process of finding, of discovering, what is within. Much of Hindu theology is an attempt to understand what lies within, whether it be an idea or an idea that actuates action. When we contemplate such an idea of interiority in Hindu theology, a multilayered notion of the human emerges. The *annamaya kosa*, the physical entity, has to be taken care of. Anyone older than an infant or not too debilitated by age or disease does so through voluntary action. Within the *annamaya* is the *pranamaya*. One's vital breath may also be voluntarily controlled — indeed, in the practice of yoga it is — but it is largely involuntary. In moving inward, we are also moving from the voluntary toward the involuntary. Within the *pranamaya* is the *manomaya kosa*, where reside our emotions and will. Here, too, there is a blending of the voluntary and the involuntary. We have only some control over our emotions and we can indeed, to some extent, shape our will. Within the *manomaya kosa* is the seat of intelligence and perception, the *vijnanamaya kosa*, whither we are led through the physical consciousness, emotion and will. But the exercise of intelligence, of *vijnana*, is difficult to chart, like the eye studying itself. The leap comes later, when the *vijnanamaya kosa* leads into the inmost *kosa* of *anandam*, the joy upon which all creation rests because it is the joy of the creative principle, the first cause itself. This leap within, from the *vijnana* to the *anandam*, cannot be voluntarily willed. When it comes, it is a gift. We must therefore follow the divine command to humans: "*Datta*" (give), to be able to receive the gift of *anandam*.

When we perform service, whether in a hospice or in an orphanage, we are involved in an attempt to care for the *annamaya kosa* of those whom we seek to serve.

But within the *annamaya kosa* is the *pranamaya kosa*, and the vital breath of the same individual is also served even as we take care of some very basic needs. Even small children, infants, the very old or sick, or teenagers immersed in their own problems may be reached through service that connects with their *manomaya kosa*. The word "*mano*" implies not only "will," but the seat of emotions; what we might simply call "the heart." This, then, touches and connects with the *vijnanamaya kosa*, the sheath of inner consciousness and intelligence that opens to what has been poetically and metaphorically described as the "lotus within the heart," the inner sanctum, if you will: the *anandamaya kosa*. The *anandam* that resides within, which we try to reach within ourselves and others, is what unites us to *Brahman*, and to each other. Service therefore touches all the interior aspects of a person that are held important in Hindu theology. These are also precisely the reasons that service without thought, mere action without reflection, becomes meaningless. Man does not live by *anna* alone.

Service connects our *anandam* with those of others and is all contained within the supreme *anandam* of the *Brahman*. By affirming the connective bliss (*anandam*), we share happiness. When we serve the *Brahman* within others, it is the opposite of civil war; it is the cure for civil strife, the basis of peace. Such service is also a path of knowing, of seeing the connections between things, people, and ideas. The addition of service to education connects education with everything and makes education purposive by being connective.

Service is thus connected to all the constituent parts of the human being: the *annamaya, pranamaya, manomaya, vijnanamaya,* and thus to the *anandamaya.* For example, when service-learning students help feed, nurse, converse with, or reach a sense of understanding with those whom they serve, they are connecting with the *annamaya, pranamaya, manomaya,* and the *vijnanamaya* parts of those people. The ultimate aim is, through these actions and through preparatory and continuous reflection, to reach the *anandam* of others — through which the *anandam* within their own selves may be reached.

Students do not only give through service and thus end up feeling altruistic and superior. It is by reaching the *anandam* of others that they touch and remain in touch with their own *anandam.* Thus, it may be said that those they serve give them a better and ineffable gift. They give the students their own *anandam.* With *anandam* comes a great measure of humility, for it puts those serving in the vicinity of the *Brahman.* This is how the pedagogy of service-learning, by uniting action and contemplative learning, leads the student across the currently debated "fault lines" of different civilizations into the interiority of Hinduism. The parting words should, appropriately, be those of the medieval Indian poet-saint:

> Unless you build,
> space will not get inside
> a house;
>
> unless the eye sees,
> mind will not decide
> on forms;

without a way
there's no reaching
the other...[66]

NOTES

1. Notwithstanding the hideous racial implication of the Nazi use of the term "Aryan" (according to responsible scholars as diverse as Kosambi, famed for his knowledge of archaeology, or Suniti Kumar Chatterii, one of Asia's most famous linguistics scholars), there was an "Aryan" tribe in the distant past. Darius I, who died in 486 B.C.E., describes himself as "an Aryan of Aryan descent." He may have descended from one of the branches. Scholars speculate that several names, such as Iran and Erin (Ireland), originated from a tribal diaspora. Sir William Jones, the eighteenth-century scholar and founder of the Asiatic Society, showed important linguistic links between Sanskrit (and its predecessor Prakrit) and early European languages such as Greek and Latin, and thus between later derivative languages on both continents. The Aryan kinship terminology is striking in its uniformity: "Mother," "father," "widow," "brother," "daughter" and many other basic words are recognizably similar in all these languages, as are other basic and commonly used words, such as the numbers. The Aryans measured wealth in cattle. (It is interesting to note that the Sanskrit word "duhita" for daughter — which has cognates in most western European languages — is derived from "she who milks cattle.")

2. D. D. Kosambi, *The Culture and Civilisation of Ancient India* (New Delhi: Vikas Publishing, 1997), p. 77.

3. Kosambi, p. 64.

4. Kosambi, p. 64.

5. Suniti Kumar Chatterii, "Race Movements and Prehistoric Culture," in *The History and Culture of the Indian People: The Vedic Age*, ed. R. C. Majumdar (Mumbai: Bharatiya Vidya Bhavan, 1996), p. 167.

6. Chatterii, "Race Movements and Prehistoric Culture," p. 144.

7. Quoted in Chatterii, "Race Movements and Prehistoric Culture," p. 153.

8. Wendy Doniger O'Flaherty, trans., *The Rig Veda* (Harmondsworth, England: Penguin Books, 1981), p. 216.

9. O'Flaherty, pp. 25–26.

10. A. L. Basham, *The Wonder That Was India* (New York: Grove Press, 1959), p. 248.

11. Juan Mascaro, trans., *The Upanishads* (Harmondsworth, England: Penguin Books, 1965), p. 51.

12. Mascaro, p. 127.

13. Mascaro, p. 127.

14. Mascaro, p. 131.

15. S. N. Dasgupta, *History of Indian Philosophy*, vol. 1 (Cambridge: Cambridge University Press, 1973), p. 45.

16. Quoted in Dasgupta, p. 45.

17. Dasgupta, p. 45.

18. Mascaro, p. 49.

19. A. K. Ramanujan, compiler and trans., *Speaking of Siva* (New York: Penguin Books, 1973), p. 108.

20. Mascaro, p. 117.

21. Mascaro, pp. 113–114.

22. Mascaro, pp. 64–65.

23. Mascaro, p. 90.

24. Barbar Stoller Miller, trans., *The Bhagavad Gita* (New York: Bantam, 1986), p. 94.

25. Mascaro, p. 140.

26. Mascaro, pp. 138–139.

27. Mascaro, pp. 61–63.

28. Miller, p. 86.

29. Dasgupta, p. 18.

30. Translation by Kalyan Ray.

31. *Speaking of Siva*, p. 105.

32. *Speaking of Siva*, p. 104.

33. Translations by Kalyan Ray, from Kabir's original poems in *Kabir – Gatha* (Allahabad: Nirala Prakasan, 1962), unpaginated.

34. L. Subramanyam, trans., *Vemana Samgraha* (Nellore, 1954), p. 66.

35. Translation by Kalyan Ray, from *Tukaram Samuha* (Varanasi: Hindi Prachar Samiti, 1966), p. 37.

36. Swami Prabhananda, "Reflections on Vivekananda's Doctrine of Service" in *Swami Vivekananda: A Hundred Years Since Chicago* (Belur, West Bengal: Ramakrishna Math and Ramakrishna Mission, 1994), p. 398.

37. Swami Prabhananda, p. 401.

38. Swami Prabhananda, p. 403.

39. Swami Prabhananda, p. 407.

40. Swami Prabhananda, p. 411.

41. Swami Prabhananda, p. 412.

42. Swami Prabhananda, p. 415.

43. Swami Prabhananda, p. 415.

44. Swami Prabhananda, p. 415.

45. Arnold J. Toynbee, *Civilization on Trial* (New York: Oxford U. Press, 1948), p. 262.

46. O'Flaherty, pp. 68–69.

47. Miller, pp. 36–39.

48. Mascaro, p. 49.

49. *The Complete Works of Swami Vivekananda* (Mayavati Memorial Edition), Vol. 3 (Calcutta: Advaita Ashrama, 1989), pp. 141–142.

50. *The Complete Works of Swami Vivekananda,* (Mayavati Memorial Edition), Vol. 5 (Calcutta: Advaita Ashrama, 1989), p. 51.

51. *The Complete Works of Swami Vivekananda,* Vol. 3, p. 189.

52. Swami Vivekananda's letter to Chakravarti, July 3, 1897.

53. *The Complete Works of Swami Vivekananda,* p. 313.

54. *Speaking of Siva,* p. 88.

55. Swami Prabhananda, p. 417. In this context see also Swami Gambhirananda, "Sri Ramakrishna and the ideal of Seva," *Prabuddha Bharata,* December 1966, pp. 516–518; and Gwilym Beckerlegge, "Social Service as Sadhana," *Religion and Society,* Vol. XXXIII, No. 4, December 1986.

56. Basham, p. 33.

57. Miller, p. 64.

58. Miller, pp. 36–38.

59. Miller, p. 58.

60. Miller, p. 99.

61. Miller pp. 115–116.

62. Miller, pp. 117–118.

63. Miller, p. 119.

64. Miller, p. 146.

65. Miller, p. 149.

66. *Speaking of Siva,* p. 108.

HINDUISM

Sacred Writings

&

Questions to Consider

THE VEDAS

Creation Hymn (*Nasadiya*)

There was neither non-existence nor existence then; there was neither the realm of space nor the sky which is beyond. What stirred? Where? In whose protection? Was there water, bottomlessly deep?

There was neither death nor immortality then. There was no distinguishing sign of night nor of day. That one breathed, windless, by its own impulse. Other than that there was nothing beyond.

Darkness was hidden by darkness in the beginning; with no distinguishing sign, all this was water. The life force that was covered with emptiness, that one arose through the power of heat.

Desire came upon that one in the beginning; that was the first seed of mind. Poets seeking in their heart with wisdom found the bond of existence in non-existence.

Their cord was extended across. Was there below? Was there above? There were seed-placers; there were powers. There was impulse beneath; there was giving-forth above.

Who really knows? Who will here proclaim it? Whence was it produced? Whence is this creation? The gods came afterwards, with the creation of this universe. Who then knows whence it has arisen?

Whence this creation has arisen—perhaps it formed itself, or perhaps it did not—the one who looks down on it, in the highest heaven, only he knows—or perhaps he does not know.

(*The Rig Veda*, translated by Wendy Doniger O'Flaherty [Harmondsworth, England: Penguin Books, 1981])

Yajur Veda

O God, make me great.
May all men perceive me a friend;
May I see all others as friends;
May we all be friends.

(*Yajur Veda*, 36.18, translated by Kalyan Ray)

THE UPANISHADS

Chandogya Upanishad

OM. There lived once a boy. Svetaketu Aruneya by name. One day his father spoke to him in this way: "Svetaketu, go and become a student of sacred wisdom. There is no one in our family who has not studied the holy Vedas and who might only be given the name of Brahman by courtesy."

The boy left at the age of twelve and, having learnt the Vedas, he returned home at the age of twenty-four, very proud of his learning and having a great opinion of himself.

His father, observing this, said to him: "Svetaketu, my boy, you seem to have a great opinion of yourself, you think you are learned, and you are proud. Have you asked for that knowledge whereby what is not heard is heard, what is not thought is thought and what is not known is known?"

"What is that knowledge, father?" asked Svetaketu.

"Just as by knowing a lump of clay, my son, all that is clay can be known, since any differences are only words and the reality is clay;

Just as by knowing a piece of gold all that is gold can be known, since any differences are only words and the reality is only gold;

And just as by knowing a piece of iron all that is iron is known, since any differences are only words and the reality is only iron."

Svetaketu said: "Certainly my honoured masters knew not this themselves. If they had known, why would they not have told me? Explain this to me, father."

"So be it, my child. Bring me a fruit from this banyan tree."

"Here it is, father."

"Break it."

"It is broken, Sir."

"What do you see in it?"

"Very small seeds, Sir."

"Break one of them, my son."

"It is broken, Sir."

"What do you see in it?"

"Nothing at all, Sir."

Then his father spoke to him: "My son, from the very essence in the seed which you cannot see comes in truth this vast banyan tree. Believe me, my son, an invisible and subtle essence is the Spirit of the whole universe. That is Reality. That is Atman. Thou art that."

(From *The Upanishads*, translated by Juan Mascaro [Harmondsworth, England: Penguin Books, 1965], p. 113 ff.)

Brihad-Aranyaka Upanishad

From delusion lead me to Truth.

From darkness lead me to Light.

From death led me to immortality.

This universe is a trinity and this is made of name, form, and action.

The source of all names is the word, for it is by the word that all names are spoken. The word is behind all names, even as Brahman is behind the word.

The source of all forms is the eye, for it is by the eye that all forms are seen. The eye is behind all forms, even as Brahman is behind the eye.

The source of all actions is the body, for it is by the body that all actions are done. The body is behind all actions, even as Brahman is behind the body.

Those three are one, ATMAN, the Spirit of life; and ATMAN, although one, is those three.

The Immortal is veiled by the real. The Spirit of Life is the immortal. Name and form are the real, and by them the Spirit is veiled.

(*The Upanishads*, pp. 127 ff.)

Isa Upanishad

Behold the universe in the glory of God: and all that lives and moves on earth. Leaving the transient, find joy in the Eternal: set not your heart on another's possession.

Working thus, a man may wish for a life of a hundred years. Only actions done in God bind not the soul of man.

Karma

According as a man acts and walks in the path of life, so he becomes. He that does good becomes good; he that does evil becomes evil. By pure actions he becomes pure; by evil actions he becomes evil.

And they say in truth that a man is made of desire. As his desire is, so is his faith. As his faith is, so are his works. As his works are, so he becomes. It was said in this verse:

A man comes with his actions to the end of his determination.

Reaching the end of the journey begun by his works on earth, from that world a man returns to this world of human action.

Thus far for the man who lives under desire.

(*The Upanishads*, p. 49 ff.)

Kena Upanishad

May quietness descend upon my limbs,
My speech, my breath, my eyes, my ears;
May all my senses wax clear and strong.
May Brahman show himself unto me.
Never may I deny Brahman, nor Brahman me.
I with him and he with me—may we abide always together.
May there be revealed to me,
Who am devoted to Brahman,
The holy truth of the Upanishads.
OM... Peace—peace—peace.

At whose behest does the mind think? Who bids the body live? Who makes the tongue speak? Who is that effulgent Being that directs the eye to form and color and the ear to sound?

The Self is ear of the ear, mind of the mind, speech of speech. He is also breath of the breath, and eye of the eye. Having given up the false identification of the Self with the senses and the mind, and knowing the Self to be Brahman, the wise, on departing this life, become immortal.

Him the eye does not see, nor the tongue express, nor the mind grasp. Him we neither know nor are able to teach. Different is he from the known, and different is he from the unknown. So have we heard from the wise.

That which cannot be expressed in words but by which the tongue speaks—know that to be Brahman. Brahman is not the being who is worshipped of men.

That which is not comprehended by the mind but by which the mind comprehends—know that to be Brahman. Brahman is not the being who is worshipped of men.

That which is not seen by the eye but by which the eye sees—know that to be Brahman. Brahman is not the being who is worshipped of men.

That which is not heard by the ear but by which the ear hears—know that to be Brahman. Brahman is not the being who is worshipped of men.

That which is not drawn by the breath but by which the breath is drawn—know that to be Brahman. Brahman is not the being who is worshipped of men.

If you think that you know well the truth of Brahman, know that you know little. What you think to be Brahman in your self, or what you think to be Brahman in the gods—that is not Brahman. What is indeed the truth of Brahman you must therefore learn. I cannot say that I know Brahman fully. Nor can I say that I know him not. He among us knows him best who understands the spirit of the words; "Nor do I know that I know him not."

He truly knows Brahman who knows him as beyond knowledge; he who thinks that he knows, knows not. The ignorant think that Brahman is known, but the wise know him to be beyond knowledge.

He who realizes the existence of Brahman behind every activity of his being—whether sensing, perceiving, or thinking—he alone gains immortality. Through knowledge of Brahman comes power.

Through knowledge of Brahman comes victory over death.

Blessed is the man who while he yet lives realizes Brahman. The man who realizes him not suffers his greatest loss. When they depart this life, the wise, who have realized Brahman as the Self in all beings, become immortal.

> (*The Upanishads: Breath of the Eternal,* translated by Swami Prabhavananda and Frederick Manchester [New York: New American Library, Penguin Putnam, 1948] pp. 30–31)

Mundaka Upanishad

Like two birds of golden plumage, inseparable companions, the individual self and the immortal Self are perched on the branches of the selfsame tree. The former tastes of the sweet and bitter fruits of the tree; the latter, tasting of neither, calmly observes.

The individual self, deluded by forgetfulness of his identity with the divine Self, bewildered by his ego, grieves and is sad. But when he recognizes the worshipful Lord as his own true Self, and beholds his glory, he grieves no more.

When the seer beholds the Effulgent One, the Lord, the Supreme Being, then, transcending both good and evil, and freed from impurities, he unites himself with him.

The Lord is the one life shining forth from every creature. Seeing him present in all, the wise man is humble, puts not himself forward. His delight is in the Self, his joy is in the Self, he serves the Lord in all [human beings]. Such as he, indeed, are the true knowers of Brahman.

> (*The Upanishads: Breath of the Eternal,* pp. 46–47)

THE BHAGAVAD GITA

Knowing nature and the spirit of man,
as well as the qualities of nature,
one is not born again —
no matter how one now exists.
By meditating on the self, some men
see the self through the self;
others see by philosophical discipline;
others by the discipline of action.

Others, despite their ignorance,
revere what they hear from other men;
they too cross beyond death,
intent on what they hear.

Arjuna, know that anything
inanimate or alive with motion
is born from the union
of the field and its knower.

He really sees
who sees the highest lord
standing equal among all creatures,
undecaying amid destruction.

Seeing the lord standing
the same everywhere,
the self cannot injure itself
and goes the highest way.

He really sees who sees
that all actions are performed
by nature alone and that the self
is not an actor.

When he perceives the unity
existing in separate creatures

and how they expand from unity,
he attains the infinite spirit.

Beginningless, without qualities,
the supreme self is unchanging;
even abiding in a body, Arjuna,
it does not act, nor is it defiled.
Just as all-pervading space
remains unsullied in its subtlety,
so the self in every body
remains unsullied.

Just as one sun
illumines this entire world,
so the master of the field
illumines the entire field.

They reach the highest state
who with the eye of knowledge know
the boundary between the knower and its field,
and the freedom creatures have from nature.

(*The Bhagavad Gita*, translated by Barbara
Stoller Miller [New York: Bantam, 1986])

VISHNU PURANA

At that time there will be monarchs, reigning
over the earth; kings of churlish spirit, violent temper,
and ever addicted to falsehood and wickedness. They
will inflict death on women, children, and cows; they
will seize upon the property of their subjects; they
will be of limited power, and will for the most part
rapidly rise and fall; their lives will be short, their
desires insatiable, and they will display but little
piety.

Wealth and piety will decrease day by day, until the world will be wholly depraved. Then property alone will confer rank; wealth will be the only source of devotion; passion will be the sole bond of union between the sexes; falsehood will be the only means of success in litigation; and women will be objects merely of sensual gratification. Earth will be venerated but for its mineral treasures; the Brahmanical thread will constitute a Brahman; external types (as the staff and red garb) will be the only distinctions of the several orders of life; dishonesty will be the universal means of subsistence; weakness will be the cause of dependence; menace and presumption will be substituted for learning; liberality will be devotion; simple ablution will be purification; mutual assent will be marriage; fine clothes will be dignity; and water afar off will be esteemed a holy spring. Amidst all castes he who is the strongest will reign over a principality thus vitiated by many faults. The people, unable to bear the heavy burdens imposed upon them by their avaricious sovereigns, will take refuge amongst the valleys of the mountains, and will be glad to feed upon wild honey, herbs, roots, fruits, flowers, and leaves: their only covering will be the bark of trees, and they will be exposed to the cold, and wind, and sun, and rain. No man's life will exceed three and twenty years. Thus in the Kali* age shall decay constantly proceed, until the human race approaches its annihilation.

(*Vishnu Purana*, translated by H. H. Wilson [London: Juhn Murray, 1840])

* Kali is the last avatar before the dissolution of the *yuga* or epoch, and not to be confused with the Goddess Kali.

TENTH, ELEVENTH, AND TWELFTH CENTURY ITINERANT INDIAN POET-SAINTS

Basavanna

The rich
will make temples for Siva.
What shall I,
a poor man,
do?

My legs are pillars,
the body the shrine,
the head a cupola
of gold.

Listen, O lord of the meeting rivers,
things standing shall fall,
but the moving ever shall stay.

*   *   *

Does it matter how long
a rock soaks in the water:
will it ever grow soft?

Does is matter how long
I've spend in worship,
when the heart is fickle?

Futile as a ghost
I stand guard over hidden gold,

O lord of the meeting rivers.

*   *   *

The eating bowl is not one bronze
and the looking glass another.

Bowl and mirror are one metal.
Giving back light
one becomes a mirror.

Aware, one is the Lord's;
unaware, a mere human.

Worship the lord without forgetting,
the lord of meeting rivers.

*   *   *

Make of my body the beam of a lute
    of my head the sounding gourd
    of my nerves the strings
    of my fingers the plucking rods.

Clutch me close
    and play your thirty-two songs
    O lord of the meeting rivers!

Devara Dasimayya

The earth is your gift,
the growing grain your gift,
the blowing wind your gift.

What shall I call these curs
who eat out of your hand
and praise everyone else?

*   *   *

Unless you build,
Space will not get inside
a house;

unless the eye sees,
mind will not decide
on forms;

without a way
there's no reaching
the other;

O Ramanatha
how will men know
that this is so?

*   *   *

I'm the one who has the body,
you're the one who holds the breath.

You know the secrets of my body,
I know the secret of your breath.

That's why your body
is in mine.

You know
and I know, Ramanatha,

the miracle

of your breath
in my body.

Allama Prabhu

Looking for your light,
I went out:

it was like the sudden dawn
of a million million suns,

a ganglion of lightnings
for my wonder.

O Lord of Caves,
if you are light,
there can be no metaphor.

       *   *   *

A running river
   is all legs.

A burning fire
   is mouths all over.

A blowing breeze
   is all hands.

So, lord of the caves,
for your men,
every limb is Symbol.

       *   *   *

If it rains fire
   you have to be as the water;

if it is a deluge of water
   you have to be as the wind;

if it is the Great Flood,
    you have to be as the sky;

and if it is the Very Last Flood of all the worlds,
    you have to give up self

and become the Lord.

Mahadeviyakka

Like an elephant
lost from his herd
suddenly captured,

remembering his mountains,
    his Vindhyas,
        I remember.

A parrot
come into a cage
remembering his mate,
    I remember.

O lord white as jasmine
show me
your ways.
    Call me: Child, come here,
        come this way.

(*Speaking of Siva*, compiled and translated
by A. K. Ramanujan [New York: Penguin
Books, 1973])

THE TEACHINGS OF SWAMI VIVEKANANDA

Swami Vivekenanda was a nineteenth-century Hindu saint and reformer who insisted that social service (*seva*) was service of God.

No man is born into any religion; he has religion in his own soul.

To the Hindu, man is not travelling from error to truth, but from truth to truth—from lower truth to higher truth. To him all religions, from the lowest fetishism to the highest absolutism, mean so many attempts of the human soul to grasp and realize the Infinite, each determined by the conditions of its birth and association; and each of these attempts marks a stage of progress.

Religious quarrels are always over the husks. When purity, when spirituality, goes, leaving the soul dry, then quarrels begin, and not before.

Man has an idea that there can be only one religion, that there can be only one Prophet, that there can be only one Incarnation; but that idea is not true. By studying the lives of all these great Messengers, we find that each was destined to play a part, as it were, and a part only; that the harmony consists in the sum total, and not in one note.

There never was my religion or yours, my national religion or your national religion. There never existed many religions; there is only one Religion. One infinite Religion has existed all through eternity and will ever exist, and this Religion is expressing itself in various countries in different ways.

There is one principle which underlies all the various manifestations of religion and which has already been mapped out for us. Every science must end where it finds a unity, because we cannot go any farther. When a perfect unity is reached, then science has nothing more of principles to tell us. So with religion. The gigantic principle, the scope, the plan, of religion was already discovered ages ago, when man found the last words, as they are called in the Vedas, "I am He" — that there is One in whom this whole universe of matter and mind finds its unity, whom they call God, or Brahman, or Allah, or Jehovah, or by any other name. We cannot go beyond that.

The end of all religions is the realizing of God in the soul. If there is one universal truth in all religions, I place it here, in realizing God. Ideals and methods may differ, but that is the central point. There may be a thousand different radii, but they all converge upon the one centre, and that is the realization of God — something behind this world of the senses.

Vedanta says that you are pure and perfect and that there is a state beyond good and evil, and that that is your own nature. It is higher than good. Good is only a lesser differentiation than evil. We have no theory of evil. We call it ignorance.

Now, in my little experience I have collected this knowledge: In spite of all the devilry that religion is blamed with, religion is not at all at fault; no religion ever persecuted men, no religion ever burnt witches, no religion ever did any of these things. What then incited people to do these things? Politics, but never religion. And if such politics takes the name of religion, whose fault is it?

Suppose we all go with vessels in our hands to fetch water from a lake. One has a cup, another a jar, another a bucket, and so forth, and we all fill our vessels. The water in each case naturally takes the form of the vessel carried by each of us. So it is with religion. Our minds are like those vessels. God is like the water filling the different vessels. And in each vessel the vision of God comes in the form of the vessel. Yet He is One; He is God in every case.

That religion which is only a means to worldly well-being is not religion, whatever else it may be.

There is no "I" and no "you"; it is all one. It is either all "I" or all "you." This idea of duality, of two, is entirely false, and the whole universe, as we ordinarily know it, is the result of this false knowledge. When discrimination comes, and man finds there are not two, but One, he finds that he himself is this universe.

The seeing of many is the great sin of the world. See all as the Self and love all; let the idea of separateness go.

Our salutations go to all the past Prophets, whose teachings and lives we have inherited, whatever may have been their race, clime, or creed. Our salutations go to all those God-like men and women who are working at present to help humanity, whatever be their birth, colour, or race. Our salutations go to those who are coming in the future — living Gods — to work unselfishly for our descendants!

It is generally said that he is an atheist who does not believe in God. Vedanta says that he is an atheist who does not believe in himself. But this is not selfish faith, because Vedanta, again, is the doctrine of Oneness. It means faith in all because you are all.

Not one atom in the universe can move without dragging the whole world along with it. There cannot be any progress without the whole world's following in its wake; and it is becoming clearer every day that the solution of any problem can never be attained on racial or national or any narrow grounds.

I am thoroughly convinced that no individual or nation can live by holding itself apart from the community of others; whenever such an attempt has been made, under the false notion of greatness, policy, or holiness, the result has always been disastrous to the one who thus secluded himself.

All that unites with the universe is virtue. All that separates is sin.

When you hurt anyone you hurt yourself, for you and your brother are one.

Not one can be happy until all are happy.

I have understood this as the real truth: God is present in every jiva*; there is no other God besides that. He who serves the jiva serves God indeed.

> (From *The Complete Works of Swami Vivekananda* (Mayavati Memorial Edition) [Calcutta: Advaita Ashrama, 1989])

* Note: "*jiva*" in Sanskrit means "living being," hence, "human." It is neither masculine nor feminine.

SWAMI VIVEKANANDA ON SERVICE

This is the gist of all worship: to be good and to do good to others. He who sees Siva in the poor, in the weak, and in the diseased really worships Siva; and if he sees Siva only in the image, his worship is but preliminary. He who has served and helped one poor man, seeing Siva in him, without thinking of his caste or creed or race, or anything, with him Siva is more pleased than He is with the man who sees Him only in temples.

Do you love your fellow men? Where should you go to seek for God — are not all the poor, the miserable, the weak, Gods? Why not worship them first? Why go to dig a well on the bank of the Ganges?

First bread and then religion. We stuff them too much with religion, when the poor fellows have been starving. No dogmas will satisfy the cravings of hunger. There are two curses here: first, our physical weakness, secondly, our jealousy, our dried-up hearts. You may talk doctrines by the millions, you may have sects by the hundreds of millions; ay, but it is all nothing until you have the heart to feel. Feel for them, as Your Veda teaches you, till you find they are parts of your bodies, till you realize that you and they, the poor and the rich, the saint and the sinner, are all parts of one infinite Whole, which you call Brahman.

You must all set your shoulders to the wheel! Your duty at present is to go from one part of the country to another, from village to village, and make the people understand that mere sitting about idly won't do any more. Make them understand their real condition, and say: "O ye brothers all, arise! Awake! How much longer will you remain asleep?" Go and advise them how to improve their own condition, and make them comprehend the sublime truths of the scriptures by presenting them in a lucid and popular way. Also instruct them, in simple words, about the necessities of life, and in trade, commerce, agriculture, and so on. If you cannot do this, then fie upon your education and culture, and fie upon your study of the Vedas and Vedanta!

In the first place, I would ask mankind to recognize this maxim: Do not destroy. Break not, pull not anything down, but build. Help if you can. Do not injure if you cannot render help. Secondly, take a man where he stands, and from there give him a lift.

It is our privilege to be allowed to be charitable, for only so can we grow. The poor man suffers that we may be helped. Let the giver kneel down and give thanks; let the receiver stand up and permit. See the Lord back of every being and give to Him.

(From *The Complete Works of Swami Vivekananda* (Mayavati Memorial Edition) [Calcutta: Advaita Ashrama, 1989])

SELECTIONS FROM MAHATMA GANDHI

Why should there be so many different faiths? The Soul is one, but the bodies which she animates are many. We cannot reduce the number of bodies: yet we recognize the unity of the Soul. Even as a tree has a single trunk but many branches and leaves, so is there one true and perfect Religion, but it becomes many, as it passes through the human medium. The one Religion is beyond all speech. Imperfect men put it into such language as they can command and their words are interpreted by other men equally imperfect. Whose interpretation is to be held to be the right one? Every one is right from his own standpoint, but it is not impossible that every one is wrong. Hence the necessity for tolerance, which does not mean indifference towards one's own faith but a love for it. Tolerance gives us spiritual insight, which is as far from fanaticism as the North Pole is from the South. True knowledge of religion breaks down the barriers between faith and faith. Cultivation of tolerance for other faiths will impart to us a truer understanding of our own.

Man does not pray to God through speech alone but through thought, word and deed. If any one of these three aspects is missing, there is no devotion.

How and where should man, who has a physical form, worship God? He is omnipresent. Hence the best and most understandable place where He can be worshipped is a living creature. The service of the distressed, the crippled and the helpless among living things constitutes worship of God.

Service is not possible unless it is rooted in love or *ahimsa*. True love is boundless like the ocean and rising and swelling within one spreads itself out and crossing all boundaries and frontiers envelopes the whole world. This service is again impossible without bread labour, otherwise described in the *Gita* as *yajna*. It is only when a man or woman has done body labour for the sake of service that he or she has a right to live.

Again, one dare not be negligent in service, or be behindhand with it. He, who thinks that one must be diligent only in one's personal business, and unpaid public business may be done in any way and at any time one chooses, has still to learn the very rudiments of the science of sacrifice. Voluntary service of others demands the best of which one is capable, and must take precedence over service of self. In fact, the pure devotee consecrates himself to the service of humanity without any reservation whatever.

A life of service must be one of humility.

My uniform experience has convinced me that there is no other God than Truth. And if every page of these chapters does not proclaim to the reader that the only means for the realization of Truth is non-violence, I shall deem all my labor in writing to have been in vain. And, even though my efforts in this behalf may prove fruitless, let the readers know that the vehicle, not the great principle is at fault. After all, however sincere my strivings after *Ahimsa* may have been, they have still been imperfect and inadequate. The little fleeting glimpses, therefore, that

I have been able to have of Truth can hardly convey an idea of the indescribable luster of Truth, a million times more intense than that of the sun we daily see with our eyes. In fact what I have caught is only the faintest glimmer of that mighty effulgence. But this much I can say with assurance, as a result of all my experiments, that a perfect vision of Truth can only follow a complete realization of *Ahimsa*.

To see the universal and all-pervading Spirit of Truth face to face one must be able to love the meanest of creation as oneself. And a man who aspires after that cannot afford to keep out any field of life. That is why my devotion to Truth has drawn me into the field of politics; and I can say without the slightest hesi-tation, and yet in all humility, that those who say that religion has nothing to do with politics do not know what religion means.

Identification with everything that lives is impossible without self-purification; without self-purification the observance of the law of *Ahimsa* must remain an empty dream; God can never be realized by one who is not pure of heart. Self-purification therefore must mean purification in all the walks of life. And purification being highly infectious, purification of oneself necessarily leads to the purification of one's surroundings.

But the path of self-purification is hard and steep. To attain to perfect purity one has to become absolutely passion-free in thought, speech, and action; to rise above the opposing currents of love and hatred, attachment and repulsion. I know that I have not in me as yet that triple purity, in spite of constant ceaseless striving for it. That is why the world's praise fails to move me, indeed it very often stings me. To conquer the subtle passions seems to me to be harder far than the physical conquest of the world by the force of arms.

I do justify entire non-violence, and consider it possible in relation between man and man and nation and nation; but it is not "a resignation from all real fighting against wickedness." On the contrary, the non-violence of my conception is a more active and more real fighting against wickedness than retaliation whose very nature is to increase wickedness. I contemplate a mental, and therefore a moral, opposition to immoralities. I seek entirely to blunt the edge of the tyrant's sword, not by putting up against it a sharper-edged weapon, but by disappointing his expectation that I should be offering physical resistance. The resistance of the soul that I should offer instead would elude him. It would at first dazzle him, and at last compel recognition from him, which recognition would not humiliate him but would uplift him. It may be urged that this again is an ideal state. And so it is. The propositions from which I have drawn my arguments are as true as Euclid's definitions, which are none the less true, because in practice we are unable even to draw Euclid's line on a blackboard.

I do not believe that an individual may gain spiritually while those who surround him suffer. I believe in *advaita*; I believe in the essential unity of man and, for that matter, of all that lives. Therefore, I believe that if one man gains spiritually, the whole world gains with him, and if one man falls, the whole world falls to that extent.

I have such implicit faith in my mission that, if it succeeds—as it will succeed, it is bound to succeed—history will record it as a movement designed to knit all people in the world together, not as hostile to one another but as parts of one whole.

Causes of hatred everywhere obtrude themselves on one's gaze. The Seers of old saw that the
only way of dealing with the Situation was to
neutralize hatred by love.

Hatred ever kills, love never dies. Such is the vast
difference between the two. What is obtained by love
is retained for all time. What is obtained by hatred
proves a burden in reality, for it increases hatred. The
duty of a human being is to diminish hatred and to
promote love.

The Allah of Islam is the same as the God of
Christians and the Ishwara of Hindus. Even as there
are numerous names of God in Hinduism, there are
many names of God in Islam. The names do not
indicate individuality but attributes, and little man
has tried in his humble way to describe mighty God
by giving Him attributes, though He is above all
attributes, Indescribable, Immeasurable. Living faith
in this God means acceptance of the brotherhood of
mankind. It also means equal respect for all religions.
If Islam is dear to you, Hinduism is dear to me and
Christianity is dear to the Christians. It would be the
height of intolerance — and intolerance is a species of
violence — to believe that your religion is superior to
other religions and that you would be justified in
wanting others to change over to your faith.

(From Mahatma Gandhi, *Collected Works*
[Delhi: Publications Division, Ministry of
Information and Broadcasting, Govern-
ment of India, 1958])

Questions

The following questions address concepts and texts discussed in both the chapter on Hinduism and the excerpts from the sacred writings.

The earliest of the Hindu Sacred Texts are full of questions. What questions would you add to the ones in the "Nasadiya?"

Is it comforting or threatening to be able to ask questions? What paradigm of authority is implied by this text? Does it encourage plural views and tolerance for diversity of views? Why do you think so? If not, why not?

Hinduism lays great emphasis on the individual vision and the art of questioning. If you were to write your own version of the creation myth, what would it be? How would you situate the human within nature and within the moral universe? What relationship would humans have with nature and with each other?

In the Upanishads, is there a distinction made between people? Between "us" and "them"? Between strangers and neighbors? Who are regarded as strangers?

How do you see gender differences within this culture? Do the people in the culture see the same differences? What have you observed in the sacred texts? What have you observed in practice in the society where you are serving?

The idea of "*sruti*" texts iterates that there are certain truths we *hear* within ourselves. Do you find that credible? How would you characterize the questions asked in the *Kena Upanishad*, "Who is the Spirit behind the eye and the ear?"

The *Chandogya, Katha,* and *Isa Upanishads* deal not oniy with the transcendent but with the immediate. How then should we relate to the world and to the people in it?

What is the point of the Svetaketu story in the *Chandogya Upanishad*? What does the example of the banyan seed illustrate?

How does the lesson of the *Chandogya Upanishad* influence our own societal, political, familial, and even interpersonal relationships?

Now let us look at the old question again: Who do you regard as neighbors? Who are strangers? Who are regarded as neighbors and who as strangers in the community in which you are serving?

In what ways is the responsibility for your actions and intentions influenced by the philosophic view in the Upanishads? How does this consciousness interact with "the spirit behind the eye and the ear" (quoted from *Kena Upanishad*)?

How do the concepts of *Atman* and *Brahman* figure in these considerations?

How is the stranger or neighbor to be thought of in these contexts?

What is properly the true context of human action?

What is not service? What is service? How can one tell the difference? Do the ancient Hindu texts help in trying to tell the difference?

What is the concept of *"ahimsa"*? How is it connected to the idea of service?

Where should we perform service? Are there designated places? Discuss this in the context of the poems of Kabir.

What is the philosophy of the service organization where you work? Who do you serve? Are others serving you? Who, and in what ways?

The *Taittiriya Upanishad* explains the various *kosas* that make up the human being. Which are the different *kosas* (your own, and in those you serve) of which you are most aware during and after your service?

What role does language (verbal and nonverbal) play at different levels in your service? Please explain and relate to the sections on the *Taittiriya Upanishad.*

What is the most valuable part of your service? Why is it valuable? For whom is it valuable?

If you are serving in a culture not your own, how does this add to your experience of life?

Does a lack of a commonality in language form a barrier? Is it a barrier that can be negotiated? In what way? Discuss this in detail.

Does the idea of the *kosas* in *Taittiriya Upanishad* help in the context of service? How does it influence the context of your learning? What kind of experiential and analytical learning has it encouraged in you?

Are you beginning to construct a new grammar of learning and experience when you serve in a foreign culture?

Which of the texts or thinkers (e.g., *Kena Upanishad, Chandogya Upanishad*, Ramakrishna, or Gandhi) did you turn to? Which were of most value? If you are encountering these thinkers and ideas in their indigenous culture and tradition, does this help you situate yourself better within that culture?

Are there any particular texts that you found outlandish when you first came upon them? What did you find strange? Did they contradict assumptions from your primary culture? Are these differences you can live with—even if they are irreconcilable? Does the experience of service contribute to your ability to deal with contradictions? Explain as far as possible, with specific instances, from your service experience and the theoretical bases of your readings.

How do you deal with the idea of trinity in Hinduism? What about polytheism? How do alien religious beliefs affect your attitude toward a culture? Do you enjoy diversity, or is it sometimes frightening? What do you learn from it?

Can you use the concepts of karma and dharma in your primary society? How does it affect your attitude to others? What about your concept of "the stranger?" What is your duty to the "stranger?" What is your duty to your neighbor? Is there a difference? What do the Upanishads say about differences and unity?

Where do "service" and "*ahimsa*" fit in the construct of the society where you grew up? What are the concepts in your society that come closest to those in India and its sacred texts?

If you could change one thing in your life, what would it be? Why? If you were asked the same question five years ago, what would you have said? What has changed in these years? Can you explain that change in the context of the *Taittiriya Upanishad* or any other sacred Indian text?

What are the ways in which you expected the experience of service to change or affect you? Were there surprises? How were these related to what you were learning? Has your attitude toward learning changed in the process? How is it different?

BUDDHISM

John Butt

INTRODUCTION

Few, if any, individual human beings in history have had greater influence on how persons have understood and lived their lives than a religious "wanderer" named Siddhattha Gotama. This creative religious genius lived most of his life in areas that are now Nepal and northeastern India sometime around the middle of the first millennium B.C.E.[1] His given name was Siddhattha or Siddhartha,[2] and he belonged to the Gotama or Gautama clan. But he is better known in history and to the millions who have revered and followed him as the Buddha.

The word "Buddha" is a title, not a name, and it means one who has "awakened" or become "enlightened." It refers specifically to one who has discovered the "truth." Truth here is used in a comprehensive sense to refer to truth about oneself, truth about the condition of all other human beings, truth about the universe, and truth about ultimate reality. The designation "Buddha" also indicates one who has been transformed by that truth into a new being.

The impressive charismatic power of Siddhattha's personality, coupled with the compelling cogency of his teachings, soon convinced many of those who had contact with him that he was no ordinary man, but rather a very special one who deserved the title of "Buddha." They became convinced that here was a man who had indeed discovered the truth about reality and about how human beings should think and live. They also believed that his life embodied and exemplified that truth.

The religious movement that dates back to the Buddha eventually spread to all parts of Asia and today encompasses the entire world. Buddhist contributions to Asian art, literature, philosophy, beliefs, and practices have been tremendous and continue to influence significantly the lives of many Asian

97

peoples. Indeed, much of Asian culture and civilization, both past and present, has been inspired at least in part by the influence of the Buddhist religion.

Over the centuries, as the Buddhist movement spread throughout Asia and to other parts of the world, it developed many different ideas, organizational forms, and social expressions. Some of the different historical and geographical embodiments of the movement seem almost incompatible or even contradictory. But the variety of different forms and expressions found in the Buddhist religion is actually a proof of the movement's creative power.

In this chapter we shall focus on the Theravada Buddhist tradition, which appears to have arisen in ancient India perhaps as early as a century or so after the time of the Buddha. It then spread to Sri Lanka, where it received its definitive forms, and onward to Southeast Asia, where it is still the dominant and most prominent form of religion.[3]

We shall focus on the Theravada tradition for two reasons. First, this tradition claims, with some justification, to be the oldest existing form of Buddhist religion and the form that most closely resembles the original. Second, it presents a form of religion that in many ways stands in sharpest contrast to those forms found in the West, and therefore it may present the most intriguing and challenging form of Buddhist religion for the Western reader.

We begin by looking at the life of the Buddha as it is presented by the Theravada tradition. The earliest accounts of his life are found in the Tipitaka, the name for the Theravada Buddhist scriptural canon. These accounts are for the most part legendary or mythical, but from these stories one can also catch a glimpse of the "historical" person who stood behind and gave rise to the myth, the one who was called "the Buddha."

THE BUDDHA

The exact date of Siddhattha's birth is not known. Until fairly recently, Western scholars tended to place it around 566 B.C.E. Recent research, however, has caused some scholars to reconsider their previous reckoning and to move the date of the birth later in time by perhaps as much as one hundred years. The traditional date set by most Buddhists is almost two hundred years earlier than the new Western date, and it is this traditional earlier date that is still observed by Buddhists in Southeast Asia.[4]

This entire period of Indian history was an age of social turmoil, political and economic upheaval, and cultural and religious transition. The India in which the Buddha lived was undergoing profound changes that affected every area of human life. In order to better understand these changes, one must look back to events that occurred almost a millennium prior to the Buddha's birth.

At that time, several waves of nomadic tribal peoples from the steppes of Central Asia moved into and began to occupy the northwestern part of the Indian subcontinent. These invaders from northwest Asia called themselves Aryans. Over the next thousand years, they gradually conquered the indigenous peoples who had previously lived in the area surrounding the Indus River. Throughout this thousand-year period, the Aryans proceeded to move slowly southward and eastward until they had reached the basin of the Ganges River.

During the time of their movement eastward and southward, the cultural life of the Aryans was slowly but surely being disrupted and transformed by the land and the peoples whom they had conquered. The pastoral and nomadic way of life that they had embraced when they lived in the steppes of Central Asia and that they had still maintained when they entered the Indian subcontinent was gradually replaced by an agricultural and then, later, by an urban society. In this new situation, the tribal social customs and moral norms that had previously governed Aryan life began to break down and disappear.

Values and truths that had once been considered eternal and had given meaning and significance to life now often seemed irrelevant and unworkable. Even religious teachings and practices that had once provided answers to fundamental questions about human life became less and less cogent and compelling in the new agricultural and urban settings. Instead of providing a key that opened the door to the meaning of life, as had once been the case, religious beliefs and practices now offered little help to a confused and distraught generation. Instead of solving problems and providing answers, religion had itself become problematic and questionable.[5]

The widespread disillusionment, anxiety, and despair that increasingly prevailed throughout Aryan society caused religion in many cases to degenerate further into magical rituals and ignorant superstition. Not all persons, however, were content to rely on magical and superstitious rituals. Some, driven by the inability of past religious beliefs and practices to explain and demonstrate an authentic and fulfilling human existence, began to search for new answers to the meaning of life.

Some of these searchers for truth became forest hermits engaged in philosophical and religious discussions about what was truly real and what kind of life was genuinely and authentically "human." These persons became the creators of the ideas and teachings found in the Upanishads, which became the intellectual foundation for later Hindu religion.

Others took up a wandering life. Dressed in rags taken from the cremation grounds and existing on food given to them by those living in the villages and towns through which they passed, they traveled from place to place seeking that which was truly real and really true. Finding one who claimed to have discovered the truth or who showed promise of finding it, they would gather around him and become his disciples. It was with this group of "wanderers" that the Buddha became associated when he began his own search for enlightenment and truth. And it was from them that most of his early followers came.

The Buddhist traditions claim that the Buddha was born at a site called Lumbini, which is now just across the Indian border in Nepal. His father, named Suddhodana, was purportedly the ruler of a relatively small tribal "kingdom" inhabited by a people known as the Sakyas.[6]

Northeastern India was at this time one of the frontiers of Aryan expansion. The Aryans themselves and their customs and civilization were new arrivals in the area. Indigenous beliefs and practices were still present and often seem to have exerted considerable influence on the people's thoughts and lives. The more developed and sophisticated forms of Aryan culture and life, represented by the Vedic traditions and rituals and the advanced speculations of the Upanishads, had probably not yet penetrated very much into this region but were found primarily in areas farther to the west.

The Ganges basin and the surrounding areas were places where one would have been exposed to a multitude of new ideas about reality and what was true. The disillusionment and despair about past traditions were certainly also present, but in addition there was a plethora of creative new ideas and new alternative ways of life. The intellectual and religious ferment concerning what it meant to be and to live as a true human being would have been experienced by the future Buddha from an early age. Not only was he exposed to this creative and protean social and mental environment, he would later make a significant contribution to it.

Although we probably think of the story of the Buddha's life beginning with his birth, many Buddhists do not. For them, the story begins in the distant past, many, many aeons ago, when a Brahman or Indian priest named Sumedha met a former Buddha named Dipankara. Sumedha was greatly impressed by this Buddha, and made a vow that he too would henceforth strive to become a fully enlightened Buddha. Henceforth, he would be a "bodhisatta," or one destined for Buddhahood.[7]

Over the aeons that followed and during more than 550 subsequent rebirths that are recorded in a collection of Buddhist stories called the *Jataka Tales*, this bodhisatta who had once been Sumedha gradually perfected the various virtues and character traits that would prepare him for enlightenment. These stories of the past lives of the Buddha are intended to show his exceptional character and virtue. They also demonstrate that the path to enlightenment is not an easy or quick one but requires much preparation and effort. The stories also illustrate in a dramatic and memorable fashion the types of preparation and effort that are required.

Especially important are the last ten lives prior to the bodhisatta's final rebirth as Siddhattha. During these ten lives, he perfected the ten most important virtues that are prerequisites to the attainment of enlightenment. The climax is reached with the story of Prince Vessantara, who perfects the virtue of "*dana*," or giving.[8] The bodhisatta is then reborn in Tusita Heaven, where he will remain until he is reborn as Prince Siddhattha.

Many of the details concerning Siddhattha's life may strike the modern student as implausible and far-fetched. For example, the Buddhist tradition states that immediately after his birth he took seven steps and proclaimed to all within hearing that he was the foremost of all human beings, that in this life he would become enlightened, and that thereafter he would experience no more rebirths. Of course, stories about a newborn baby walking and talking strike many modern readers as preposterous and ridiculous. But what the student needs to remember regarding this story and other similar unbelievable episodes from the Buddha's life is that they were not intended to be literal accounts or video records of what happened.

In the mind of the creators and transmitters of these stories, the Buddha was the greatest and most important person ever to have lived on earth. Because, according to their thinking, he was so extraordinary, they believed that extraordinary things must have taken place in his life; in fact, they expected this. Their accounts of the Buddha's life should therefore not be read as literal renditions of what happened, but as confessions of their own faith in this very special person. For them he was himself miraculous, and so they believed that his life must have also been filled with miraculous events. An ordinary, literal version of what took place would fail to do justice to who the Buddha really was, what he truly represented, and how he lived.

Soon after Siddhattha's birth, he was visited by an Indian seer or holy man who, while in a meditative trance, is supposed to have observed great rejoicing taking place in the heavens. After inquiring about the cause of this celebration, he was told that a very special child had just been born on earth. Wishing to see this special person, the holy man sought out the newborn child. When he entered King Suddhodana's palace, the child levitated, and both the holy man and the parents paid obeisance to the child. This was of course a reversal of ordinary behavior, in which a child pays respect to his or her parents and a younger lay person shows reverence to a holy man. The point of the story is that this was no ordinary child.[9]

A story concerning Prince Siddhattha's childhood has the same theme. On the occasion of a royal plowing ceremony over which King Suddhodana was presiding, the seven-year-old prince was left seated under a tree near where the ceremony was taking place. As the royal plow dug into the earth and turned over the soil, many earthworms were exposed, and soon birds began to congregate and swoop down to devour them. The young prince, observing the birds eating the worms, became very distraught by this cruelty of nature. In order to calm himself, he began to focus on his in-breathing and out-breathing and soon fell into a meditative trance. Although the sun continued to move across the sky, the shadow of the tree beneath which the young prince was seated remained firmly fixed on the spot that he occupied. The royal babysitters, noticing that the shadow had not moved, summoned the prince's parents, who came and once again paid him reverence.

This story, in many ways similar to the story of the boy Jesus in the temple, shows the superior and extraordinary nature of the young prince. It demonstrates first of all Siddhattha's great sensitivity to suffering. It also shows his power over the forces and laws of nature. Later in his life, shortly before his enlightenment, Siddhattha would recall this incident and again focus on his breathing as a means of stilling and centering his thoughts and feelings.

A major event occurred in Siddhattha's life when he reached the age of twenty-nine. Accompanied by his personal attendant, he went for a ride in his chariot through a park near the palace. On this and subsequent outings the prince encountered an old man, an extremely sick person, and a human corpse.[10] Supposedly this was the first time that the prince had ever seen people in these conditions.

The tradition explains that his father had shielded and protected him from all such sights since the time of his birth. This was because the astrologers who had predicted the child's future had all agreed that Suddhodana's son was endowed with an extraordinary nature and had unusual potential. They predicted that he would become either a universal political ruler (*Cakkavatti/Chakravartin*) or a fully enlightened religious leader (a Buddha) whose teachings would save the world.

When the father inquired what would determine which of these two courses would be the one his son would follow, he was told that if the child were ever exposed to suffering (*dukkha*), he would renounce the throne and go in search of enlightenment. King Suddhodana apparently preferred to have his son become a universal ruler, and from that day onward he sought to shield his son from all contact with every kind of suffering. Indeed, he even forbade all elderly, sick, and dying people from entering the vicinity of the palace.[11] It was only through the miraculous intervention of supermundane or heavenly beings posing as an old man, an invalid, and a corpse that the prince was finally made aware of these three forms of suffering.[12]

This confrontation with aging, sickness, and death at first startled the prince, who was puzzled and confused as to why anyone should be in such conditions. When his attendant explained to him that this was the common destiny of all human beings and that someday in the future even the prince would experience these same three conditions, Siddhattha was overcome with despair and despondency.

As he continued through the park, however, he came upon a fourth person. This fourth encounter was to alter Siddhattha's own life and to affect human history forever. The fourth encounter was with a religious wanderer dressed in rags but with an appearance and bearing that deeply impressed the prince. When he inquired from his attendant who this person was, his attendant responded that this was one of those who had left society and gone in search of an answer to the enigmas of human existence represented by aging, sickness, and death. At that exact moment, Siddhattha resolved that he too would follow this example and take up the life of a religious wanderer.

When the prince and his attendant returned to the palace, King Suddhodana was informed about what his son had seen. He immediately summoned the prince and tried desperately to persuade him not to renounce the throne for the life of a religious wanderer. Finally, Siddhattha agreed to remain in the palace and continue as the heir to his father's throne if his father would agree to grant him a request. Eagerly, King Suddhodana agreed, but when he asked his son what it was that he wanted, Siddhattha replied that his request was never to experience old age, sickness, and death.

In desperation, King Suddhodana ordered the gates of the palace shut in an effort to prevent Siddhattha from leaving. He then summoned the most skilled, beautiful, and sensual female dancers and musicians in the royal household to come and entertain his son, hoping that this entertainment would distract and divert him from his intention to leave the palace.

The dancers and musicians entertained the prince late into the night, but their performances had little or no effect on him. And as the night grew late, one by one the performers fell asleep. Soon their beautiful and seductive hair and clothing became disheveled. Some began to snore. Saliva ran down the cheeks of others. And as the prince gazed upon the sleeping women before him, rather than seeing a seductive and diverting scene, he was instead reminded of the decaying corpse that he had encountered earlier that day.

Rising from his seat, Siddhattha took a farewell look at his sleeping wife and newborn son.[13] Then the prince mounted his horse, and together with his attendant and with help from the supermundane beings, he left the palace. As Siddhattha departed the palace, he was confronted by the demon Mara,[14] the Buddhist personification of suffering and death, who unsuccessfully tried to block and prevent the prince's "going forth." But the bodhisatta was not to be stopped. He would continue until he had found the truth about reality and discovered how to overcome suffering and death.

This "Great Going Forth," as it is called in the Buddhist tradition, took place on the night of the full moon during the month that usually corresponds to the month of May in the modern Western calendar. This event has been reenacted many millions of times in the countries of Southeast Asia during the ensuing centuries. Young Buddhist youths dressed in clothes resembling that of an Indian prince have, like Siddhattha, mounted a horse when one was available or ridden on the shoulders of a male relative when one was not and left their homes to go to a nearby Buddhist temple. There they have shaved their heads, donned the yellow robes of Buddhist novices or monks (today's equivalent of religious wanderers) and, following Siddhattha's example, begun their own quest for enlightenment.[15]

After leaving the palace, Siddhattha spent the next several months studying with two famous teachers who belonged to the wanderers' community. From them he learned how to meditate and soon gained the ability to attain the higher meditative trances. But he still lacked that for which he was searching, namely, the truth about the human condition of suffering (*dukkha*), its causes, and its remedy. Leaving the two teachers, he next embarked upon a six-year period of severe asceticism, during which he endured extreme austerities.

His ascetic efforts eventually gained him five disciples who were impressed by his dedication and resolve to find an answer to the human predicament. His efforts also resulted in his becoming severely emaciated and weakened — so weakened, in fact, that he drew closer and closer to death. Finally, one day he fell into a coma and was thought by his companions to have died, but he then revived and resumed his meditations.

Suddenly, as he meditated, he heard in his mind the playing of an Indian stringed instrument.[16] Listening to the sounds of this instrument, he reflected that in order to achieve the proper note the strings must be neither too taut nor too loose. It occurred to him that the same principle applied to the search for truth and enlightenment.

As a child and young man he had been protected, pampered, and indulged by his parents. He had enjoyed a life of luxury and ease. But such a life had not resulted in the eradication of suffering. He knew that old age, sickness, and death still awaited him. Now, in an effort to avoid and conquer these conditions, he had gone to the opposite extreme and was engaging in excessive and destructive austerities. But rather than saving him from death and suffering, these austerities had merely caused him to suffer more and they were now about to cause his death. At that moment, he came to the conclusion that neither a life of indulgence and luxury nor a life of severe asceticism was the way that would lead to truth and enlightenment. The right path was the "Middle Way" between these two extremes.

Coming to this realization, Siddhattha announced to his companions that he was giving up his ascetic practices. His companions, feeling that Siddhattha was a "quitter" and a "loser," now left him to go in search of another religious guide.

Alone and weak, but with new inspiration and hope, Siddhattha resumed his search for the truth.

While wandering in the vicinity of Bodhgaya, Siddhattha was given a nourishing meal by a female householder.[17] Strengthened and refreshed by this food, he was now ready to embark on the final stages of his quest for enlightenment. Recalling the peace and tranquility that he had experienced as a young child when he had focused on his breathing, he decided that he would once again use this form of meditation in a final effort to reach his goal.

He prepared a place to meditate under a species of tree that would later become known as the Bodhi tree or the "Tree of Enlightenment." Siddhattha resolved that he would remain there seated in meditation focusing upon his breathing until he had discovered and understood the truth about suffering, its causes, and the way to eradicate those causes.

However, before beginning to meditate, he decided to take his alms bowl to the bank of a nearby stream to confirm that his new course of action was the correct one. If he were now on the right path, he wanted a sign to confirm that this was the case. When he placed the bowl in the water, he received the sign: the bowl began to move upstream, against the current. Siddhattha now knew that he was following the correct path.

The bodhisatta's bowl slowly filled with water and sank to the bottom of the stream. As it reached the bottom it hit the alms bowls of the previous Buddhas, who had also sat at this very same spot when they reached enlightenment. This story informs us that the bodhisatta was at a very special and sacred place. This place should be understood not in a geographical sense but in a religious or existential sense. Although Siddhattha, no doubt, did sit beneath a tree in the forest in the vicinity of Bodhgaya at the time of his enlightenment, the alms bowls of all the previous Buddhas at this spot reveals the deeper religious meaning of this place and the event that occurred there.

Religious scholars sometimes refer to such a place as the *axis mundi*, or the "center of the world or the universe." This is not a geographical reference but a spiritual or religious one. The *axis mundi* is not a spot that can be located on a map. The place of enlightenment can be anywhere. In the case of Siddhattha, it happened to be beneath a tree in a forest in northeast India near the town called Bodhgaya. But it might be anywhere, a spot on a road, or a stall in a market, or a desk in an office or library. It is wherever one happens to be when one penetrates and understands the truth about reality. That is why the alms bowls of all those who have become enlightened were at this spot.

This understanding of the place of enlightenment also helps to explain what happened next. Siddhattha was now attacked once again by the demon Mara. Mara and Siddhattha engaged in a struggle over who had the right to sit beneath the tree. This was not a fight over who got to sit under a shady tree in the forest on a hot day. It was a struggle to determine who sits at the symbolic center, and is therefore Lord of the universe. The struggle was to determine whether suffering and death, as represented by Mara, or peace, serenity, truth, and life, as represented by the future Buddha will dominate the universe and human existence.

Mara first attempted to prevent Siddhattha's enlightenment by attacking him with an army of demons and hideous animals in an effort to frighten him and thereby force him to give up his pursuit of enlightenment. When the attack failed, Mara attempted to dissuade him by pointing to the great multitude of demons and animals supporting Mara's claim to rule over the universe. He then challenged Siddhattha to support his own claim by producing an equal or superior amount of support.

In what was to become the basis for one of the most popular mudras (symbolic gestures) of Buddhist iconography, Siddhattha responded by pointing to the ground with his right hand. Immediately, the earth goddess emerged from the depths of the earth, and from her hair poured forth a flood of water that washed away Mara and his host. This story employs a very powerful and meaningful religious imagery.

In India and the Buddhist areas of Southeast Asia, good deeds or acts of virtue and religious merit were, and still are, confirmed ritually by pouring water over the hand of the recipient. This water, of course, is then absorbed into the ground. What is symbolized in this story is the reemergence from the earth of all the water that had been absorbed during the time when the bodhisatta had been pursuing enlighten-ment. The water represents all the virtuous deeds and merit previously accumulated by the bodhisatta. These good deeds and merit are what have earned Siddhattha the right to reach and sit at the place of enlightenment.

It should be noted, however, that although good deeds or meritorious actions bring one to the point of enlightenment, they do not produce enlightenment itself. In order to discover the truth one must go beyond the doing of good and virtuous acts. One must be able also to penetrate and realize the truth through meditation.

Mara made one final attempt to prevent Siddhattha from meditating. He sent his three daughters, who represent lust, greed, and anger, to seduce and entice Siddhattha away from the place of enlightenment. When this ploy also failed, Mara left, and the bodhisatta began to meditate.

After having gained a state of concentration by focusing on his breathing, he next focused his attention on the human condition. As he meditated, he gradually came to understand the cycle of birth, death, and rebirth to which all beings are subject. He now clearly saw and fully understood the human predicament. Seeing repetitive rebirths and re-deaths and the suffering (*dukkha*) that they entailed caused Siddhattha to experience a deep sense of aversion.

Next he turned his attention to understanding the causes of that predicament and discovered that the root causes were ignorance (*avijja*) and selfish desire (*tanha*). He understood the true nature of the universe and the processes by which it operates, and this insight or knowledge allowed him to experience a powerful sense of detachment or nonattachment (*viraga*) to himself and to the world about him.

Finally, during the early hours of the morning just before the sunrise, he came to a full realization of how to eradicate suffering and its causes. This realization created within him a feeling and experience of liberation (*vimutti*). As the first rays of the morning sun shone over the horizon, Siddhattha opened his eyes and saw everything from a new perspective. He saw things as they really and truly are. He had discovered the truth about himself, about the human condition, and about ultimate reality. He had become "enlightened." But even more significantly, not only did he now possess the truth; the truth also possessed him. His discovery was a transforming experience that resulted in his becoming a new person, a new being, a "Buddha."

The Buddha now began to share his discovery with others. The first ones to receive the "good news" that a cure for suffering had been discovered or rediscovered[18] and was now once again available were the five "wanderers" who had previously been his companions. He sought them out and met them at a deer park in the vicinity of Varanasi. The five ascetics had previously resolved not to have anything more to do with this "quitter." But now, in spite of their resolution, they found themselves respectfully listening to his message.

One by one the five also discovered the truth and became transformed by it. They attained the status that Buddhists call *Arahat*.[19] Experientially, this indicates that one has attained a level of understanding that is no different from the enlightenment experience of the Buddha. It differs from his experience only in that *Arahat*s attain enlightenment through the Buddha's teaching, whereas, according to Buddhists, the Buddha's enlightenment resulted solely from his own efforts.

For the next forty-five years, the Buddha and his growing circle of disciples, many of whom became *Arahat*s, proclaimed and shared their message of "good news" with the people of northeastern India. Many of those to whom the message was proclaimed found it convincing. No doubt, like the first five *Arahat*s, they were also persuaded not only by the power of the teaching but also by the charisma of the ones who proclaimed it. They in turn became followers of the Buddha, the Dhamma (his teaching), and the *Sangha* (his enlightened disciples).

These three, the Buddha, the Dhamma, and the *Sangha*, became the "Triple Gems" or "Triple Treasures" of the Buddhist community. For Buddhists these three represent the objects of highest value and worship. They also represent the "Three Refuges" on which Buddhists rely and in which they place their faith and trust.

During the period immediately after the enlightenment and also during the remaining forty-five years of his life, the Buddha began to formulate, articulate, and organize his thoughts and insights into a body of teachings that could be communicated to others. This process was continued by the *Arahat*s and by Buddhist scholar-monks in the centuries that followed until at last there was a giant compendium of

Buddhist teachings and commentary that now represents Buddhist doctrine, or the Dhamma.

At the same time that the Dhamma was being given shape, the monastic community (*Sangha*) was also being organized and structured. Disciplinary rules governing almost every imaginable situation were being formulated that would ensure the community's purity and its continued growth and well-being in the years ahead. Although most of the Buddhist teachings and rules were intended for the community of monks, some attention was also given to those persons who admired and respected the Triple Gems but who were unable or not yet ready to join the monastic community. For such persons, who composed an increasingly large lay community, the Buddha formulated special teachings that included advice on methods of practice and living that would be suitable for them and that would contribute to their progress toward enlightenment.

The Buddha's life ended when he was eighty years old. While traveling in a region located in the far north of India, the Buddha experienced severe intestinal pains. For some time his health seems to have been in decline, and he now found that he was too weak to continue his journey. Physically exhausted, he lay down between two trees. Although it was not the season for them to be in bloom, they suddenly burst into flower, and showered his body with blossoms. After giving some final instructions and encouragement to the large group of followers who were with him, the Buddha fulfilled his destiny and attained what Buddhists call *parinibbana* or the "fullness and completion of *nibbana*."

Westerners and those who are not Buddhists might refer to this event as the Buddha's death. But for Buddhists, as for most Indians (Hindus), death implies rebirth. In the case of the Buddha, however, no rebirth took place. The cycle of existence that is characterized by suffering to which he had been chained was now ended. In fact, that chain had already been broken at the time of his enlightenment under the Bodhi tree when he was thirty-five years old. He had remained alive and in this world for another forty-five years only in order to teach and help others.

His mission had been to share with them the "good news" that there was a cure for human suffering and to help them to discover that cure for themselves. But although he had been *in* the world for the last forty-five years of his life, he had not been *of* it. Even when he experienced physical pain, as was the case during his last days, Buddhists do not view such pain as *dukkha*. The enlightenment under the Bodhi tree had removed the "sting" from pain that causes it to turn into suffering or *dukkha*. Thus, the Buddha, though experiencing physical pain, could nonetheless end his life peacefully and serenely.

In the next section we shall examine the contents of some of the Buddha's major teachings.

THE DHAMMA

In the previous section, the word "Dhamma" or "dharma" has been translated sometimes as "truth" and sometimes as "teaching." In fact, the term has both these meanings.

The word comes from the Sanskrit root "*dhr*," meaning "to hold up" or "to support." Its most primary meaning is that which upholds a structure or forms a foundation. In the Buddhist case, what is being held up is everything that exists. The word thus refers to the basic structure of all that is, and probably the best translation is either "reality" or perhaps "truth." A secondary meaning derived from this basic meaning is the "teaching" about reality or truth.

Beneath the Bodhi Tree the Buddha experienced and realized "Ultimate or Transcendent Reality and Truth." Buddhists call this truth and reality the Dhamma. In the weeks that followed his discovery, the Buddha formulated and articulated this Dhamma so that it might be communicated and taught to others. This teaching is also called the Dhamma. This Dhamma in the latter sense is found in the Buddhist scriptures (the Tipitaka) and the commentaries and other writings that interpret the scriptures.

The Tipitaka is divided into three sections or, literally, "baskets." The first contains the Rules of Discipline or *Vinaya* for those who belong to the various monastic groupings of the *Sangha* (monks, nuns, and novices). The second consists of sermons and teachings delivered by the Buddha during the forty-five years of his ministry. The third section, called the *Abhidhamma*, is composed of metaphysical and psychological interpretations and classifications of the Teachings. This section was composed at a considerably later date than the first two.

The Buddhist tradition claims that the first two sections of the Tipitaka were formulated shortly after the Buddha's "passing away." A council that included almost all of his enlightened disciples (*Arahats*) met together to decide on a definitive version of the teachings and monastic rules that had been laid down by the Buddha. This assembly became known as the First Buddhist Council, and its main result was the creation of the *Vinaya* and *Sutta* sections of the Tipitaka.

The *Abhidhamma* was formulated and recited at another council (the Third Buddhist Council), which took place about 200 years later. Many Buddhists, however, regard the entire Tipitaka as the Word of the Buddha (*Buddha-vacana*). That is, they believe that all three baskets accurately reflect what the Buddha communicated and taught when he was alive.[20]

116

There are several summaries of the Dhamma in the Buddhist scriptures. One is a simple formula contained in a sermon that the Buddha delivered to over a thousand of his enlightened followers on the occasion of a full moon night about nine months after his enlightenment. The formula says:

Avoid evil.
Do that which is good.
Purify the mind.
This is the teaching of all Buddhas.

These three principles summarize in a simple and straight-forward way the purpose and content of all the Buddha's teachings and monastic rules.

Another well-known summary of the Buddha's teachings is found in the first sermon that he delivered following his enlightenment. This sermon was given to the five ascetics who had previously been his companions during the period when he had practiced austerities. The summary found in this sermon is known as "The Four Noble Truths." Whether or not this formula actually constituted the Buddha's first sermon, its inclusion in the canonical version of the Buddha's first sermon shows that his early enlightened disciples believed that the Four Noble Truths expressed the essential points in the Buddha's teachings. We shall use this summary as a guide in considering the basic contents of the Buddha's message.[21]

The Four Noble Truths seem to be patterned after a medical model. Ancient Indian medical writings often consisted of four statements. First, the physician would state the nature of the illness and describe its symptoms. Second, he would diagnose the cause(s) of the illness. Third, he would set forth the alternative to this unhealthy condition by de-scribing what the condition of the patient would be after she or he had been cured. Fourth and finally, the physician would write out the prescription for the medicine(s) or the instructions about the treatment that would bring about a cure. The Buddha's first sermon uses a similar formula, probably based on this medical one, to present the truth he had discovered.

THE FIRST NOBLE TRUTH: "ALL IS *DUKKHA*"

The Buddha began his sermon by declaring that "All compounded things are *dukkha*."[22] The word "*dukkha*" has usually been translated into English as "suffering." Although "suffering" is part of its meaning, such a translation is somewhat misleading and may give the wrong impression.

For example, the claim that "all is *dukkha*" should not be understood as a denial of pleasure. Human beings certainly experience periods of happiness and pleasure. Along with tears, there is laughter; along with sorrow, joy; along with disappointment, hope. The Buddha never denied this. But all these positive emotions and experiences occur in the context of *dukkha* and, indeed, contribute to *dukkha*'s continuation and increase. All of our pleasant experiences must finally come to an end, and when this deprivation occurs, we are left only with sorrow, nostalgia, and a longing for their return.

The Buddhist understanding of the human condition (*dukkha*) may be compared to having a noose about our necks and being subjected to repeated hangings as we experience rebirth and death over and over again. As we fall through space after having been born, some very nice things may happen in our lives. We may, for example, enjoy beauty, fall in love, and experience success. But while all these nice things are taking place, we are also falling through space with a noose around our necks. When we realize that this is our situation, what was previously considered delightful and pleasant takes

118

on a new meaning and significance. No longer can these things be seen and experienced as simply pleasure. They are instead tainted with the bittersweet knowledge that they are a part of and contribute to *dukkha*.

The Buddhist term denotes a much more pervasive and broader meaning than mere physical, or even mental, suffering, however. It refers to the imperfect and flawed nature of all human existence. There is something fundamentally and intrinsically wrong with our lives.

The word "*dukkha*" was used originally to refer to a wheel that was off-center and out of alignment and which, as a result, did not turn smoothly. Or, we might compare it to gears that do not mesh and therefore grind against one another. In a similar way, the Buddha realized that our lives are warped, distorted, and deviant from what they should be. The result is that we are not in harmony with the natural state of things or with reality. When this is the case, disharmony — or grinding of the gears — and suffering are inevitable.

The full meaning and significance of the term "*dukkha*" is perhaps best conveyed in English by using words such as "imperfection" or "distortion" or even "error." Nonetheless, to say that "all" is imperfect or distorted or in error is a startling and somewhat upsetting statement. Certainly many Westerners would find it objectionable. Most would probably agree that some things are imperfect or distorted or in error, but to say that "all" things are thus is for many persons unacceptable and itself a distortion of the truth.[23]

Basic to the Western outlook on life is the belief that people should be and therefore can be happy. Happiness is viewed as an achievable goal. The "pursuit of happiness" mentioned in the American Declaration of Independence is not seen as an impossible endeavor whose goal is unattainable. Most Westerners believe that if one seriously perseveres in her or his pursuit of happiness, she or he will find it.[24] The Buddha's statement seems to deny this.

Certainly our behavior seems to confirm our unwillingness to accept the Buddha's diagnosis of our human condition. Not only do we refuse to accept his diagnosis; we also go to great lengths to prove that he was wrong. When happiness does not seem to be obtainable, many modern Westerners are prone to resort to stimulants and/or alcohol to convince themselves and others that happiness is a human possibility and that they themselves are happy. And we attempt to deny all those things that might suggest otherwise.

We try to deny, for example, the aging process by expending large sums of money on face-lifts, hair transplants, and weight-reduction programs to convince others and ourselves that we are still young. We engage in sexual affairs and sometimes marriages with younger people in an effort to prove our youth. And, finally, we try to remove from our sight and consciousness those once near and dear to us, who have now become elderly and are painful reminders that we, too, are growing older. Aging spouses are removed by divorce. Elderly parents and relatives are placed in nursing facilities where they will not be constant reminders of what we too soon will become.

As for death, the denial of death has become not only an obsession but also a major business. We "pretty-up" corpses at great expense and then compliment their "beautiful" appearances. We speak of the dead as being "asleep" and "resting peacefully." We pay exorbitant amounts of money on coffins and funeral arrangements to ensure that the dead will be "comfortable." We create elaborate pictures of life after death, and we speak with great assurance about our own personal immortality and everlasting life.

In all these things our behavior is very much like that of the Buddha's father, who attempted to protect his son from the realities of old age, sickness, and death. We, too, attempt to deny these realities by pampering ourselves with luxuries and indulging ourselves in countless ways to prove that we are happy. Despite minor flaws here and there, we want to believe that everything is fundamentally all right.

But Siddhattha even before his enlightenment knew better. He sensed early on in his life that something was inherently wrong with human existence and with the natural order. He did not yet see the full implications and repercussions of this belief and feeling; these he would come to understand at his enlightenment. However, already as a result of his early encounters with aging, sickness, and death, he knew that something was fundamentally wrong with human existence and needed changing.[25] His ensuing search for enlightenment was motivated by the desire to find out what exactly was wrong and how to fix it.

THE SECOND NOBLE TRUTH: THE ROOTS OF SUFFERING ARE IGNORANCE AND DESIRE

The Buddha was not alone in claiming that "All is *dukkha.*" A great many Indians at that time felt this and would have agreed. Indeed, it was this feeling that had given rise to the wanderers' movement. Unlike the modern Westerner's refusal to agree with the Buddha's claim that "All is *dukkha*," many Indians in his day would have responded, "Yes, we know!" But they would have then asked, "Why is this so?" and more importantly, "What can we do about it?"

The Buddha's unique contributions to the religious scene in India and to the history of humankind were the answers he gave to these last two questions. In the Second Noble Truth

121

he explained why "all is *dukkha*." In the Third Noble Truth he revealed an alternative to *dukkha*. And in the Fourth Noble Truth he proclaimed how we can reach that alternative.

The Second Noble Truth states that the basic reason we experience *dukkha* is that we are ignorant. We misunderstand and distort our true nature and that of the world and reality. And because we misunderstand, we act inappropriately. The inevitable result of such actions is *dukkha*, or suffering. Thus, both *dukkha* and our inappropriate actions are rooted in and spring from our ignorance.

Of what are we ignorant? The Buddha claimed that there are three inherent truths that characterize the human condition as we now experience it. They are "*anicca*" (impermanence), "*anatta*" (no substantial and enduring entities), and "*dukkha*" (imperfection or suffering). Failure to recognize these three attributes of human existence is the primary and original source of *dukkha* as well as the reason for its continuation.

We are ignorant first of all that we are diseased. We fail to notice the noose around our necks. Therefore, we go on living as if nothing were wrong. But something is wrong, and if we fail to recognize this fact, we are doomed to suffer not just in this life but in future lives as well. Our ignorance and denial of *dukkha* results in our condition becoming continually worse and our plight ever more serious. Why is this the case? Again, ignorance is the answer. For we are not only ignorant of the fact that we are suffering but also of the causes and conditions that give rise to that suffering. Thus, without knowing it we are continually contributing to the continuation of our suffering.

Second, we are ignorant of the impermanent nature of all ordinary and compounded things (*aniccca*). As Siddhattha surveyed the human situation and the world in which we live, he came to the conclusion that everything is always changing.

Nothing is permanent. All existence is fleeting and ephemeral. Once again, as was the case with the First Noble Truth, the word "all" is important and should be stressed. There are no exceptions.[26] The transient nature of the universe extends to everything and everyone that we daily experience.

This leads to the conclusion that "all is *anatta*." This is the third matter of which we are ignorant. Since nothing compounded is in itself permanent, there are no eternal or immortal entities, no permanent and enduring substances, existing within the realm of ordinary human experience. This means that the possibility of our being or possessing an "immortal soul" is excluded. Since perhaps earliest prehistoric times, most human beings have believed that they consisted of a body and a soul or souls. They have also believed that although the body obviously undergoes changes and finally perishes at death, the soul continues and is reborn or transmigrates into another existence. The soul has been seen as immortal, eternal, and often unchanging.

The Buddha vehemently denied this commonly held belief. He maintained that the idea of an immortal soul was a delusion. Moreover, he saw it as a pernicious delusion. He claimed that the mistaken belief that we are essentially immortal, consisting of a temporal body but possessing an eternal soul, is the root cause of human suffering. The fallacy that our true and essential self is unchanging and immortal results in our being obsessed with protecting and gratifying that self. Because we believe that we are or have a "self," we become "selfish." We see everything from our own perspective, from the perspective of "I" and "Mine," measuring what is in it for "me."

In contrast to the common view that sees human beings consisting of a changing and temporal body that houses an immortal and unchanging soul or self, the Buddha maintained that we human beings consist of five factors, all of which are interrelated, mutually conditioned, and constantly changing. The first of these factors is the physical body, but in place of an immortal soul the Buddha posited four other factors, none of which is immortal or unchanging.[27] And since all human experience can be explained and accounted for by these five factors, there is no need to posit the existence of an immortal soul as a sixth factor. The immortal soul has been shown to be an unnecessary delusion, a product of our ignorance about the true nature of the self.

Not only is there no individual soul; there is also no extra-terrestrial and supernatural Soul residing somewhere up in the sky or in heaven. "God" is also an unnecessary delusion. Deities, like human beings and all other living and conscious beings, are composed of constantly changing and interrelated physical, mental, and emotional components. There is no "immortal and invisible God(s)." The Buddha does not deny the existence of divine beings, but he lowers their status so that they are no longer eternal or immortal, no longer omnipotent or omniscient. They remain as very important beings of the universe, but because they, like everyone and everything else, are compounded and changing, they, too, in time will pass away and be reborn in a new condition.

It was this insight into our human nature and into the nature of the universe that the Buddha discovered on the night of his enlightenment. The principle of the mutually conditioned co-dependent origination of all things (*paticca-samuppada*) is spelled out in a formula called the "twelve links in the chain of causation." The first link in this chain is "*avijja*" (ignorance) about the true nature of reality. Especially dangerous and pernicious is the deluded notion, which has no basis in fact, that we are or have immortal selves or souls.

124

This self-centered ignorance eventually gives rise to "*tanha*" (desire that is rooted in selfish ignorance), which in turn gives rise to "*upadana*" (selfish grasping or holding onto), and so on, until finally all these elements generate birth, old age, and death, that is *dukkha* or suffering. Notice that birth itself is seen as leading to and being a part of the cycle of *dukkha*. Therefore, the elimination of *dukkha* will require the eradication of birth and rebirths.

The "twelve links" formula can be briefly summarized as follows: Because we believe we are or have a self, we become selfish, self-centered persons, who are always looking out for ourselves. We are constantly viewing everyone and everything else from the perspective of our own self-interest. Self-survival and self-gratification become the two great motivating and compelling, as well as propelling, forces in our existence. We not only desire whatever will contribute to our own survival and pleasure, we also grasp and cling to such things.

Of course, in a universe in which everything is impermanent and constantly changing, it is impossible to grasp and hold on to anything. All such attempts are doomed to failure and frustration. A way of life that focuses on "self-preservation" and "self-gratification" will not work or be successful because it is counter to the true nature of reality. Such an outlook and way of life are based on and rooted in ignorance, and the inevitable outcome will always be *dukkha*.

If the disease afflicting humankind is caused by the "I and Mine" virus, clearly the way to effect a cure is by destroying this virus. If ignorance about the true nature of reality is the root of the disease, the cure must be the establishment of wisdom (*panna*) or right understanding about our own true nature and the nature of the universe.[28] But before the Buddha prescribed how we should go about establishing wisdom and gaining enlightenment, he first described what the enlightened state or the healthy condition of the patient would be like. This description is found in the Third Noble Truth.

THE THIRD NOBLE TRUTH: THE ENLIGHTENED STATE OR *NIBBANA*

The Buddha referred to the enlightened state as "*nibbana*" or "nirvana." This term was commonly used to refer to the extinguishing of a fire or a lamp. Usually this was accomplished by depriving the fire or flame of further fuel or by covering it and thereby depriving it of oxygen.

Early scholarly studies of the Buddhist religion in the West did not treat this doctrine kindly. Nor has it received a sympathetic understanding in popular explanations. Many Westerners have equated *nibbana* with the annihilation of the self or soul, and the Buddhist religion is then accused of teaching a negative and nihilistic philosophy and way of life.

In response to these accusations, it should be noted first of all that the Buddha denied the existence of an immortal soul or self. So, *nibbana* could hardly be the annihilation of something that never existed. Second, the Buddha explicitly denied several times that he taught a doctrine of annihilation or nihilism. If *nibbana* does not refer to the extinction of the self or the soul, to what then does it refer?

In many of his sermons and teachings, the Buddha compared the selfish desires and passions that spring from our ignorance to a blazing fire, out of control and destroying all in its path. It is to the extinguishing of these desires and passions that the term *nibbana* refers. It represents not only the extinquishing of the outward and inward symptoms of *dukkha* but also the eradication of the virus (ignorance) that causes the diseased and unhealthy condition of human life.

The negative interpretations of *nibbana* have been supported by the fact that *nibbana* is usually described almost entirely in negative terms. But this does not mean that *nibbana* itself is negative. The reason for the use of negative language results from the fact that all our human experience and therefore all our human language arises from within the context of *dukkha*. No other language is available, and it is thus necessary to use negatives when trying to describe or point to the opposite of *dukkha*. It is impossible to describe a perfect or healthy state such as *nibbana* in positive terms when one is using a language that was created to be used to describe an unhealthy condition such as *dukkha*. The healthy state is one that completely transcends and differs from the unhealthy one. In such a case, all one can say is that the healthy state is unlike the diseased one.

This is why the Buddha, when asked to talk about the nature of *nibbana*, would sometimes simply remain silent. On other occasions he would employ negative language. And sometimes he would assert that the question was not an appropriate one. This last response probably indicates that the question was being asked for the wrong reasons. For example, questions about life after death are usually asked in order to find out if there is anything in it for us. Similar questions about *nibbana* that are asked in hopes that the answer will satisfy our selfish desire for immortality are also asked for the wrong reason. The question itself is counterproductive to reaching the goal of *nibbana*. This is why the Buddha refused to answer it.

In spite of negative language associated with *nibbana*, it should always be remembered that for the Buddha and Buddhists, *nibbana* represents a very positive goal. It is the very opposite of *dukkha*. And it is the "pearl of great price" for which one should strive above all else. *Nibbana* is health, and therefore our salvation.

In spite of the negative language used to describe *nibbana*, its positive and desirable nature nonetheless shows through. No place is this truer and more evident than in the life of the Buddha himself. He first attained the state of *nibbana* at the time of his enlightenment. During the remaining forty-five years of his life, he exhibited in his personal life the positive nature of *nibbana*. Certainly for most of those who knew him, his life was not something negative and undesirable. Rather, it was a state of life to be emulated. Even among those who considered the attainment of such a life as beyond their present capacity, many embraced it as a future goal. Moreover, their deep reverence for the Buddha and his enlightened followers points to the high esteem in which those who had attained *nibbana* were held.

Far from being a negative and gloomy religion, as it is sometimes pictured in the Western world, the Buddhist religion proclaims that there is an alternative to the diseased and unhealthy condition that we now experience. We do not have to continue in *dukkha*. The alternative is called *nibbana*, and the Buddha's own life following the enlightenment reveals a foretaste of what *nibbana* is and will be. The completed and fulfilled state of *nibbana* — that is, the state of the Buddha following his passing away — is beyond our ability to conceive or verbalize. Nonetheless, this ultimate and final state should certainly be seen not as a negation or a rejection of the Buddha's life up until that time but rather as his life's fulfillment and completion.

Thus, the Buddha's proclamation of *nibbana* is a proclamation of "Good News." The Buddha's message is a "Gospel" of good tidings for all people. That is why on the face of Buddha images one sees not tears but the trace of a smile, not despair but a peaceful countenance exuding confidence and hope, not grief but an expression of complete joy and serenity.

THE FOURTH NOBLE TRUTH: THE PATH

Although dependent on the preceding three Truths, the Fourth Truth should be considered the most important. For it represents the prescription and treatment that will produce a healthy condition (salvation).

The Path consists of eight parts. Although they form a sequence, they do not represent separate and independent steps. Each step influences and supports the others. In a sense, the beginning or first step in the Path (Right Understanding and Right Views) is also its end and final conclusion. In fact, another popular version of the Buddha's prescription (see below) places Wisdom or Right Understanding last in the order.

The Eightfold Path mentioned in the Buddha's first sermon consists of the following components:

1. Right Understanding and Views
2. Right Intentions and Thoughts
3. Right Speech
4. Right Actions
5. Right Livelihood
6. Right Effort
7. Right Awareness
8. Right Concentration

The other formula, known as the Threefold Perfections, consists of:

1. Morality (*sila*)
2. Concentration (*samadhi*)
3. Wisdom (*panna*)

These two formulas represent the way to create a "nibbanic" existence. They are the prescribed medicines or the treatment and therapy that will eradicate selfish ignorance and desire. If followed correctly as prescribed, they are guaranteed to eventually produce health or salvation.

Before beginning the treatment, however, one must first have sufficient "faith" (*sraddha*) in the physician and the treatment that he or she prescribes to be willing to try it. Although *sraddha* here involves to a certain extent "belief" (right views), it goes beyond simply "believing." It also entails "commitment" (right intentions) to act upon what one believes.

Buddhists express their faith by taking "refuge" in the "Three Buddhist Gems or Treasures." "Taking refuge" is accomplished by repeating the following formula:

"I go to the Buddha for refuge.
I go to the Dhamma for refuge.
I go to the *Sangha* for refuge."

Both monks and laypersons recite this formula communally at most Buddhist services. It is also often recited by Buddhists individually and in private one or more times a day. The recitation of this formula signifies that the person believes in and values the Buddha, his Teaching, and the "Company of Enlightened Followers" who have embraced and fulfilled his Teaching. It means further that a person reciting the formula views these "Three Gems" as revelations of that which is truly real and really true. The recitation also is an expression of an individual's commitment to live in a way that reflects his or her faith in the Three Buddhist Gems.

It is believed that if a person possesses genuine faith in the truth and values represented by the Buddha, the Dhamma, and the *Sangha*, that person is ensured of eventually attaining *nibbana*. Also, such persons are guaranteed of never being reborn in a lower state than their current one. Even though such faith is highly important and a necessary prerequisite for entering and progressing along the path to enlightenment, it is not a substitute for wisdom. Rather, it is the seed from which wisdom will grow.

The formula of the Eightfold Path begins with Right Understanding and Views (Step 1), which indicates the content or object of faith. Initially, such understanding and views are elementary, imperfect, and incomplete. The goal of the Path is to perfect and complete one's understanding, or, in other words, to become enlightened. But this will happen only after one has completed the treatment prescribed by the Buddha.

Step 2, consisting of the development of Right Intentions and Thoughts, is the basis for all that will follow as one proceeds along the pathway toward enlightenment. Underlying all of our actions, speech, and means of earning a livelihood are our thoughts. Right thought leads to right action, right speech, and right livelihood. As the opening verses of the Dhammapada say, "The thought is the parent of the deed."[29]

The first visible signs of faith are a change in one's conduct. This behavioral change corresponds to Morality (*sila*) in the formula of the Three Perfections and to steps 3, 4, and 5 of the Noble Eightfold Path.

Right Speech (Step 3) emphasizes telling the truth or not lying, but this prescription also involves refraining from using slanderous and abusive language, engaging in malicious and or idle gossip, and contributing to unfounded rumors. A very large percentage of our speech falls into one or more of these categories. No wonder then that Buddhists value silence. It is better not to speak at all than to speak wrongly.

Just as the thought or idea is the source of our words and speech, so speech often gives birth to actions. Right Action (Step 4) is action that benefits others and contributes to the welfare of other beings. The Buddhist explanation of right action also includes a number of actions that should be avoided, such as killing, stealing or dishonesty, and sexual misconduct.

Right Livelihood (Step 5) prohibits becoming involved with any harmful occupations. These include trafficking in weapons, intoxicants, poisons, slaves, animals (for the purpose of slaughter), engaging in deceptive and fraudulent occupations, such as soothsaying or magic, and being involved in usury. In contrast, right occupations are those that contribute to the welfare and happiness of others and society.

These moral precepts or *sila* are the basis of the Buddhist way of life. Unless they are observed, further spiritual progress will be impossible, and if attempted, will fail. *Sila* is given concrete expression in the recitation of the "Five Precepts," which are recited by all Buddhists during most communal services. This recitation reminds Buddhists of how they should live their lives to progress toward enlightenment and *nibbana*. The precepts are:

> I shall refrain from the taking of life.
> I shall refrain from taking that which is not mine.
> I shall refrain from sexual misconduct.
> I shall refrain from false speech.
> I shall refrain from taking intoxicants.

Although these rules correspond to ethical and moral precepts found around the world and in all the major world religions, here they fit into the scheme of therapy or treatment being prescribed by the Buddha in order to eradicate *dukkha*.

Just as a person suffering from heart or lung disease may be told to lose weight, stop smoking, and begin exercising, so the Buddha emphasizes that by following the above precepts one will be able and ready to proceed toward a life free from *dukkha*.

As the Buddhist continues along the path toward enlightenment, she or he does not leave morality behind but continues to practice the moral precepts. Moral actions, however, are in themselves not sufficient. They are a necessary prerequisite for progress toward enlightenment, but they do not produce enlightenment. In order to reach the desired goal, one must not only do good but also practice mental concentration.

Developing mental concentration is not an easy task. That is perhaps why "Right Effort" (Step 6) is placed directly before those steps concerning meditation or concentration in the Eightfold Path. In fact, right effort is required for performing all the items in the Eightfold Path, but it is especially important and necessary for developing mental concentration. For this reason the list of the Threefold Perfections also includes right effort under the category of Concentration (*samadhi*).

In the formula of the Eightfold Path, the development of mental concentration consists of two steps: "Right Awareness" (Step 7) and "Right Concentration" (Step 8). The aim of "Right Awareness" is to attain the ability to concentrate solely on "one-point." Various aids may be employed to assist one in achieving this goal. For example, one may focus one's attention on the flame of a candle or the end of a stick of burning incense. Another possibility is to place a round colored object a short distance in front of the meditator, who will then focus on this shape.

The preferred method, however, is the one that was used by the Buddha prior to and during his enlightenment. Recalling the event that occurred when he was seven years old, he began to meditate upon his breathing, focusing on the in-breath and then the out-breath. This method, called *anapanasati*, is recommended as the simplest, easiest, and most effective way of achieving one-pointedness. Moreover, this method can also continue to be used in practicing "Right Concentration" or the higher forms of meditation and insight.

Anapanasati consists of focusing one's attention on the air passing in and out at the tip of the nostrils. (An alternative technique is to focus on the rising and falling of the abdomen.) Sometimes a mantra is used to assist the meditator in focusing, or he or she may simply count the in-breaths and out-breaths up to a certain number and then back down to one. In the case of using a mantra, very often the word "Bud-dha" is silently and repeatedly thought. With the in-breath the meditator repeats mentally the first syllable and with the out-breath the last syllable. If the meditator's attention becomes distracted, she or he should simply note or register awareness of this distraction and then resume focusing on breathing.

This practice has several results. At a very practical level, it produces a sense of peaceful relaxation that is beneficial to a person's physical and mental health. It also results in greater control over one's mind and thinking. The attention span is increased and expanded, and can then be applied to the performance of various tasks such as reading, writing, or one's daily work. But more important from the Buddhist perspective, it also allows a person to become mentally focused so that she or he can then advance to the higher stages of meditation that will be necessary in order to attain enlightenment.

"Right Concentration" (Step 8) also can be divided into two types. Each leads to enlightenment, but one is more direct while the other is more indirect. One might compare these two ways to two highway routes leading to one's destination. One is an Interstate super highway. On such a highway the route is direct, there are few distractions, and one can travel at a much greater speed. The other is a meandering roadway filled with many interesting sights and side roads that offer various enticements that may delay or even prevent the traveler from reaching the intended destination.

The latter is the form of meditation or concentration that includes higher mystical states known as the Four Absorptions (*jhanas*). It was this form of meditation that Siddhattha first learned from his two teachers, but that he then later rejected as being unable to lead one to *nibbana*. These states are created and conditioned by the mind. They are therefore not the same as *nibbana*. But there is the very real danger that they may be mistaken and substituted for it.

In these higher states of trance, the meditator may see signs and visions or become able to perform unusual and supernatural feats. Such visions and powers can become temptations to the meditator to remain at this level and fail to progress on toward enlightenment. Also, the experience of supernatural manifestations can generate a selfish thirst for worldly popularity and power. Over the centuries, not a few Buddhist monks and meditators have fallen into this trap.

The other form of higher concentration that is distinctively Buddhist is called *vipassana*.*Vipassana* means "insight meditation" and refers to "seeing directly into" the true nature of reality. It is this ability to see things as they really and truly are that constitutes *nibbana*. *Vipassana* is based upon and represents a continuation of the awareness already attained in Step 7. That awareness or one-pointedness is now used to analyze various components of reality in order to see things as they really are.

The basic Buddhist text on this analytic method of meditation is the *Satipatthana-sutta*. This text recommends focusing and meditating on four subjects. One should begin with one's own physical body, and then continue to analyze one's feelings and thoughts. Finally various moral and intellectual subjects may be analytically examined. Such subjects might include, for example, the teachings of the Buddha, such as the Four Noble Truths or other Buddhist doctrines.

Beginning with the physical body and especially with one's breathing is important because these two things are more immediate and more easily controlled. Meditating analytically upon one's body and breathing builds upon and utilizes the breathing technique already established in Step 7. The one-pointedness attained in Step 7 is now directed to various aspects of reality, allowing the meditator to see deeply into the nature of things as they truly and really are.

As we have seen, the Buddhist understanding of the human condition (*dukkha*) may be compared to having a noose about one's neck and being subjected to repeated hangings as one experiences rebirth and death over and over again. The Second Noble Truth analyzes the nature and causes of *dukkha*. And the Third Noble Truth announces that there is an alternative to this predicament. Now the Fourth Noble Truth informs us how we can escape our situation and attain the alternative.

It is as if we are told that we have always had a knife in our possession that can be used to cut through the noose that encircles our necks. We ourselves are able to free ourselves from *dukkha*. (In fact, we *must* do so, for there is no one else who is able to do it for us.) The knife represents our mental abilities to alter our situation. But for this to happen, one must first become aware that the noose is around one's neck and that one possesses a knife that is able to cut through the noose. Next, one must take out the knife and sharpen and ready it for use. In addition, we ourselves must learn how to use it correctly. Finally, there is the action of using the knife to cut through the rope.[30]

Step 7 (developing mindful awareness) may be compared to sharpening and preparing the knife for use. Step 8 corresponds to cutting through the noose of ignorance and gaining insight into the true nature of reality. By this action we discover and realize that indeed all things are *anicca, anatta,* and *dukkha.* And this truth sets us free.

Such insight is the equivalent of obtaining Wisdom or *"panna,"* the final component of the Threefold Perfections. In the formula of the Eightfold Path one has now returned to "Right Views and Understanding." But no longer are such views and understanding a preliminary step toward enlightenment. They now represent the attainment of complete and perfect understanding and wisdom. The fullness of enlightenment and the corresponding healthy condition of *nibbana* have been reached. The journey is now complete.

Such understanding and wisdom is not simply theoretical knowledge about our human condition and the true nature of reality. It is an insight into the truth of reality that completely transforms us. This transforming wisdom entails not just an increase in what we know, but effects a complete transformation of our conscious thinking as well as our subconscious and unconscious mind, of our outer actions and speech as well as our innermost feelings and the depths of our being. To experience this transformation fully is to experience *nibbana.* It is to become an Enlightened Being, a Buddha or an *Arahat.*

THE *SANGHA*

The number of the Buddha's disciples and admirers apparently increased dramatically during his lifetime and certainly continued to grow in the centuries that followed. Nonetheless, it is probable that initially other communities among the wanderers were larger and more prominent than the Buddhist one. The eventual triumph of the Buddhist community over its rivals was probably due to several factors.[31]

First, there was the indisputable attraction of the Buddha's charisma and personality. Although there are indications that at times he did encounter opposition and rejection, it is clear that most found him to be an attractive and powerful personality.

Second, the truth that he had discovered and his formulation and proclamation of that truth in his teachings clearly had great appeal both to members of the wandering communities as well as to those who remained in ordinary society. Both groups found not only his personality but also his message compelling, inviting, and convincing.

Third, many of the Buddha's early followers seem to have been persons endowed with extraordinarily high intellectual, moral, and personal qualities. In addition, they seem to have possessed unusual capabilities for leadership and organization. As the Buddhist movement developed and expanded, these early leaders were replaced by people who were equally impressive. The quality of life and learning as well as the dedication and abilities of these early leaders of the *Sangha* must surely have made a deep and positive impression on the general population, and contributed significantly to the community's growth and expansion.

After almost two centuries of gradual growth and development, in the middle of the third century B.C.E., the Buddhist community experienced a period of extraordinary expansion and flowering. The person primarily responsible for this surge of creativity and growth was an exceptional individual by the name of Asoka. Asoka was the third ruler of the Mauryan dynasty and appears to have been one of the truly great kings of India and the ancient world.[32] During his reign, the Mauryan Empire grew to new dimensions and eventually came to include the entire Indian subcontinent.

The Buddhist traditions picture Asoka as having been a ruthless and power-hungry tyrant during his early life. But after gaining control of the throne (perhaps illegitimately) and then waging a bloody war of expansion that further extended the boundaries of his empire, Asoka apparently became attracted to the Buddha's teachings and practices and experienced a complete change of heart.[33]

Although he had been acquainted with the Buddhist religion for some time, he now began to show a new and serious interest in trying to follow Buddhist teachings and practices in his own life. He apparently tried to apply Buddhist ideals and values in governing the empire. He seems to have been particularly attracted to those teachings that were intended especially for laypersons, and he soon began to make those teachings the ideological basis for his new extended empire.[34]

He also appears to have become a great supporter of the Theravada Buddhist monastic community. According to some Buddhist historical accounts, he was even ordained and lived as a monk for a short time. Later, he purportedly organized a major assembly of monks to revise and correct the Buddha's teachings. This council, the Third Buddhist Council, also reformed and purified the *Sangha* by expelling a large number of monks who were found to be unworthy in their conduct and/or heretical in their views. The remaining pure and orthodox monks, who constituted the reformed and purged Buddhist *Sangha* are identified by the Theravada tradition as being the true Theravada monks.

At the conclusion of the Third Council, missionaries were dispatched to spread throughout the empire and to areas beyond its borders the newly purified and reformed version of the Buddhist religion. It was at this time that the Buddhist religion first entered Sri Lanka. Indeed, Asoka's son and later his daughter, both of whom were ordained members of the Buddhist *Sangha*, are said to have played pivotal roles in introducing the Buddhist religion to that island kingdom. It is also traditionally claimed that the origins of the Buddhist religion in Southeast Asia date from this same time.[35]

The expansion of the Buddhist religion into new geographical areas exacerbated the divisions that had already begun to appear in the Buddhist *Sangha* several centuries earlier. These divisions had arisen as a result of different interpretations of the teachings and also because of different religious practices.

The First Buddhist Council, which met shortly after the Buddha's passing away (*parinibbana*), was necessitated by disagreements over exactly what the Buddha had taught and which rules were binding on his followers. In order to settle these disagreements, the First Council produced the first two "baskets" of the Pali Canon, the *Vinaya* (monastic rules) and the *suttas* (sayings or teachings of the Buddha). These represented what was considered the definitive and authoritative version of the Buddha's teachings. They are still considered by Theravada Buddhists to be the *Buddha-vacana* or "Word of the Buddha."[36]

About one hundred years later, a Second Buddhist Council was called to deal with similar problems concerning the monastic rules. This Council ended with the *Sangha* splitting into two separate groups, one of which upheld a stricter and more literal interpretation of the rules and teachings, the other advocating a more lenient and liberal view. The Theravada tradition identifies with the more conservative group and believes that it represents the orthodox position. The liberal group, which was probably the larger of the two, may be the forerunner of a more serious split within the Buddhist community that would occur several centuries later and that is still evident today.

This serious division occurred sometime around the first century B.C.E. with the appearance in India of a new form of Buddhist teaching and practice. The new movement was given the name Mahayana. All other Buddhists were lumped together and called Hinayana.[37] In general, Hinayana groups represented older and more conservative forms of Buddhist teachings and practices. The Theravada tradition was one of those included among the conservative groups.

Both sides of this major division within the Buddhist community viewed and to some extent still today consider the other side as representing an inferior and/or heretical form of the Buddha's teachings. Eventually, all but one of the different groups listed under the label Hinayana declined and finally ceased to exist. The one exception was the Theravada community.

The Theravada branch continues to be the overwhelmingly predominant form of Buddhist religion found in Sri Lanka and mainland Southeast Asia. Mahayana also spread from India into these areas, but eventually disappeared there and was replaced by the Theravada forms of belief and practice. In Central Asia, however, Mahayana was more successful. It remained dominant there for many centuries, until it was finally supplanted by the Islamic religion, following the arrival of and conquest by the Muslims. In Tibet and East Asia (China, Korea, Japan, and Vietnam), it is still the predominant form of the Buddhist religion.

Within India itself, the Buddhist religion continued to grow and develop until about the twelfth century C.E. During the first millennium of the Common Era, most of the various branches of the Buddhist religion continued to exist in India and to interact with various forms of the Hindu religion until in some respects the two religious streams became almost indistinguishable. The chief difference that continued to

separate Buddhists from Hindus and to give them an independent identity was the religious organization of the *Sangha*
and the community of Buddhist monks.

When the Muslim invaders took control of much of
northern India during and around the twelfth century, they
destroyed many of the Buddhist monasteries and killed a large
number of Buddhist monks. Thus, the distinguishing feature
that characterized the Buddhist religion in India was elim-
inated. The almost total obliteration of the monasteries and
the disruption in religious life caused by the disappearance of
the Buddhist monks effectively marked the end of Buddhist
religion in the land of its birth.[38]

In the nineteenth and twentieth centuries, both the
Mahayana and Theravada Buddhist communities were
reintroduced into India. But the return of the Buddhist religion
to the land where it originated has been for the most part
symbolic, and has not resulted in a large number of converts.[39]
Perhaps more significant for the future of the Buddhist religion
has been the spread of both Mahayana and Theravada
Buddhist communities into the West. Almost every Western
country now has active Buddhist teaching and missionary
centers.

The appeal of the Buddhist religion to many Westerners
has been heightened by the precipitous decline of the Christian
religion in Europe and North America. A significant and
perhaps increasing number of Westerners now see the
Buddhist religion as an attractive religious alternative to
traditional forms of Western spirituality and religion. It also
appears that the new geographical and cultural settings
provided by the West may result in the emergence of creative
and innovative changes within the Buddhist religion itself. It
remains to be seen how this will all work out in the future.

THE BUDDHIST RELIGION AND SERVICE

The Buddhist religion has often been labeled "other-worldly" and described as being uninterested and uninvolved in society and worldly affairs. In fact, this is a misunderstanding and misrepresentation of the Buddhist religion as it is understood, lived, and practiced by Buddhists themselves. This misunderstanding arises in part from the interpretation of *nibbana* as an otherworldly goal that has nothing to do with ordinary daily life lived in society. *Nibbana*, however, should not be viewed in this way. Although it represents an entirely and completely different sphere from that which we experience in this world in our ordinary daily lives, it is very much related to our life in this world.

The Buddha never advocated even for the wanderers or for the later monks that they should completely remove themselves from society. The Buddhist wanderers who lived in the forest needed to be close enough to villages to receive alms and to teach the villagers the Dhamma. This was also true later, when the Buddhist wanderers became monks and began to live in monasteries. Such monasteries were to be built within easy walking distance of towns and villages, and daily contact between monks and villagers was considered necessary and beneficial both to the laity and to the monks.

Some scholars have made a sharp distinction between what they call kammatic Buddhist religion and nibbanic Buddhist religion. Kammatic Buddhist religion focuses on doing good deeds in order to acquire merit that will result in one's being reborn in a more desirable realm of existence in a future life or in gaining future prosperity and happiness in this one. Indeed, the overwhelming majority of Buddhists, both laypersons and monks, are involved in and focus on this type of Buddhist religion. It is wrong, however, to separate the concerns and practices of kammatic Buddhist religion from the pursuit of *nibbana*.[40]

Buddhists see their merit-making activities and good deeds as contributing to their progress toward the ultimate goal of *nibbana*. Although meditation leading to insight into the true nature of reality is the primary and ultimate means of achieving *nibbana*, merit-making and good karmic actions also play an important and necessary preparatory and supportive role. And it should be remembered that the practices of meditation as well as the gaining of insight both occur in this world and are a part of the daily lives of those who have become fully enlightened or are striving to become so.

Buddhist religious practices described in the formula of The Threefold Perfections do not consist only of meditation (*samadhi*) and the cultivation of wisdom (*panna*); also included is morality (*sila*). And the Eightfold Path includes Right Speech, Right Action, and Right Livelihood as well as those items concerning meditation and insight or understanding.

The moral injunctions for both laypersons and monks include the theme of service. Buddhist morality is built upon the ideas of universal love and compassion that involve service both to other individuals and to society as a whole. Although service may be understood as contributing to advancement toward an otherworldly goal, it is both advocated and performed in this world, here and now.

Service in the Buddhist religion takes several forms. In all these forms it is an expression of compassion (*karuna*) and loving kindness (*metta*).[41] Compassion is one of the basic components of enlightenment. Although enlightenment is often identified with wisdom, equally important are the elements of purity and compassion.

Compassion and wisdom complement and correct each other. Without compassion, wisdom can become dry and scholastic, and can easily degenerate into selfish intellectual pride. Without wisdom, compassion can turn into a possessive and grasping kind of love or into merely a sentimental emotion. Buddhists recognize that true wisdom must be compassionate wisdom, and true love must be enlightened love.

Service, according to the Buddhist view, should spring from such enlightened love and compassion. In the case of the monks this takes two forms. First and most important, the monks serve others by teaching them the Dhamma. Sharing the truth with others is the greatest service that anyone can perform for another. No other gift even comes close to this one. For one suffering from a horrible and terminal disease, there can be no greater gift than the news of a cure and no greater service than providing the sick person with that cure.

The Buddhist *Sangha* is the repository of the most important truth there is—the truth that destroys *dukkha* and results in *nibbana*. Monks have no greater duty toward others than that of sharing with them the Dhamma. Whenever the laity request monks to preach the Dhamma, as they usually do in almost every Buddhist ritual service, it the responsibility of the monks to do so. Such missionary and pastoral preaching or teaching represents the ultimate service that monks can provide to the laity.

Monks also serve the laity by providing them with an opportunity to make merit. The best way for laypersons to make merit is by presenting offerings of food, robes, and other items to the monks (the *Sangha*). Serving others is always a virtuous and meritorious action, but when the recipient of the service is an individual monk or the whole *Sangha*, the amount of merit is multiplied many times. That is why the Buddha once described the monks and the *Sangha* as "the best field of merit."

The daily morning alms-round of the Buddhist monks vividly illustrates how they provide laypersons an opportunity to make and accumulate merit. In Thailand, for example, Theravada Buddhist monks usually arise well before dawn and then walk through the streets and lanes near their temples collecting food from laypersons for their morning and midday meals. Some Westerners refer to this practice as begging, but if one observes closely, one will see that this is far from being the case.

Long before the monks arrive, the laity has prepared special food for them, and the laypeople then wait in front of their houses or on the street for the monks to pass. When the monks approach, it is not the monks who request an offering of food, but the laypeople who indicate that they wish to present the monks with food. And it is not the monks who thank the laity for the offering that they have received, but the laypeople who express gratitude and respect to the monks by word and gesture as they present their offerings.

The morning alms-round is a ritual that serves almost as "a means of grace" for the laity. The gracious compassion of the monk in receiving this gift allows the layperson to earn merit. By giving to the monks, the laypeople profess their faith and show their support of the monks' quest for enlightenment. Also, by their action of giving, they themselves are able to share and to participate in that quest. Such action is highly meritorious for the layperson. At the same time, the monks, by showing gracious compassion toward the laity, are also making merit for themselves.

The greatest gift and service that a layperson can offer to the *Sangha*, however, is the gift of oneself by becoming a novice or a monk. In many Southeast Asian Buddhist countries, the hope of every mother and father is that their sons will become ordained as Buddhist novices or monks. In some countries, such as Thailand, the amount of time spent in the *Sangha* may be just a few months or even only several weeks or days. The ideal, however, was and is for every young male to become ordained, even if for only a short time. The act of entering the *Sangha*, and thereby giving or dedicating oneself to the quest for enlightenment, was seen as highly meritorious, and was considered both necessary and desirable for a young man's future in society. Although today ordination is less common than in the past, it still remains the ideal and goal for a large part of the Buddhist population.[42]

In addition to giving food to the monks and listening to their sermons, or becoming a novice or a monk, laypersons can also make merit by providing financial support to the Buddhist *Sangha*. Particularly important and efficacious in this regard are donations contributed for the construction and maintenance of buildings or other edifices that will be used by the monastic community. Building reliquaries (*chedhis* or *stupas*) to enshrine relics of the Buddha or the remains of important Buddhist figures is considered to be especially meritorious.

Service by the laity also extends to daily life and inter-actions with others. Keeping the Five Precepts, for example, is an expression of compassionate goodwill toward others that both makes merit for oneself and at the same time serves and benefits others. Acts of kindness and love in any form provide service to others and society; they also contribute to one's own advancement toward the immediate goal of a better future and rebirth and toward the ultimate goal of *nibbana*.

Many of the stories concerning the lives of the Buddha before his rebirth as Prince Siddhattha focus on the bodhisatta's great compassion and loving kindness. The stories, for example, of the bodhisatta and the hungry tigress and the account of Prince Vessantara's generosity are examples of the future Buddha's willingness to serve and help others by giving to them what they needed even to the point of sacrificing his own life.[43]

Following his enlightenment, the Buddha continued to exemplify compassionate service to others on numerous occasions. Sometimes such service consisted of words to help others to see the truth and thereby attain a more peaceful and enlightened state, and sometimes it took the form of actual physical service.

Illustrative of the first kind of service is the story of the Buddha and Lady Gotami. Having just lost her only son, whom she loved dearly to a virulent disease, she brought his body to the Buddha to ask him to restore life to her child. The Buddha promised her that he would do so, if she would go back into the city and find a mustard seed from a house in which no one had yet died, and then return with the seed and the body of her son. Hopefully she rushed back into the city and spent the entire day looking for a seed from such a house. Finally, at the end of the day, exhausted and sorrowful, she took the body of her son to the place of cremation and placed it on the ground. She then spoke to her dead son, saying, "Little child, I had thought that death and suffering came only to you. But now I see that it the common lot of all human beings." Rising and leaving the body of her son, she then made her way back to where she had met the Buddha that morning.

When the Buddha noticed her approaching, he called out to ask if she had found the seed. She replied, "That quest is ended. Grant me refuge as your disciple." The Buddha had not sent her to find a seed, but to find the truth, the First Noble Truth, that "all is *dukkha*; all is suffering."

At first glance, it may seem that the Buddha was being cruel in deceiving and playing a trick on Lady Gotami. But in fact he was being compassionate and merciful by causing her to find out for herself the truth of suffering. He had given her an opportunity to learn the first insight that leads one to enlightenment and *nibbana*. Having recognized the pervasiveness and inevitability of suffering, she was now ready to progress toward the goal of overcoming and removing suffering. She was now prepared to become the Buddha's disciple.[44]

An inspiring example of physical service by the Buddha is found in the story of a visit that he made to a group of his monastic followers. One was extremely sick and unable to rise from his bed. The other monks, however, had paid no attention to him and had left him to lie in his own filth while they pursued their religious duties and goals. The Buddha reprimanded these monks for their neglect of their sick colleague, and proceeded himself to bathe and clean the sick monk. His own behavior became an example to the monks of how they should serve others.

Another example of the Buddha's serving others through his teaching is his message to a layman named Singala. This *sutta*, which is the most important passage dealing with the morality of the laity in the Pali scriptures, both demonstrates and emphasizes service to others. Its theme is the importance of developing and maintaining good and appropriate human relations. Six different kinds of human relations and the proper behaviors for each are mentioned and compared to the six directions. Performing sincere and respectful services for others as well as exhibiting compassionate and considerate attitudes and proper behavior toward one's fellow human beings are set forth as the right way for a Buddhist layperson to live and as the means by which she or he can attain a better rebirth.

Another example of how the Buddha's teachings inspired service to others is found in the edicts and inscriptions of

Asoka. In these edicts and inscriptions, which clearly reflect the Buddhist lay teachings, the emperor describes some of the humanitarian projects that he undertook to benefit, serve, and improve society and the lives of his subjects. His concern for the welfare of his subjects was demonstrated in many simple and practical ways. He initiated, for example, a program of planting trees and digging wells along major highways in order to make taking a journey more pleasant for travelers. He discouraged the hunting and slaughter of animals. He established hospitals for both animals and human beings. He encouraged his subjects to work hard at their jobs, exercise thrift and frugality in their living, avoid drinking and gambling, and show respect to superiors and compassion to inferiors. Asoka's ideals and actions as ruler became the model for future Buddhist kings in Sri Lanka and Southeast Asia.

These examples show that service to others should not be understood as something foreign or alien to the Buddhist religion. Service is an indispensable part of the religious truth that the Buddha discovered, embodied, and taught. The Buddha himself both in his past lives and during the period following his enlightenment revealed the importance of helping others. And he also provided by both word and deed an incomparable example of what it means to serve others in the Buddhist sense.

The underlying motivation for Buddhist service is compassion, and that compassion is an essential attribute or component of the ultimate truth and reality that was manifest in the Buddha and is the Dhamma.

NOTES

I wish to express my appreciation to Professor Saeng Chandrangam for his reading of this chapter and for his helpful comments on its contents. He also collected most of the scriptural passages concerning and illustrating service in the Theravada Buddhist tradition. Also, I am grateful to Ms. Ana Yoerg for helping with proofreading the text and for making helpful stylistic and grammatical suggestions.

1. The exact dates are uncertain. Until recently, most modern Western scholars tended to date the Buddha's "passing" or death (*parinibbana*) at 486 or 483 B.C.E. Recently, however, some scholars have moved the date more than a century later. Southeast Asian Buddhists, on the other hand, place the date much earlier. In Thailand, for example, the date of the Buddha's "passing" is calculated to be 543 B.C.E. and the current year based on this reckoning is 2546 C.E. (2003 C.E.). The Buddhist tradition claims that he was eighty years old at the time of his "passing."

2. "Siddhattha" is the Pali spelling and "Siddhartha" the Sanskrit one. Since this chapter focuses primarily on the Theravada Buddhist tradition, the canon of which was written in the Pali language, religious and technical terms will usually be given according to the Pali spellings.

3. The Pali term "*Theravada*" (literally meaning "Teaching of the Elders" or enlightened followers of the Buddha), or its Sanskrit equivalent "*Sthavira-vada*," first appears in the accounts of the Second Buddhist Council, which took place about a hundred years after the Buddha's passing away (*parinibbana*). It is used to describe the minority reformist group that emerged following the Second Council. This group was stricter and more conservative than the other group, called the Mahasanghika, which apparently was the majority group. Theravada Buddhists today identify themselves with the reformist group, but also believe that their form of practice and teachings date back to the First Council, which took place about three months after the Buddha's *parinibbana* and is claimed to represent the original teachings of the Buddha.

4. See Peter Harvey, *An Introduction to Buddhism: Teachings, History and Practices* (Cambridge: Cambridge University Press, 1990), p. 9.

5. It is unnecessary to elaborate on the similarities between the age in which the Buddha lived and our own age. Both represent

"axial ages" or pivotal turning points in the history of humankind. And in both periods many persons considered traditional religious teachings and practices to be irrelevant or even untrue.

6. Although the Buddhist traditions refer to Suddhodana as a king, his status was probably more like that of an ancient Scottish clan chieftain. Although he may have been in fact a ruler of the Sakya people, he most likely ruled in consort with other elders of the tribe. His role was therefore probably more like that of the leader of a council of elders than that of a great king or emperor. The picture presented by the Theravada tradition reflects a later period in Indian history, when larger and more powerful kingdoms and finally the great Mauryan Empire had been established. For additional information about the Buddha's life, see the Suggested Readings.

7. The term "bodhisatta" in the Theravada tradition refers to the life of the historical Buddha from the time of his having made the vow to attain enlightenment until his realization of that vow. The Sanskrit spelling of this word (*bodhisattva*) is used in the Mahayana Buddhist tradition to refer to what Mahayana Buddhists see as an alternative and higher ideal than the Theravada ideal of the "*Arahat*."

8. The story of Prince Vessantara is immensely popular in Theravada Buddhist countries such as Thailand. Murals depicting scenes from his life are found in many temples, and sermons and stories relating his sacrifices and virtues play a prominent and influential role in Thai religious life.

9. The theme and purpose of this story resembles the story of the "wise men" in Matthew's description of the birth of Jesus. The wise men, like the Hindu seer, are given a heavenly vision or sign of the birth of an extraordinary person. They, too, seek out the child to pay him homage and reverence. In both cases, the point of the story is to emphasize the special status and nature of the newborn child.

10. Some accounts say that four months elapsed between each of the first three encounters, which would mean that these three signs occurred over a period of one year. Others accounts say all took place on the same day.

11. King Suddhodana's behavior in trying to protect his son from the reality of *dukkha* (suffering) is similar to that of most human beings who attempt to deny and avoid all reminders of our susceptibility to sickness and disease and of the inevitability of aging and death. King Suddhodana's denial of *dukkha* is not unlike our own response to the Buddha's later teaching that "all is *dukkha*."

12. These heavenly beings are identified as Hindu deities. Although they are usually called "gods," the Sanskrit term for such

a being is "*deva*" meaning "shining one." In the Buddhist tradition, their divine status is considerably devalued and lowered. Their main function in the account of Siddhattha's life, both here and elsewhere, is to move the story along. It is probably a mistake and misleading to label these beings "gods."

13. Westerners sometimes criticize the future Buddha's leaving of his wife and child as being callous and irresponsible. The Buddhist answer to such criticisms is that by seeking and finding a remedy for the suffering (*dukkha*) that afflicts all humankind, he was doing far more for his family, and for all human beings, than if he had remained with his wife and child in the palace.

14. The name or title "Mara" is derived from the word "*marana*," meaning death. The confrontation and later battle between the bodhisatta and Mara thus represents a struggle between Life and Death (and the suffering or *dukkha* that Death represents and entails). Mara also represents many negative mental states. Mara's appearance on this occasion may mean that Siddhattha was experiencing feelings of reluctance and a wavering of mind about whether or not to leave the palace and his family.

15. An excellent discussion of the Buddhist ordination ceremony and of how it relates to the "Great Going Forth" of the future Buddha is found in Wilfred Cantwell Smith, *The Faith of Other Men* (New York: Harper Torchbooks, 1972), Chapter Three.

16. In the Theravada tradition it is a deity who plays the instrument. Once again these beings serve to move the story along.

17. The scene of the woman's offering food to the bodhisatta is featured prominently in many Thai temple murals depicting the life of the Buddha. It is a reminder of the importance of giving to and supporting those on the way to enlightenment, namely novices and monks. It represents a powerful and vivid "stewardship sermon" to the Buddhist viewer. And it emphasizes that giving and service are key Buddhist values.

18. The Buddha did not invent or create the truth (Dhamma). Nor was he the first to discover it. All Buddhas or enlightened beings, past, present, and future, and all Arahats have found and experienced the same truth. Siddattha's discovery was in fact a rediscovery of the eternal truth.

19. In Pali, the mental achievement itself is called *arahattaphala*. The person who has attained this state is always called *Arahanta* or *Arahant*. The Sanskrit spelling for such a person is *Arhat*.

20. The Theravada tradition claims that once during his ministry the Buddha visited the heaven where his mother had been reborn,

and there preached to her the *Abhidhamma* or Third Basket of the Pali Canon. This is a legendary way of affirming that the third section of the canon as well as the other two represent the authentic teachings of the Buddha. Historically, however, Theravada Buddhists and modern scholars maintain that the *Abhidhamma* section appeared during or around the time of the Third Buddhist Council. See below.

21. Two excellent presentations and interpretations of the Four Noble Truths from the Theravada perspective are mentioned in the Suggested Readings. One is by Walpola Rahula, a Sinhalese Buddhist monk, and the other by Buddhadasa Bhikkhu, a Thai Buddhist monk.

22. According to the Theravada Buddhist understanding, all things are compounded except for empty space and the experience of *nibbana*. Thus, this statement applies to all of our ordinary human experiences.

23. Another possible translation would be the theological term "sin," and especially the way in which this term is presented and interpreted in the doctrine of "original sin." The Christian tradition claims that all persons are by their nature "sinners" and that all creation is tainted with sin. But, like the Buddhist claim that all is *dukkha*, the Christian teaching that all persons are sinners, including even newborn babies, is not exactly a popular or readily accepted view in the Western world today.

24. The importance of perseverance in obtaining happiness is also emphasized in Buddhist teachings. But in the Buddhist case, it is perseverance in following the Path that leads to enlightenment and *nibbana*. In the Western case, happiness is understood in a very different sense, as is the means of achieving it.

25. Although the traditional story claims that Siddhattha never experienced these things until he was an adult, such a claim cannot be accepted as the literal truth. We are told, for example, that his mother died when he was only a few days old, and we have seen that at the age of seven his experience of the birds devouring the earthworms caused him to become greatly distressed and distraught.

26. The only exceptions are empty space and *nibbana*, neither of which applies to our ordinary human experiences in our present diseased condition. All of life as we currently experience it is impermanent and constantly changing. Change itself is the only constant.

27. The other four factors or aggregates (*khandhas*) in addition to the material body are feelings or emotions, cognition or perception,

volition, and consciousness. See Harvey, pp. 49–50 and Rahula and Bhikku for a more detailed discussion of the *khandha*s.

28. Notice how our language contributes to our misunderstanding and ignorance. Personal and possessive pronouns and self-reflective pronouns reenforce the idea that we are or have an enduring "self " or essence.

29. The Dhammapada is one of the most popular and influential subsections of the Pali Canon. There are several easily available English translations of this text.

30. Professor Saeng Chandrangam has pointed out that in Thailand the parts of a knife are often compared with the three components mentioned in the formula of the Three Perfections: *sila, samadhi*, and *panna*. *Sila* is compared with the handle; *samadhi* with the blade or crest; and *panna* with the cutting edge of the blade. It is the last of these three, the cutting edge, that actually does the cutting, but without the handle and crest the cutting cannot take place.

31. The reasons for the Buddhist community's growth and success correspond to the Triple Gems of the Buddhist religion: the Buddha, the Dhamma, and the *Sangha*.

32. The Mauryan Empire was the culmination of a political process that had been going on in India for almost a millennium. Following their arrival in the Indian subcontinent, the various Aryan tribes, through a process of intertribal fighting and conquest of native peoples, had gradually become united into several large and powerful kingdoms. Alexander the Great's victories over some of these kingdoms and the subsequent withdrawal of his armies left a power vacuum in the subcontinent that was soon filled by a newcomer on the Indian political scene by the name of Candragupta Maurya. Candragupta was the founder of the Mauryan dynasty and the grandfather of Asoka. For more information about the history of this period and Asoka, see A. L. Basham, *The Wonder That Was India* (New York: Hawthorn Books, Inc., 1963), pp. 49–58.

33. The Buddhist tradition's description of Asoka as an evil and diabolical human being prior to his having come under the influence of the Buddhist religion is probably an exaggeration intended to dramatize the great change that the Buddhist religion effected in his life. Bloodthirsty acts, however, were not uncharacteristic of ancient [and, sometimes, modern] rulers. But Asoka's later compassionate and enlightened actions certainly were uncharacteristic of most rulers both past and present. For more about Asoka, see the Suggested Readings.

34. Asoka's embracing of the Buddhist religion was perhaps motivated, at least in part, by his need for a new political and moral ideology to unify his vast and diverse empire and to legitimize his rule over it. The Buddhist lay ethic seems to have provided just what he needed and was looking for. His edicts and inscriptions suggest that he was either not familiar with or at least not very interested in the major Buddhist teachings and doctrines, such as *dukkha, anatta,* and *nibbana,* which formed the heart of the Buddha's teaching for his monastic disciples. Asoka's new political ideology (Dhamma), as expressed in his pillar edicts and rock inscriptions, is strangely silent about these doctrines. On the other hand, the message of the edicts and inscriptions seems to be almost exactly the same as that intended for Buddhist laypersons.

35. Although most Buddhists in Southeast Asia believe that the Buddhist religion arrived in Southeast Asia during the reign of Asoka, there is no firm historical evidence to support such a claim. Apart from Buddhist records compiled several centuries later in Sri Lanka stating that the Third Buddhist Council dispatched missionaries to Suvannabhumi (an area that is now believed to refer to somewhere in Southeast Asia), there is no factual historical evidence of the Buddhist religion reaching Southeast Asia until several centuries later.

36. The traditions formulated during the First Council were oral and continued to be passed on in this form for several centuries. The Pali Canon was first put into writing in Sri Lanka around 80 B.C.E. See Harvey, pp. 3–4. The Third Council was responsible for adding the third "basket" (the *Abhidhamma*) to the Pali Canon. According to the Theravada tradition, several years after the Buddha's enlightenment, he visited the heaven where his mother had been reborn and preached the contents of this third basket to her. The *Abhidhamma* section is therefore also seen together with the Vinaya and the *suttas* to be the *Buddha vacana* or "Word of the Buddha."

37. The term "*Maha-yana*" literally means the "Great Vehicle," whereas the term "*Hina-yana*" is often translated as the "Small Vehicle." Some persons have explained the use of these two terms by pointing out that over the centuries Mahayana beliefs and practices flourished in a larger geographical area and were espoused by many more people than was the case with Hinayana. Actually, however, the term "Hinayana" is derogatory and refers in a disparaging way to the "inferior" nature of the beliefs and practices espoused by this group of Buddhists. The term "Mahayana," on the other hand, means "great" in the sense of "superior." Obviously,

these two terms were developed and used by the Mahayana Buddhists in order to contrast themselves favorably with other Buddhist groups.

38. Theravada Buddhist communities continued to exist in the extreme part of South India for several more centuries, but these communities eventually withdrew to the island of Sri Lanka.

39. A mass conversion of Indian "untouchables" to the Buddhist religion did occur during the latter half of the twentieth century. But these conversions were motivated by social and racial or ethnic concerns more than by religion. They represented a social statement against the caste system more than a genuine religious conversion to Buddhist beliefs and practices.

40. Melford Spiro, in his book *Buddhism and Society: A Great Tradition and Its Burmese Vicissitudes* (New York: Harper & Row, 1970), draws a sharp distinction between various types of Buddhist religion that he found practiced in Burma in the latter part of the twentieth century. Prominent among these types was what he labeled nibbanic Buddhism and kammatic Buddhism. See H. B. Aronson, *Love and Sympathy in Theravada Buddhism* (Delhi: MB, 1980) for a criticism of what he views to be an excessively sharp distinction and division between these two types of Buddhist practice both by Spiro and by Winston King. See King, *In Hope of Nibbana: An Essay on Theravada Buddhist Ethics* (LaSalle, Ill.: Open Court, 1964).

41. See Aronson, *Love and Sympathy in Theravada Buddhism* for a detailed discussion of these two concepts in the Buddhist religion.

42. The fact that ordination is no longer possible for women presents a major problem here. The order of nuns ceased to exist in the Theravada world during the first millenium C.E. The official position of the *Sangha* is that women must wait for the coming and enlightenment of the next Buddha to obtain permission to reestablish the Order of Nuns (*bhikkuni*). In Thailand, a small number of women wear white clothing, shave their heads, and are called "nuns," but in fact these are only devout laywomen. The term in Thai for these women is "*mae chi*," not *bhikkuni*. Recently, one former female professor was ordained a *bhikkuni*, but her ordination is not considered valid or recognized by the Thai *Sangha*. For more on the role of women in Buddhist religion, see the Suggested Further Reading.

43. See Sacred Writings and Questions to Consider.

44. The Buddha's teaching of the Dhamma to others often involved what might be considered trickery. His teaching method, or *upaya* (translated into English as "skill in means"), was sometimes

a way of deceiving the listeners so that they might discover the truth. Already in his response to his father when he was about to leave the palace we see him using this technique. It is again evident in the interaction with his cousin Nanda on the day that Nanda was to be married, and also in the Buddha's response to his own wife when she requested him to bless their son, Rahula, by bestowing upon him the Buddha's legacy as heir apparent. In the case of Nanda, the Buddha convinces him to forego marriage with a beautiful woman and be ordained as his disciple so that he can be reborn in a "heavenly or V.I.P. penthouse" where there will be a multitude of "heavenly beauties" for Nanda to enjoy. This deception actually results not in Nanda's being reborn in this sensual V.I.P. penthouse but in his eventually becoming enlightened and attaining *nibbana*. In the case of Rahula, the Buddha agrees to his wife's request to bestow on their son his legacy, but then announces that his legacy is the truth of the Dhamma, and proceeds to ordain his son as the first Buddhist novice.

BUDDHISM

Sacred Writings

&

Questions to Consider

The following passages from the Buddhist tradition illustrate the value placed on service and ways of serving.

A god asks:

> Say of what folk by day and night
> Forever does the merit grow?
> In righteousness and virtuous might
> What folk from earth to heaven go?

The Buddha replied:

> Planters of groves and fruitful trees,
> And they who build causeway and dam,
> And wells construct and watering sheds,
> And (to the homeless) shelter give —
> Of such as these by day and night
> Forever does the merit grow.
> In righteousness and virtuous might
> Such folk from earth to heaven go.

(*Samyutta-nikaya* II p. 45–46 [PTS])

Questions

In the above passage, what are the specific acts that result in a person's attaining heaven?

Is heaven a desirable goal in the Buddhist religion? Is it the most desirable? Explain.

In the Buddhist view, how are *nibbana*/nirvana and heaven different and how are they related?

How do the means of reaching these two goals differ? How are they related?

In the above passage, a "god" (deity/*deva*) asks the Buddha which people accumulate merit and go to heaven. How is the "god" in the above passage different from and similar to "God" in Judaism? In Christianity? In Islam? In Hinduism?

Explain how the "god" in the above passage differs from the Buddha in nature and status. Which, if either, is more similar to "God" in the Abrahamic religious traditions (Judaism, Christianity, Islam)? Explain.

If you know or work with Buddhists, what do you know of their religious goals? Do they share the outlook on reaching heaven described in this passage? If you do not know or work with Buddhists, have you known or worked with anyone who seems to hold this outlook on reaching heaven, even if it is not expressed in Buddhist terms?

There are four ways of serving other people:

1. By giving
2. By nice words
3. By being of use to others
4. By maintaining integrity

(*Dighanikaya* III: 152, 232;
Anguttaramikaya II: 32, 248)

Questions

In order of importance, how would the Buddhists you know and with whom you work rank the ways of serving others mentioned in this passage? How would you rank these four ways of serving?

Describe the content of each of the ways mentioned above, and explain how each way provides service to others. Can you cite examples from your service experience of individuals serving others in each of the four ways? What about your agency as an institution? Are there clearly stated policies regarding each of these? Is there a strong, unwritten code of behavior for staff, volunteers, and clients with regard to each? Is your agency failing in any of these four ways of serving? How does a failure affect the mission of the agency? Can you recall instances where you have served in any or all of these four ways? Can you recall instances where you failed because of what you did or failed to do? How did your acts of service or failures affect your effectiveness as a volunteer?

❀   ❀   ❀

There are ten ways of making merit. One of them is to render service to others.

(Commentary to *Dighanikaya* III: 999; *Abhidhammathasangaha* 146)

Questions

Among Protestant Christians, "making merit" has often been viewed negatively in comparison to the concept of "grace." How do you understand the difference between "merit" and "grace"? Do you see any evidence of "grace" or something comparable to "grace" in the Theravada Buddhist religion? Explain. In your own opinion, how are "grace" and "merit" related, and what is the relation of each to your work and service?

Cite examples from your service experience in which merit was the motivation. Cite examples of grace. What is your own motivation to serve?

A certain monk was suffering from dysentery. He lay fallen in his own excrements without anyone to tend him. The Buddha on his routine inspection tour of the lodgings with Ananda brought water, washed the sick monk over, clothed him and laid him down on the couch.

On that occasion the Lord had the order of monks convened and instructed them thus,

"Monks, you have not a mother, you have not a father who might tend you. If you, monks, do not tend one another, then who is there who will tend you? Whoever, monks, would tend me, he should tend the sick."

(*The Book of the Discipline* [PTS] IV.432)

Questions

In the Buddhist religion, what is the source and motive for compassionate acts of mercy and kindness?

On one occasion, the Buddha identified himself with the Dhamma/dharma. In this passage, he identifies himself with the sick. Explain how these two identifications are related.

Compare the parable of the last judgment, found in Matthew 25 in the New Testament of the Christian Bible (see page 320), and the parable of the Good Samaritan, found in Luke 10:25–37 (see page 315), with the passage quoted above. What are the differences and similarities?

A young man named Nandiya in Varanasi was a devout Buddhist who gave alms regularly not only to Buddhist monks but also distributed food to orphans and travelers at the gate of his home. He was highly praised by the Buddha.

(Commentary to the *Dhammapada* Verse 173)

Questions

The Buddha taught that the *Sangha* or Order of Monks and Nuns was the "best field of merit." Explain this teaching. Explain why you agree or disagree with this teaching.

Is "giving" always a good practice? Are there cases when it may be detrimental to either the giver or the receiver, or both? Have you seen examples of "service" that you believe was actually detrimental? Describe such a situation. Was it an isolated incident or is it a frequent occurrence or even a policy? From your knowledge of the social problems of the culture in which you are serving, are there national policies and programs that you consider "detrimental service?" Argue your case.

There was a young man named Magha in Acala Village of the kingdom of Magadha. Every day he went around clearing empty spaces, making them pleasant spots for poor people to stay. Later on he cleaned the village streets and pruned the trees along the streets. In cold season he made fire for the poor and in hot season he provided them with water.

Afterwards thirty-two young men joined him in his good work. They served the community with more difficult tasks like building roads and rest houses for travelers at intersections.

At the ends of their lives all the thirty-three young men were born in the Tavatimsa heaven.

(Commentary to the *Dhammapada* Verse 21)

Questions

How does being "born in heaven" in the Buddhist view differ from "going to heaven" in the Western view?

In the Buddhist religion, does the goal of *nibbana* detract from service and other acts that would enable one to attain heaven? Explain.

Is it sufficient to do good on one's own; or is it also necessary to organize society to perform good deeds? From the history of your service agency, describe how the work and organization has grown and attracted supporters. How is it failing in respect to growth and support? If it is failing, what might the agency do to change that? What might you do to help? How is the larger society of your nation organized to perform good deeds and assist those in need? Who does it neglect to serve? How do you see the intersection between religion and government in respect to taking care of social problems and human needs? Between the individual volunteer and social structures?

What has attracted you to the service you have chosen?

The Buddhist ideal of service was fully implemented with political power by Asoka, the great Buddhist emperor in the third century B.C.E. His own words on public service are found on the Girnar Rock Edict No. 2. The edict reads as follows:

> Everywhere within the dominion of His Sacred and Gracious Majesty the King, and likewise among [those peoples who reside in the areas on the frontiers of the empire], have been instituted by his Sacred and Gracious Majesty the King two kinds of medical treatment — medical treatment of man and medical treatment of beast. Medical herbs also, those wholesome for man and wholesome for beast, have been caused to be imported and to be planted in all places where they did not exist. Roots also, and fruits have been caused to be imported and to be planted everywhere wherever they did not exist. On the roads, wells also have been caused to be dug and trees caused to be planted for the enjoyment of man and beast.

> (Radhakumud Mookerji, *Asoka*, [Delhi: Motilal Banarsidass Publishers Private Ltd., 1995], p. 131–132)

Questions

Theravada Buddhists view King Asoka as the ideal model of a Buddhist ruler. How is his view of government similar to and different from your own view of the role of government in society?

How does the Mauryan Empire under King Asoka differ from a welfare state? How should government social services be related to religious social services? For example, in the United States, the two major political parties have traditionally taken opposite stances on the desirability of having government involved in the care of the poor, the sick, and the elderly. Which side of the argument would you take? Give reasons for and against each position.

Asoka has been compared to the Roman Emperor Constantine in Christian history, and like Constantine he has been viewed by some as a religious hero and ideal model and by others as one who caused the religion to become corrupted and to decline. Discuss how these two historical figures are similar and different. How do you evaluate their roles in the history of the Buddhist and Christian religious communities?

From what you have learned about the history of your agency, describe how the work and organization have grown. Who have been the leaders in guiding this growth? What actions have they taken to ensure growth in their service and sustainability so the organization may serve in the future? What personal qualities do they possess? Or has the agency failed to grow? If so, what might be done to revitalize the organization? Has the agency in any way promoted the concept of "cascading," in which those served now serve others? In your agency, has success been because of the example set by one or some (as in the case of the Buddhist monk cited in the passage), or has it been accomplished by a campaign of public information, relations, and promotion? What attracted you to service? Can you cite someone whose example inspired you? Can you cite learning about a problem or need to which you then felt compelled to respond with action?

What is the relationship between your service agency and local government? Between your agency and national government? What government regulations is your agency obligated to follow? Does your agency receive government funding? How does this affect, negatively or positively, the mission of your agency? Is there conflict between your agency and local and/ or national government?

His Holiness, Somdet Phra Ngyanasangworn, the Supreme Patriarch of Thailand, has said:

> People in the world are interrelated at all levels: at the family level, at the national level and at the global level. The relationship is both physical and mental, both constructive and negative.
>
> There are many factors that have helped unite the people. The most widely used is the political or military might. But it has forced people to surrender in fear and hatred. It always incurs hostility, resistance and violence.
>
> Buddhism offers Dhamma, instead of force, to unite people. The uniting Dhamma consists of giving (*dana*), nice speech (*piyavaca*), services (*atthacariya*), and integrity (*samanattata*).
>
> (Sermon on the Red Cross Day, May 8, 2525 [1982])

Questions

Buddhadasa Bhikkhu, one of Thailand's most respected and creative religious thinkers in the twentieth century, has emphatically stated that religion and ethics are not the same. And he continues that Buddhism is a religion. How do you distinguish between religion and ethics? Is the passage above a religious passage or an ethical passage? Explain.

Discuss how the teaching of codependent origination (the interrelatedness of all things) is related to doing good and service to others. Cite an example of the interrelatedness of all things in the work of your agency and/or in the social problems facing your host nation. In what respects has globalization affected the clients served by your agency? Has it affected the agency itself and its staff?

Discuss how you see and have experienced the interrelationship of service and learning.

In Buddhism there is a close relationship or inter-dependence between the internal and the external. Loving kindness (*metta*) and compassion (*Karuna*) are the internal virtue; giving (*dana*) and social services (*atthacariya*) are the external, social action. Social action, in order to be pure, sincere and really of benefit, must be based on compassion.

> (Pra Dhammapidok (P. A. Payutto), *Buddhadharma*, [Bangkok: Mahachula-longkorn University], p. 756)

Questions

What is the Buddhist motive for doing good and serving others?

How does Buddhist "compassion" compare with such concepts as love and mercy in each of the four other religions discussed in this book?

In the Buddhist context, how does one become compassionate? In the Buddhist understanding of compassion, cite examples of belief in or acts of compassion that you have experienced in your agency — by clients, by staff, by you. Have you been the recipient of an act of compassion — by a client or a member of staff?

You selected a program of service-learning or volunteer service, which implies compassion. Describe how you became a compassionate person. Does your development in compassion follow the path to compassion as understood in Buddhism?

JUDAISM

Elliot N. Dorff

WHO ARE THE JEWS?

The Jewish tradition traces its roots to Abraham. The patriarchal stories of the Bible reflect the migration of the ancient Hebrews from Mesopotamia to Canaan and from there to Egypt. Jewish history continues with the Exodus from Egypt (c. 1250 B.C.E.); the revelation of God at Mount Sinai; the gradual conquest of Canaan during the period of Joshua, the Judges, and the Kings; the building of the First Temple and, with it, the first Jewish commonwealth under Solomon; the splitting of the Jewish commonwealth into northern and southern kingdoms around the year 930 B.C.E.; the conquest and dispersion of the northern kingdom by Assyria in 722 B.C.E., the conquest and exile of the southern kingdom by the Babylonians in 586 B.C.E., and with that the destruction of the First Temple and the first Jewish commonwealth. All of these events are depicted in the Bible.

Jews established a strong community in Babylonia (modern-day Iraq) that continued to exist for another fifteen hundred years under the Persians and then the Muslims. A number of Jews returned to rebuild the Temple in 516 B.C.E. and with that established the second Jewish commonwealth. It continued to exist in Israel through Greek and Roman conquests until 70 C.E., when the Romans destroyed the Second Temple and, with it, the second Jewish commonwealth.

Jews continued to exist in Israel in fairly large numbers for the next three hundred years, but their situation became increasingly dire, and the focus of Jewish history shifted to the community in Persia. The Persian Jewish community was at the forefront of the world Jewry through the Muslim period, extending to approximately 1050 C.E., but there were sizable Jewish communities in Israel, North Africa, southern Europe, India, and China during that time.

Beginning around the year 1000 C.E. and extending to the fifteenth century, the Jewish communities of North Africa and western Europe became the major centers of Jewish culture. Jews, expelled from the eastern Mediterranean region and western Europe in the fourteenth and fifteenth centuries, moved to eastern Europe and the eastern Mediterranean basin, where they were concentrated until the late nineteenth and early twentieth centuries. At that time, because of persecution in Russia and the development of Zionism, a movement to reconstitute Jewish national life in the ancient homeland, many Jews moved to America and Israel, although the majority of them remained in eastern Europe until they were slaughtered in the Nazi Holocaust.

It is difficult to determine exactly how many Jews there are in the world today, in part because there are major disputes about who is a Jew. Jewish law defines someone as Jewish if he or she was born to a Jewish woman or converted to Judaism; but groups of Jews differ as to the proper standards of conversion, and the Reform movement in Judaism officially recognizes as Jewish the child of a Jewish father even if the mother is not Jewish. In any case, the fact that classic Jewish law defines a Jew in terms of birth to a Jewish woman makes it clear that, in contrast to Christians and Muslims, Jews do not need to affirm specific beliefs to be Jewish; Judaism certainly has core beliefs, as will be described below, but Jewish identity, based as it is on birth, is more national or ethnic than religious. In that way it is similar to national identity, where one is a citizen of the nation in which one is born, even if one does not know the predominant language or who the national heroes are. Furthermore, some people identify themselves as Jews without converting to Judaism even though neither of their parents was Jewish. Demographers generally count the "core Jewish population," which includes all people who identify themselves as Jews, regardless of what makes them believe that they are Jews. Under that definition, there are, at last estimate, 13,254,100 Jews in the world.[1] This means that while Jews have had and continue to have an immense influence on Western culture, they constitute only 0.2 percent of the world's population. (Christians, by contrast, are about a third of the world's people, and Muslims are twenty percent.[2])

The largest Jewish community lives in the United States (approximately 5.7 million), and the second largest lives in Israel (approximately 4.9 million). There are also large Jewish communities numbering in the hundreds of thousands in France, the Former Soviet Union, Canada, the United Kingdom, and Argentina, and there are sizable but somewhat smaller Jewish communities in Germany, Australia, Brazil, South Africa, Hungary, and Mexico.[3] It can be said truthfully that Jews live in almost every country of the world, including those that are currently hostile to Judaism and Israel. That is the result of the remarkable fact that Jews lived without a homeland for close to nineteen hundred years, the only people to survive under those conditions.

Traditional and liberal manifestations of Judaism exist in most countries. In the United States, there are four movements: Reform, Reconstructionist, Conservative, and Orthodox. All segments of religious Judaism affirm some form(s) of the classical Jewish beliefs in God (except "Secular Humanist Judaism"), the sacred status of Torah (the Five Books of Moses) together with rabbinic interpretations of it throughout history, and concern for the Jewish people as a group together with an interest in studying and developing Judaism's cultural products. The movements differ with regard to how they understand the Torah and its authority.

Orthodox Jews believe that the Torah is the literal word of God and that Jewish law contained in it, as interpreted by rabbis over the centuries, is to be obeyed as nothing less than the direct command of God. It is therefore not to be changed, but only applied to modern circumstances as need be.

Conservative Jews believe that all Jewish sources must be understood in their historical context. When you study the history and historical context, you discover that the Torah itself was written over centuries and edited later on, and it, like later books of the Jewish tradition, was influenced by the cultures among whom Jews lived at the time. Therefore, while Conservative Jews consider Jewish law binding, they are more willing than Orthodox Jews to make changes in its content in response to modern values and needs, seeing that as continuing historically authentic Judaism.

Reconstructionist and Reform Jews do not consider Jewish law to be binding, although many voluntarily choose to observe sections of it and both movements in recent times have done more to encourage their members to do so. The Reconstructionist movement possesses a greater sense of community than the Reform movement does and hence offers more encouragement to adopt the folkways of the Jewish people. Autonomy is a central value for Reform Judaism. Thus for Reform Jews, Jewish law is at most a resource that the individual may choose to consult in making a decision; it is certainly not the authoritative command of God.

These approaches represent the positions of the rabbis of the various movements, but, for the lay people, family history, convenience, and friendships are at least as important in choosing an affiliation as ideology and personal Jewish practice are. Therefore, Jews might be members of a given synagogue affiliated with a particular movement even though their own personal philosophies and practices do not coincide with those of that synagogue. Furthermore, only some of those who identify themselves as Jews do so in religious as well as ethnic terms, which is always a puzzle to Christians and Muslims, for whom religious affirmations are a requirement for identification as such.

SOME CORE JEWISH BELIEFS

God

Classical Jewish belief centers on the creation of the world by God, the revelation of God at Sinai contained in the Torah, the historical relationship of God to the Jewish people from the time of Abraham through the Exodus and on to the present day, and the hope for an ideal future and life after death. Thus, while there are many Jewish theologies, all but a few affirm a personal God who created everything and cares for all He created, including all human beings. Even though Jews do not always understand God's actions, as evidenced most graphically in the biblical book of Job, Judaism affirms that God is just and moral and demands the same of us:

> The Rock [God]! — His deeds are perfect,
> Yea, all His ways are just;
> A faithful God, never false,
> True and upright is He.
>
> (Deuteronomy 32:4)

> He has told you, O man, what is good,
> And what the Lord requires of you:
> Only to do justice
> And to love goodness.
> And to walk modestly with your God.
>
> (Micah 6:8)

The Chosen People

As the Bible tells it, though, God has chosen the people Israel to be "a kingdom of priests and a holy people" (Exodus 19:6), "a light unto the nations" (Isaiah 49:6) — that is, a model people of whom God demands more than of all other people. Thus, instead of the seven laws which, by Jewish tradition, God demands of all descendants of Noah ("the Noachide Covenant") — namely, prohibitions against murder, adultery and incest, idolatry, blasphemy, eating a limb from a living animal, and theft, together with the positive command to establish a system of justice, including laws and courts — Jews are commanded to observe a total of 613 commandments articulated in the Torah as interpreted (and often expanded) by the rabbis over the generations. This is "the Chosen People concept," which is all too often seen as a mark of Jewish haughtiness and exclusivity, but when understood rightly is just the opposite; for God choose Israel not for special privilege, but for special responsibility:

> Hear this word, O people of Israel,
> That the Lord has spoken concerning you,
> Concerning the whole family that I brought up from
> the land of Egypt:
> You alone have I singled out of all the families of the
> earth;
> That is why I will call you to account for all your
> iniquities.
>
> (Amos 3:1-2)

Thus Jews have a special mission in life, to make this world a better place through abiding by the many extra commandments that God imposes on them. This is the root of the activist stance toward life mentioned earlier, felt even by otherwise nonreligious Jews and carried out in a variety of social-action projects.

The Torah (literally, Instruction) that God gave to the People Israel to articulate the terms of the Covenant between God and Israel applies only to Jews. That part of the Jewish Covenantal notion should be fairly easy for people of other faiths to understand because every religion sees itself as the optimal way to live life—at least for themselves and possibly for all other people as well.

What is probably harder to communicate to Christians and Muslims is the fact that the Jewish tradition does not claim that it is the only way in which people can fulfill God's will for mankind and be "saved." (Incidentally, in Christianity the promised salvation is from sin, but Jews instead look forward to liberation from the dangers and limitations of life, including rule by others.) On the contrary, historically, Judaism has not been missionary and has even made it hard for people to convert to Judaism, for, as the biblical prophet Micah (4:5) proclaimed, even in the eschaton, the ultimate stage in human history, while all nations will learn Torah from Jerusalem, "all peoples will walk each in the names of its gods, and we will walk in the name of the Lord our God forever and ever." Furthermore, according to the Rabbis, if non-Jews abide by the Seven Commandments given to Noah and seek to be righteous, they have done all that God wants of them. "The pious and virtuous of all nations participate in eternal bliss," the Rabbis said.[4] Even at the prime moment of nationalistic triumph, the Exodus from Egypt, the Rabbis picture the ministering angels singing songs of praise over the destruction of the Egyptians in the Red Sea, but God rebukes them, saying, "My children lie drowned in the sea, and you sing hymns of triumph?"[5] Thus, the Jewish Covenant does not entail exclusivity or triumphalism.

The Rabbis even maintained that the righteous among the idolaters of ancient times shall inherit a place in the World to Come.[6] This, of course, has direct implications for the relationships of Judaism to truly idolatrous faiths. Judaism would never embrace polytheism as a vision of the truth or idolatry as appropriate worship. Nevertheless, idolaters remain creatures of God and must be respected as such; indeed, some of them may be among the "the righteous of the nations" (*hasidei u'mot ha-olam*).

It is not easy, though, to balance the firmly held belief that, as God's creatures, all people are the object of His concern and eligible for His favor with a sense of appreciation and pride in being God's Covenanted people, following God's preferred way. Historically, largely depending upon the particular circumstances in which Jews found themselves, the tensions involved meant inevitably that sometimes Jewish nationalism and sometimes Jewish universalism was dominant. Overall, though, from ancient times to our own, Jews have tried to strike a balance between their nationalism and their universalism.

The Messiah

Both the tensions and the balance are probably best illustrated in the Jewish notion of Messianism. The ultimate aim, as the biblical prophet Isaiah declared, is that all people worship God so that there will be universal peace among people and in nature, even to the extent that the wolf will lie down with the lamb.[7] But Israel has a special role to play as "a light of the nations,"[8] and, as several biblical prophets asserted, it is Israel's God that all people will ultimately worship and Israel's Torah that they will practice.[9] Moreover, according to the Rabbis, in Messianic times Jews will be rewarded for their efforts to make God's will known by the renewed union of the tribes of Israel in the land of Israel, the rebuilding of Jerusalem, the restoration of Jewish political autonomy, and general prosperity—so much so that non-Jews will seek to convert to Judaism to take advantage of Jews' new status but will not be allowed to do so because their motive is not disinterested.[10] Still, all righteous people are to participate in the human fulfillment of Messianic times and the Hereafter.

Why do Jews not accept Jesus as the Messiah? Ultimately, it is because Jesus did not produce the results that the Messiah was supposed to bring. That is, from the time of Jesus to our own day, human life has not been marked by the peace, prosperity, and love promised by Isaiah and other biblical prophets. Instead we still have wars, poverty, and prejudice. Jews say that we are still waiting for the Messiah who will redeem us from the maladies of human life.

Torah

The Torah given at Mount Sinai is, according to Jewish tradition, not only the Five Books of Moses that constitute the Written Torah, but also the Oral Torah, the tradition's interpretations of the written word and the practices and customs of the Jewish people. The first published form of the Oral Torah is the Mishnah, edited by Rabbi Judah, President of the Sanhedrin (the Supreme Court), around 200 C.E. Because that work articulated the tradition's understanding of the Written Torah and also defined Jewish practice as amplified by the Oral Torah, and because it was organized conveniently by topic, discussions of Jewish law thereafter were based on the Mishnah. The deliberations in Israel were edited together in approximately 400 C.E. in what is known as the Jerusalem (or Palestinian) Talmud; those in Babylonia were edited about one hundred years later in what is known as the Babylonian Talmud, the more extensive and authoritative of the two. After that time, rabbis wrote commentaries on the Talmud and rabbinic rulings (*"responsa," teshuvot*) on the specific cases that came before them, and the Oral Tradition has continued in those forms to our own day.

This parallels the process in Christianity and Islam: Christianity is based on the Bible as defined by the Church Fathers (who added the books of the New Testament to the Hebrew Bible) and as interpreted by them (they maintain that biblical law, for example, was superceded by the Spirit once Jesus arrived); similarly, Islam is based on the Bible as retold by Muhammad and as interpreted by imams from his time to ours. Thus, all three of the Western religions are not the religion of the Bible; they are rather traditions, based on holy scriptures which themselves are chosen and declared holy by the religion's leaders and then interpreted and applied by them and by the people who try to live their lives by them.

The Torah that God gave at Mount Sinai was not to be added to or subtracted from (Deuteronomy 4:2; 13:1), and so no new legislation was to be admitted that would change biblical law. In each generation, though, judges were to interpret the law according to their own insights and needs (Deuteronomy 17:8-13). The Rabbis of the Mishnah and Talmud, who were concerned that Judaism remain relevant through the generations, expanded the judicial mandate so as to enable Jewish law to apply to new circumstances and moral perceptions. Thus, while "judge-made law" is frowned upon by certain legal scholars because elected legislatures are chosen to make laws, in Judaism, where no such legislatures exist, judge-made law is the standard operating procedure. That is why most of Jewish law is based on rabbis' rulings on specific cases over the centuries.

Finally, Judaism goes further than most other traditions in attempting to define moral duties in legal terms, for law gives moral norms definition, authority, and seriousness. It is one thing to announce general moral norms like "Love your neighbor as yourself" (Leviticus 19:18) and "Justice, justice shall you pursue" (Deuteronomy 16:20), both of which the Torah demands of us; it is another to spell out what love and justice mean in the concrete events of human relationships. Only if those moral values are defined in specific actions do the norms take effect and become meaningful, for life itself is not abstract and general but concrete and specific. Hence the Talmud and later Jewish law go into great detail to define what it means to love our neighbor and do justice, what is required of us and what is not. (The latter — what is not required of us — is also a crucial element of determining the scope of moral norms.) Law has some drawbacks as a mechanism to identify what is moral, and Jewish sources take steps to diminish them; but in the end, Judaism uses law to give morals definition and authority.[11]

For all its focus on translating moral norms into legal terms, the Jewish tradition nevertheless recognizes a realm of morality beyond the scope of the law (*lifnim m'shurat ha-din*). The Torah commands, "You shall do the right and the good in the eyes of the Lord" (Deuteronomy 6:18), which the Tabbis interpret to mean that one must do the moral thing even if not required by law.[12] In fact, the Rabbis of the Talmud maintained that the Second Jewish Commonwealth was destroyed by the Romans in 70 C.E. because Jews failed to go beyond the letter of the law in their treatment of each other.[13] Thus Jews are required to obey the law, which itself establishes a high moral standard, and, beyond that, Jews are required to aspire to ideal moral behavior by going beyond what is required of them by law.

JEWISH MORALS

Why do religions have anything specific to say about morality? The reason is inherent in the very word "religion." The "lig" in that word comes from the Latin root meaning bonds or linkages, the same root from which we get the word "ligament," which is connective tissue. Religions describe the ties that we have to our families, our community, the rest of humanity, the environment, and the transcendent. In so doing, religions give us conceptual eyeglasses, as it were, through which we look at the world. Secular philosophies like liberalism, Marxism, or existentialism do that too, but philosophies, qua philosophies, are purely intellectual. Religions, on the other hand, by their very nature embody their views of life in myths and rituals and thereby form communities of people connected to each other and to their shared vision of what is and what ought to be. Such religious communities provide camaraderie, strength, and meaning in the ongoing aspects of life—the life cycle, the seasonal cycle, and, indeed, the progress of each day and week; they furnish moral education in a variety of formats; and they also work together toward realizing their ideals. Religions, then, are related to morality by virtue of the fact that they provide pictures of the way the world is, visions of what it ought to be, and communities to teach morality and work toward moral goals.

Religions, though, do not all present the same moral view. Some norms, of course, are virtually universal, such as prohibitions against murder and theft, and demands to help others. Even for such universal rules, though, the exact definition varies; thus the Quakers, for example, maintain that all killing of human beings constitutes murder, while Jews assert that while peace is to be actively sought, killing an enemy in war or in self-defense is not only permissible but mandatory. Furthermore, even when a norm is defined in the

186

same way by two religions, each of them may give a different degree of emphasis to it. Finally, some positive duties or prohibitions are affirmed by some religions and not by others.

As a result of these variations, each religion presents a picture of reality and of the ideal that is distinctive in degree or kind. Each of the religions also uses various methods to inculcate its conception of morality in its youth and adults. To understand Jewish morality, then, it will be helpful to describe some important elements of Judaism's vision of the real and the ideal.

The Human Being

We begin with several Jewish convictions about the individual:

The body belongs to God.

For Judaism, God, as Creator of the world, owns everything in it, including our bodies.[14] God loans our bodies to us for the duration of our lives, and we return them to God when we die. Consequently, God can and does assert the right to restrict how we use our bodies according to the rules articulated in Jewish law.

One set of these rules requires us to take reasonable care of our bodies. Rules of good hygiene, sleep, exercise, and diet are not just words to the wise designed for our comfort and longevity, but rather commanded acts that we owe God.[15]

Just as we are commanded to maintain good health, so we are obligated to avoid danger and injury.[16] Indeed, Jewish law views endangering one's health as worse than violating a ritual prohibition.[17] So, for example, Conservative, Reform, and some Orthodox authorities have prohibited smoking as an unacceptable risk to our God-owned bodies.[18]

187

Being created in God's image imparts value to life, regardless of the individual's level of capacity or incapacity.

Some ways of thinking are thoroughly pragmatic: a person's value is a function of what that person can do for others. In sharp contrast, three times in its opening chapters, the Torah declares that whatever we are able or unable to do, God created each of us in the divine image, from which we each gain ultimate worth.[19] Even those guilty of a capital offense have the image of God embedded in them; the Torah therefore prescribes that after such people are executed for their crimes, we must honor the divinity of their bodies (and the holiness of the land of Israel) by burying them quickly.[20]

The Rabbis took this concept further. That we were created in God's image is a manifestation of God's love for us; our awareness of the divine image within us is a mark of yet more divine love:

> Beloved is man, for he was created in the image of God; but it was by a special love that it was made known to him that he was created in the image of God, as the Torah says, "For in the image of God He made man" (Genesis 9:6).[21]

Exactly which feature of the human being reflects this divine image is a matter of debate within the tradition. The Torah itself seems to tie it to humanity's ability to make moral judgments—that is, to distinguish good from bad and right from wrong, to behave accordingly, and to judge one's own actions and those of others on the basis of this moral knowledge.[22] Another human faculty connected by the Torah and by the later tradition to divinity is the ability to speak.[23] Maimonides claims that the divine image resides in our capacity to think, especially discursively.[24] Locating the divine image within us may also be the Torah's way of acknowledging that we can love, just as God does,[25] or that we are at least partially spiritual and thus share God's spiritual nature.[26] Finally, a deservedly famous passage in the Mishnah states that just as God is unique, so too is each human being. Just as an original Picasso is worth more than any copy, so too, then, does our uniqueness impart ultimate value to every human being, with direct relevance to our duty to aid people:

> For this reason was Adam created alone: to teach you that with regard to anyone who destroys a single soul, Scripture imputes guilt to him as though he had destroyed a complete world; and with regard to anyone who preserves a single soul, Scripture ascribes merit to him as though he had preserved a complete world....Additionally, [Adam was created alone] to proclaim the greatness of the Holy One, blessed be He: for if a man strikes many coins from one mold, they all resemble one another, but the Supreme King of kings, the Holy One, blessed be He, fashioned every person in the stamp of the first person, and yet not one of them looks the same as anyone else. Therefore every single person is obligated to say: "The world was created for my sake."[27]

Thinking that the world was created for your sake can, of course, produce more than a little arrogance. The following, lovely Hasidic saying introduces an appropriate balance:

> A person should always carry two pieces of paper in his/her pockets. On one should be written, "For me the world was created," and on the other, "I am but dust and ashes" [quoting Genesis 18:27].[28]

Still, the Mishnah, like the other sources cited, expresses the immense worth that each individual has due to the specific way in which the Torah describes God's creation of human beings.

Not only does this doctrine describe aspects of our nature; it also prescribes behavior. The Torah itself prohibits murder on this basis: "Whoever sheds the blood of man, by man shall his blood be shed; for in His image did God make man" (Genesis 9:6). Similarly, the Rabbis maintain that because human beings are created in God's image, we affront God when we insult another person.[29] Consider also the traditional blessing to be recited when seeing someone with a disability: "Praised are you, Lord our God, *meshaneh ha-briyyot*, who makes different creatures," or "who created us different." Precisely when we might recoil from a deformed or incapacitated person, or thank God for not making us like that, the tradition instead bids us to embrace the divine image in such people—indeed, to bless God for creating some of us so.[30] The same considerations apply to oneself:

> Rabbi Akiba said: "You shall love your neighbor as yourself" (Leviticus 19:18) [implies that] you should not say that inasmuch as I am despised, let my fellow-man be despised with me, inasmuch as I am cursed, let my fellow-man be cursed with me. Rabbi Tanchuma said: If you act in this manner, know Who it is you despise, for "in the image of God made He man" (Genesis 1:27).[31]

The body is morally neutral and potentially good.

The body is neither bad nor good. Rather, its energies, like those of our mind, will, and emotions, are morally neutral. All our faculties can and should be used for divine purposes as defined by Jewish law and tradition. Within these constraints, the body's pleasures are God-given and are not to be shunned, for to do so would be an act of ingratitude toward our Creator. This is in sharp contrast to the asceticism advocated by some elements of other religions in order to conquer the body's penchant to lead us to sin.[32] On the other end of the spectrum, this is also in sharp contrast to secular culture, where the body is simply a source of physical pleasure. For Judaism we must take care of and use our bodies not just for pleasure, but to serve God, as Maimonides (1135–1204) makes clear:

> He who regulates his life in accordance with the laws of medicine with the sole motive of maintaining a sound and vigorous physique and begetting children to do his work and labor for his benefit is not following the right course. A man should aim to maintain physical health and vigor in order that his soul may be upright, in a condition to know God....Whoever throughout his life follows this course will be continually serving God, even while engaged in business and even during cohabitation, because his purpose in all that he does will be to satisfy his needs so as to have a sound body with which to serve God. Even when he sleeps and seeks repose to calm his mind and rest his body so as not to fall sick and be incapacitated from serving God, his sleep is service of the Almighty.[33]

The Family

The family is a critical unit in Jewish ideology and practice, for it serves several purposes:

Providing for adult needs.

Ever since the Torah's story about the creation of Eve out of Adam's side, the Jewish tradition has considered it to be God's plan that "a man leaves his father and mother and clings to his wife and they become one flesh" (Genesis 2:24). They "become one flesh" not in the ontological way of understanding that phrase—that is, one being, never to be rent asunder through divorce—for divorce, while often sad, is both permissible, as Deuteronomy 24 makes clear, and sometimes the right thing to do. They instead "become one flesh" in several other important ways.

Physically, they become one flesh when they have sexual relations together; marriage and family are designed, in part, to satisfy the sexual needs of both spouses. Judaism, from its earliest sources, assumes that women have sexual needs just as much as men do. A husband has rights to sex within marriage too, and if his wife consistently refuses to have sex with him, he may gradually reduce the amount of money he would have to pay her in a divorce settlement until he does not have to pay her anything.[34] Both parties may agree to have sexual relations as often or as seldom as they wish, but these provisions in Jewish law establish clearly that both partners to a marriage are entitled to have their sexual needs satisfied.

The spouses "become one flesh" psychologically as well. Thus, the Rabbis declare that "although a man may have many children, he must not remain without a wife," for, as God declares in the Garden of Eden story, "it is not good for a person to live alone."[35] Moreover, the Rabbis affirm, "a man without a wife lives without blessing, without life, without joy, without help, and without peace."[36] They therefore disparage bachelorhood[37]—a far cry from the ideal of asceticism in other cultures. Thus, marriage, in the Jewish view, is the optimal context for human development and for meeting all of our adult needs.

Since a major objective of marriage and family is mutual love and support, spousal, parental, or child abuse, aside from being violations of Judaism's laws prohibiting assault and battery, are a total undermining of what family relations should be. They are also desecrations of the divine image inherent in each of us and a failure to respect those so created. Such acts are therefore condemned and punished.

Creating, educating, and supporting the next generation.

Sex within marriage has two distinct purposes: companionship and procreation. Thus, on the one hand, sexual relations are valued as a form of human love even when the couple cannot, or is not planning to, have children. On the other hand, procreation is an important activity—so important, in fact, that it is the very first commandment mentioned in the Torah: "God blessed them [the first man and woman] and God said to them: 'Be fruitful and multiply...'" (Genesis 1:28). The Rabbis later defined that obligation as the duty to have two children at a minimum, although, like all obligations, it does not apply to those who cannot comply—in this case because of problems of infertility—and the ideal is to have as many children as one can.[38]

Marriage not only provides the venue for having children; it is also, in the Jewish view, the context in which they are educated. The Torah specifically makes Jewish education—including Jewish morals—the duty of parents.[39] Parents may use schools to help them fulfill that duty, but they must periodically check to make sure that their children are in fact learning what they should because, ultimately, the duty to educate children remains theirs. Moreover, much of the Jewish tradition can only be taught at home, for this is a tradition that is not restricted to the synagogue or school: it intends to influence virtually every detail of life.

Education

Education is not only for children; it is a lifelong activity in Judaism. Thus, in the Torah, "Moses summoned all the Israelites and said to them: Hear, O Israel, the laws and rules that I proclaim to you this day! Study them and observe them faithfully!"[40] Moreover, the Torah requires that once every seven years all the Israelites — "men, women, and children" — gather to hear the entire Torah read.[41] Later Jewish tradition would make this instead a weekly reading from the Torah on each Sabbath, with smaller sections read on the market days of Mondays and Thursdays as well. From the very beginning, then, this was not to be an esoteric tradition, kept as a secret by the few privileged to know it; it was, rather, to be an open, public tradition, studied and interpreted by Jews of both sexes and all ages.

Jews for generations identified this commandment with studying the Jewish tradition, convinced that one should "turn it over, and turn it over again, for everything is included in it."[42] As Jews interacted with other cultures that were making progress in science, medicine, law, and other fields, however, a number of them learned those lessons and integrated their new knowledge into their practice and understanding of Judaism. This became considerably more pronounced after the Enlightenment, when Jews were allowed into the mainstream of society. It is not an accident, then, that Jews in far higher percentages than the general American population attend college and graduate school;[43] this is arguably, at least in part, an offshoot of the traditional Jewish commitment to education. Nowadays, in fact, the great need is for Jews to deepen their knowledge of Jewish sources and thought.

The Community

If the family is the primary unit in Jewish life, the community follows close behind. Communities are necessary, in part, for practical purposes, for only through living in a community can one have what one needs to live life as a Jew — synagogues, schools, kosher food, a person skilled in circumcision, a cemetery, and more. Furthermore, only in a community can all the duties of Judaism be fulfilled, for justice, care for the poor, education, and many other Jewish demands require other people.

The community, though, is important not only for practical purposes, but for theological ones. The People Israel stood at Sinai as a community, and it is as a group that they made the Covenant with God. From then on, each Jew, as the Passover ritual powerfully states, is to see himself "as if he himself left Egypt" and stood at Sinai, thereby sharing in God's work of liberation and God's Covenant with all other Jews in all generations. Judaism, contrary to Enlightenment ideology, does not see us as isolated individuals with rights; it sees us rather as members of a community, who have duties to each other and to God.

This sense of community is much stronger than the kinds of communities we are accustomed to in modern, post-Enlightenment societies. In Jewish law, once I am Jewish by birth or conversion, I am Jewish for life. If I convert to another religion, I am an apostate, and I lose the privileges of being Jewish (such as being married or buried as a Jew, or being counted as part of the prayer quorum), but I retain all the obligations of being Jewish. This is, then, not a voluntary sense of community, but a corporate sense, in which I am part of the body of the Jewish community and cannot be severed from it.[44]

This strong sense of community in Covenant with God is symbolized by the minyan, the prayer quorum consisting of ten Jewish adults. Jews may pray or study individually, but some parts of the liturgy can only be recited, and the official Torah reading can only be accomplished in the presence of ten Jewish adults, the minimum number for a community. Only as such can we bless and sanctify God fully, and only as such can we hear and study God's word adequately.

The following talmudic list of facilities and people that are to be part of any Jewish community fit for a rabbi to reside there reveals the nature of what a community is for the Jewish tradition:

> It has been taught: A scholar should not reside in a city where [any] of the following ten things is missing: a court of justice which can impose flagellation and monetary penalties; a charity fund, collected by two people and distributed by three [to ensure honesty and wise policies of distribution]; a synagogue; public baths; toilet facilities; a circumciser; a doctor; a notary [for writing official documents]; a slaughterer [of kosher meat]; and a schoolmaster. Rabbi Akiba is quoted [as including] also several kinds of fruit [in the list] because they are beneficial for eyesight.[45]

The community must thus provide facilities and people necessary for justice (a court and a notary), Jewish religious life (a synagogue, a circumciser, and a kosher slaughterer), Jewish education (a rabbi and a schoolmaster), charity, and health care, including public baths and toilets (remember that this was written before the advent in the past century of indoor plumbing), a doctor, and, according to Rabbi Akiba, even the foods necessary for health. If the Jewish community of talmudic times did not live under foreign rule, this list would undoubtedly also have included other factors that the rulers took care of, such as defense, roads, and bridges. In many times and places, Jewish communities had semiautonomy, with the powers of taxation and policing that that implied. For example, Jewish law requires that communities appoint inspectors of the weights and measures used by merchants, to insure honesty.[46]

Social Action and the Messianic Future

All of these elements of Jewish life—the individual, the family, education, and the community—are necessary for the ongoing life of Jews, but they are also intended to enable Jews to carry out the Jewish mission. Jews believe that the Messiah has not yet come, that the world is still broken and fragmented by war, disease, poverty, meanness, and the like. Only God can ultimately bring the Messiah; in the Aleinu, the prayer that ends every Jewish worship service, we express our hope that God will "utterly destroy false gods and fix the world through the reign of the Almighty."[47] Nevertheless, we are to help God in that task as His agents and partners in the ongoing repair of the world. This includes research into preventing or curing disease, political steps to avoid war and reenforce peace, political and economic measures to stop hunger, legal methods to assure justice, and educational efforts to teach morality and understanding. Jews have been and continue to be heavily involved in social action; indeed, they overwhelmingly see it as the most important factor in their Jewish identity.[48] This commitment to repair the world stems from the conviction that the world is not now redeemed, that we must act in order to help God bring about the messianic hope for the future.

JEWISH VALUE-CONCEPTS RELEVANT TO CONCERN FOR THE POOR

Why should we help the poor and others in need? The Jewish tradition provides some strong reasons to do so. To see that these reasons are not obvious, it is important to note that there are very good reasons *not* to help the poor and others in need. These include the following:

(1) The poor often do not work for a living and therefore do not deserve our help.

(2) It may ultimately be detrimental to the poor to offer them aid, for they may come to depend on it and never take the initiative to extricate themselves from poverty.

(3) Sometimes giving money to the poor actually contributes to their harmful habits and thus injures them immediately and physically; too many poor people use money that they beg for for alcohol or drugs.

(4) When people on the streets ask for a handout, you never know whether they really need it.

(5) Worse, beggars on the streets might even pose a danger to you, for if they do not get what they want, they may attack you—especially if they are on drugs.

(6) Even if beggars do not pose a physical threat, they are surely bothersome. Society as a whole, and businesses in particular, have an interest in making sure that people can walk the streets without being accosted by beggars.

(7) Part of the reason that pandering is bothersome is that beggars instill a sense of guilt in us. Even if we earned each penny of our own resources legitimately, the vast majority of us are not rich, and we surely cannot support everyone in the world who needs help. But how can I walk past a particular person who seems so needy? My duty to help others, coupled with sheer compassion for the plight of the truly unfortunate, makes me want to give money to each and every one I pass.

Pandering thus makes it hard to make good decisions about how to spend that part of our own private resources that we can devote to helping the poor.

(8) Begging is inherently demeaning, and as individuals and as a society we do not want to encourage behavior that cheapens our sense of the dignity of human beings. If people need money, we should help them with education and jobs, not alms.

In light of these and other reasons to refuse to help the poor, why should we ever think of coming to their aid? One can easily think of humanitarian reasons to support the needy, but general rationales and good wishes tend to lack color and staying power. Religions do not guarantee moral action, but they can provide an ideological and social context for thinking seriously about moral issues and strong motivations to carry out our moral resolves. Therefore it is helpful to plumb Jewish priorities and attachments that foster advocacy for the poor.

Piqquah Nefesh (Saving or Guarding Human Life)

The major Jewish concern in relation to the poor and others who need help is to make sure that people can sustain themselves. Saving life and health is of paramount importance in the Jewish tradition, taking precedence over all but three of the biblical commandments.[49]

Jews take for granted that life is a supreme value, but other cultures definitely do not. Stalin's Russia, Mao's China, Hitler's Germany, and the "killing fields" of Cambodia are stark twentieth-century examples of whole societies that valued life very little, even when their own citizens' lives were at stake. The Jewish tradition not only values Jewish lives, but non-Jewish ones as well. Indeed, on Passover night we diminish the cup of joy for our Exodus because some of God's children (the Egyptians) had to be killed in order for the Exodus to happen, and Jewish sources on just wars (including contemporary discussions in Israel on "pure wars") are concerned about unnecessary deaths on either side.[50] Other traditions value life too, but very few value life as much as the Jewish tradition does. This, then, is not only a deeply-rooted value of Judaism, but a distinctive one, in degree, if not in kind.

Community

One conceptual underpinning of the Jewish value of caring for the poor and for others in need is that such behavior exemplifies and expresses our existence and character as a community. Feeding, sheltering, clothing, and educating the poor are part of our social contract, for such activities help the community as a whole. In addition to that practical consideration, community is a theological value, for God made His Covenant with the whole People Israel and demanded that as a community we care for each other. God also created all human beings and demands that we care for those outside our community as well.

Over the ages, care for the poor became nothing less than a defining characteristic of Jews, a manifestation of what it means to be a Jewish community. Maimonides went so far as to say, "We have never seen nor heard of an Israelite community that does not have a charity fund."[51] Jewish law required members of the community to contribute — the equivalent of a tax in our society. The amounts varied with the wealth of the individual, but there was no escaping this obligation. "The court may even seize his property in his presence and take from him what it is proper for that person to give. It may pawn possessions for purposes of charity, even on the eve of the Sabbath."[52] The degree to which a person was obligated to contribute to the poor became the mark of membership in a community:

> One who settles in a community for thirty days becomes obligated to contribute to the charity fund together with the other members of the community. One who settles there for three months becomes obligated to contribute to the soup kitchen. One who settles there for six months becomes obligated to contribute clothing with which the poor of the community can cover themselves. One who settles there for nine months becomes obligated to contribute to the burial fund for burying the community's poor and providing for all their needs of burial.[53]

According to Jewish law, at least two people must approach a donor to collect funds for the poor, and a minimum of three must jointly distribute the funds, so as to convey to all concerned that the entire community is collecting and distributing money in fulfillment of its corporate obligation.[54] In our own day, when Jews differ sharply in beliefs, practices, and customs, and when we live and work among non-Jews to a much greater extent than in times past, the shared work of collecting and distributing charity is a significant mechanism through which individual Jews become a Jewish community.[55]

Individuals are also held responsible for helping the needy, but an individual is not normally required to shoulder the burden of financing the total needs of a petitioner; that is a collective responsibility. Only if the community will not or cannot cooperate in giving assistance is the individual liable to satisfy all of a petitioner's needs—assuming, of course, that the donor can afford the requisite aid.

The rule became one of concentric circles: one must see to one's own needs first, then those of one's family, then close friends, then the poor of one's own community, and then the poor of other communities.[56] Concentrating on one's own family and community makes sense, for one is best equipped to know both the problems and the resources in one's own area, and the ties that one feels to others who are near and dear are a powerful motivation to help. Even so, the record of medieval and modern Jewish communities that put themselves out for refugees fleeing persecution and expulsion is truly impressive.

Empathy

Compassion is probably the primary motive for the many private groups that engage in poverty-relief efforts. It is clearly an important Jewish motivation too, but Judaism goes beyond basic humanitarian feelings. Jews are enjoined not so much to have sympathy but, more important, empathy, as the following biblical passage makes clear:

> You shall not subvert the rights of the stranger or the fatherless; you shall not take a widow's garment in pawn. Remember that you were a slave in Egypt and that the Lord your God redeemed you from there; therefore do I enjoin you to observe this commandment.... When you gather the grapes of your vineyard, do not pick it over again; that shall go to the stranger, the fatherless, and the widow. Always remember that you were a slave in the land of Egypt; therefore do I enjoin you to observe this commandment.[57]

In the ancient world, even among Jews, one way people became slaves was by falling into debt.[58] Consequently, the imagery in this passage from Deuteronomy is very powerful: Jews care for the poor because Jews have known the slavery and indignity to which poverty subjects a person.

God's Commandment

The ultimate Jewish reason for assisting the poor and others in need is that in many different places in the Torah, God commands us to do so. For many, that is enough: if God, who is all-knowing and all-wise, commands such action, then it is the proper thing to do. For others, the belief that God will enforce His commandments through reward and punishment is the crucial factor. For most Jews, both aspects of this divine imperative are operative.

Membership in God's Covenanted People

Aside from belief in an all-wise God and in God's enforcement of His laws, the Bible presents many other reasons for obeying God's laws—including God's laws on aiding the needy. One prominent biblical reason is that Jews have established a special relationship with God through the Covenant. The mutual promises between God and our ancestors morally and legally bind us to the Covenant's obligations. Moreover, the Covenant creates an eternal, personal relationship between God and the Jewish people. Like marriage among human beings, the Covenant relationship produces obligations even stronger than those of a promise or a contract. Its duties carry the authority of love.[59] Thus, we care for the needy not only because God commands us to do so, but out of love for our Covenanted Partner.

Acknowledgment of God's Dominion over the Earth and Humanity

Another theological reason to obey God's commands is grounded in God's creation and ownership of the entire universe. Human beings may, at God's behest, own property, but ultimately God owns everything. Thus, those who refuse to provide for the poor effectively deny God's sovereignty, for such people dispute God's ultimate legal claim to all the earth and God's right to demand that some of His property be redistributed to the poor. Consequently, the Rabbis deemed refusal to assist the poor nothing less than idolatry.[60]

Assisting the poor in biblical times took the form not only of direct aid, but also of relief from servitude, and that too was rooted in respect for God's ownership of the world. While an Israelite could be sold into slavery to another Israelite in order to pay a debt, the master was required to set the slave free within six years, even if the debt was not totally redeemed by that time. If the slave chose to remain in servitude, he could do so, but only until the Jubilee year, when even the reluctant slave had to go free, "For it is to Me that the Israelites are servants; they are My servants, whom I freed from the land of Egypt, I the Lord your God."[61]

Gratitude to God

Another basis for giving to those in need is gratitude for what one has. As the historian S. D. Goitein has noted, after the year 70 C.E., when "there was no longer the Temple where one could express one's gratitude toward God or seek his forgiveness by sacrifices, gifts to the poor served as substitutes. This idea, so impressively expounded in Talmudic and medieval literature, was taken literally and seriously."[62]

The Dignity of Being Created in God's Image

The fact that each person was created in the image of God requires that we preserve not only the lives of those in need, but their dignity as well.[63] So, for example, if someone injures another person, Jewish law requires the attacker to compensate the victim for the injury itself (lost capital value), the pain involved, medical expenses, time lost from work, and also degradation.[64] When discussing payment for degradation, the Talmud's basis for comparison is the embarrassment involved in poverty. That is, the clear case of degradation, to which other cases can be instructively compared, is the embarrassment involved in being in need.[65]

The imperative to preserve a needy person's dignity underlies Maimonides' famous list of the degrees of charity:

> There are eight degrees of charity, one higher than the other. [1] The highest degree, exceeded by none, is that of the person who assists a poor person by providing him with a gift or a loan or by accepting him into a business partnership or by helping him find employment—in a word, by putting him where he can dispense with other people's aid. With reference to such aid, it is said, "You shall strengthen him, be he a stranger or a settler, he shall live with you" (Leviticus 25:35), which means strengthen him in such a manner that his falling into want is prevented.
>
> [2] A step below this stands the one who gives alms to the needy in such manner that the giver knows not to whom he gives and the recipient knows not from whom it is that he takes....Similar to this is one who drops money in the charity box. One should not drop money in the charity box unless one is sure that the person in charge is trustworthy, wise, and competent to handle the funds properly...
>
> [3] One step lower is that in which the giver knows to whom he gives but the poor person knows not from whom he receives....[4] A step lower is that in which the poor person knows from whom he is taking but the giver knows not to whom he is giving....
>
> [5] The next degree lower is that of him who, with his own hand, bestows a gift before the poor

person asks. [6] The next degree lower is that of him who gives only after the poor person asks. [7] The next degree lower is that of him who gives less than is fitting but gives with a gracious mien. [8] The next degree lower is that of him who gives morosely.[66]

Since poverty is an affront to the dignity inherent in us as creatures of God, all those who can are obliged to help. By the same token, the poor themselves must take care to protect their own dignity. One way of doing this is to give charity — no matter what one's economic state. "Even a poor person who lives entirely on charity must also give charity to another poor person."[67] Also, the poor who need aid are encouraged to apply to the community fund and are discouraged from door-to-door begging because it would diminish their own dignity.[68]

Aspirations for Holiness

Finally, and perhaps quintessentially, Judaism bids us to care for the poor and others in need in order to be holy. The Hebrew term "*qadosh*," which we translate as "holy," denotes something set apart from the usual and mundane, something special or even Godlike. Many of the biblical laws regarding poverty occur in the sections of Leviticus that scholars call the Holiness Code. Chapter 19 of Leviticus, where some of the poverty provisions appear, begins: "The Lord spoke to Moses, saying: Speak to the whole Israelite community and say to them: You shall be holy (*qadosh*), for I, the Lord your God, am holy" (Leviticus 19:1-2).

What does it mean to be holy like God? In part, the Bible says, it requires caring for the poor and the needy, for God does just that. God will not forget the poor, the widow, and the orphan. He pities, comforts, and cares for them.[69] In biblical legal and prophetic literature, God seeks social justice for such people and warns against oppressing them.[70] These passages put the laws requiring us to help such people in a striking theological context: you shall care for the poor because that is part of what it means to be holy, to be like God. The ancient Rabbis spelled it out even more clearly:

> Rabbi Hama, son of Rabbi Hanina, said: What is the meaning of the verse, "You shall walk behind the Lord your God" (Deuteronomy 13:5)?...[It means that] a person should imitate the righteous ways of the Holy One, blessed be God. Just as the Lord clothed the naked,...so too you must supply clothes for the naked [poor]. Just as the Holy One, blessed be God, visited the sick,...so too you should visit the sick. Just as the Holy One, blessed be God, buried the dead,...so too you must bury the dead. Just as the Holy One, blessed be God, comforted mourners,...so too you should comfort mourners.[71]

The very word for charity in Hebrew, *tzedakah*, is a derivative of the word *tzedek*, meaning justice. In contrast, the Latin root of the English word "charity" means affection, indicating that our charitable acts come out of our love for others and they are beyond the call of duty. The Hebrew word *tzedakah* instead indicates that for Judaism we must help others because it is the only right and just thing to do. We are not being superior human beings in helping others; we are simply doing what God expects of us. Acting for the welfare of the poor and others in need is thus perceived as a way of doing God's will and at the same time imitating God.

JEWISH POVERTY PROGRAMS

Biblical Provisions for the Poor

The Bible treats the support of the poor primarily in two sections: parts of the Holiness Code, especially Leviticus 19 and 23; and sections of the laws of Deuteronomy, especially in chapters 14 to 15 and 23 to 26.

Ongoing biblical aid took several forms. Farmers were to leave for the poor the corners of the fields (*pe'ah*), sheaves or fruit forgotten while harvesting (*shekhihah*), the stalks that fall aside from the edge of the farmer's sickle (*leket*), grapes separated from their clusters (*peret*), and defective clusters of grapes or olives (*olelot*). During the Sabbatical year (*shevi'it*), when fields were to lie fallow, the poor had first rights to the Sabbatical fruits. During the third and sixth years of the Sabbatical cycle, a tithe of one's crops was to be designated for the poor (*ma'aser oni*, "the tithe of the poor"). During the Sabbatical year, everyone had an open privilege to eat from a neighboring vineyard or field. The first tithe (*ma'aser rishon*), given yearly to the Levites, was also a form of aid to the poor, since the Levites had no other income.[72] Finally, the Bible provides that every fifty years, during the Jubilee year, all land reverts to its original owners; this was intended to prevent permanent impoverishment.[73]

In addition to these agricultural gifts, several other provisions of biblical law helped to prevent poverty. Specifically, workers were to be paid promptly,[74] and those who had money were to extend loans to their fellow Israelites in need without usury.[75] In the Sabbatical year, debts are to be canceled altogether; despite that, Israelites are not to "harbor the base thought" of refusing to loan money to needy Israelites when the Sabbatical year is near.[76] Clothing taken as a pledge for a loan had to be returned each evening for use by the poor person at night. When collecting such a pledge, the creditor had to stand outside the poor person's home, thus reinforcing that person's abiding dignity despite his or her poverty.[77] It was the duty of the judge to protect the rights of the downtrodden, although not at the price of fairness.[78]

It is not at all surprising that biblical provisions for the poor focus primarily on agricultural gifts, for most Jews of that time earned their living through farming. A monetary economy was not well established until later times.

What is surprising is that there is any provision for the poor at all. No other ancient law code stipulates gifts for the poor based on each year's crops, as the Torah does.[79] Until modern times, in fact, most law codes made the assumption that poor people were not just unfortunate; their poverty was caused by some moral fault of theirs, and they therefore did not deserve to be helped. On the contrary, in many legal systems, the poor were to be punished. In England and the United States, for example, debtors' prisons were common until the nineteenth century, and even when they were theoretically abandoned at that time, imprisonment on other charges, such as concealment of assets or vagrancy, continued some of the substance of the idea that debtors should be imprisoned for their wrongdoing.[80] Thus, these biblical laws proclaiming that the poor are not to be blamed but rather helped are truly unprecedented and innovative, and they can only be explained on the basis of the Israelites' theological convictions described in the previous section.

Rabbinic Poverty Law

By the time of the Talmud, Jews had become involved in commerce and trades, and so Rabbinic law provides for the urban poor as well as the rural poor. This included a number of curative and preventative measures.

Curative measures: the forms of assistance.

There were three Rabbinic forms of relief: the soup kitchen (*tamhui*), medical attention (*rippui*), and the charity fund (*kuppah*).

The Mishnah establishes the requirement that each community have a soup kitchen for the daily dietary needs of the poor. It also prescribes that a traveling poor person be given no less than a loaf of bread; if he or she stays overnight, the townspeople must supply enough food for a night's lodging, and if the stay includes a Sabbath, the locals must give the traveler three meals.[81] In the Middle Ages, synagogues were the site of daily food distribution to the local and traveling poor. This system was gradually superseded by three other forms of aid that included dietary assistance: reception of poor travelers in the homes of the rich; provision for vagrants in communal hostelries or inns; and aid offered by benevolent societies for strangers and the resident poor.[82]

Although there was no institution to give medical care to the poor, physicians gave their services freely. The Talmud approvingly notes the example of Abba, the bleeder, who:

> placed a box outside his office where his fees were to be deposited. Whoever had money put it in, but those who had none could come in without feeling embarrassed. When he saw a person who was in no position to pay, he would offer him some money, saying to him, "Go, strengthen yourself (with food after the bleeding operation)."[83]

There are similar examples among medieval Jewish physicians, and the ethic must have been quite powerful because it is not until the nineteenth century that a rabbi rules that the communal court should force physicians to give free services to the poor if they do not do so voluntarily.[84] Moreover, the obligation to heal the poor devolves upon the community as well as the physician. The sick, in fact, enjoy priority over other indigent persons in their claim to private or public assistance, and they may not refuse medical aid out of pride or a sense of communal responsibility.[85]

The most substantial form of assistance to the poor is the charity fund. Eligibility for its beneficence is generally limited to the resident poor, rather than to passers-through.[86] It is clearly defined in other regards as well:

> Whoever possesses two hundred zuz [i.e., enough money to support himself for a full year, from one harvest season to the next] may not collect gleanings, forgotten sheaves, [crops from] the corners of the fields, or poor man's tithe. If he possesses two hundred zuz less one dinar [i.e., 199 zuz], even if one thousand [householders each] give him [one dinar] all at the same time, this person may collect [produce designated for the poor]. If he possesses two hundred zuz [that he cannot freely use because the money serves as] collateral for a creditor or for his wife's marriage contract, this person may collect [produce designated for the poor.] They may compel him to sell neither his house nor the tools [of his trade so that he might acquire through his sale 200 zuz in cash].[87]

Along with food, the community authorities arranged for shelter. Jewish communities fulfilled this obligation through a compulsory hospitality rotation, wherein the townspeople were required to take turns providing lodging for guests.[88] The charity fund also provided clothing, although food for the starving took precedence over clothes for the naked.[89]

Curative measures: the hierarchy of recipients

Family members are to be aided first, then close friends, then the poor of one's own community, and then the poor of other communities.[90] Jewish law provides that, as a general rule, women are to be aided before men — assuming that there is not enough for both — because "it is not unusual for a man to go begging, but it is unusual for a woman to do so."[91] This assumed gender differentiation probably is based on, or combined with, fear for the physical safety of a begging woman. Women take precedence over men because men can beg with less danger to themselves and, in the judgment of the Rabbis, with less loss of dignity.[92]

Redeeming captives (*pidyon shevu'im*), though, takes precedence over helping anyone else in need, for those in captivity, even more than the homeless and the destitute, are in danger of sexual violation and, ultimately, of losing their lives:

> Redeeming captives takes precedence over sustaining the poor and clothing them, and there is no commandment more important than redeeming captives. Therefore, the community may change the use of any money it collected for communal needs for the sake of redeeming captives... Every moment that one delays redeeming captives where it is possible to do so quickly, one is like a person who sheds blood.[93]

Because Jews were a prime target for kidnappers, Jewish communities had to establish limits as to how much they would spend so as not to encourage future kidnapping of Jews, but they routinely erred on the side of redeeming the current captives at too high a price despite the implications.

Jewish law required Jews to support the non-Jewish poor as well "for the sake of peace."[94] One must remember that until the twentieth century, most Jews lived in societies that were corporately organized, in which each ethnic or religious group within a nation had responsibility for dealing with its own internal affairs. Moreover, under Muslims and Christians, Jews were generally second-class citizens who were rarely cared for and routinely persecuted. That Jewish law should require Jews to give charity to non-Jews at all—even if it is only for the political motive of maintaining peace—is therefore remarkable.

Curative measures: the extent of assistance

On the basis of Deuteronomy 15:8, "You shall open your hand [to the poor person] and provide him sufficient for his need, whatever it may be," the Rabbis ruled that those managing the community's charity fund must take cognizance of the standard of living poor people enjoyed before falling into poverty. The fund must then afford whatever they need to regain their dignity—even if that means providing a horse and herald.[95] This does *not* mean, though, that the community was obligated to restore the poor to their former wealth.[96] Instead, the officers who distribute funds must differentiate between the *legitimate* call to sustain a poor person's honor and an *illegitimate* demand on the part of the poor to live lavishly at the community's expense.

Another factor obviously plays a role in how much aid the poor receive, namely, the funds available. Throughout history, most Jewish communities were themselves poor. Consequently, few poor people, if any, were provided with "a horse to ride upon and a slave to run before him," or the equivalent. Indeed, the limited resources of Jewish communities made it especially imperative that they balance the individual needs of each poor person with due regard for their obligation to aid *all* the needy.[97] No wonder the Talmud says that the distribution of charitable funds is more onerous than the collection![98]

The hierarchy of needs embedded in the sources, then, is this:

(1) Redemption from captivity — especially for women — for captives were at risk of loss of life and physical violation.

(2) Medical care for people who need it, for even those who maintain that building and supporting a synagogue take precedence over normal charity to individuals nevertheless give precedence to providing for the sick among the poor. Life and health take precedence over all other communal priorities, in accordance with the value of *piqquah nefesh*.

(3) Food for those without it.

(4) Clothing and housing. Starvation was seen as more of a risk to a person's life than clothing or housing, at least in the Middle Eastern countries where the Talmud and the Mishnah were written. In northern climates during the winter, though, clothing and housing become more urgent, sometimes even more than food.

(5) Dowries and other necessities for indigent brides.

(6) Whatever is necessary to sustain a person's dignity.

Preventive measures

Jewish family law is one mechanism by which the classical Rabbis sought to prevent poverty. According to Jewish law, fathers are obligated to teach their sons not only the Torah, but a trade as well. A father may delegate this responsibility to a teacher who is paid for taking the boy as an apprentice, but the father remains responsible to make sure that the son acquires a remunerative skill.[99] As Rabbi Judah put it, failure to do that is effectively teaching your son to steal.[100]

Jewish law requires Jewish communities to supply indigent young women with a dowry. Historically, that insured that there would be few unmarried women and therefore, it was hoped, few women who would need to go begging.[101]

The Rabbis also used their power over the marketplace to prevent poverty. They imposed a profit limit of one-sixth for merchants selling foodstuffs and other commodities essential to human life. Concessions to the market may have undermined the effectiveness of this law at times. We see that in the provisions in Jewish law allowing merchants to include in the base price, for purposes of this law, not only the price at which they bought an item but also their costs in selling it and reasonable payment for their time and effort. Moreover, vendors were always permitted to sell at the current market price, even if it was more than a sixth over the base. Nevertheless, the Rabbis' intent in establishing the regulation was to insure that the necessities of life would be available to everyone. The one-sixth profit margin provided an incentive for businesspeople to produce and sell basic necessities while keeping the price of those commodities within reach of most of the population.[102]

Rabbinic law also seeks to prevent poverty through making loans easily available to the poor. The Bible demands that Jews lend money interest-free to a needy fellow Jew. In order to insure obedience to that command, the Rabbis actually altered the court's procedural rules "so as not to lock a door in front of potential borrowers."[103]

Another important way to prevent poverty is to provide job opportunities for all, the highest form of charity on Maimonides' list. Historically, the extended family, as the basic social unit within the community, took primary responsibility for affording employment to those of its members who were out of work or unskilled, but if that failed, the community as a whole became responsible. This obligation was often not easy to fulfill. One historian estimates that between the fifteenth and eighteenth centuries, approximately twenty percent of the Jewish community was unemployed or poverty-stricken.[104]

In our own day, Richard Rubenstein has argued vigorously that this traditional demand to find employment for those able and willing to work will become harder and harder to meet. He claims that contemporary unemployment is a chronic condition fed by massive overpopulation, which itself is the product of the high value placed on human manipulation of the environment. This, in turn, is rooted in the biblical perception that human beings, following God's instructions to Adam, are to rule nature. Rubenstein thinks that socio-political triage, in which whole nations and entire segments of nations (especially the poor and unemployed) are deprived of food, shelter, medical attention, and other necessities, will increasingly become the way rich nations solve the problem of too many people in the world and too few resources.[105] Whether or not he is correct in measuring the extent of poverty and unemployment or in tracing our attitudinal problems back to the Bible, he is certainly right in underscoring the contemporary urgency of the traditional Jewish demand to provide employment.[106]

The responsibilities of the poor

If donors and distributors have obligations, so do the poor. The goal of Jewish charity is to help the poor become self-supporting. This objective is based on the assumption that the poor will work diligently to earn themselves out of poverty in order to avoid the disgrace inherent in begging.[107] Jewish law does not require the poor to sell their homes or tools, nor does it force them to sell their fields at a substantial loss. Poor people are, however, obligated to work and to sell off any of their luxurious possessions in a good-faith effort to become independent of public assistance.[108] Moreover, Jewish law requires even the poor to give charity, and it presumes that people will strive heartily to avoid the embarrassment of being on the dole.

The law makes this assumption in part because respect for labor runs deep within the Jewish tradition. In contrast to many in the ancient world — including the Greek philosophers — Jews were not to disdain labor or the working classes but were rather to "love work and hate lordship."[109] Jews were not permitted to wage war or engage in robbery or piracy to earn a living, as many other peoples did. It was also forbidden to simply rely upon God to provide:

> A person should not say, "I will eat and drink and see prosperity without troubling myself since Heaven will have compassion upon me." To teach this, Scripture says, "You have blessed the work of his hands" (Job 1:10), demonstrating that a man should toil with both his hands and then the Holy One, blessed be God, will grant divine blessing.[110]

The ideal for a human being, according to the Rabbis, is "Torah with gainful employment" — i.e., knowledge and continuing study of the tradition combined with constructive work.[111] People should work not only for their own livelihood, but also for the inherent dignity of labor and the ongoing effects of work on generations to come. A popular story recounts that the Emperor Hadrian was walking near the city of Tiberias when he saw an old man breaking up the soil to plant trees.

> Hadrian said to him, "Old man, if you had worked earlier, there would be no need for you to work so late in life." He replied, "I have toiled both early and late, and what was pleasing to the Master of

Heaven God has done with me." Hadrian asked him how old he was, and the answer was one hundred. He then exclaimed, "You are a hundred years old, and you stand there breaking up the soil to plant trees! Do you expect to eat of their fruit?" He replied, "If I am worthy, I will eat; but if not [and I die], as my fathers labored for me, so I labor for my children."[112]

In addition to these moral, theological, and historical dimensions of labor, the Rabbis were sensitive to its psychological effects: "Great is work, for it honors the workers."[113] Work was not a human punishment inherited from Adam in the Garden of Eden; it was instead our path to respect and self-worth. The Rabbis' esteem for the value of work was so great that at one point they interpreted God's sweeping commandment, "Therefore choose life" (Deuteronomy 30:19), to mean "acquire a handicraft"[114] — a terse, but forceful expression of the connection of life itself to work.

This work ethic in the Jewish tradition is a strong factor in explaining why Jewish sources do not express the worry, as some writers and lawmakers do, that providing too much in welfare will serve as a disincentive for the poor to become self-sustaining. Another factor is that those on welfare in Jewish communities were not richly provided for, and so there was little to recommend staying on the dole. But in addition to that negative motivation to become self-sustaining, the positive value of work and the dignity that accompanies it have historically motivated Jews to get off welfare.

Respect for the poor

When a poor person requests a job, a loan, or outright aid, the Jewish tradition insists that the dignity of the person asking be preserved. The Torah demands that creditors not

218

enter the homes of those from whom they are collecting pledges,[115] and the Rabbis take this further. One must remember, they say, that "God stands together with the poor person at the door, and one should therefore consider Whom one is confronting."[116] Yose b. Johanan of Jerusalem, one of the earliest rabbinic authorities, went further still, saying "Let the poor be members of your household."[117]

Even if you cannot help a beggar, rabbinic law insists that you preserve the person's sense of dignity by speaking kindly with him or her. You may certainly not yell at beggars or even pass them by as if they are not worth notice, for "God...will not despise a contrite and crushed heart" (Psalms 51:17). Thus, as Maimonides asserts and repeats, "Woe onto him who embarrasses a poor person—woe onto him!"[118]

TRANSLATING FROM THEN TO NOW[119]

In a variety of ways, our contemporary situation differs greatly from the circumstances when most Jewish laws and customs of charity distribution were established. First, who is responsible to provide for the poor? Today, we try to aid them through massive and far-reaching social and governmental institutions. Thus, the respective obligations of the individual, the Jewish community, and governments to aid the poor need to be reevaluated and adjusted. Do our taxes, or a portion of them, fulfill part of our religious obligations to provide for the poor? If so, do we now have a religious as well as a civic duty to get involved in government to insure that the funds are equitably, honestly, and wisely apportioned?

The answer to both questions is "yes." Some of the poverty provisions in the Torah's laws are, after all, nothing less than taxes on a person's income. Since a percentage of taxes in most countries is used for aiding the poor, parallel to the use of some biblical taxes, one can legitimately argue that at least part of the duty to care for the poor is fulfilled through paying current taxes. At the same time, the social policy of most nations in the world today specifically presumes that the safety net for the poor will *not* be created by government alone; private charity must also play a significant role in this effort. Tax provisions permitting deductions for charity make this intention explicit. Jews therefore can only fulfill a *part* of their obligations to the poor through their taxes; they must also contribute some of their income to the charities of their choice. And, indeed, it is a mark of pride for Jews to be among the most generous segments of the general population, an ethic that all Jews should foster through their own giving.

Second, who should be the beneficiaries of our aid? Jewish law's preference for the poor near at hand over those far away is much harder to define and justify in a world of instant communications. Within the North American Jewish community, some of the most pressing and costly needs concern Jews in places as distant as Israel, Argentina, and the former Soviet Union. Both morally and strategically, First World powers must be concerned with Third World poverty. We may still have primary responsibility for the poor who belong to our own community, but it is not as simple to apply that criterion as it was when people knew little of conditions far away from home and when what happens far away affects us directly. "To increase learning is to increase heartache," as Ecclesiastes says.[120]

Third, the level of assistance that we expect to provide the poor has also changed substantially. Except for making the indigent downright rich, Jewish law specifies virtually no limit on what a community should afford poor people to retain the dignity of their former social and economic status. That is an impossible standard to maintain in modern times, as it undoubtedly also was in centuries past.

Fourth, many of the details described in the law for collection and distribution of aid are out of place in the modern world. Designating three people to decide how to distribute the community's charitable resources, as Jewish law does, seems blatantly autocratic to us; thirty is even too small a number for the boards of directors of many of our larger charitable organizations, to say nothing of governmental agencies. Moreover, delivery of the aid is more efficiently and honorably done through the mail or through direct deposits in bank accounts rather than by delegations traveling door-to-door. This is a laudable development, in keeping with Maimonides' ladder of charity that prefers gifts given and received anonymously over those where giver and/or recipient know each other's identity.

Fifth, Jewish law gives the court legal power to force people to give an amount commensurate with their income and the community's needs, and it also assigns the court legal authority to seize the property of those who renege on a pledge. However tempting these measures may be to modern fund-raisers, Jewish communal officials no longer have such power. Government agents do have that power, of course, and collecting and distributing aid for the poor through governmental agencies is the rough equivalent of the power granted Jewish courts in pre-Enlightenment times.

Despite these differences between earlier eras and our own in the circumstances of poverty and the remedies for alleviating it, Jewish sources and the concepts and values embedded in them can have a significant impact on the way we think about poverty in our own time and on the ways we respond to it. Specifically, first, we are indeed our brother's (and sister's) keeper, as God made clear to Cain at the outset of the Bible[121] and as Jewish law delineates in detail. This fundamental imperative to help others sets the stage for all ancient and modern discourse on the needy.

Second, the priorities set by Jewish law and values as to which needs we should meet first remain persuasive. Specifically, we must seek first to save life and health, in part by providing medicine and in part by supplying food, clothing, and shelter. We must then seek to provide the skills and tools to enable people to become self-sufficient. Our methods for accomplishing these ends will surely differ in many respects from those used in former eras, but even the classical *tamhui* (soup kitchen) is a project of many Jewish communities today through organizations such as Jewish Family Service, Sova, and Mazon, and Jewish communities in the twentieth century accomplished major feats of redeeming Jews from Nazi Europe, the Soviet Union, Arab countries, and Ethiopia.

Third, everything we do for the needy must be done with discretion and respect. Since the best type of aid by far is prevention of poverty in the first place, the clear mandate of the Jewish tradition is to support governmental and private programs of education in general, and job training in particular. These programs pay multiple dividends, keeping whole groups of the population from a life of unemployment, degradation, and often crime, and enabling them to become productive and dignified members of society. This duty to teach children a form of gainful employment first devolves on parents and then, by extension, on the community, and it puts into practice the top rung of Maimonides' hierarchy of charity, by which we help someone to help themselves.

If assistance is necessary, for both practical and moral reasons it is better to proffer employment, a loan, or investment capital to poor people than to give money as a dole. A loan or investment has the potential for making the poor person self-supporting, thus eliminating the drain on the community's resources. It also preserves the dignity of the poor person now and, if the venture succeeds, for the long term.

Even so, a poor person seeking aid from an individual cannot be denied enough for immediate sustenance. However we may react to being confronted by street beggars, Jewish law requires that we give food to those who ask for it without investigating to make sure that they are not deceiving us in stating their need; if they ask for clothing or housing, which is more expensive, we may not investigate if we recognize the beggar but we may if we do not. In any case, we must treat the beggar kindly.[122] These laws, though, demand that we provide *food, clothing*, and *shelter* for the hungry; we need not give beggars money when we have good evidence that it will not be used for that purpose. Most commonly, this occurs when the people asking are clearly inebriated or under the influence of drugs and when the money would in all likelihood be used to feed their habit. Indeed, to give them money under those circumstances would be "placing a stumbling block before the blind," a violation of Leviticus 19:14 as the Rabbis interpreted it.[123] To avoid this problem, some people keep on their person a ready supply of food coupons redeemable at various restaurants or supermarkets so that they can be sure that their contribution to a beggar will indeed be used for a legitimate purpose. Others maintain that giving people even such a specified voucher encourages them to continue on the dole and that the morally responsible thing to do is to direct them (or help them get to) a communally run program that will provide for their basic needs while simultaneously taking steps to help them become self-supporting. If you have neither the time nor the information to help the person reach a responsible agency, it is probably best to give him or her something. Even though the person may be deceiving you and even though you may even be contributing to a bad habit of panhandling, it is better to take those risks than to pass by someone who is truly in need.

On the other hand, nobody is obliged by Jewish law to supply people who ask for help with large sums of money; a small donation is all that is called for. Anything more than that undermines our concern to dissuade people from begging; we want them instead to get help from the public and private agencies created to supply assistance with continuity and with the professional expertise to assess and respond to their actual needs. Similarly, on a communal level, immediate sustenance should be available for the truly destitute with few, if any, questions asked, through food pantries, soup kitchens, food stamps, or supermarket vouchers.

Jewish communities of the past made arrangements of varying sorts for housing the poor. For example, since the 1980s, severe cutbacks in American government support for mental-health facilities and for housing programs for the poor have forced thousands of people to live on the streets, a phenomenon that has occurred in other countries as well. From a Jewish perspective, this is simply intolerable; it is, indeed, a national disgrace. Housing must be provided for the homeless, preferably on an ongoing basis but at least on nights with cold or inclement weather. If poor people have housing of their own, they should be permitted to retain it even while getting public assistance to pay for their rent and food. Welfare programs should also allow the poor to retain their tools of employment since the ultimate social goal of these programs is to help people become self-sufficient.

One important way to prevent poverty is through education. In this world that increasingly requires skills of communication and technology, teenagers who drop out of school all too often find out that unskilled jobs are few and low-paying. Major efforts, then, must be devoted to keeping teenagers in school and to improving the education students obtain there. In addition to the many other good reasons we want our children to be well educated, education must be seen as an important tool to avoid poverty.

Collectors and distributors of public assistance have the responsibility to act honestly, discreetly, and wisely in their sacred tasks. This includes striking a delicate balance between assuring that those asking for aid are truly in need while simultaneously preserving their privacy and honor as much as possible. It also includes an absolute duty to handle the money collected honestly and responsibly.

The poor have duties of their own. They must responsibly manage whatever resources they have, and, if at all possible, work to secure training and employment that will extricate them from poverty. That is, the ideal of making the poor self-sufficient is an ideal not only for donors, but for recipients as well. Those who cannot work or find employment must try to contribute to the community in some other ways. Communal officials have the right and duty to ensure that people receiving aid are living up to these responsibilities, but they must do so tactfully and respectfully.

AN ONGOING CHALLENGE

While "the poor will never cease from the land" (Deuteronomy 15:11), we are not permitted to sit back and apathetically let that situation persist. Hence the verse continues: "That is why I command you: open your hand to the poor and needy kinsman in your land." Judaism has accepted the continuous nature of the problem of poverty, but it is anything but fatalistic about it. On the contrary, in both theory and practice, Jews have assumed throughout history that it is within our ability to provide for the poor and that it is our sacred task to do so.

In aiding the poor and other needy people, Jewish theoretical convictions about the divine source of the Torah and the moral norms and ideals articulated in it give Jews a sense of why they should serve others and how, even in the radically changed world of today. Jewish moral beliefs about the nature of the human being, the family, the community, and the future define what is important in life and motivate Jews to try to achieve those moral goals. Specific Jewish demands to provide food, clothing, and shelter to the destitute and to respect the disabled give these theoretical convictions practical import. Fulfilling such concrete duties to care for the needy makes it possible for a fellow human being to escape the slavery of poverty and live as a respected member of the community, thereby gaining the status of free individual that we all need and deserve. Preventing poverty and honorably assisting the poor are therefore nothing short of holy activities. In making these aims our priority, we act as human beings should and imitate no less an exemplar than God:

> If your brother, being in straits, comes under your authority,...let him live with you as your brother....I the Lord am your God who brought you out from the land of the Egyptians to be their slaves no more, who broke the bars of your yoke and made you walk erect.
>
> (Leviticus 25:35–36; 26:13)

NOTES

In all of the following notes,

M. = Mishnah (edited c. 200 C.E.)
T. = Tosefta (edited c. 200 C.E.)
J. = Jerusalem [Palestinian] Talmud (edited c. 400 C.E.)
B. = Babylonian Talmud (edited c. 500 C.E.)
M.T. = Maimonides' code, the *Mishneh Torah* (1177 C.E.)
S.A. = Joseph Karo's code, the *Shulhan Arukh* (1565 C.E.)

1. Sergio Della Pergola, "World Jewish Population 2001," in the *American Jewish Yearbook 2001*, David Singer and Lawrence Grossman, eds. (New York: American Jewish Committee, 2001), pp. 532–569, esp. p. 540.
2. "Top Ten Organized Religions of the World." Infoplease.com. © 2002 Family Education Network, August 7, 2003. <http://infoplease.com/ipa/A0904108.html>.
3. Della Pergola, pp. 540, 565.
4. *Sifra* on Leviticus 19:18.
5. B. *Megillah* 10b.
6. T. *Sanhedrin* 13:2, and, in regard to the children of Gentiles, T. *Sanhedrin* 13:1. Later Jewish tradition follows Rabbi Joshua in both passages. See also M. *Avot* 4:29 and *Lamentations Rabbah* on Lamentations 3:23, both of which seem to assure life after death to people generally, and B. *Eruvin* 19a and *Ecclesiastes Rabbah* to Ecclesiastes 3:9, both of which promise the Garden of Eden to the righteous and Gehinom to the wicked, without mention of any restriction to Jews. One source, in fact, specifically limits the punishment of Gehinom to the children of *wicked* gentiles: "With respect to the children of wicked gentiles, all agree that they will not enter the World to Come" (B. *Sanhedrin* 110b). Some Rabbinic sources express the opposite extreme: "The Resurrection is reserved for [the People] Israel" (*Genesis Rabbah* 13:6; cf. M. *Sanhedrin* 10:1). These undoubtedly reflect times in which gentiles were oppressing Jews and the consequent need during such times to reinforce Jewish commitment with the promise of future reward; they may also reflect the concern of Jewish leaders that some of their number would be attracted to Hellenistic or Christian beliefs and practices. Restricting the reward of the World to Come to Jews alone would encourage Jews to persevere in their faith, despite oppression or the lures of foreign ideas. That does not erase, though, the remarkably

universalistic passages that appear in Rabbinic literature, some of which are cited at the beginning of this note, and the clear aversion to missionary activities embedded in Jewish law and practice for at least the last two thousand years.

7. Isaiah 11:6; cf. generally Isaiah 2:2–4; 11–12.

8. Isaiah 49:1–6; 51:4.

9. Isaiah 2:2–4; 19:23–24; Zephaniah 2:11, 3:8–9; Zekhariah 14:9.

10. *Leviticus Rabbah* 36:2; B. *Avodah Zarah* 3b.

11. For a discussion of the advantages and disadvantages of translating moral norms into legal terms, see Elliot N. Dorff, *To Do the Right and the Good: A Jewish Approach to Modern Social Ethics* (Philadelphia: Jewish Publication Society, 2002), Appendix B, pp. 262–285; and *Loving Your Neighbor and Yourself: A Jewish Approach to Modern Personal Ethics* (Philadelphia: Jewish Publication Society, 2003), chapter 1.

12. See, for example, the commentary of Nahmanides (1194–c. 1270) on Deuteronomy 6:18.

13. B. *Bava Metzia* 30b. For examples of specific cases in which people did act beyond the letter of the law, see B. *Ketubbot* 97a; B. *Bava Kamma* 99b–100a; B. *Bava Metzia* 24b. God can be addressed in prayer to act beyond the letter of the law in dealing with His human creatures (B. *Berakhot* 7a), at least when there is no call to do a true judgment (B. *Avodah Zarah* 4b).

14. See, for example, Exodus 19:5; Deuteronomy 10:14; Psalms 24:1. See also Genesis 14:19, 22 (where the Hebrew word for "Creator" [*koneh*] also means "Possessor," and where "heaven and earth" is a merism for those and everything in between) and Psalms 104:24, where the same word is used with the same meaning. The following verses have the same theme, although not quite as explicitly or as expansively: Exodus 20:11; Leviticus 25:23, 42, 55; Deuteronomy 4:35, 39; 32:6.

15. Bathing, for example, is a commandment according to Hillel: *Leviticus Rabbah* 34:3. Maimonides summarized and codified the rules requiring proper care of the body in M.T. *Laws of Ethics (De'ot)*, chapters 3 and 5. He spells out there in remarkable clarity that the purpose of these positive duties to maintain health is not to feel good and live a long life, but rather to have a healthy body so that one can then serve God.

16. B. *Shabbat* 32a; B. *Bava Kamma* 15b, 80a, 91b; M.T. *Laws of Murder* 11:4 5; S.A. *Yoreh De'ah* 116:5 gloss; S.A. *Hoshen Mishpat* 427:8 10.

17. B. *Hullin* 10a; S.A. *Orah Hayyim* 173:2; S.A. *Yoreh De'ah* 116:5 gloss.

18. Elliot N. Dorff and Arthur Rosett, *A Living Tree: The Roots and Growth of Jewish Law* (Albany: State University of New York Press, 1988), pp. 337–362, where Orthodox, Reform, and Conservative rabbinic rulings regarding smoking are reprinted.

19. Genesis 1:27; 5:1–2; 9:6.

20. See Deuteronomy 21:22–23.

21. M. *Avot (Ethics of the Fathers)* 3:18.

22. See Genesis 1:26–27; 3:1–7, 22–24.

23. See Genesis 2:18–24; Numbers 12:1–16; Deuteronomy 22:13–19. Note also that "*ha-middaber,*" "the speaker," is a synonym for the human being (in comparison to animals) in medieval Jewish philosophy.

24. Maimonides, *Guide for the Perplexed*, Part I, Chapter 1.

25. See Deuteronomy 6:5; Leviticus 19:18, 33–4, and note that the traditional prayer book juxtaposes the paragraph just before the Shema, which speaks of God's love for us, with the first paragraph of the Shema, which commands us to love God.

26. Consider the prayer in the traditional, early morning weekday service, "*Elohai neshamah she-natata bi,*" "My God, the soul (or life-breath) which you have imparted to me is pure. You created it, You formed it, You breathed it into me; You guard it within me...." Harlow (1985), pp. 8–11. Similarly, the Rabbis describe the human being as part divine and part animal, the latter consisting of the material aspects of the human being and the former consisting of that which we share with God; see *Sifre Deuteronomy*, par. 306; 132a. Or consider this rabbinic statement in *Genesis Rabbah* 8:11: "In four respects man resembles the creatures above, and in four respects the creatures below. Like the animals he eats and drinks, propagates his species, relieves himself, and dies. Like the ministering angels he stands erect, speaks, possesses intellect, and sees [in front of him and not on the side like an animal]."

27. M. *Sanhedrin* 4:5.

28. Rabbi Bunam, cited by Martin Buber, *Tales of the Hasidim* (New York: Schocken, 1948), Vol. II, pp. 249–250.

29. *Genesis Rabbah* 24:7.

30. For a thorough discussion of this blessing and concept in the Jewish tradition, see Carl Astor "...*Who Makes People Different*": *Jewish Perspectives on the Disabled* (New York: United Synagogue of Conservative Judaism, 1985).

31. *Genesis Rabbah* 24:7. Consider also: "Great is human dignity, for it overrides a negative prohibition of the Torah" (B. *Berakhot* 19b, etc.) "The Holy One, blessed be He, has concern for the honor of all His creatures, including non-Jews and even wicked people like Balaam" (*Numbers Rabbah* 20:14). "All the Holy One, blessed be He, created, He created for His own honor" (B. *Yoma* 38a, based on Isaiah 43:7).

32. Romans 6–8, especially 6:12; 7:14–24; 8:3, 10, 12–13; Galatians 5:16–24; I Corinthians 7:2, 9, 36–38.

33. M.T. *Laws of Ethics (De'ot)* 3:3.

34. M. *Ketubbot* 5:6–7.

35. Genesis 2:18; B. *Yevamot* 61b.

36. *Genesis Rabbah* 17:2; B. *Yevamot* 62b–63a; *Midrash Psalms* on Psalms 59:2.

37. B. *Kiddushin* 29b–30a.

38. The minimum of two: M. *Yevamot* 6:6 (61b); M.T. *Laws of Marriage* 15:4; S.A. *Even Ha'ezer* 1:5. The ideal of having more: B. *Yevamot* 62b, basing it on Isaiah 45:18 and Ecclesiastes 11:6; M.T. *Laws of Marriage* 15:16.

39. Deuteronomy 6:7, 20–25; 11:19. This was already one of Abraham's duties: Genesis 18:19.

40. Deuteronomy 5:1.

41. Deuteronomy 31:10–13.

42. M. *Avot* 5:24.

43. Close to a quarter (24 percent) of American Jewish adults 18 years of age and older have received a graduate degree, and 55 percent have earned at least a bachelor's degree. The current comparable numbers for non-Jews are 5 percent and 28 percent. "U.S Jewish Population Fairly Stable Over Decade, According to Results of National Jewish Population Survey, 2000–2001," www.ujc.org/njps, p. 4.

44. For more on this, see Elliot N. Dorff, "Training Rabbis in the Land of the Free" in *The Seminary at 100*, Nina Beth Cardin and David Wolf Silverman, eds. (New York: Jewish Theological Seminary of America, 1987), pp. 11–28, esp. 12–19; and Milton R. Konvitz, *Judaism and the American Idea* (New York: Schocken Books, 1978), chapter 5.

45. B. *Sanhedrin* 17b.

46. B. *Bava Batra* 89a; M.T. *Laws of Theft* 8:20; S.A. *Hoshen Mishpat* 231:2.

47. This prayer is found in the prayer books of all Jewish denominations, but see, for example, *Siddur Sim Shalom*, Jules Harlow,

ed. (New York: Rabbinical Assembly and United Synagogue of America, 1985), pp. 162 f.

48. Half of Ameican Jews polled across the nation by the *Los Angeles Times* listed a commitment to social equality as the factor most important to their sense of Jewish identity, whereas only 17 pecent cited religious observance and another 17 percent cited support for Israel. See Robert Scheer, "Jews in U.S. Committed to Equality," *Los Angeles Times*, April 13, 1988, Section I, pp. 1, 14–15.

49. B. *Sanhedrin* 73a.

50. For a discussion of some of the sources on Judaism's view of war, see Elliot N. Dorff, *To Do the Right and the Good: A Jewish Approach to Modern Social Ethics* (Philadelphia: Jewish Publication Society, 2002), chapter 7.

51. M.T. *Laws of Gifts to the Poor* 9:3.

52. M.T. *Laws of Gifts to the Poor* 7:5, 10. Maimonides' sources: B. *Ketubbot* 50a (one fifth maximum); *Sifre* on Deuteronomy 14:22 (tithe applied to money); B. *Bava Batra* 9a (a third shekel minimum); B. *Gittin* 7b (poor must give); B. *Bava Batra* 8b (compulsion applied, but cf. Tosafot there for minority views). Cf. also S.A. *Yoreh De'ah* 248:1 2.

53. M.T. *Laws of Gifts to the Poor* 9:12. Cf. T. *Pe'ah* 4:9; J. *Bava Batra* 1:4; B. *Bava Batra* 8a.

54. B. *Bava Batra* 8b; M.T. *Laws of Gifts to the Poor* 9:5.

55. Jacob Neusner, *Tzedakah: Can Jewish Philanthropy Buy Jewish Survival?* (Chappaqua, N.Y.: Rossel Books, 1982), pp. 32, 67 ff.

56. *Sifre* on Deuteronomy 15:7; M.T. *Laws of Gifts to the Poor* 7:13; S.A. *Yoreh De'ah* 251:3.

57. Deuteronomy 24:17–18, 21–22.

58. See Exodus 21:2–11; Leviticus 25:39 ff.

59. Hosea 2:4–22 and Jeremiah 2:2 are two famous examples that link the metaphor of marriage to the relationship between God and Israel. Deuteronomy 6:4–8; 7:6–11; 11:1, 22; etc. all speak of obedience out of love.

60. T. *Pe'ah* 4:20.

61. Leviticus 25:55; see also verses 42–43.

62. S. D. Goitein, *A Mediterranean Society: The Jewish Communities of the Arab World as Portrayed in the Documents of the Cairo Genizah* (Berkeley: University of California Press, 1971), Vol. II, p. 143.

63. Deuteronomy 24:10–11; M. *Ketubbot* 13:3; S.A. *Yoreh De'ah* 251:8; *Even Ha-Ezer* 112:11; B. *Ketubbot* 43a; S.A. *Even Ha-Ezer* 112:16; 93:4.

64. M. *Bava Kamma* 8:1.

65. B. *Bava Kamma* 86a.

66. M.T. *Laws of Gifts to the Poor*, 10:7–14. Translated in *A Maimonides Reader*, Isadore Twersky, ed. (New York: Behrman House, 1972), pp. 136–137. See also S.A. *Yoreh De'ah* 249:6. Goitein, however, notes that jobs, loans, and investments were generally given first to relatives or those who had not yet taken alms; cf. Goitein, *A Mediterranean Society*, Vol. II, p. 142.

67. B. *Bava Kamma* 119a; B. *Gittin* 7b; M.T. *Laws of Gifts to the Poor* 7:5; S.A. *Yoreh De'ah* 248:1; 251:12.

68. B. *Bava Batra* 9a; S.A. *Yoreh De'ah* 250:3 4.

69. God will not forget the poor: Psalms 9:12; 10:12; etc. God pities and comforts the poor: Psalms 34:6; Isaiah 49:13; etc. God cares for the poor: Jeremiah 20:13; Psalms 107:41; 132:15; Job 5:15; etc.

70. God seeks social justice for the poor: Deuteronomy 10:17–18; II Samuel 22:28; Isaiah 25:4; Amos 2:6; 4:1; etc. God forbids oppressing the poor: Exodus 23:3; Leviticus 19:15; Isaiah 1:23; Ezekiel 22:7; Micah 2:2; Malachi 3:5; etc.

71. B. *Sotah* 14a.

72. Cf. Mordecai Katz, *Protection of the Weak in the Talmud* (New York: Columbia University Press, 1925), p. 80. See also B. *Rosh Hashanah* 12b and the commentary of Rashi there.

73. Most of these laws appear in the passages cited at the beginning of this paragraph. Third-year tithes are also mentioned in Deuteronomy 14:28–29 (in addition to 26:12–13). That Sabbatical produce should be given to the poor is in Exodus 23:11 (although in Leviticus 25:6–7 it is the owner of the land together with his slaves and hired workers who are entitled to it), and the Jubilee laws appear in Leviticus 25:8ff.

74. Deuteronomy 24:14–15.

75. Leviticus 25:36–37; Deuteronomy 23:20.

76. Deuteronomy 15:1–2, 7–11.

77. Exodus 22:25–26; Deuteronomy 24:10–15.

78. Exodus 23:6–9; cf. Deuteronomy 16:18–20; 23:17–18; cf. Psalms 82:3, etc. The poor, though, were not to be preferred in their cases just because they were poor any more than the rich were to be given special consideration; rather, fairness to all litigants was to be the rule: Leviticus 19:15; Deuteronomy 1:17.

79. The closest we have to anything like that is not in a law code but rather in The Instruction of Amen-Em-Opet, a letter from some time between the tenth and the sixth centuries B.C.E. similar in tone to the biblical Book of Proverbs. The *advice* given there is to permit the widow to glean unhindered and to give gifts of oil to the

poor as conduct approved by the gods, but *not* required by them—and certainly not by human governing authorities. See *Ancient Near Eastern Texts Relating to the Old Testament*, James B. Pritchard, ed. (Princeton: Princeton University Press, 1955), p. 424.

80. For a brief account, see "Debt" in *The New Illustrated Columbia Encyclopedia* (New York: Columbia University Press, 1979), 6:1850.

81. M. *Pe'ah* 8:7. Cf. T. *Pe'ah* 4:8, 10; J. *Eruvin* 3:1 (20d); B. *Shabbat* 118a; B. *Bava Metzia* 8b–9a; B. *Sanhedrin* 17b.

82. Israel Abrahams, *Jewish Life in the Middle Ages* (New York: Atheneum, 1969), p. 311.

83. B. *Ta'anit* 21b. Cf. Goitein, *A Mediterranean Society*, Vol. II, p. 133.

84. Rabbi Eleazar Fleckeles, *Teshuvah Me'ahavah*, III, *Yoreh De'ah* 336.

85. S.A. *Yoreh De'ah* 249:16; 255:2.

86. T. *Pe'ah* 4:9.

87. M. *Pe'ah* 8:8.

88. Cf. the gloss of Moses Isserles on S.A. *Hoshen Mishpat* 163:1; *Arukh Hashulhan, Hoshen Mishpat* 163:1.

89. B. *Bava Batra* 9a; S.A. *Yoreh De'ah* 251:7.

90. *Sifre* on Deuteronomy 15:7; M.T. *Laws of Gifts to the Poor* 7:13; S.A. *Yoreh De'ah* 251:3.

91. B. *Ketubbot* 67a; S.A. *Yoreh De'ah* 251:8.

92. S.A. *Yoreh De'ah* 251:7–8.

93. S.A. *Yoreh De'ah* 252:1, 3.

94. B. *Gittin* 61a; M.T. *Laws of Gifts to the Poor* 7:7. According to B. *Gittin* 59b, obligations that are for the sake of peace have pentateuchal authority.

95. T. *Pe'ah* 4:10–11.

96. B. *Ketubbot* 67b. M.T. *Laws of Gifts to the Poor* 7:3, 4; S.A. *Yoreh De'ah* 250:1.

97. M.T. *Laws of Gifts to the Poor* 7:3, 4; S.A. *Yoreh De'ah* 250:1.

98. B. *Shabbat* 118a.

99. Cf. Goitein, *A Mediterranean Society*, Vol. II, p. 191.

100. B. *Kiddushin* 29a.

101. M. *Ketubbot* 6:5; cf. B. *Ketubbot* 67a–67b; B. *Megillah* 3b; B. *Makkot* 24a; S.A. *Yoreh De'ah* 250:2; 251:8.

102. B. *Bava Batra* 90a; Falk, *Sma*, to S.A. *Hoshen Mishpat* 231, note 36; cf. Aaron Levine, *Free Enterprise and Jewish Law* (New York: KTAV and Yeshiva, 1980), pp. 91–95. Falk seems to include clothing and rent as well as food in this rule.

103. B. *Sanhedrin* 3a.

104. Arcadius Kahan, "The Early Modern Period," in Salo W. Baron, et. al., eds., *Economic History of the Jews* (New York: Schocken, 1975), p. 68.

105. Richard Rubenstein, *The Age of Triage* (Boston: Beacon Press, 1983), especially chapters 1, 9, and 10.

106. In April, 1997, the Rabbinical Assembly, the organization of Conservative rabbis, passed a "Resolution on Global Poverty and the Deteriorating Global Environment," calling for "our governments to scrutinize the dynamics and practices of their respective economies with a view to balancing the battle against poverty with environmental protection so that humankind live within the bounds of the regenerative, absorptive, and carrying capacities of the earth and in such a way that the needs of current and future generations can be met." *Proceedings of the Rabbinical Assembly 1997* (New York: Rabbinical Assembly, 1998), pp. 254–255.

107. Based on God's words to Adam, "By the sweat of your brow shall you get bread to eat" (Genesis 3:19), the Rabbis asserted that people have a moral right to eat only if they earn it by their own effort. B. *Bava Batra* 110a; *Genesis Rabbah* 14:10.

108. M. *Pe'ah* 8:8; B. *Ketubbot* 68a; M.T. *Laws of Gifts to the Poor* 9:14–17.

109. M. *Avot* 1:10. Cf. Rav's "pearl" in B. *Berakhot* 17a.

110. *Tanhuma*, "Vayetze," Section 13.

111. M. *Avot* 2:2.

112. *Leviticus Rabbah* 25:5.

113. B. *Nedarim* 49b.

114. J. *Pe'ah* 15c.

115. Deuteronomy 24:10–11.

116. *Leviticus Rabbah* 34:9.

117. M. *Avot* 1:5.

118. B. *Bava Batra* 9b; M.T. *Laws of Gifts to the Poor* 10:5.

119. I am indebted to Jacob Neusner for the idea for this section and some of its substance. Cf. Neusner, *Tzedakah*, pp. 45–52.

120. Ecclesiastes 1:18.

121. Genesis 4:9.

122. B. *Bava Batra* 9a; M.T. *Laws of Gifts to the Poor* 7:6. See also note 68 above and the text at that point in the essay.

123. The Rabbis understood that verse to apply not only to a physical stumbling block being put before a physically blind person, but also to moral stumbling blocks put before a morally blind person — and even to giving false information to someone who can be harmed by it. See, among others, *Sifra* on Leviticus 19:14 (in

regard to giving inappropriate or dangerous advice); B. *Pesahim* 22b (in regard to giving wine to a Nazarite or a limb from a living animal to a non-Jew, thus tempting each of them to violate laws that apply to them); B. *Mo'ed Katan* 5a (in regard to marking grave sites so as to avoid stepping on them); B. *Mo'ed Katan* 17a (in regard to striking a grown child, thus tempting him to strike his parent back and be subject to the death penalty according to Exodus 21:15); and B. *Bava Metzia* 75b (in regard to lending money without witnesses).

JUDAISM

Sacred Writings

&

Questions to Consider

RATIONALES FOR SERVICE

God Creates and Owns Everything and Demands that We Save the Lives and Welfare of His Creatures (*piqquah nefesh*).

Deuteronomy 10:14: Mark, the heavens to their uttermost reaches belong to the Lord your God, the earth and all that is on it!

Mishnah, *Sanhedrin* **4:5**: For this reason was [the first] man created alone: to teach you that with regard to anyone who destroys a single soul, Scripture imputes guilt to him as though he had destroyed a complete world; and with regard to anyone who preserves a single soul, Scripture ascribes merit to him as though he had preserved a complete world. Furthermore, [man was created alone] for the sake of peace among men, that one might not say to his fellow, "My father was greater than yours."... Additionally, [man was created alone] to proclaim the greatness of the Holy One, blessed be He: for if a man strikes many coins from one mold, they all resemble one another, but the Supreme King of kings, the Holy One, blessed be He, fashioned every person in the stamp of the first person, and yet not one of them looks the same as anyone else. Therefore every single person is obligated to say: "The world was created for my sake."

Deuteronomy 24:6: A handmill or an upper millstone shall not be taken in pawn, for that would be taking someone's life in pawn.

Babylonian Talmud, *Sanhedrin* **74a**: Rabbi Johanan said in the name of Rabbi Simeon bar Yehodzadak: By a majority vote, it was resolved in the upper chambers of the house of Nithza in Lydda [where the Sanhedrin, the Supreme Court, was meeting during the Emperor Hadrian's persecutions of the Jews in the years after 135 C.E.] that in every other law of the Torah, if a person is commanded [by a Roman or a criminal], "Transgress [a particular commandment of God] or I will kill you," he may transgress so not to be killed, except for idolatry, incest/adultery, and murder [where the Jew must suffer death rather than commit such acts].

Babylonian Talmud, *Sanhedrin* **73a**: On the basis of what biblical verse do we know that if a man sees his neighbor drowning, mauled by beasts, or attacked by robbers, he is bound to save him? From the verse, "You shall not stand idly by the blood of your neighbor" (Leviticus 19:16). — [Objection:] But is it derived from that verse, or from elsewhere? Specifically, how do we know [that one must save his neighbor] from the loss of himself [that is, from dying]? From the verse, "And you shall restore him to himself" [Deuteronomy 22:2, which the Rabbis are reading out of context, but in accordance with a possible reading of the Hebrew words, to refer not to a lost object but to the man himself]. From that verse I might think that it is only a *personal* duty [because Deuteronomy says "and *you* shall restore him to himself"], but that he is not bound to take the trouble of hiring men [if he cannot save the victim on his own]; therefore, this verse [Leviticus 19:16] teaches us that he must [even hire others to save someone from attack]. Jerusalem Talmud *Terumot* 7:20: Caravans of [Jewish] men are walking down a road, and they are accosted by non-Jews who say to them: "Give us one from among you that we may kill him; otherwise we shall kill you all." Though all may be killed, they may not hand over a single soul of Israel. However, if the demand is for a specified individual like Sheva, son of Bikhri [who, according to the biblical story in II Samuel 20, was convicted of a capital crime], they should surrender him rather than all be killed.

Questions

We should help the poor in order to save their lives and welfare. In a secular way of thinking (that is, without considerations of God or the transcendent element of experience), why should we do that? In a Jewish way of thinking, why should we do that? Describe the strengths and weaknesses of both of those rationales for helping the needy to preserve their lives.

Is the rationale for service of the agency where you are working like that of Judaism or is it secular? What is your agency's motivation/rationale for service? What sources have you used to determine the rationale: mission statement, interview(s) with chief supervisor, annual report, brochures?

The first human being was created alone, according to the Mishnah, to teach us several lessons, one of which is that whoever destroys a single person destroys a whole universe and whoever preserves a single person preserves a whole universe. Explain how that is so. Is the meaning of "preserve" here restricted to maintaining a person's life, or do you think that it has broader meanings, such as preserving a person's dignity through lifting that person out of poverty or giving that person an education?

How does your agency "preserve life," and does your agency define the preservation of life narrowly or broadly? What choices have been made at your agency that demonstrate the broad or narrow definition? Is the action of the agency consistent with its rhetoric?

Deuteronomy 24:6 prohibits taking in pawn the tools by which a person earns a living. Explain how that very specific command of God is connected to God's ownership of all of us. Can you think of other specific things that one should do or refrain from doing to protect people's life and health?

Have those whom your agency serves had the tools by which they or their forebears earned a living taken away? If so, by whom and under what conditions? For example, agricultural workers who migrate to the city are often left with no "tools" — training or skill — to earn a living.

After the failure of the Bar Kokhba revolt against the Romans, the Emperor Hadrian made it a capital crime to practice Judaism or teach anything about Judaism. The Sanhedrin, meeting in secret, had to find a way to balance the competing goods of life itself and living life according to God's commandments as understood in Judaism. Their solution was to say that life takes precedence over almost anything — so, for example, you should violate the laws of the Sabbath or even the laws prohibiting theft to save your life or that of someone else. If a Roman (or some other person) says that he will kill you unless you murder someone else or bow to idols in public or commit incest or adultery, you must prefer to die at his hands rather than to engage in such acts. Life that included such acts is, for the Rabbis, not worth living. Would you draw the line in the same place? Under what circumstances, if any, would you refuse to do something even if it meant that you would lose your life? Conversely, what risky things would you do in the name of some ultimate goal? (Think, for example, of people who volunteer for military service or give aid to those who live in dangerous circumstances.) Notice that these considerations put a limit even on the value of life itself.

Did choosing to engage in a service-learning program reflect your belief in the purpose and value of human life — your own and those whom you are serving? Have your beliefs changed through your experience of service?

The Talmud requires us to take active steps to save someone else in need, even to the extent of hiring other people to assist us in the process. This is in sharp contrast to the laws in all but two American states (Wisconsin and Vermont) and in many other countries, where you have no legal duty to assist others and cannot be prosecuted for failing to do so. There was a famous case — the Kitty Genovese case — in which a woman in

New York was murdered outside an apartment complex, screaming all the while, and it turned out that twenty-three people had heard her and had not even bothered to telephone the police, an act that would not have threatened their own lives. In fact, until recently, when many American states enacted "Good Samaritan laws," someone who tried to save someone else could be sued if the victim suffered harm in the process. The Talmud here takes the exact opposite approach: we have an affirmative duty to help others in need. At the same time, we must, as we saw earlier, preserve our own lives. If someone is drowning, then, or being attacked by robbers, what should you do according to Jewish law? (Incidentally, those who have taken lifesaving courses may remember that the motto of the American Red Cross in such courses is "Throw, tow, row, go" — that is, first try to help the person by throwing him or her a life jacket; then try to throw the victim a rope and tow him or her to shore; then, if necessary, row out to the person in a boat and try to get the person into the boat; and then, only if no other possibility exists, swim out to the person to try to save him or her. That is, endanger yourself as little as possible in the process of saving others.) What about ministering to patients with a communicable disease?

Does your agency have policies governing the staff and volunteers related to self-protection? What have you observed about the behavior of staff in this regard? Do staff members observe precautions? Along the spectrum from no responsibility for others to disregard for one's own safety and well-being, where do individuals who work in your agency fall? Speculate on why there may be differences. Is the work for some agency employees only a means of earning a living while for others it is a moral imperative?

The selection from the Jerusalem Talmud presents a very hard case. If you were asked to rule, and you decided to rule on a utilitarian basis (that is, the greatest good for the greatest number), how would you rule? Why does the Talmud rule differently? Why does the Talmud make an exception if the enemy identifies a person who has been condemned to death in court?

Does your agency operate out of a philosophy of the "greatest good for the greatest number," or does it restrict those whom it serves?

Being Part of a Community

Deuteronomy 22:1–4: If you see your fellow's ox or sheep gone astray, do not ignore it; you must take it back to your fellow. If your fellow does not live near you or you do not know who he is, you shall bring it home and it shall remain with you until your fellow claims it; then you shall give it back to him. You shall do the same with his ass; you shall do the same with his garment; and so too shall you do with anything that your fellow loses and you find: you must not remain indifferent. If you see your fellow's ass or ox fallen on the road, do not ignore it; you must help him raise it.

Exodus 23:5: When you see the ass of your enemy lying under its burden and would refrain from raising it, you must nevertheless raise it with him.

Babylonian Talmud, *Sanhedrin* 17b: It has been taught: A scholar should not reside in a city where [any] ofthe following ten things is missing: (1) a court of justice which can impose flagellation and monetary penalties; (2) a charity fund, collected by two people and distributed by three [to ensure honesty and wise policies of distribution]; (3) a synagogue; (4) public baths; (5) toilet facilities; (6) a circumciser; (7) a doctor; (8) a notary [for writing official documents]; (9) a slaughterer [of kosher meat]; and (10) a schoolmaster. Rabbi Akiba is quoted [as including] also several kinds of fruit [in the list] because they are beneficial for eyesight.

Maimonides' *Mishneh Torah*, **Laws of Gifts to the Poor 9:12 (based on Tosefta** *Pe'ah* **4:9; Jerusalem Talmud** *Bava Batra* **1:4; Babylonian Talmud** *Bava Batra* **8a):** One who settles in a community for thirty days becomes obligated to contribute to the charity fund together with the other members of the community. One who settles there for three months becomes obligated to contribute to the soup kitchen. One who settles there for six months becomes obligated to contribute clothing with which the poor of the community can cover themselves. One who settles there for nine months becomes obligated to contribute to the burial fund for burying the community's poor and providing for all their needs of burial.

Leviticus 19:33–34: When a stranger resides with you in your land, you shall not wrong him. The stranger who resides with you shall be to you as one of your citizens; you shall love him as yourself, for you were strangers in the land of Egypt: I the Lord am your God.

Questions

Deuteronomy 22 insists that for people in our community, even those we do not know, we must not remain indifferent to their losses but must rather assist them in retrieving them. We must also help any other member of the community to raise his or her fallen animal. For modern examples of that, think of helping someone with a disabled car or, more metaphorically, any kind of disability that the person suffers, whether physical, financial, emotional, or anything else. Why should we do this?

What behavior of clients indicates that at the agency they feel, or do not feel, that they are part of a community? Do they help each other or are they estranged from or indifferent to each other? Are the clients and agency employees a community of mutual support or are they two separate communities?

What does Exodus 23 add to what we learned in Deuteronomy 22? Why is that important for our sense of community? Should I help out of a sense of community — of what people in a given community do for each other as part of what it means to be a community — or because God commanded me to do this, whether I feel that sense of community or not — or both? Imagine cases in which one or the other of these rationales would be appropriate.

What motivated the founder(s) of your agency? What motivates the current chief executive officer or governing board? What motivates you?

The Talmud describes what every community must have for a scholar (rabbi) to live there — and, by implication, what any community worthy of the name must provide. Which of these things are relevant to helping the needy? (Notice that while not all of the items on the Talmud's list are intended to help the needy, some do so directly and some offer indirect help.) In modern times, what would you add to this list to enable the community to fulfill its communal obligations to the needy?

Does the community served by your agency possess the requirements for a community as listed in the Talmud? What does your community need that it now lacks? How might you and others provide for it?

Maimonides delineates what an individual owes a community, making it depend on how long the person has lived there. Think about parallels in our own time: What do visitors to your country owe it? Temporary residents? Permanent residents? Citizens? Would your country make any of these classes of people legally responsible to help the needy, as Jewish law does? Why or why not?

If you are serving in a community or country not your own, did you choose service-learning so that you could give and not just take from the community? In your judgment, is it all right or morally wrong for academic institutions to use communities as laboratories without contributing to their well-being? Are you satisfied that the service you and others are providing is equal to what you are receiving/learning?

The Torah expands our usual understanding of our duties to visitors and resident aliens saying that we not only may not oppress the stranger, but must love him or her as ourselves. According to the Torah, there are two reasons for this: we ourselves were strangers, and God commands us to do so. Explain how each reason demands that we love the stranger in our midst. How does this command expand our duties to help others? What would this say, for example, about our duty to provide education and health care to illegal immigrants?

Who are considered to be "strangers" in the community where you are working? What rights do "strangers" have in the community? Are there those who are seeking to take away these rights? What does your agency do by way of direct service or advocacy for the rights of these "strangers"?

Empathy from Your Experience of Needing Service

Exodus 23:9: You shall not oppress a stranger, for you know the feelings of the stranger, having yourselves been strangers in the land of Egypt. [See also Exodus 22:21.]

Deuteronomy 10:19: You must love the stranger, for you were strangers in the land of Egypt.

Deuteronomy 24:17–22: You shall not subvert the rights of the stranger or the fatherless; you shall not take a widow's garment in pawn. Remember that you were a slave in Egypt and that the Lord your God redeemed you from there; therefore do I enjoin you to observe this commandment. When you reap the harvest in your field and overlook a sheaf in the field, do not turn back to get it; it shall go to the stranger, the fatherless, and the widow — in order that the Lord your God may bless you in all your undertakings. When you beat down the fruit of your olive trees, do not go over them again [to pick up the olives that you missed the first time you harvested the olives of a given tree]; that shall go to the stranger, the fatherless, and the widow. When you gather the grapes of your vineyard, do not pick it over again [to gather the grapes that you missed the first time]; that shall go to the stranger, the fatherless, and the widow. Always remember that you were a slave in the land of Egypt; therefore do I enjoin you to observe this commandment.

Questions

When have you been a stranger, and has your experience helped you to reach out to others in your service? Have staff or agency personnel reached out to you? Have the agency's clients?

Deuteronomy 10 goes further: like Leviticus 19, it requires that we not only desist from harming a stranger, but actually love the stranger, presumably meaning that we must provide positive benefits to him or her. In both verses, the rationale given is that we were slaves in Egypt. Explain the reasoning involved in going from the experience of being slaves in Egypt to the command to love the stranger.

Is love for the stranger a value of your agency? How is it expressed and demonstrated in word and action?

With whom is the stranger grouped in the laws of Deuteronomy 24? Why? What are some of the concrete duties to the stranger that Jews have, according to this source?

What are the concrete duties of your agency? What are your concrete duties as a volunteer/service-learning student?

The Bible assumes an economy that is primarily agricultural. What would be some parallel duties to those in Deuteronomy 24 in an economy that is mercantile or industrial, such as many countries have now?

Is your agency addressing the real needs of the clients? Is it in any way working from a model that is no longer operative? Cite arguments that you have heard on both sides.

God's Commandment

Exodus 22:25–27: If you lend money to My people, to the poor among you, do not act toward them as a creditor: exact no interest from them. If you take your neighbor's garment in pledge, you must return it to him before the sun sets; it is his only clothing, the sole covering for his skin. In what else shall he sleep? Therefore, if he cries out to Me, I will pay heed, for I am compassionate.

Exodus 22:22–24: You shall not ill-treat any widow or orphan. If you do mistreat them, I [God] will heed their outcry as soon as they cry out to Me, and My anger shall blaze forth and I will put you to the sword, and your own wives shall become widows and your children orphans.

Isaiah 1:16–20: Wash yourselves clear; Put your evil doing away from My sight. Cease to do evil; learn to do good. Devote yourselves to justice; aid the wronged, uphold the rights of the orphan; defend the cause of the widow. "Come, let us reach an understanding," says the Lord, "Be your sins like crimson, they can turn snow-white; Be they red as dyed wool, they can become like fleece." If, then, you agree and give heed, you will eat the good things of the earth; But if you refuse and disobey, you will be devoured by the sword. For it was the Lord who spoke. [For similar sentiments, see also Isaiah 10:1–4 and many other passages in the Prophets.]

Deuteronomy 15:7–11: If there is a needy person among you, one of your kinsmen in any of your settlements in the land that the Lord your God is giving you, do not harden your heart and shut your hand against your needy kinsman. Rather, you must open your hand and lend him sufficient for whatever he needs. Beware lest you harbor the base thought, "The seventh year, the year of remission [of debts] is approaching," so that you are mean to your needy kinsman and give him nothing. He will cry out to the Lord against you, and you will incur guilt. Give to him readily and have no regrets when you do so, for in return the Lord your god will bless you in all your efforts and in all your undertakings. For there will never cease to be needy ones in your land, which why I command you: open your hand to the poor and needy kinsman in your land.

Questions

These four sources all indicate that God will punish those who harm the needy. What aspect of God is at work here — His love, His justice, or both?

What does your agency believe about punishment by God or by the secular laws/courts for those who harm the needy? What do the clients seem to believe? Are they confident that justice will come to them from God and/or the authorities, in this world or the next, or are they cynical about the possibility of justice?

The first three sources deal with subverting the rights of the needy, which God will punish. They do not speak to our affirmative duty to help the needy. That is expressed in other sources, such as Leviticus 19, cited below, and Deuteronomy 15. What aspects of God are involved in decreeing that positive duty?

Is the work of your agency that of defending rights or is it engaged in extending benefits?

Human Beings are Created in the Image of God

> **Genesis 1:27**: And God created the human being in His image, in the image of God He created him: male and female He created them.

> **Genesis 5:1–2**: This is the record of Adam's line. When God created man, He made him in the likeness of God; male and female He created them. And when they were created, He blessed them and called them Human.

> **Genesis 9:6**: Whoever sheds the blood of man, by man shall his blood be shed; for in His image did God make man.

> *Numbers Rabbah* **20:14**: The Holy One, blessed be He, has concern for the honor of all His creatures, including non-Jews and even wicked people like Balaam.

Deuteronomy 21:22–23: If a man is guilty of a capital offense and is put to death, and you impale him on a stake, you must not let his corpse remain on the stake overnight, but must bury him the same day. For an impaled body is an affront to God [literally, "a curse of God"]: you shall not defile the land that the Lord your God is giving you to possess.

Genesis Rabbah **24:7**: Rabbi Akiba said: "You shall love your neighbor as yourself" (Leviticus 19:18) [implies that] you should not say that inasmuch as I am despised, let my fellow-man be despised with me, inasmuch as I am cursed, let my fellow-man be cursed with me. Rabbi Tanchuma said: If you act in this manner, know Who it is you despise, for "in the image of God made He man" (Genesis 1:27).

Babylonian Talmud, *Yoma* 38a, based on Isaiah 43:7: All the Holy One, blessed be He, created, He created for His own honor.

Questions

What do you think it means to be created in the image of God? That is, in which aspect(s) is each of us Godlike?

What individuals or groups believe about themselves is important in determining how they experience life. Many service-learning students have expressed wonder that people in poverty or with disabilities are so positive about life despite their problems. What attitudes do you see in the people you are serving?

For the Bible, is it only men who are created in the image of God, or are women too? Are people of only one particular race or creed created in the image of God? Explain.

How does your community view gender and racial differences? If they are religious in tradition and practice, does their religion account for their point of view?

Why, as Genesis 9 asserts, is the image of God relevant to the rule that murderers should be put to death?

How are murderers viewed and treated in your community? Are there different points of view, and do these have a religious base?

For the story of Balaam, see Numbers 22:2–24:25; 31:16; and Deuteronomy 23:4-6. According to the Midrash in *Numbers Rabbah*, God has concern for the dignity of all his people, including non-Jews, and including even wicked people like Balaam, who lead others morally astray by putting them in tempting situations. Notice how that is borne out in Deuteronomy 21, which asserts that a man put to death for a capital offense must be removed from the stake on which he was executed before nightfall because to leave him there would show disrespect for the image of God still in him and therefore constitute an affront to God. What do these texts say about the relationship of the image of God in us to our actions? Note that the image God within a person does not save him from being executed if he commits a capital crime. What is the import of these passages for serving prisoners in various ways—or people outside of prison who are less than paragons of virtue?

What is the attitude of your agency and community to those who commit crimes against others? Does your agency or community believe that there is the possibility of rehabilitation? Is there a general belief that people are either wicked or righteous or that all people have some of each quality? Who are identified as the wicked by your community?

Note that, according to *Genesis Rabbah* 24:7, loving your neighbor as yourself does not permit you to ignore his or her welfare if you do not like yourself, for God intends that you respect and love yourself and that you extend that same love to your neighbor. What do these texts say about how we should treat people who are self-loathing or even just depressed?

Do religious beliefs affect attitudes toward self? What appears to be the most important determinant to self-worth—religion, family, community, ethnic identity? Some believe that service is deprecating to self-esteem; others have found that service that is based on respect and mutuality is ennobling not only to the server but also to the served. How are you experiencing your service-learning program vis à vis the clients and community? Some people who struggle with feelings of low self-esteem discover that in serving, in finding they are useful to others and to society, their own sense of self-worth is increased. Similarly, when community members, even those in serious need, are allowed and encouraged to help others, their own sense of despair is reduced. Have you seen examples of this where you are serving? Does the agency encourage its clients to help each other, the agency employees, and you, the volunteer?

Imitating God in Our Aspirations for Holiness

Deuteronomy 10:17–18: For the Lord your God is God supreme and Lord supreme, the great, the mighty, and the awesome God, who shows no favor and takes no bribe, but upholds the cause of the fatherless and the widow, and befriends the stranger, providing him with food and clothing.

Psalms 146:5–10:
Happy is he who has the God of Jacob for his help,
whose hope is in the Lord his God,
maker of heaven and earth,
the sea and all that is in them;
who keeps faith forever;
who secures justice for those who are wronged,

gives food to the hungry.
The Lord sets prisoners free;
the Lord restores sight to the blind;
the Lord makes those who are bent stand straight;
the Lord loves the righteous;
the Lord watches over the stranger;
He gives courage to the orphan and widow,
but makes the path of the wicked tortuous.
The Lord shall reign forever,
your God, O Zion, for all generations. Hallelujah
    [praise the Lord].

Sifre Deuteronomy, **Ekev**: "To walk in all His ways" (Deuteronomy 11:22). These are the ways of the Holy One: "gracious and compassionate, patient, abounding in kindness and faithfulness, assuring love for a thousand generations, forgiving iniquity, transgression, and sin, and granting pardon..." (Exodus 34:6). This means that just as God is gracious and compassionate, you too must be gracious and compassionate. "The Lord is righteous in all His ways and loving in all His deeds" (Psalms 145:17). As the Holy One is righteous, you must be righteous. As the Holy One is loving, you too must be loving.

Babylonian Talmud, *Sotah* **14a**: "Walk after the Lord your God" (Deuteronomy 13:5). What does this mean? Is it possible for a mortal to walk after God's Presence, for has it not been said, "For the Lord your God is a devouring fire" (Deuteronomy 4:24)? The verse means to teach us that we should follow the attributes of the Holy One, praised be He. As He clothes the naked, for it is written, "And the Lord God made for Adam and for his wife coats of skin and clothed them" (Genesis 3:21), you too should clothe the naked. The Holy One, blessed be He, visited the sick, for it is written, "And the Lord appeared to him near the oaks of Mamre" [after Abraham's circumcision] (Genesis

18:1); you too should visit the sick. The Holy One, blessed be He, comforted those who mourned, for it is written, "And it came to pass after the death of Abraham, that God blessed Isaac, his son" (Genesis 25:11); you too should comfort those who mourn. The Holy One, blessed be He, buried the dead, for it is written, "And He buried him [Moses] in the valley" (Deuteronomy 34:6): you too should bury the dead.... Rabbi Simlai taught: The Torah begins with deeds of kindness and ends with deeds of kindness. It begins with deeds of kindness, as it is written, "And the Lord God made for Adam and for his wife garments of skins and clothed them" (Genesis 3:21). It ends with deeds of kindness, as it is written, "And He buried him [Moses] in the valley in the land of Moab" (Deuteronomy 34:6).

Leviticus 19:1–2, 9–10, 14–15, 32–36: And the Lord spoke to Moses, saying: Speak to the whole community of Israel and say to them: You shall be holy, for I, the Lord your God, am holy....When you reap the harvest of your land, you shall not reap all the way to the edges of your field, or gather the gleanings of your harvest. You shall not pick your vineyard bare, or gather the fallen fruit of your vineyard; you shall leave them for the poor and the stranger: I the Lord am your God....You shall not insult the deaf, or place a stumbling block before the blind. You shall fear your God: I am the Lord. You shall not render an unfair decision: do not favor the poor or show deference to the rich; judge your kinsman fairly....You shall rise before the aged and show deference to the old; you shall fear your God; I am the Lord. When a stranger resides with you in your land, you shall not wrong him. The stranger who resides with you shall be to you as one of your citizens; you shall love him as yourself, for you were strangers in the land of Egypt: I, the Lord, am your God. You shall not falsify measures of length, weight, or capacity. You shall have an honest balance, honest weights, an honest *ephah* [a dry measure], and an honest *hin* [a liquid measure]. I the Lord am your God who freed your from the land of Egypt. You shall faithfully observe all My laws and all My rules: I am the Lord.

Questions

How is God depicted in Deuteronomy 10 and Psalms 146? Note that these verses present a theistic God, one with a personality and a will and one deeply concerned with what goes on in our human world, rather than a deistic God, a creative force that has no personality or will and therefore cannot care for us. How does the theistic character of God in the Jewish tradition add authority to the imperative that we help others?

The Rabbis, in *Sifre Deuteronomy*, Ekev, and Babylonian Talmud, *Sotah* 14a, make specific what was implied in Deuteronomy 10 and Psalms 146 — namely, that God's attributes are a model for us. Notice, though, that the Rabbis have chosen some specific attributes of God for us to model and not others that are also manifest in the Bible — e.g., that God is jealous (as in Exodus 5; Hosea 2), and that God is sometimes at least apparently unjust (Book of Job). This is an important point about how traditions develop: the Jewish tradition, just like the Christian and Muslim traditions, consists of a *choice* of which books constitute holy scripture, which parts of holy scripture should serve as our focus and which to ignore, and ultimately of how to interpret holy scripture and apply it to our times. In the Rabbis' view, then, what aspects of God should serve as a model for us? Why do you think that they made that choice?

What human attributes are most valued at your agency? Are they the same or different from those valued by Judaism?

Leviticus 19 begins with a general principle: You shall be holy because I, the Lord your God, am holy. The rest of the chapter then defines what holiness means for Jews. It includes both moral and ritual commandments, including a number, cited here, that apply directly to those in need. Finally, it ends with the admonition that we obey God's commandments in gratitude for redeeming us from Egypt. Thus, as a mark of gratitude to God we have the *duty* to aspire to holiness. It is not simply something noble to do; it is an obligation of ours to aspire to be Godlike in fulfilling these laws. Does that add to your motivation to help the needy? Is it a consideration of others (employees, community members, volunteers) who work at your agency?

JEWISH DIRECTIONS FOR HELPING THE NEEDY

How One Should Give: Priorities among Methods of Providing Service

> Maimonides' *Mishneh Torah*, **Laws of Gifts to the Poor 10:7–14 (see also *Shulhan Arukh*, Yoreh De'ah 249:6):** There are eight degrees of charity, one higher than the other. (1) The highest degree, exceeded by none, is that of the person who assists a poor person by providing him with a gift or a loan or by accepting him into a business partnership or by helping him find employment—in a word, by putting him where he can dispense with other people's aid. With reference to such aid, it is said, "You shall strengthen him, be he a stranger or a settler, he shall live with you" (Leviticus 25:3–5), which means strengthen him in such a manner that his falling into want is prevented.
>
> (2) A step below this stands the one who gives alms to the needy in such manner that the giver knows not to whom he gives and the recipient knows not

from whom it is that he takes....Similar to this is one who drops money in the charity box. One should not drop money in the charity box unless one is sure that the person in charge is trustworthy, wise, and competent to handle the funds properly...

(3) One step lower is that in which the giver knows to whom he gives but the poor person knows not from whom he receives...(4) A step lower is that in which the poor person knows from whom he is taking but the giver knows not to whom he is giving....

(5) The next degree lower is that of him who, with his own hand, bestows a gift before the poor person asks. (6) The next degree lower is that of him who gives only after the poor person asks. (7) The next degree lower is that of him who gives less than is fitting but gives with a gracious mien. (8) The next degree lower is that of him who gives morosely.

Questions

The underlying values in Maimonides' list are the dignity and privacy of all concerned. Why are those values important from a secular point of view? In addition to those concerns, why else are those values important from a Jewish point of view, given Judaism's conceptions of God and human beings? Are dignity and privacy valued by your agency? How are employees trained or not trained to treat clients with dignity and respect their privacy? Are there rules such as confidentiality of records that ensure respect and privacy?

How would modern charity programs, both private and government-sponsored, fit into Maimonides' list — or fail to do so? How could those that fail to satisfy Maimonides' requirements be changed in order to preserve the dignity and privacy of all concerned?

For What One Should Give: Priorities among Kinds of Service

Shulhan Arukh, **Yoreh De'ah 249:16**: There are those who say that the commandment to [build and support] a synagogue takes precedence over the commandment to give charity [*tzedakah*] to the poor, but the commandment to give money to the youth to learn Torah or to the sick among the poor takes precedence over the commandment to build and support a synagogue.

Shulhan Arukh, **Yoreh De'ah 251:7-8**: One must feed the hungry before one clothes the naked [since starvation is taken to be a more direct threat to the person's life than exposure]. If a man and a woman came to ask for food, we put the woman before the man [because the man can beg with less danger to himself]; similarly, if a man and woman came to ask for clothing, and similarly, if a male orphan and a female orphan came to ask for funds to be married, we put the woman before the man.

Redeeming captives takes precedence over sustaining the poor and clothing them [since the captive's life is always in direct and immediate danger], and there is no commandment more important than redeeming captives. Therefore, the community may change the use of any money it collected for communal needs for the sake of redeeming captives. Even if they collected it for the sake of building a synagogue, and even if they bought the wood and stones and designated them for building the synagogue, such that it is forbidden to sell them for another commanded purpose, it is nevertheless permitted to sell them for the sake of redeeming captives. But if they built it already, they should not sell it…

Questions

What are the underlying values and priorities in Jewish law's determination of who should be first on our list to help? Do you share those values? Does your agency? Would you use other values in making your decisions as to who should get our first attention? If so, which, and how would you then change Jewish law's list of priorities? How would your agency assess the Jewish list of priorities?

Would modern circumstances lead you to prioritize those who should get our services differently? If so, why? If not, why not? Have you had to reconcile your values in this regard with those of the community in which you are serving?

Even if some category of persons is low on our list of priorities, we may still have a duty to do what we can to help the person in need. Is there a way of addressing that need, even if we cannot do so fully? Have you seen your agency meet needs that are not part of the central mission? Have you responded to needs beyond those duties that you have been assigned?

To Whom One Should Give: Priorities among Recipients

Maimonides' *Mishneh Torah*, Laws of Gifts to the Poor 7:13: A poor person who is his relative takes precedence [in one's gifts to the needy] over anyone else. The poor of one's household take precedence over those of his city. The poor of his city take precedence over the poor of another city, as the Torah says, "to your brother, your poor, and the poor of your land" (Deuteronomy 15:11).

Babylonian Talmud, *Gittin* 61a: Our Rabbis taught: We support the poor among non-Jews along with poor of the people Israel, and we visit the sick among non-Jews along with the sick of the people Israel, and we

261

bury the poor [for whom there is nobody to pay funeral expenses] among non-Jews along with the poor of the people Israel in the interests of peace.

Questions

Do you agree with this concept of concentric circles in establishing whom you must help first? If so, why? If not, why not? How does your agency determine who it will or will not serve?

Note that Jewish law for almost 2,000 years has required Jews to help non-Jews, despite the fact that Jews had already suffered persecution by the Romans and others. Can you think of other religions or cultures that demand that its adherents help people outside their own group? If so, what is the rationale for doing so? In addition to the interests of peace, which the Talmud cites here, what other Jewish theological convictions about the nature of God and human beings do you think motivate this requirement of Jewish law to help non-Jews in need as well as Jews?

Does your agency place restrictions by age, gender, race, religion, or other criteria on who will be served? If so, why?

CHRISTIANITY

David Kwang-sun Suh

BELIEVING AND WORKING

The first Christians made it abundantly clear that having faith alone is not enough for salvation in the Christian religion. According to the writings of Jesus' disciples such as James and John, faith without action is incomplete. James asks a hard question of the readers of the New Testament: "What good is it, my brothers and sisters, if you say you have faith but do not have works? Can faith save you?...So faith by itself, if it has no works, is dead" (James 2:14–15, 17).

John is even more challenging. "Those who say, 'I love God,' and hate their brothers or sisters, are liars. For those who do not love a brother or sister whom they have seen, cannot love God whom they have not seen" (I John 4:20). While John says that the commandment of Jesus was clear enough: "those who love God must love their brothers and sisters also" (I John 4:21), James declares that "Religion that is pure and undefiled before God, the Father, is this: to care for orphans and widows in their distress, and keep oneself unstained by the world" (James 1:27).

THE JUDEO-CHRISTIAN TRADITION

This Christian tradition of relating faith and work or loving God and loving one's neighbors is deeply rooted in the Hebrew tradition. According to the Hebrew teaching in the Old Testament, God is closely related to the world, including human beings. God created the world and everything in it. God created human beings in God's own image. God punished the human beings who disobeyed God's commandments. Since the beginning of human history, there is no time that God has had nothing to do the world: God is with the world and in the world in all of human affairs. When the Hebrews were slaves of Egypt, God was there with them, and, seeing the misery of the people of Egypt, heard their cries (Exodus 3:7). The Book of Exodus has recorded the account of God's action in the world: God liberated the Hebrews from bondage. God has acted in the world, in human history. God's action in the world is the model for human beings in the world. Human beings must act in the world as God has worked in the world—for liberation, for justice, for reconciliation, and for peace. As God has worked for the slaves, the poor, and the despised, human beings must be on the side of the poor and the oppressed.

The Hebrew prophets were the critics of the Hebrew religion, especially when the people went astray in the name of religion. One of the Hebrew prophets, Amos, was most strong on the issue of false religion—that is, religion that has nothing to do with the world and with the poor and the oppressed. Amos said in very strong words:

> I hate, I despise your festivals,
> and I take no delight in your solemn assemblies.
> Even though you offer me your burnt offerings
> and grain offerings,
> I will not accept them,
> and the offerings of well-being of your fatted animals
> I will not look upon.
> Take away from me the noise of your songs;
> I will not listen to the melody of your harps.
> But let justice roll down like waters,
> and righteousness like an ever-flowing stream.
> (Amos 5:21–24)

Religious worship with songs, musical instruments, and all kinds of offerings to God is nothing to God. God despises them all. Worship that comes out of one's sincere faith with a total love and devotion was denied and rejected by God. What God demands of the worshippers is action—an action for justice, to "let justice roll down like waters, and righteousness like an ever-flowing stream."

GOD'S EMPTYING OF GODSELF

At the center of Christian faith, there is Jesus. The Christian faith is about Jesus. Christian faith confesses that Jesus is the son of God, or God coming into the world as a human being. Faith in God, for Christians, is faith in Jesus.

Jesus was born in Palestine, then a part of the Roman Empire, in c. 4–6 B.C.E. and lived until c. 30 C.E. He was born into a Jewish family and spent his adult life teaching, preaching, healing, and serving the poor and the dispossessed. Although he was a faithful Jew and extremely knowledgeable about his religious tradition, in his teaching and action he challenged those who adhered to the law of the faith without an accompanying humility and who ignored those in need. When it came to a choice between serving human needs — such as by healing — and fulfilling the law — such as not healing on the day of rest, as it was considered to be work — he choose to serve human needs.

The number of his followers grew, and so did opposition to him. Powerful Roman and Jewish officials saw him as a rabble-rouser, inciting the people against their authority. Finally, he was arrested, tried, and put to death by the cruelest of methods — crucifixion. As was the custom of the time, his body was wrapped in a shroud and placed in a cave or tomb with a huge stone rolled in front of the entrance.

The story of Jesus' life is recorded in what are called the four Gospels, a word that means the "Good News"; they are attributed to the writers Matthew, Mark, Luke, and John. These narratives make up the first four books of the sacred writings of Christians, the New Testament. The Gospels describe how in the days following Jesus' death, some women who were among his most devoted followers went to the tomb, found the stone rolled away, and the tomb empty. A figure appeared to them, asking "Why do you seek the living among the dead? He whom you seek has risen." They recalled how, in his life, Jesus had told them that he would die and then return to his heavenly Father (God). In the days following Jesus' death, others among his disciples (followers) believed that he appeared to them and that finally he told them he was ascending to his Father's throne, and that they were to carry on his message and his work of teaching, healing, and forgiving.

Devotion to Jesus and his message of hope spread first among the Jews of the area who saw him as their long-awaited Messiah, the One who saves. But soon his following included many others and spread through the lands of the Eastern Mediterranean, extending finally to Rome itself. Most notable among the converts to this new religion of Christianity was Saul of Tarsus, called Paul. Paul's letters to the churches in various cities of the region are included in the New Testament.

For the first three hundred years following Jesus' death, the Roman authorities bitterly opposed Christianity and put to death many of these early Christians. But despite the persecution, the religion grew. Finally, in 313 c.e., the Roman Emperor Constantine made Christianity an officially tolerated religion of the Roman Empire. In the years following, Christianity spread throughout what is now Europe, to parts of North Africa, and east into what is now Russia. Today, Christianity, the world's largest religion, is also predominant in the Americas, much of Africa, and the Philippines, and is growing in Africa, Asia, and elsewhere.

According to the Christian faith, Jesus is fully human and at the same time fully divine. His coming into the world as a human being is called "incarnation," meaning that God became flesh, in order to be God's concrete, physical manifestation in the world.

The Gospel according to John has interpreted Jesus as God's coming into the world as follows:

> In the beginning was the Word, and the Word was with God, and the Word was God. He was in the beginning with God. All things came into being through him, and without him not one thing came into being.
>
> (John 1:1–3)

> And the Word became flesh and lived among us, and we have seen the glory, the glory as of a father's only son, full of grace and truth.
>
> (John 1:14)

"The Word" in Greek is *logos*, meaning reason. (Some feminist theologians argue that it should be translated as *Sophia*, or wisdom, in order to reduce the masculinity of the character of the Word or God). John's confession is that Jesus is God made flesh. In this sense, Jesus is believed to be truly God and truly human. What is important in the belief is that God has come to the world among us human beings.

This belief, at the center of the Christian religion, is expressed in the birth story of Jesus. When Jesus' mother, Mary, conceived out of wedlock, Mary's husband-to-be, Joseph, began to reconsider their marriage. An angel appeared in Joseph's dream and told him: "Do not be afraid to take Mary as your wife, for the child conceived in her is from the Holy Spirit. She will bear a son, and you are to name him Jesus" (Matthew 1:20–21). The story continues: "All this took place to fulfil what the Lord had spoken by the prophet: 'Behold, a virgin shall conceive and bear a son, and his name shall be called Emmanuel' (which means God, with us)" (Mathew 1:23). God has come into the world as a human being and dwelt among us.

This faith was once again affirmed in St. Paul's letter to the Philippians:

> [Christ Jesus] who, though he was in the form of God, did not regard equality with God as something to be exploited, but emptied himself, taking the form of a slave, being born in human likeness. And being found in human form, He humbled himself and became obedient to the point of death, even death on a cross.
>
> (Philippians 2:6–8)

God has "emptied himself"; that is, God has given up God's almighty, highest and absolute position in heaven. God has become a human being and a slave for humanity. And the God-human Jesus came to live in the world as Emmanuel, "God with us."

THE LIFE AND TEACHING OF JESUS

The Birth of Jesus

The Gospels of Mathew, Mark, Luke, and John present a variety of images of Jesus. Some stories within each of these narratives of the life, teachings, and actions of Jesus overlap each other, while others give a totally different picture. Nonetheless, one may pick out noticeably visible and outstanding features of Jesus' life, work, and teachings.

First, Jesus was born into the poor family of the carpenter Joseph — a royal lineage, but in a poor and despised region of Galilee in Palestine. According to the Gospel of Luke, Jesus' parents had to go down to Bethlehem for the census registration of the Roman Empire at the time when Mary was ready to deliver her baby. They were not able to find a decent place for the child's birth; "there was no place in the inn" (Luke 2:7b). "She gave birth to her firstborn son and wrapped him in bands of cloth, and laid him in a manger" (Luke 2:7a). When Jesus came to the world, he came to a humble stable, among the animals in a shack.

This is an amazing story of Jesus told by the first authors of the Christian Bible. He is on the one hand a God incarnate, Godself, born in the royal lineage, but on the other hand, he was born in the poorest circumstances. This story is quite similar to the story of Buddha: Buddha was born in a royal family, but he had to leave the royal palace to seek truth and live among the poor. Like Buddha, Jesus gave up his divine and royal status. For the sake of the world, he emptied himself of his status and lived among the poor.

Jesus had to become a political refugee soon after his birth. King Herod, according the account of the Gospel of Matthew, attempted to assassinate the baby Jesus. King Herod was a Jewish king at the time of Jesus' birth, and he was told by "wise men from East" (Matthew 2:1 ff.) that a certain star was a sign showing the birth of a king of Jews. King Herod, a despot, ordered all the children in and around Bethlehem who were two years old or under to be killed, thereby hoping to kill Jesus among them. Joseph, the father of Jesus, had a dream in which an angel ordered him to take Mary and the baby Jesus to Egypt for the time being, in order to escape from Herod's assassination attempt.

After King Herod died, an angel appeared again in Joseph's dream and ordered him to take his family back to Palestine. But Herod's successor, Archelaus, was even worse than Herod. Joseph was instructed by the angel to go to the land of Galilee, up in the rugged northwestern mountain areas, and not to Judea, the district of Jerusalem. Jesus' family settled in a town called Nazareth, and "Jesus was called a Nazarene" (Matthew 2:23b).

The Devil's Temptations

According to tradition, Jesus stayed in Nazareth as a village carpenter helping his father Joseph until he came of age at thirty years old. Before his public life, he went to the river Jordan to be baptized by John the Baptist. John the Baptist's mother was a close friend—some say cousin—of Mary, mother of Jesus.

After his baptism, Jesus went into the wilderness for meditation without food or drink for forty days. Toward the end of his meditation, according to the Gospel accounts, he was tempted by a devil three times. The first temptation that the devil put before Jesus was to suggest that Jesus turn stones into bread. This was an interesting and most attractive temptation, for Jesus was famished from his fasting. But it was attractive to Jesus not only for his own sake; such a miracle could be an easy and great solution for the poor and hungry people of Palestine at the time. One may say that this is a "materialist" or "capitalist" temptation, believing that bread and bread alone would solve all the problems in the world. Jesus rejected this "materialist" or "capitalist" suggestion of the devil by saying that "One does not live by bread alone" (Luke 4:4). The suggestion was a pernicious one. It was not a suggestion coming from God, but from the devil himself, an enemy of the people, and especially of the poor. This suggests that Jesus is for the poor, but he would not collaborate with the devil for the solution to the problem of poverty in the world.

The second temptation was the devil's offer of political power, a suggestion even more pernicious: "If you will worship me now, all the glories and authority over the world will be yours." The devil said that political power and glory had been given to him, the devil; they belonged to the devil, who said, "To you [Jesus] I will give their glory and all this authority; for it has been given over to me, and I give it to anyone I please" (Luke 4:6). This is a chilling statement about political power: it was coming from the devil, and it was given to anyone who would please the devil and work for his cause in the world.

The second temptation was also attractive to Jesus: He could solve many political problems, especially for the Jewish people who were suffering from the harsh and oppressive colonial rule of the Roman Empire. Take the political and military power, and chase the Romans out from this land of Israel. For liberation, one could collaborate even with the devil on the theory that "the end justifies the means."

Jesus' answer was clear and strong: "Worship the Lord your God, and serve only him." He rejected the devil's temptation not because he was against all politics but because he was against the devil's claim that political power was given to him. Jesus knew that all political power is from God. Any power that puts itself above God is coming from the devil. Any power that claims to be absolute and puts itself above God is idolatry. All political power ought to come under the commandment of God. Any political power that is coming from the devil and that refused to obey God's commandment is nothing but an idol. Jesus' answer to the devil is the strongest iconoclastic stance against political power that makes itself absolute over and beyond God and humanity.

The third temptation was a religious temptation, implying that religion could enable Jesus to do anything he wanted. The tempting devil was clever by suggesting that even if Jesus jumped down from the pinnacle of the temple, God's angels would lift him up and he would remain unharmed. The devil was testing Jesus' faith, trying to tell Jesus that he was a "man of little faith." Jesus was not trapped into the devil's scheme. No, the devil's suggestion that Jesus throw himself off the temple was not a test of Jesus' faith. It was testing God and therefore was blasphemy.

Jesus' "Mission Statement"

After his spiritual dual with the devil in the wilderness, Jesus appeared in his hometown synagogue to preach. He spoke about his ministry by quoting the prophet Isaiah:

"The Spirit of the Lord is upon me,
because he has anointed me to
bring good news to the poor.
He has sent me to proclaim
release to the captives
and recovery of sight to the blind,
to let the oppressed go free,
to proclaim the year of the Lord's favor."

(Luke 4:18–19)

This was Jesus' mission statement. He came to proclaim the liberation of the poor, the blind, and captives. It was another answer to the devil who tempted him in the wilderness. It was Jesus' political statement over against the devil's political temptation. It was a political statement of liberation that came from God for the reign of God.

Healing and Care of the Sick

The most outstanding and visible public activity of Jesus was healing the sick. When John the Baptist sent his disciples to Jesus asking questions about him: "Are you the one who is to come, or are we to wait for another?" Jesus' answer was direct and clear:

Go and tell John what you have seen and heard: the blind receive their sight, the lame walk, the lepers are cleansed, the deaf hear, the dead are raised, the poor have good news brought to them.

(Luke 7:22)

According to the Gospel accounts, at least twenty-six healing events took place in Jesus' three years of ministry. He raised three from the dead. The Gospel narratives tell us that besides his teachings with parables to the disciples, to small and big audiences, and arguing and debating with his adversaries (most of whom were religious leaders of the time), Jesus' time was spent in a ministry of healing.

Jesus healed those with the dreaded disease of leprosy, a paralyzed man, a lame man sitting by a pool, a blind and mute man, a man born blind, a man with dropsy, and a blind beggar. Jesus cured women as well: a bleeding woman suffering for some twelve years approached Jesus for cure, a girl possessed by a demon was healed, and a crippled woman stood up and walked.

He was acting as a miracle doctor—Jesus healed diseases for which there was no cure. Jesus gave hope to the hopeless. It should be noted that no other religious leaders had this kind of "medical service" to the poor and the sick. We cannot find a story of Buddha doing this kind of healing service to his people in India. There is no mention of Confucius dealing with the poor and the sick. An outstanding, unique feature of the Christian religion is that its "founder," Jesus, lived with and worked on behalf of the poor, the sick, and the dead. Jesus' actions and work for the poor and sick are remarkable and visible as much as his verbal teachings.

Jesus also sent out his disciples—one time some seventy of them—to every town and place where he himself intended to go (Luke 10:1–20). They were commissioned to "cure the sick who are there" (Luke 10:9). And when the seventy returned to Jesus, they were joyful, saying, "Lord, in your name even the demons submit to us" (Luke 10:17). According to New Testament scholars, the Jesus movement started by itinerant wandering preachers who would go around from one town to another and enter a house that welcomed them. They preached about Jesus, cured the sick, and cared for the poor.

Friends of the Poor and the Despised

Jesus was born into a poor family. He himself was poor. Once he said to his disciples about his poverty: "Foxes have holes, and birds of the air have nests; but the Son of Man has nowhere to lay his head" (Luke 9:58). He himself was a wanderer. He was practically "homeless."

Jesus was not only poor, he was with the poor and for the poor as well. Twentieth-century Latin American "liberation theologians" talk about Jesus as having a "preferential option" for the poor. That is to say that Jesus would rather associate himself with the poor than with the rich and powerful. He attracted multitudes of the poor in his preaching. He declared to them:

> Blessed are you who are poor,
> for yours is the kingdom of God.
> Blessed are you who are hungry now,
> for you will be filled.
> Blessed are you who weep now,
> for you will laugh.
>
> (Luke 6:20–21)

And he condemned the rich and powerful in the same breath:

> But woe to you who are rich,
> for you have received your consolation.
> Woe to you who are full now,
> for you will be hungry.
> Woe to you who are laughing now,
> for you will mourn and weep.
>
> (Luke 6:24–25)

In an amazing miracle story, Jesus fed five thousand men (along with women and children) with two fish and five loaves of bread. He fed the poor and hungry people. His disciples were mostly poor fishermen.

Jesus dined with people such as tax collectors, who were despised by others as betrayers. A tax collector by the name of Levi, son of Alphaeus, was one of them. As Jesus was dining with Levi, there were many tax collectors, friends of Levi and sinners (according to the religious leaders' standards). When the scribes of the Pharisees saw this, they asked Jesus' disciples, "Why does he eat with tax collectors and sinners?" Jesus answered them directly by saying, "Those who are well have no need of a physician, but those who are sick; I have come to call not the righteous, but sinners" (Mark 2:17).

Jesus did not discriminate against women. Rather, he was on the side of women. Many women who had been cured of evil spirits and infirmities such as Mary Magdalene, Joanna, Susanna, and others were with Jesus and his disciples (Luke 8:1–3). There is a remarkable story of a Samaritan woman by the well. Jesus asked for water from the well from which the woman was drawing water. And he spoke with her, which was illegal behavior for a Jewish man at that time. As he liberated himself from the patriarchal Jewish law against woman, he liberated her also (John 4:7–15). Jesus did not refuse to heal women on many occasions. When an adulterous woman was brought to Jesus for punishment, he released her from her accusers (John 8:1–11). A prostitute poured a very expensive ointment of nard on Jesus, and he welcomed her act of tribute (Mark 14:3–9).

Who Is My Neighbor?

Once a rich young man came to Jesus and asked him, "Good teacher, what must I do to inherit eternal life?" (Luke

18:18 ff.). Jesus asked him back whether he kept the commandments, and his reply was "Yes, I have kept all these since my
youth." Jesus told him very straight: "There is still one thing
lacking. Sell all that you own and distribute the money to the
poor, and you will have treasure in heaven; then come, follow
me" (Luke 18:22). The rich young man, deeply disturbed, turned
away and and left. Jesus required radical action for the rich to
share their wealth with the poor and become poor themselves.
This is the Jesus way of life—emptying oneself for others and
for the poor and needy. Jesus instructed this rich young man
to act on his faith, a radical action at that, and to give up his
possessions and follow Jesus.

Jesus asked for a turning back, or turning around, from an
old style of life—from rich to poor, from oppressing to liber-
ating, and from being aggressors to becoming victims. Jesus
did not ask the poor to become rich, and the powerless to
become powerful. He asked always people to come down from
top to bottom, from above to below. When a very influential
Pharisee, a leader of Jews, came at night to visit Jesus in secret
asking for the sign of the kingdom of God, Jesus' answer was
typical, "No one can see the kingdom of God without being
born anew" (John 3:3). To be born anew or to be born again
means to turn around from one's old lifestyle, to have, in
modern terminology, a "paradigm shift" in one's life. In a
religious language, we call it "repentance."

How can we have a new life or the kingdom of God or
eternal life? Jesus was asked this perennial question by the
people, especially rich and powerful ones of his time. The most
famous story Jesus told concerning this question is that of the
good Samaritan. A lawyer stood up with arrogance asking Jesus
a question: "Teacher, what must I to do to inherit eternal life?"
(Luke 10: 25 ff.) Jesus replied to his question with a question,
"What is written in the law?" This was a very appropriate

question, for he was after all, speaking to a lawyer, a specialist on the Jewish religious laws. This lawyer's answer was clear and to the point: "You shall love the Lord your God with all your heart, and with all your soul, and with all your strength, and with all your mind, and your neighbor as yourself" (Luke 10:27). Jesus acknowledged that this was the correct answer, but, typically called the lawyer to action: "This do, and you will inherit eternal life." But the lawyer persisted with his questions, perhaps hoping to trick Jesus. He asked, "And who is my neighbor?" (Luke 10:29) Jesus' response was to tell the story of the good Samaritan.

The story is a dramatic story, well told by Jesus, about a man who was robbed on his way from Jerusalem to Jericho on a rugged mountain road—a road that is still rugged today. He was not only robbed but also stripped, beaten, and left half dead. Jesus told the story with sharp criticism against religious and intellectual leaders of the community at the time—a priest and a Levite—who passed by the half-dead man on the road. But a Samaritan, who was supposed to be an enemy of the Jews, had pity on the robbed Jewish man. According to the story, the Samaritan "went to him and bandaged his wounds, having poured oil and wine on them. Then he put him on his own animal, brought him to an inn, and took care of him" (Luke 10:34). That was not all. He gave money to the innkeeper to take care of him until he could come back, saying if the money was not enough he would reimburse him for any additional expenses.

Jesus made it clear to the lawyer what to do to inherit eternal life. The Gospel of Luke, in which the story of the good Samaritan appears, does not tell us whether the lawyer did or did not put what he learned from Jesus into practice. Knowing the laws and commandments by heart, and asking clever questions are not enough. Jesus urges his followers to act. As some theologians say, "doing" theology is more important than "knowing" theology. This is to say, as James told us, faith without action or work is nothing. "Faith in action," or "action in faith" is what Jesus and the first Christians were urging us to practice.

To Serve, Not to Be Served

The posture of Jesus was deeply and constantly on the side of the poor and with the sick and suffering. Jesus made it clear to his disciples over and over again that he came to serve and not to be served (Mark 10:45). He gave up on his divine position in heaven to come to the world as a human being.

As a human being, Jesus did not take the position of political power to rule and dominate over the people. Rather, he served the people as a suffering servant.

When the mother of John and James came to Jesus asking for high positions for her sons, Jesus said, "You do not know what you are asking" (Matthew 20:22). Jesus denounced the position-seekers and the rulers of the world, saying, "You know that the rulers of the Gentiles lord it over them, and their great ones are tyrants over them but I tell you that whoever wishes to be great among you must be your servant, and whoever wishes to be first among you must be your slave" (Matthew 20:26–27).

In the last chapters of the Gospel of John, there is a moving scene of Jesus kneeling down to wash his disciples' feet (John 13:1–20), a task usually assigned to the lowest servant. By performing this act himself, Jesus was demonstrating that to serve others, even in the humblest ways, is never demeaning and we should not be ashamed to take on such a task on behalf of another. (This act of foot-washing has been incorporated into the ritual of many Christian churches. On the night before Good Friday, the day commemorating the death of Jesus, the head of the parish or church washes the feet of the people of the parish. In Rome, the Pope himself washes the feet of those who serve him at the altar.) Foot-washing is not the place and posture of a powerful ruler. But Jesus came to the world as a humble servant of the people — particularly those who are poor, humble, hungry, sick and needy. He was the lowest of all: he lived and worked for and with the lowest class of people.

Jesus died by crucifixion. An execution on the cross was the most cruel form of punishment of the Roman Empire, imposed upon political criminals against the Emperor and upon runaway slaves. Jesus was accused of being an agitator of the people because he spent his time with the people and on the side of the people and by word and action declared himself against the Jewish political rulers and religious leaders of his time. His "preferential option" for the poor was costly. His choice to live among the poor and oppressed, to serve them, and to challenge others to do the same, ended with his suffering and death on the cross.

Following Jesus

During his life, Jesus on many occasions called people to follow him. Many responded, living with him and working with him until his death on the cross and after his resurrection. Today, Christians confess that to be a Christian is to follow Jesus, and that to follow the way of Jesus brings us into the presence of Jesus. To believe in Jesus can mean praying to Jesus the Divine, reading the Gospels of Jesus, studying and learning the difficult passages in the Bible, going to churches regularly, fasting, and following the church calendars to observe special events such as the festivals of Easter Sunday and Christmas. But when Jesus was telling the people to follow him, he was urging them to do and act as he did. That is, Jesus called his followers to serve the people, heal the sick, and give sight to the blind, and to liberate the oppressed and exploited in the real sociopolitical life.

To believe in Jesus as a Christian is to serve Jesus by serving people. Christians believe that Jesus Christ is with us when we serve people and work for the poor, the sick, and the oppressed. Christian faith does not stop in the recitation of prayers and the Bible passages. Christian faith grows and becomes strong in action on behalf of others, especially those in need.

According to the famous Chapter 25 of the Gospel of Matthew, just before Jesus was arrested, tried, and crucified, he spoke a parable about the last judgment. In it, he told how the king will separate people one from another as a shepherd separates the sheep from the goats. And he would speak to the sheep on his right-hand side: "Come, you that are blessed by my Father, inherit the kingdom prepared for you from the foundation of the world; for I was hungry and you gave me food, I was thirsty and you gave me something to drink, I was a stranger and you welcomed me, I was naked and you gave me clothing, I was sick and you took care of me, I was in prison and you visited me" (Matthew 25:34–36).

The people on the right-hand side of the king were shocked to hear this, for they did not remember that they had done all of these things for Jesus; they had never seen or met Jesus in their lifetime in this world. So, they questioned the king: "Lord, when was it that we saw you hungry and gave you food, or thirsty and gave you something to drink?" (Matthew 25:37) The king's answer was clear enough: "Truly I tell you, just as you did it to one of the least of these who are members of my family, you did it to me" (Matthew 25:40).

The presence of Jesus, the Christian presence, is where there are those who are hungry, thirsty, naked, sick, strangers, or in prison. To follow Jesus is to follow him in his presence among the poor and the sick. To believe in Jesus and confess him to be Christ, the savior, the liberator, and the Messiah, is to work with him as a servant of the suffering people in the world.

A BRIEF HISTORY OF THE CHRISTIAN MOVEMENT IN THIS LIGHT

The history of the Christian movement since the time of Jesus and of his disciples and followers may be very well characterized as a history of the people who lived out the way of Jesus—following Jesus and serving others. At times, especially when the Christian religion became a state religion and earned the position of power, Christianity and the church went astray and forgot about the way of Jesus as servant to the poor and the oppressed.

However, when the true believers of Jesus saw the crisis, they spoke out. Eventually, the Christian movement turned around and changed its course and reformed itself to more nearly become the true followers of Jesus and live the way of Jesus. The history of Christianity may be described as a long process of struggle to realize the way of life that Jesus taught and acted throughout his life and death.

One important development in this struggle to follow Jesus and imitate the life of Jesus was the monastic movement, the history of which is as rich and long as the history of the Christian movement itself. It began in the Christian world from the third century when the persecution of Christians by the Roman emperors became severe and unbearable. The persecuted Christians took refuge in the wilderness of Egypt and of the Middle East to meditate on God as hermits totally separated from the mundane. But the movement grew even after the Roman Empire, under the emperor Constantine the Great, recognized Christianity as an official state religion, in 313 C.E.

The monastic movement then spread to Western Europe and the islands of Great Britain and Ireland, especially in the period of Medieval Christendom, producing such leaders as Anthony, the first founder of a monastery in Egypt, in the third century, and Benedict, Basil, Dominic, and Francis of Assisi, all of whom contributed greatly to the formation of the monastic life in the thirteenth century. In the twelfth and thirteenth centuries, there were notable monastic movements initiated and run by women, such as Clare of Assisi and Hildegard of Bingen, which spread throughout Europe.

The philosophy of the early monastic movement was to leave the secular world and live alone as a hermit, to meditate on God and salvation alone. (The word "monastery" came from the Greek word *"mono,"* or "alone.") But later, like-minded people gathered together to live in a community, that is, in a monastery or, in the case of women, in a convent. Their focus was — and is — to follow the way of Jesus and live like Jesus himself. They vow to become poor, chaste, and to obey God. This is a radical commitment to the way of Jesus. Monks and brothers and sisters are those who give up the world and worldly possessions and pleasures to follow the way of Jesus.

There were many types of monasteries in the medieval period in the Western world that have continued throughout the centuries. The life of the monasteries is centered around worship from dawn to dusk, praying, singing, chanting, silent meditation, reading books, and copying the Bible.

Some monasteries, however, made themselves famous and notable for their service in the community. While they were the medieval centers of learning and of spiritual and intellectual life, they were also the agents of service to the poor and the afflicted. They were not only secluded from the world for service to God, but they were also open to the world for the life of service.

Perhaps the most remarkable personage in the monastic movement is Francis of Assisi. Francis (1182–1226) founded a monastic order that carried his name, the Franciscans. He was born into the family of a wealthy Italian cloth merchant, lived well in his youth, and even joined the military to fight as a soldier in a local war. But he could not find meaning in his life as a soldier, and went on a pilgrimage to Rome. In the streets of Rome he met a beggar with whom he exchanged sleeping places for a day. And later, to test himself as a follower of Jesus, he embraced a leper. Upon his return home, he helped build the local church with his wealth, and lived the solitary life of a hermit.

A dramatic turn happened when he encountered the words in Matthew 10:7–10, Jesus' instructions to the disciples when they were sent out to the world: "As you go, proclaim the good news, 'The kingdom of heaven has come near.' Cure the sick, raise the dead, cleanse the lepers, cast out demons. You received without payment; give without payment. Take no gold, or silver, or copper in your belts, no bag for your journey, or two tunics, or sandals, or a staff; for laborers deserve their food." Francis took the passage as a direct message from Jesus himself. He became a beggar and gave freely to the poor.

Later in his life, he joined the Crusades and went to the Holy Land to convert the Muslims. But he was appalled by the cruelty of the crusaders against the Arabs. He tried to stop the Christian crusaders' behavior, but failed. Upon his return home he worked among the lower- and middle-class lay people in his community. He was inspired by a wealthy woman from Assisi, Clare, who herself had founded an order for women called the Poor Clares. Pope Innocent III gave Francis permission to found a monastery to work among the poor. The Franciscan order had two rules: live by the Gospel, and possess nothing. They worked in their local contexts as the Scripture directed them.

Among the women in this period, Hildegard of Bingen (1098–1179) is the most outstanding example of the work of women in the medieval convents. She was born in a family of ten children, and was educated in German Benedictine convents. She was to become the first administrator of the Benedictine community in Bingen. She preached the need for reform in the life of the clergy and monasteries alike. Her most outstanding gift was her miraculous healing through her practice of medicine. She was the author of many books, among them *Causes and Cures*.

As we have seen, the ideal of monastic life is to combine learning and service, prayers and works. It is to actualize the life and work of Jesus — the true Christian living in the world for others.

THE REFORMERS AND MODERN CHRISTIANS

The movement in Western Europe in the sixteenth and seventeenth centuries known as the Reformation may be called a "secularization" of the medieval monastic movement. That is, the Reformers attempted to bring the life of monasteries into the secular world, introducing the monastic principles of poverty, chastity, and obedience into the everyday life of ordinary believers. This attempt was manifested most notably among Protestant Puritans, who practiced an ascetic life in the secular world. The trend was also strong in the Reform movement of John Calvin (1509–1564) in Geneva. Another aspect of the Reform movement was to preach the Gospel of Jesus Christ to the dispossessed, and to work on behalf of the poor. This movement was initiated in London by John Wesley (1703–1791), who later became the leader of the Christian denomination called the Methodists.

In the period of the Industrial Revolution, a new technology for mass production was introduced, creating the problem of a labor force with a rapidly growing gap between the rich and the poor. In the midst of rising industries and wealth, poverty was the basic condition for the mass of the people in a newly developing Europe. The political economist Karl Marx (1818–1883) began expounding communist theories that envisioned a world in which the working class would rule and dictate the socioeconomic affairs. The *Communist Manifesto*, which Marx helped draft in 1848, called for the unity of all working-class people around the world.

This was the time when various Christian movements arose apart from the institutional church. One example was the Young Men's Christian Association (YMCA) movement (and later the Young Women's Christian Association). It was initiated in the laborers' ghetto in London in 1844, to help young workers pouring into London from rural England in search of various factory jobs. A student organization at Oxford University began this movement by providing lodging and sports facilities for homeless young strangers to the city. Later, the Association was formed, and membership grew to hundreds and then thousands. This was a prime and enduring example of university students going into the world and serving the poor and homeless.

This type of Christian social-service movement became known as the Social Gospel movement in the newly industrialized America in the late nineteenth century. It was a theological movement initiated by the Reverend Walter Rauschenbusch (1861–1918). Deeply disturbed by the life of the neighborhood around his parish church in Detroit, Michigan, he developed a theology that expounds on the building of the kingdom of God on earth by transforming the socioeconomic system of the capitalistic society. He named himself a Christian Socialist. His theology and action among the poor workers influenced Reinhold Niebuhr's (1892–1971) Christian social ethics in the twentieth century.

A notable example of Christian involvement in social and political activities is the German theologian, Dietrich Bonhoeffer (1906-1945), who died in a Gestapo prison for his political activism against Nazi Germany during its cruel campaign of extermination of European Jews. Bonhoeffer raised a daring prophetic voice in wartime Germany. He worked not only on behalf of the Jews, but also for peace in Europe in the midst of the Second World War. He was a radical activist, following the way of Jesus. He said this was a costly discipleship—sometimes even demanding one's life for defense of and service to the oppressed and despised. He showed by his example that following the way of Jesus is not an easy thing.

Another outstanding example of a costly discipleship is that of Martin Luther King, Jr. (1929–1968), who led the American civil-rights movement in the 1960s until he was assassinated in 1968. He had moved out of his comfortable pulpit to preach the Christian Gospel, and walked into the dangerous streets to say "no" to American racism and injustice. He moved against police lines and walked into jail to proclaim the good news for African-Americans to liberate themselves and claim the equality that American ideals proclaimed. He followed the way of Jesus and in doing so, he suffered beatings, tear gas, attacks by dogs, and imprisonment. He was killed for his beliefs and actions, following the example of Jesus' death. All the people around the world who are oppressed and discriminated against share the vision described in his speech in Washington, D.C., which began with the sentence "I have a dream..." and continued with King's description of a world in which justice, equality, and peace prevailed.

ACTION AND FAITH

A Medieval theologian, St. Anselm, once defined theology as "Faith seeking understanding." But many Latin American theologians who have advocated "liberation theology" in recent decades put a strong emphasis on action, work, or praxis in social and political contexts. They put action for social change and liberation of the poor and the oppressed at the center of "doing" theology and suggest that theological reflection follows action. They have changed Anselm's definition to "Faith acting in social transformation." A clearer and stronger theological understanding of Christian faith comes only with action and involvement in the world among the poor and suffering. For faith in Jesus is to follow Jesus and live the way of Jesus for the kingdom of God.

CHRISTIANITY

Sacred Writings

&

Questions to Consider

The following Old Testament and New Testament excerpts are from the Bible, Revised Standard Version.

OLD TESTAMENT

Isaiah 58:6–12: "Is not this the fast that I choose: to loose the bonds of wickedness, to undo the thongs of the yoke, to let the oppressed go free, and to break every yoke? Is it not to share your bread with the hungry, and bring the homeless poor into your house; when you see the naked, to cover him, and not to hide yourself from your own flesh? Then shall your light break forth like the dawn, and your healing shall spring up speedily; your righteousness shall go before you, the glory of the LORD shall be your rear guard. Then you shall call, and the LORD will answer; you shall cry, and he will say, Here I am.

"If you take away from the midst of you the yoke, the pointing of the finger, and speaking wickedness, if you pour yourself out for the hungry and satisfy the desire of the afflicted, then shall your light rise in the darkness and your gloom be as the noonday. And the LORD will guide you continually, and satisfy your desire with good things, and make your bones strong; and you shall be like a watered garden, like a spring of water, whose waters fail not. And your ancient ruins shall be rebuilt; you shall raise up the foundations of many generations; you shall be called the repairer of the breach, the restorer of streets to dwell in."

Questions

What does Isaiah say God will do for those who respond to people in need? Have you met those in your service agency who seem to be "like a spring of water, whose waters fail not," despite limited agency resources? What gives them the energy and will to continue?

Isaiah 61:1–3: The Spirit of the Lord GOD is upon me, because the LORD has anointed me to bring good tidings to the afflicted; he has sent me to bind up the brokenhearted, to proclaim liberty to the captives, and the opening of the prison to those who are bound; to proclaim the year of the LORD's favor, and the day of vengeance of our God; to comfort all who mourn; to grant to those who mourn in Zion—to give them a garland instead of ashes, the oil of gladness instead of mourning, the mantle of praise instead of a faint spirit; that they may be called oaks of righteousness, the planting of the LORD, that he may be glorified.

Amos 5:7–11: O you who turn justice to wormwood, and cast down righteousness to the earth! He who made the Pleiades and Orion, and turns deep darkness into the morning, and darkens the day into night, who calls for the waters of the sea, and pours them out upon the surface of the earth, the LORD is his name, who makes destruction flash forth against the strong, so that destruction comes upon the fortress. They hate him who reproves in the gate, and they abhor him who speaks the truth. Therefore because you trample upon the poor and take from him exactions of wheat, you have built houses of hewn stone, but you shall not dwell in them; you have planted pleasant vineyards, but you shall not drink their wine.

Questions

The passages from Isaiah and Amos contrast God's action toward the oppressed and the oppressor. What have you observed and experienced in your community regarding justice?

Jonah1:1–17: Now the word of the LORD came to Jonah the son of Amittai, saying, "Arise, go to Nineveh, that great city, and cry against it; for their wickedness has come up before me." But Jonah rose to flee to Tarshish from the presence of the LORD. He went down to Joppa and found a ship going to Tarshish; so he paid the fare, and went on board, to go with them to Tarshish, away from the presence of the LORD.

But the LORD hurled a great wind upon the sea, and there was a mighty tempest on the sea, so that the ship threatened to break up. Then the mariners were afraid, and each cried to his god; and they threw the wares that were in the ship into the sea, to lighten it for them. But Jonah had gone down into the inner part of the ship and had lain down, and was fast asleep. So the captain came and said to him, "What do you mean, you sleeper? Arise, call upon your god! Perhaps the god will give a thought to us, that we do not perish."

And they said to one another, "Come, let us cast lots, that we may know on whose account this evil has come upon us." So they cast lots, and the lot fell upon Jonah. Then they said to him, "Tell us, on whose account this evil has come upon us? What is your occupation? And whence do you come? What is your country? And of what people are you?" And he said to them, "I am a Hebrew; and I fear the LORD, the God of heaven, who made the sea and the dry land." Then the men were exceedingly afraid, and said to him, "What is this that you have done!" For the men knew that he was fleeing from the presence of the LORD, because he had told them.

Then they said to him, "What shall we do to you, that the sea may quiet down for us?" For the sea grew more and more tempestuous. He said to them, "Take me up and throw me into the sea; then the sea will quiet down for you; for I know it is because of me that this great tempest has come upon you." Nevertheless the men rowed hard to bring the ship back to land, but they could not, for the sea grew more and more tempestuous against them. Therefore they cried to the LORD, "We beseech thee, O LORD, let us not perish for this man's life, and lay not on us innocent blood; for thou, O LORD, hast done as it pleased thee." So they took up Jonah and threw him into the sea; and the sea ceased from its raging. Then the men feared the LORD exceedingly, and they offered a sacrifice to the LORD and made vows.

And the LORD appointed a great fish to swallow up Jonah; and Jonah was in the belly of the fish three days and three nights.

Questions

Why do you think Jonah resisted the call to go to Nineveh to preach against wickedness? From your study of religions and history, can you name other leaders who at first resisted such a call?

When trying to decide whether or not to be engaged in service or service-learning, did you have moments of wanting to "flee to Tarshish?"

When things go wrong, we often look for a scapegoat—someone to blame—as did the sailors on Jonah's ship. Have you seen examples in your community or in your group of volunteers or service-learning students of someone who continually looks for someone else to blame? What about you? Have you accepted a situation—and your responsibility for it—without blaming others? (If so, congratulate yourself on your maturity!)

Proverbs 11:24–25: One man gives freely, yet grows all the richer; another withholds what he should give, and only suffers want. A liberal man will be enriched, and one who waters will himself be watered.

Proverbs 19:17: He who is kind to the poor lends to the LORD, and he will repay him for his deed.

Proverbs22:9: He who has a bountiful eye will be blessed, for he shares his bread with the poor.

Questions

Have you seen people in your community or agency who give generously of their time and resources? How are their lives enriched by their giving?

Exodus 3:1–14: Now Moses was keeping the flock of his father-in-law, Jethro, the priest of Midian; and he led his flock to the west side of the wilderness, and came to Horeb, the mountain of God. And the angel of the LORD appeared to him in a flame of fire out of the midst of a bush; and he looked, and lo, the bush was burning, yet it was not consumed. And Moses said, "I will turn aside and see this great sight, why the bush is not burnt." When the LORD saw that he turned aside to see, God called to him out of the bush, "Moses, Moses!" And he said, "Here am I." Then he said, "Do not come near; put off your shoes from your feet, for the place on which you are standing is holy ground." And he said, "I am the God of your father, the God of Abraham, the God of Isaac, and the God of Jacob." And Moses hid his face, for he was afraid to look at God.

Then the LORD said, "I have seen the affliction of my people who are in Egypt, and have heard their cry because of their taskmasters; I know their sufferings, and I have come down to deliver them out of the hand of the Egyptians, and to bring them up out of that land to a good and broad land, a land flowing with milk and honey, to the place of the Canaanites, the Hittites, the Amorites, the Perizzites, the Hivites, and the Jebusites. And now, behold, the cry of the people of Israel has come to me, and I have seen the oppression with which the Egyptians oppress them. Come, I will send you to Pharaoh that you may bring forth my people, the sons of Israel, out of Egypt." But Moses said to God, "Who am I that I should go to Pharaoh, and bring the sons of Israel out of Egypt?" He said, "But I will be with you; and this shall be the sign for you, that I have sent you: when you have brought forth the people out of Egypt, you shall serve God upon this mountain."

Then Moses said to God, "If I come to the people of Israel and say to them, 'The God of your fathers has sent me to you,' and they ask me, 'What is his name?' what shall I say to them?" God said to Moses, "I AM WHO I AM." And he said, "Say this to the people of Israel, 'I AM has sent me to you.'"

Questions

God calls Moses to a great but difficult job, one Moses must have known entailed not only challenges but risks. In your studies, have you learned of ordinary people who took on extraordinary tasks? (You may want to look at the biographies of many recent Nobel Peace Prize recipients.) Are there such people associated with your university, your service agency, or the community where you are serving? Are there those in positions of authority and leadership who failed to live up to a call? What might be your challenge?

NEW TESTAMENT

Luke 2:1–20: In those days a decree went out from Caesar Augustus that all the world should be enrolled. This was the first enrollment, when Quirinius was governor of Syria. And all went to be enrolled, each to his own city. And Joseph also went up from Galilee, from the city of Nazareth, to Judea, to the city of David, which is called Bethlehem, because he was of the house and lineage of David, to be enrolled with Mary, his betrothed, who was with child. And while they were there, the time came for her to be delivered. And she gave birth to her first-born son and wrapped him in swaddling cloths, and laid him in a manger, because there was no place for them in the inn.

And in that region there were shepherds out in the field, keeping watch over their flock by night. And an angel of the Lord appeared to them, and the glory of the Lord shone around them, and they were filled with fear. And the angel said to them, "Be not afraid; for behold, I bring you good news of a great joy which will come to all the people; for to you is born this day in the city of David a Savior, who is Christ the Lord. And this will be a sign for you: you will find a babe wrapped in swaddling cloths and lying in a manger." And suddenly there was with the angel a multitude of the heavenly host praising God and saying, "Glory to God in the highest, and on earth peace among men with whom he is pleased!"

When the angels went away from them into heaven, the shepherds said to one another, "Let us go over to Bethlehem and see this thing that has happened, which the Lord has made known to us." And they went with haste, and found Mary and Joseph, and the babe lying in a manger. And when they saw it they made known the saying which had been told them concerning this child; and all who heard it wondered at what the shepherds told them.

But Mary kept all these things, pondering them in her heart. And the shepherds returned, glorifying and praising God for all they had heard and seen, as it had been told them.

Questions

In this story of Jesus' birth, Luke tells us three different times that Jesus was laid in a manger — a box holding feed for cattle and other animals. Why does he say this was necessary, rather than laying the newborn baby in a crib or a cradle? Why do you think Luke emphasizes this point about Jesus' birth? What do you think Luke, living as he did in an age that believed in the power of symbolism and prediction, was saying that this predicts about Jesus' future life?

What beliefs does your community hold about the significance of events surrounding the birth of a baby?

Where are babies delivered in the community where you are serving? Are there those who find there is "no room at the inn" for them? Do people have medical insurance? Who pays for it? What do they do if they have no insurance and cannot afford care?

Matthew 2:13–23: Now when they had departed, behold, an angel of the Lord appeared to Joseph in a dream and said, "Rise, take the child and his mother, and flee to Egypt, and remain there till I tell you; for Herod is about to search for the child, to destroy him." And he rose and took the child and his mother by night, and departed to Egypt, and remained there until the death of Herod.... But when Herod died, behold, an angel of the Lord appeared in a dream to

Joseph in Egypt, saying, "Rise, take the child and his mother, and go to the land of Israel, for those who sought the child's life are dead." And he rose and took the child and his mother, and went to the land of Israel. But when he heard that Archelaus reigned over Judea in place of his father Herod, he was afraid to go there, and being warned in a dream he withdrew to the district of Galilee. And he went and dwelt in a city called Nazareth, that what was spoken by the prophets might be fulfilled, "He shall be called a Nazarene."

Questions

Just as Luke tells the story of Jesus' birth, so Matthew tells this story of Jesus' infancy. Being a refugee — fleeing under the cover of darkness in fear of one's life — is a never-to-be-forgotten experience for families and generally affects their later family history. They often tell the story of fleeing again and again. From what you know of Jesus' life and teachings, how do you imagine this family experience influenced his ministry?

Are there refugees in your community? Did they flee their homeland for political or economic reasons? How have they been received in the community? Who, if anyone, has been there to help them? Does your agency help them? Do they want some day to return home, or have they settled for good in the new land?

Do you know or know about any refugees who have returned home specifically to serve? For example, Gandhi, Indian by birth, began his work in South Africa before deciding to return home and leading the nationalist movement for India's independence from English colonial rule.

If you are serving abroad, you elected to leave home. What role do you envision playing when you return home?

John 3:1–17: Now there was a man of the Pharisees, named Nicodemus, a ruler of the Jews. This man came to Jesus by night and said to him, "Rabbi, we know that you are a teacher come from God; for no one can do these signs that you do, unless God is with him." Jesus answered him, "Truly, truly, I say to you, unless one is born anew, he cannot see the kingdom of God." Nicodemus said to him, "How can a man be born when he is old? Can he enter a second time into his mother's womb and be born?" Jesus answered, "Truly, truly, I say to you, unless one is born of water and the Spirit, he cannot enter the kingdom of God. That which is born of the flesh is flesh, and that which is born of the Spirit is spirit. Do not marvel that I said to you, 'You must be born anew.' The wind blows where it wills, and you hear the sound of it, but you do not know whence it comes or whither it goes; so it is with every one who is born of the Spirit." Nicodemus said to him, "How can this be?" Jesus answered him, "Are you a teacher of Israel, and yet you do not understand this? Truly, truly, I say to you, we speak of what we know, and bear witness to what we have seen; but you do not receive our testimony. If I have told you earthly things and you do not believe, how can you believe if I tell you heavenly things? No one has ascended into heaven but he who descended from heaven, the Son of man. And as Moses lifted up the serpent in the wilderness, so must the Son of man be lifted up, that whoever believes in him may have eternal life."

For God so loved the world that he gave his only Son, that whoever believes in him should not perish but have eternal life. For God sent the Son into the world, not to condemn the world, but that the world might be saved through him.

Questions

What does Jesus mean by saying to Nicodemus that he must be born again and in the spirit? What does this story tell you about the incarnation—God made flesh and being? Have you met anyone who turned his or her life around, such as a recovered alcoholic?

The passage ends with the assurance that Jesus came not to condemn the world but to save it. Are there leaders in your community who criticize those in the community, and are doing so because they love and want to save rather than just to condemn?

John 4:1-26: Now when the Lord knew that the Pharisees had heard that Jesus was making and baptizing more disciples than John (although Jesus himself did not baptize, but only his disciples), he left Judea and departed again to Galilee. He had to pass through Samaria. So he came to a city of Samaria, called Sychar, near the field that Jacob gave to his son Joseph. Jacob's well was there, and so Jesus, wearied as he was with his journey, sat down beside the well. It was about the sixth hour.

There came a woman of Samaria to draw water. Jesus said to her, "Give me a drink." For his disciples had gone away into the city to buy food. The Samaritan woman said to him, "How is it that you, a Jew, ask a drink of me, a woman of Samaria?" For Jews have no dealings with Samaritans. Jesus answered her, "If you knew the gift of God, and who it is that is saying to you, 'Give me a drink,' you would have asked him, and he would have given you living water." The woman said to him, "Sir, you have nothing to draw with, and the well is deep; where do you get that living water? Are you greater than our father Jacob, who gave us the well, and drank from it himself, and his sons, and his cattle?" Jesus said to her, "Every one who drinks of this water will thirst again, but whoever drinks of the water that I shall give him will never thirst; the water that I shall give him will become in him a spring of water welling up to eternal life." The woman said to him, "Sir, give me this water, that I may not thirst, nor come here to draw."

Jesus said to her, "Go, call your husband, and come here." The woman answered him, "I have no husband." Jesus said to her, "You are right in saying, 'I have no husband'; for you have had five husbands, and he whom you now have is not your husband; this you said truly." The woman said to him, "Sir, I perceive that you are a prophet. Our fathers worshiped on this mountain; and you say that in Jerusalem is the place where men ought to worship." Jesus said to her, "Woman, believe me, the hour is coming when neither on this mountain nor in Jerusalem will you worship the Father. You worship what you do not know; we worship what we know, for salvation is from the Jews. But the hour is coming, and now is, when the true worshipers will worship the Father in spirit and truth, for such the Father seeks to worship him. God is spirit, and those who worship him must worship in spirit and truth." The woman said to him, "I know that Messiah is coming (he who is called Christ); when he comes, he will show us all things." Jesus said to her, "I who speak to you am he."

Questions

Jesus' encounter with the woman at the well is remarkable in many ways and would have shocked the people of his day.

Jesus claimed to be a good and faithful Jew, but here he violates several taboos. What were they?

Even more surprising is Jesus' revelation of who he is—the long-awaited Messiah, the Savior—not to his own people but to this Samaritan woman. Why do you think that he did so? By this encounter and example, what was Jesus telling his followers?

What divisions are there in the community where you are serving? Who does not speak to whom? Is the reason based on religion, gender, race, class, or caste? Who violates the taboos?

The Samaritan woman knew of the Jewish expectation of a Messiah. What knowledge about the "other" is known by otherwise separated groups in the community where you are serving?

Have you, through your service, encountered people previously unknown to you? Have you or they initiated the contact? What was their or your initial response—eagerness, shyness, forthrightness, suspicion? If there was resistance, how was it overcome?

John 4:46–54: So he came again to Cana in Galilee, where he had made the water wine. And at Capernaum there was an official whose son was ill. When he heard that Jesus had come from Judea to Galilee, he went and begged him to come down and heal his son, for he was at the point of death. Jesus therefore said to him, "Unless you see signs and wonders you will not believe." The official said to him, "Sir, come down before my child dies." Jesus said to him, "Go; your son will live." The man

believed the word that Jesus spoke to him and went his way. As he was going down, his servants met him and told him that his son was living. So he asked them the hour when he began to mend, and they said to him, "Yesterday at the seventh hour the fever left him." The father knew that was the hour when Jesus had said to him, "Your son will live"; and he himself believed, and all his household. This was now the second sign that Jesus did when he had come from Judea to Galilee.

Questions

Who are the healers in the community where you are serving? Is your agency engaged in healing body, mind, and/or spirit? To what extent does healing occur because the person has a strong faith in the healer?

Matthew 9:9–13: As Jesus passed on from there, he saw a man called Matthew sitting at the tax office; and he said to him, "Follow me." And he rose and followed him.

And as he sat at table in the house, behold, many tax collectors and sinners came and sat down with Jesus and his disciples. And when the Pharisees saw this, they said to his disciples, "Why does your teacher eat with tax collectors and sinners?" But when he heard it, he said, "Those who are well have no need of a physician, but those who are sick. Go and learn what this means, 'I desire mercy, and not sacrifice.' For I came not to call the righteous, but sinners."

Questions

Who in your community associates with those whom the respectable people shun? Does your agency welcome and serve those rejected by society? Is your agency criticized or itself rejected for its action, or does the community respect and value it for its work? In what ways does the community embrace and participate in the mission of your agency in welcoming the rejected?

Matthew 12:1–14: At that time Jesus went through the grainfields on the sabbath; his disciples were hungry, and they began to pluck heads of grain and to eat. But when the Pharisees saw it, they said to him, "Look, your disciples are doing what is not lawful to do on the sabbath." He said to them, "Have you not read what David did, when he was hungry, and those who were with him: how he entered the house of God and ate the bread of the Presence, which it was not lawful for him to eat nor for those who were with him, but only for the priests? Or have you not read in the law how on the sabbath the priests in the temple profane the sabbath, and are guiltless? I tell you, something greater than the temple is here. And if you had known what this means, 'I desire mercy, and not sacrifice,' you would not have condemned the guiltless. For the Son of man is lord of the sabbath."

And he went on from there, and entered their synagogue. And behold, there was a man with a withered hand. And they asked him, "Is it lawful to heal on the sabbath?" so that they might accuse him. He said to them, "What man of you, if he has one sheep and it falls into a pit on the sabbath, will not lay hold of it and lift it out? Of how much more value is a man than a sheep! So it is lawful to do good on the sabbath." Then he said to the man, "Stretch out your hand." And the man stretched it out, and it was restored, whole like the other. But the Pharisees went out and took counsel against him, how to destroy him.

Questions

Just as in the story of Jesus' encounter with the Samaritan woman at the well when he violated a number of Jewish regulations, these two stories tell of Jesus allowing his hungry followers to gather food and then of he himself healing on the day of rest. Both of these actions were considered to be work, and therefore prohibited on the sabbath. What does Jesus say about priorities?

What are the priorities of your service agency? Do you agree with them? What rules would your agency break in order to serve those in need?

Jesus responds to his accusers in a way that shows his deep knowledge of Jewish tradition and law. Do you know of anyone in your agency/community/university who has extensive knowledge and has used it to challenge prevailing laws, regulations, or traditions? Are there—or have there been—such people in the nation where you are serving? Who are they? What did they know and challenge? Were they successful?

What have you learned that has bound you to which priorities? Have you discussed this with others? Has your extended knowledge helped you in your service? Have you tried to persuade others to make changes?

Matthew 5:1–12: Seeing the crowds, he went up on the mountain, and when he sat down his disciples came to him. And he opened his mouth and taught them, saying:

"Blessed are the poor in spirit, for theirs is the kingdom of heaven.

"Blessed are those who mourn, for they shall be comforted.

"Blessed are the meek, for they shall inherit the earth.

"Blessed are those who hunger and thirst for righteousness, for they shall be satisfied.

"Blessed are the merciful, for they shall obtain mercy.

"Blessed are the pure in heart, for they shall see God.

"Blessed are the peacemakers, for they shall be called sons of God.

"Blessed are those who are persecuted for righteousness' sake, for theirs is the kingdom of heaven.

"Blessed are you when men revile you and persecute you and utter all kinds of evil against you falsely on my account. Rejoice and be glad, for your reward is great in heaven, for so men persecuted the prophets who were before you.

Questions

These sayings form part of the Sermon on the Mount and are known as the Beatitudes. In this sermon, Jesus describes a new order in which those who suffer will be restored, satisfied, and exalted. Can you think of people in the community where you are serving who can be described by any one of the attributes that Jesus mentions? Do they feel rewarded? Do they hope for rewards in their future life on earth or in an afterlife?

Would you identify yourself with any of these characteristics? What are your expectations?

Matthew 11:1–6: And when Jesus had finished instructing his twelve disciples, he went on from there to teach and preach in their cities.

Now when John heard in prison about the deeds of the Christ, he sent word by his disciples and said to him, "Are you he who is to come, or shall we look for another?" And Jesus answered them, "Go and tell John what you hear and see: the blind receive their sight and the lame walk, lepers are cleansed and the deaf hear, and the dead are raised up, and the poor have good news preached to them. And blessed is he who takes no offense at me."

Questions

How does Jesus say the Messiah can be recognized? Is this the test of authenticity that the people expected? Today, how do we recognize a leader who will do good for the community rather than exploit it for his or her own ends?

Luke 7:36–50: One of the Pharisees asked him to eat with him, and he went into the Pharisee's house, and sat at table. And behold, a woman of the city, who was a sinner, when she learned that he was at table in the Pharisee's house, brought an alabaster flask of ointment, and standing behind him at his feet, weeping, she began to wet his feet with her tears, and wiped them with the hair of her head, and kissed his feet, and anointed them with the ointment. Now when the Pharisee who had invited him saw it, he said to himself, "If this man were a prophet, he would have known who and what sort of woman this is who is touching him, for she is a sinner." And Jesus

answering said to him, "Simon, I have something to say to you." And he answered, "What is it, Teacher?" "A certain creditor had two debtors; one owed five hundred denarii, and the other fifty. When they could not pay, he forgave them both. Now which of them will love him more?" Simon answered, "The one, I suppose, to whom he forgave more." And he said to him, "You have judged rightly." Then turning toward the woman he said to Simon, "Do you see this woman? I entered your house, you gave me no water for my feet, but she has wet my feet with her tears and wiped them with her hair. You gave me no kiss, but from the time I came in she has not ceased to kiss my feet. You did not anoint my head with oil, but she has anointed my feet with ointment. Therefore I tell you, her sins, which are many, are forgiven, for she loved much; but he who is forgiven little, loves little." And he said to her, "Your sins are forgiven." Then those who were at table with him began to say among themselves, "Who is this, who even forgives sins?" And he said to the woman, "Your faith has saved you; go in peace."

Questions

Have you met people in your agency who suffered greatly (by their own doing, such as by taking drugs; at the hands of others, such as through child abuse; or from misfortune or accident) and who, having been helped, are deeply grateful? How did the "woman of the city" show her gratitude? To whom are those you know grateful and how do they show their gratitude? Is your decision to serve an act of gratitude on your part?

Luke 8:1–3: Soon afterward he went on through cities and villages, preaching and bringing the good news of the kingdom of God. And the twelve were with him, and also some women who had been healed of evil spirits and infirmities: Mary, called Magdalene, from whom seven demons had gone out, and Joanna, the wife of Chuza, Herod's steward, and Susanna, and many others, who provided for them out of their means.

Questions

Are women and their needs given equal, less, or greater care than men in your community or agency?

Matthew 14:13–21: Now when Jesus heard this, he withdrew from there in a boat to a lonely place apart. But when the crowds heard it, they followed him on foot from the towns. As he went ashore he saw a great throng; and he had compassion on them, and healed their sick. When it was evening, the disciples came to him and said, "This is a lonely place, and the day is now over; send the crowds away to go into the villages and buy food for themselves." Jesus said, "They need not go away; you give them something to eat." They said to him, "We have only five loaves here and two fish." And he said, "Bring them here to me." Then he ordered the crowds to sit down on the grass; and taking the five loaves and the two fish he looked up to heaven, and blessed, and broke and gave the loaves to the disciples, and the disciples gave them to the crowds. And they all ate and were satisfied. And they took up twelve baskets full of the broken pieces left over. And those who ate were about five thousand men, besides women and children.

Questions

Part of the meaning that Christians ascribe to the idea of "incarnation" — God made man — is that bodily needs are real and must be given attention. Does your agency provide food? Is it nutritious and tasty? What other bodily needs does it address?

Matthew 18:1-6: At that time the disciples came to Jesus, saying, "Who is the greatest in the kingdom of heaven?" And calling to him a child, he put him in the midst of them, and said, "Truly, I say to you, unless you turn and become like children, you will never enter the kingdom of heaven. Whoever humbles himself like this child, he is the greatest in the kingdom of heaven.

"Whoever receives one such child in my name receives me; but whoever causes one of these little ones who believe in me to sin, it would be better for him to have a great millstone fastened round his neck and to be drowned in the depth of the sea.

Questions

Jesus must have surprised his disciples when he told them that they would gain heaven not by achieving great power and performing noble deeds, but by becoming like a child — at least like a child in the times and culture of Jesus! What specific qualities of children does he single out?

Jesus has harsh judgment for those who fail to protect children and lead them astray. How are children led into wrongdoing in the community where you are serving? Who in the community tries to protect children?

John 7:53–8:11: They went each to his own house, but Jesus went to the Mount of Olives. Early in the morning he came again to the temple; all the people came to him, and he sat down and taught them. The scribes and the Pharisees brought a woman who had been caught in adultery, and placing her in the midst they said to him, "Teacher, this woman has been caught in the act of adultery. Now in the law Moses commanded us to stone such. What do you say about her?" This they said to test him, that they might have some charge to bring against him. Jesus bent down and wrote with his finger on the ground. And as they continued to ask him, he stood up and said to them, "Let him who is without sin among you be the first to throw a stone at her." And once more he bent down and wrote with his finger on the ground. But when they heard it, they went away, one by one, beginning with the eldest, and Jesus was left alone with the woman standing before him. Jesus looked up and said to her, "Woman, where are they? Has no one condemned you?" She said, "No one, Lord." And Jesus said, "Neither do I condemn you; go, and do not sin again."

Questions

Jesus powerfully reminds those who condemn wrongdoers that they also are sinners. Have you read or heard about, or perhaps even met, someone who was in a position to pass judgment on others and then later was discovered to have committed a crime himself or herself?

Luke 10:25–37: And behold, a lawyer stood up to put him to the test, saying, "Teacher, what shall I do to inherit eternal life?" He said to him, "What is written in the law? How do you read?" And he answered, "You shall love the Lord your God with all your heart, and with all your soul, and with all your strength, and with all your mind; and your neighbor as yourself." And he said to him, "You have answered right; do this, and you will live."

But he, desiring to justify himself, said to Jesus, "And who is my neighbor?" Jesus replied, "A man was going down from Jerusalem to Jericho, and he fell among robbers, who stripped him and beat him, and departed, leaving him half dead. Now by chance a priest was going down that road; and when he saw him he passed by on the other side. So likewise a Levite, when he came to the place and saw him, passed by on the other side. But a Samaritan, as he journeyed, came to where he was; and when he saw him, he had compassion, and went to him and bound up his wounds, pouring on oil and wine; then he set him on his own beast and brought him to an inn, and took care of him. And the next day he took out two denarii and gave them to the innkeeper, saying, 'Take care of him; and whatever more you spend, I will repay you when I come back.' Which of these three, do you think, proved neighbor to the man who fell among the robbers?" He said, "The one who showed mercy on him." And Jesus said to him, "Go and do likewise."

Questions

The Good Samaritan is, for Christians, probably the most beloved of all of Jesus' parables. Note that it begins with the lawyer's didactic question, which Jesus answered not with a legal definition but with this now famous story. The Samaritan, a man from a group to whom Jews of the time did not speak, is cited as the example of the Good Neighbor. What did the Samaritan give to the man left robbed and beaten?

The priests and Levites in the story who "passed by on the other side" without helping were the religious authorities who were most knowledgeable about Jewish law. Yet, says Jesus, they were missing the point. The highest commandment of the law that will bring eternal life is to serve those in need.

Are the religious and civil authorities in your community "passing by on the other side," or are they working to respond to human needs? What does the story of the Good Samaritan say about qualities needed in good leaders?

The good neighbor is actually a member of an outside "tribe." What does this say about looking for help? Are there outsiders—including yourself—who have been good neighbors to people in need in a particular community because they are the ones responding to needs? (Think, for example, of Mother Teresa, who was not Indian by birth.)

Matthew 20:20–28: Then the mother of the sons of Zebedee came up to him, with her sons, and kneeling before him she asked him for something. And he said to her, "What do you want?" She said to him, "Command that these two sons of mine may sit, one at your right hand and one at your left, in your kingdom." But Jesus answered, "You do not know what you are asking. Are you able to drink the cup that I am to drink?" They said to him, "We are able." He said to them, "You will drink my cup, but to sit at my right hand and at my left is not mine to grant, but

it is for those for whom it has been prepared by my Father." And when the ten heard it, they were indignant at the two brothers. But Jesus called them to him and said, "You know that the rulers of the Gentiles lord it over them, and their great men exercise authority over them. It shall not be so among you; but whoever would be great among you must be your servant, and whoever would be first among you must be your slave; even as the Son of man came not to be served but to serve, and to give his life as a ransom for many."

Questions

In this passage, the woman asks of Jesus what most mothers want for their children—success and happiness. But Jesus warns her that to partake of *his* cup may not bring her what she expects. And, once again, he overturns the normal order by saying that the greatest among them must be a servant to all and reminding them that he, the Son of Man, came not to be served but to serve.

In the community where you are serving, are there those who want to share in the success of the agency without actually contributing and serving? Have you identified any whom you consider to be great not because of their power or position but because of their outstanding service? What sacrifices have they made or risks have they taken in order to serve? How are they regarded by various members of the community?

Luke 19:1-9: He entered Jericho and was passing through. And there was a man named Zacchaeus; he was a chief tax collector, and rich. And he sought to see who Jesus was, but could not, on account of the crowd, because he was small of stature. So he ran on ahead and climbed up into a sycamore tree to see him, for he was to pass that way. And when Jesus came to the place, he looked up and said to him, "Zacchaeus, make haste and come down; for I must stay at your house today." So he made haste and came down, and received him joyfully. And when they saw it they all murmured, "He has gone in to be the guest of a man who is a sinner." And Zacchaeus stood and said to the Lord, "Behold, Lord, the half of my goods I give to the poor; and if I have defrauded any one of anything, I restore it fourfold." And Jesus said to him, "Today salvation has come to this house, since he also is a son of Abraham.

Questions

Tax collectors in Jesus' time and culture were generally considered to be dishonest extortioners. But Zacchaeus, who gave one half of his goods to the poor and made restitution to those he defrauded, was an exception. Jesus approved of Zacchaeus, thereby challenging the stereotype.

Who in your community is often judged not by individual qualities and behavior but by perceptions of a group to which he or she belongs? Do you believe the general perception is accurate? Are there many exceptions?

Jesus links generosity to the poor with salvation. Have you known anyone who appears to have been saved in this present life because of their generosity? (Perhaps you know someone who was previously addicted to drugs or alcohol who is today "clean" — saved — by dedication to serving.)

Matthew 26:6–13: Now when Jesus was at Bethany in the house of Simon the leper, a woman came up to him with an alabaster flask of very expensive ointment, and she poured it on his head, as he sat at table. But when the disciples saw it, they were indignant, saying, "Why this waste? For this ointment might have been sold for a large sum, and given to the poor." But Jesus, aware of this, said to them, "Why do you trouble the woman? For she has done a beautiful thing to me. For you always have the poor with you, but you will not always have me. In pouring this ointment on my body she has done it to prepare me for burial. Truly, I say to you, wherever this gospel is preached in the whole world, what she has done will be told in memory of her."

Questions

This passage seems at first to contradict Jesus' message that giving to the poor is more important than acts of worship. But Jesus graciously accepted the woman's expensive gift, although the money spent on it could have been used to help those in need. Jesus knew that for the woman, the gift came from love and gratitude.

Does your agency or community spend money on celebrations or other things that seem a foolish use of money to you? Upon reflection, what purpose(s) do these things serve? Do they point to differences between your sense of values and priorities and those of the community? Between your culture and theirs? Have you changed your mind about how you see the use of resources as you have come to better understand the community and culture in which you are serving?

Matthew 25:31–40: "When the Son of man comes in his glory, and all the angels with him, then he will sit on his glorious throne. Before him will be gathered all the nations, and he will separate them one from another as a shepherd separates the sheep from the goats, and he will place the sheep at his right hand, but the goats at the left. Then the King will say to those at his right hand, 'Come, O blessed of my Father, inherit the kingdom prepared for you from the foundation of the world; for I was hungry and you gave me food, I was thirsty and you gave me drink, I was a stranger and you welcomed me, I was naked and you clothed me, I was sick and you visited me, I was in prison and you came to me.' Then the righteous will answer him, 'Lord, when did we see thee hungry and feed thee, or thirsty and give thee drink? And when did we see thee a stranger and welcome thee, or naked and clothe thee? And when did we see thee sick or in prison and visit thee?' And the King will answer them, 'Truly, I say to you, as you did it to one of the least of these my brethren, you did it to me.'"

Questions

This story that Jesus told may be considered an explanation of the way he understood the corporate nature of community and society: That when we help the needy, we are helping all, even the most rich and powerful. "No man is an island." Think about the leaders of your community agency. Do they identify with those in need in such a way that they appreciate those who work on behalf of the "least of the brethren?" Does the community at large feel that it benefits, or that it is deprived of resources, when resources are directed to the needs of the poor?

James 2:1–7: My brethren, show no partiality as you hold the faith of our Lord Jesus Christ, the Lord of glory. For if a man with gold rings and in fine clothing comes into your assembly, and a poor man in shabby clothing also comes in, and you pay attention to the one who wears the fine clothing and say, "Have a seat here, please," while you say to the poor man, "Stand there," or, "Sit at my feet," have you not made distinctions among yourselves, and become judges with evil thoughts? Listen, my beloved brethren. Has not God chosen those who are poor in the world to be rich in faith and heirs of the kingdom which he has promised to those who love him? But you have dishonored the poor man. Is it not the rich who oppress you, is it not they who drag you into court? Is it not they who blaspheme that honorable name by which you are called?

Questions

In his letter, James admonishes Christians to welcome all, casting aside the world's hierarchy of who is valued and who is not. What hierarchy of worth is the generally accepted one in the community where you are serving? What determines one's place in the accepted hierarchy — age, race or skin color, education, wealth, gender, family history?

Is a mission of your agency to challenge, reinforce, or passively accept the existing hierarchy? Do you approve of its stance?

James 2:14–17: What does it profit, my brethren, if a man says he has faith but has not works? Can his faith save him? If a brother or sister is ill-clad and in lack of daily food, and one of you says to them, "Go in peace, be warmed and filled," without giving them the things needed for the body, what does it profit? So faith by itself, if it has no works, is dead.

Questions

The relationship between faith and good works has been a major trope for Christian theologians over the centuries, especially in Europe at the time of the Protestant Reformation. James states bluntly that "faith by itself, without good works, is dead." In what or who do people in your agency—staff and clients—put their faith? Is it God, government, medicine, education, the next generations, something else? How is their faith related to help for those in need? To social change?

I John 4:7–12: Beloved, let us love one another; for love is of God, and he who loves is born of God and knows God. He who does not love does not know God; for God is love. In this the love of God was made manifest among us, that God sent his only Son into the world, so that we might live through him. In this is love, not that we loved God but that he loved us and sent his Son to be the expiation for our sins. Beloved, if God so loved us, we also ought to love one another. No man has ever seen God; if we love one another, God abides in us and his love is perfected in us.

I John 4:20–21: If any one says, "I love God," and hates his brother, he is a liar; for he who does not love his brother whom he has seen, cannot love God whom he has not seen. And this commandment we have from him, that he who loves God should love his brother also.

Questions

Have you read about or met those whose expressions and acts of love seem to come from a power beyond themselves or who attribute their strength and ability to serve to a higher power? How do they express their love — in words, in action, working for what cause and what ends?

Philippians 2:5–11: Have this mind among yourselves, which you have in Christ Jesus, who, though he was in the form of God, did not count equality with God a thing to be grasped, but emptied himself, taking the form of a servant, being born in the likeness of men. And being found in human form he humbled himself and became obedient unto death, even death on a cross. Therefore God has highly exalted him and bestowed on him the name which is above every name, that at the name of Jesus every knee should bow, in heaven and on earth and under the earth, and every tongue confess that Jesus Christ is Lord, to the glory of God the Father.

Questions

In this letter of Paul to the church at Philippi, he describes a central belief of Christians — that God as Jesus gave up his powers to become a humble servant for the sake of the human family, even giving himself up to a terrible death and that for his sacrifice, God restored him to the Godhead and thus exalted him. As the "man for others," Jesus is seen by Christians as the supreme example of leadership. What examples of leadership have you studied in the history of the nation and culture where you are serving? Describe someone in that history or culture that you would identify as a servant-leader. Describe someone in the agency whom you would so describe.

1 Corinthians 13:1–3: If I speak in the tongues of men and of angels, but have not love, I am a noisy gong or a clanging cymbal. And if I have prophetic powers, and understand all mysteries and all knowledge, and if I have all faith, so as to remove mountains, but have not love, I am nothing. If I give away all I have, and if I deliver my body to be burned, but have not love, I gain nothing.

Questions

This passage from the letter of Paul to the church in Corinth is one of the most frequently quoted passages of the New Testament, committed to memory and beloved by Christians, often chosen for inclusion in wedding and funeral services. What does Paul say happens to our talents, powers, and other good qualities if we have no love? Have you known those who appear to serve for reasons other than loving those in need? How do you define love? Do you think it is possible to serve without loving, or is serving itself evidence of love?

John 13: 1–17: Now before the feast of the Passover, when Jesus knew that his hour had come to depart out of this world to the Father, having loved his own who were in the world, he loved them to the end. And during supper, when the devil had already put it into the heart of Judas Iscariot, Simon's son, to betray him, Jesus, knowing that the Father had given all things into his hands, and that he had come from God and was going to God, rose from supper, laid aside his garments, and girded himself with a towel. Then he poured water into a basin, and began to wash the disciples' feet, and to wipe them with the towel with which he was girded. He came to Simon Peter; and Peter said to him, "Lord, do you wash my feet?" Jesus answered him, "What I am doing you do not know now, but afterward you will understand." Peter said to him, "You shall never wash my feet." Jesus answered him, "If I do not wash you, you have no part in me." Simon Peter said to him, "Lord, not my feet only but also my hands and my head!" Jesus said to him, "He who has bathed does not need to wash, except for his feet, but he is clean all over; and you are clean, but not every one of you." For he knew who was to betray him; that was why he said, "You are not all clean."

When he had washed their feet, and taken his garments, and resumed his place, he said to them, "Do you know what I have done to you? You call me Teacher and Lord; and you are right, for so I am. If I then, your Lord and Teacher, have washed your feet, you also ought to wash one another's feet. For I have given you an example, that you also should do as I have done to you. Truly, truly, I say to you, a servant is not greater than his master, nor is he who is sent greater than he who sent him. If you know these things, blessed are you if you do them.

John 13:31–35: When he had gone out, Jesus said, "Now is the Son of Man glorified, and in him God is glorified; if God is glorified in him, God will also glorify him in himself, and glorify him at once. Little children, yet a little while I am with you. You will seek me; and as I said to the Jews so now I say to you, 'Where I am going, you cannot come.' A new commandment I give to you, that you love one another; even as I have loved you, that you also love one another. By this all men will know that you are my disciples, if you have love for one another."

Questions

At the heart of Christianity is Jesus, and this story of Jesus washing his disciples' feet is at the heart of the Christian teaching about service. As the passage above indicates, this washing occurred on the great Jewish holy day Passover, which commemorates God's saving of his people. It was on the night before Jesus was arrested, tried and put to death. The dinner Jesus had with his twelve disciples on that night is the meal at which he instituted what has become the major liturgical rite of the Christian Church, known by the names the Mass, Holy Communion, the Liturgy, or the Eucharist (the Thanksgiving). On the night before Good Friday, known as Holy Thursday, incorporated in the celebration of the Mass in many parts of the Christian Church is a ceremony of feet-washing in which the priest washes the feet of those who serve at the altar, then the laity wash each other's feet. In Rome, the Pope kneels on the ground to wash the feet of those who serve him. The importance of this rite indicates of the importance of this story to Christians throughout the ages.

In the time of Jesus, travelers, dirty and footsore from wearing open sandals on the dusty and rocky roads of

Palestine, would, upon entering a house, have their feet washed by the lowliest servant.

How did Peter misunderstand what Jesus was doing? Why do you think that at first he refused to allow Jesus to wash his feet? Have you seen people at your agency who cannot allow others to serve them? How do you feel when others offer to help you or otherwise perform an act of kindness on your behalf? Grateful? Embarrassed? Beholden?

Who has served you in the community you have gone to serve? Are they new acquaintances? Strangers?

Who generally performs the acts of service and hospitality in the community where you are serving? The host? Women? Servants? Who performs direct service at your agency? The supervisor? The least well-paid? Volunteers? Everyone?

Have you seen acts of service, kindness, and hospitality performed by those who normally one would not be expected to do these things? For example, one service-learning student remembered the college president helping to unload the luggage from the airport van. She claims she will never forget that act of welcome.

CHRISTIAN PRAYERS AND WRITINGS

A Prayer of Francis of Assisi

"Instrument of Thy Peace"

Lord, make me an instrument of Thy peace. Where there is hatred, let me sow love; where there is injury, pardon; where there is doubt, faith; where there is despair, hope; where there is sadness, joy; where there is darkness, light.

O Divine Master, grant that I may not so much seek to be consoled, as to console; not so much to be understood, as to understand; not so much to be loved, as to love. For it is in giving that we receive, it is in pardoning that we are pardoned, it is in dying that we are born again to eternal life.

O Lord, open my eyes that I may see the need of others, open my ears that I may hear their cries, open my heart so that they need not be without succor, let me be not afraid to defend the weak because of the anger of the strong, nor afraid to defend the poor because of the anger of the rich. Show me where love and hope and faith are needed, and use me to bring them to those places. And so open my eyes and my ears that I may this coming day be able to do some work of peace for Thee.

Help me, O Lord, to be more loving. Help me, O Lord, not to be afraid to love the outcast, the leper, the unmarried pregnant woman, the traitor to the State, the man out of prison. Help me by my love to restore the faith of the disillusioned, the disappointed, the early bereaved. Help me by my love to be witness of Thy love.

And may I this coming day be able to do some work of peace for Thee.

O Lord, help me to order my life better, help me to use my gifts more industriously, help me to turn from no one in need, help me to see You in the hungry, the sick, the prisoners, the lonely, help me this coming day to do some work of peace for You.

> From *Instrument of Thy Peace*, edited by Alan Paton (New York: Seabury Press, 1982).

Questions

In this famous prayer, Francis enumerates many human problems. Select one and describe a situation in which someone at your agency — it could be you! — has acted, perhaps bravely, when facing opposition or community disapproval, to relieve suffering. What does Francis mean by praying that he become an "instrument" of peace?

The Words of Martin Luther King, Jr.

Martin Luther King, Jr., led the civil-rights movement in the United States in the 1950s and until his assassination in 1968. He was a Christian pastor, the head of Ebenezer Baptist Church in Atlanta, Georgia. He was awarded the Nobel Peace Prize and is recognized the world over for his Christian work on behalf of the poor, the disenfranchised, and victims of racism.

In these writings, King raises a number of questions about education, its practice, and the importance we place on it.

> An individual has not started living until he can rise above the narrow confines of his individualistic concerns to the broader concerns of all humanity.

329

Every man must decide whether he will walk in the light of creative altruism or the darkness of destructive selfishness. This is the judgment. Life's most persistent and urgent question is, What are you doing for others?

Everybody can be great. Because anybody can serve. You don't have to have a college degree to serve. You don't have to make your subject and your verb agree to serve. You don't have to know about Plato and Aristotle to serve. You don't have to know Einstein's theory of relativity to serve. You don't have to know the second theory of thermodynamics in physics to serve. You only need a heart full of grace. A soul generated by love.

All too many of those who live in affluent America ignore those who exist in poor America; in doing so, the affluent Americans will eventually have to face themselves with the question that Eichmann chose to ignore: How responsible am I for the well-being of my fellows? To ignore evil is to become an accomplice to it.

As long as there is poverty in the world I can never be rich, even if I have a billion dollars.... I can never be what I ought to be until you are what you ought to be. This is the way our world is made. No individual or nation can stand out boasting of being independent. We are interdependent.

A man who won't die for something is not fit to live.

I often wonder whether or not education is fulfilling its purpose. A great majority of the so-called education people do not think logically and scientifically. Even the press, the classroom, the platform, and the pulpit in many instances do not give us objective and unbiased truths. To save man from the morass of propaganda, in my opinion, is one of the chief aims of education. Education must enable one to sift and weigh evidence, to discern the true from the false, the real from the unreal, and the facts from fiction.

The function of education, therefore, is to teach one to think intensively and to think critically. But education which stops with efficiency may prove the greatest menace to society. The most dangerous criminal may be the man gifted with reason but with no morals.

We must remember that intelligence is not enough. Intelligence plus character — that is the goal of true education. The complete education gives one not only power of concentration but worthy objectives upon which to concentrate. The broad education will, therefore, transmit to one not only the accumulated knowledge of the race but also accumulated experience of social living.

Human progress is neither automatic nor inevitable. Even a superficial look at history reveals that no social advance rolls in on the wheels of inevitability. Every step toward the goal of justice requires sacrifice, suffering and struggle; the tireless exertions and passionate concern of dedicated individuals. Without persistent effort, time itself becomes an ally of the insurgent and primitive forces of irrational emotionalism and social destruction. This is no time for apathy or complacency. This is the time for vigorous and positive action.

The belief that God will do everything for man is as untenable as the belief that man can do everything for himself. It, too, is based on a lack of faith. We must learn that to expect God to do everything while we do nothing is not faith but superstition.

A religion true to its nature must also be concerned about man's social conditions. Religion deals with both earth and heaven, both time and eternity. Religion operates not only on the vertical plane but also on the horizontal. It seeks not only to integrate men with God but to integrate men with men and each man with himself. This means, at bottom, that the Christian gospel is a two-way road. On the one hand, it seeks to change the souls of men and thereby unite them with God; on the other hand, it seeks to change the environmental conditions of men so that the soul will have a chance after it is changed. Any religion that professes to be concerned with the souls of men and is not concerned with the slums that damn them, the economic conditions that strangle them, and the social conditions that cripple them is a dry-as-dust religion. Such a religion is the kind the Marxists like to see — an opiate of the people.

> From *The Words of Martin Luther King, Jr.,* selected by Coretta Scott King (New York: Newmarket Press, 1983).

Questions

What have you experienced in your education? Has the focus been on teaching you to "sift and weigh evidence, to discern the true from the false?" Do you agree with King that education must be linked to character-building?

You chose service-learning to be a part of your education. Did you make that choice because the values it implies are consistent with the education that you have received to date, or because it stands in contrast to your previous educational experiences? (Remember that you have had many teachers — some part of formal schooling, but also and importantly, parents, religious training, camps, and clubs.)

King says that the uneducated can serve. From your service experience, cite examples of those with little formal education who have been successful in serving others.

King sets forth the Christian vision of society as inter-dependent — that is, that the well-being of any one person is related to the well-being of all. Do you believe that this view predominates in your society, or is the prevalent image one of competition? How does it compare with the interrelatedness of all in Buddhism?

Mother Teresa: In My Own Words

Mother Teresa is known throughout the world for her service to the destitute and dying, first in Calcutta, India, and then, through the religious order that she founded, the Missionaries of Charity, to those in many other parts of the world.

> Today it is very fashionable to talk about the poor. Unfortunately, it is not fashionable to talk with them.
> A way of satisfying our brethren's hunger is to share with them whatever we have—to share with them until we ourselves feel what they feel.
> Do we share with the poor, just like Jesus shared with us?
> Whoever the poorest of the poor are, they are Christ for us—Christ under the guise of human suffering.
> The Missionaries of Charity are firmly convinced that each time we offer help to the poor, we really offer help to Christ.
> When we touch the sick and needy, we touch the suffering body of Christ.
> We are at the service of the poor. But are we capable, are we willing to share the poverty of the poor? Do we identify with the poor whom we serve? Do we really feel in solidarity with them? Do we share with them just like Jesus shares with us?

The poor anywhere in the world are Christ who suffers. In them, the Son of God lives and dies. Through them, God shows his face.

All my years of service to the poor have helped me to understand that they are precisely the ones who better understand human dignity. If they have a problem, it is not lack of money, but the fact that their right to be treated humanly and with tenderness is not recognized.

Jesus comes to meet us. To welcome him, let us go to meet him.

He comes to us in the hungry, the naked, the lonely, the alcoholic, the drug addict, the prostitute, the street beggars.

He may come to you or me in a father who is along, in a mother, in a brother, or in a sister.

If we reject them, if we do not go out to meet them, we reject Jesus himself.

Poverty has not been created by God. We are the ones who have created poverty. Before God, we are all poor.

Jesus is the one we take care of, visit, clothe, feed and comfort every time we do this to the poorest of the poor, to the sick, to the dying, to the lepers, and to the ones who suffer from AIDS.

We should not serve the poor like they were Jesus. We should serve the poor because they are Jesus.

From *Mother Teresa: In My Own Words,* compiled by Jose Luis Gonzalez-Balado (New York: Gramercy Book, 1997).

Questions

How do you understand this selection of Mother Teresa's writings in relation to the Christian concept of incarnation?

Has your own experience in service and service-learning helped you to "share with them [the poor] until [you yourself] feel what they feel?"

Dietrich Bonhoeffer: Letters and Papers from Prison

Dietrich Bonhoeffer, imprisoned and put to death for publicly opposing the regime in Nazi Germany, wrote these letters and papers from prison. In them, he considers some of the most profound and troubling questions of theology, and especially of the relationship between Christian faith and the secular world.

13 September 1943

It is a strange feeling to be so completely dependent on other people; but at least it teaches one to be grateful, and I hope I shall never forget that. In ordinary life we hardly realize that we receive a great deal more than we give, and that it is only with gratitude that life becomes rich. It is very easy to overestimate the importance of our own achievements in comparison with what we owe to others.

Christmas 1943 - Morning Prayers

O God, early in the morning I cry to thee.
Help me to pray.
And to concentrate my thoughts on thee; I cannot do this
    alone.
In me, there is darkness,
But with thee there is light;
I am lonely, but thou leavest me not;
I am feeble in heart, but with thee there is help;
I am restless, but with thee there is peace.
In me there is bitterness, but with thee there is patience;
I do not understand thy ways,
But thou knowest the way for me.
O heavenly Father,
I praise and thank thee
For the peace of the night;
I praise and thank thee for this new day;
I praise and thank thee for all thy goodness
And faithfulness throughout my life.
Thou hast granted me many blessings;
Now let me also accept what is hard
From thy hand.
Thou wilt lay on me no more
Than I can bear.
Thou makest all things work together for good for thy
    children.
Lord Jesus Christ,
Thou wast poor
And in distress, a captive and forsaken as I am.
Thou knowest all man's troubles;
Thou abidest with me
When all men fail me;
Thou rememberest and seekest me;
It is thy will that I should know thee
And turn to thee.
Lord, I hear thy call and follow;
Do thou help me.

30 April 1944

If we do not want to do all that, if our final judgment
must be that the western form of Christianity, too,
was only a preliminary stage to a complete absence
of religion, what kind of situation emerges for us, for
the Church? How can Christ become the Lord of the
religionless as well? Are there religionless Christians?
If religion is only a garment of Christianity — and even
this garment has looked very different at different
times — then what is religionless Christianity? Barth,
who is the only one to have started along this line of
thought, did not carry it to completion, but arrived
at a positivism of revelation, which in the last analysis
is essentially a restoration. For the religionless
working man (or any other man) nothing decisive is
gained here. The questions to be answered would
surely be: What do a church, a community, a sermon,
a liturgy, a Christian life mean in a religionless world?
How do we speak of God — without religion, i.e.
without the temporally conditioned presuppositions
of metaphysics, inwardness, and so on? How do we
speak (or perhaps we cannot now even "speak" as
we used to) in a "secular" way about "God"? In what
way are we "religionless-secular" Christians, in what
way are we the εκκλησια [ecclesia — church], those
who are called forth, not regarding ourselves from a
religious point of view as specially favoured, but
rather as belonging wholly to the world? In that case
Christ is no longer an object of religion, but something
quite different, really the Lord of the world. But what
does that mean? What is the place of worship and
prayer in a religionless situation? Does the secret
discipline, or alternatively the difference (which I
have suggested to you before) between penultimate
and ultimate take on a new importance here?

4 May 1944

What is above this world is, in the gospel, intended to exist for this world. I mean that, not in the anthropocentric sense of liberal, mystic, pietistic, ethical theology, but in the biblical sense of the creation and of the incarnation, crucifixion and resurrection of Jesus Christ.

May 1944

We have spent too much time in thinking, supposing that if we weigh in advance the possibilities of any action, it will happen automatically. We have learnt, rather too late, that action comes, not from thought, but from a readiness for responsibility. For you, thought and action will be confined to your responsibilities in action. With us, thought was often the luxury of the onlooker; with you it will be entirely subordinated to action. "Not every one who says to me, 'Lord, Lord,' shall enter the kingdom of heaven, but he who does the will of my Father who is in heaven," said Jesus (Matt. 7.21).

25 May 1944

Here again, God is no stop-gap; he must be recognized at the center of life, not when we are at the end of our resources; it is his will to be recognized in life, and not only when death comes; in health and vigour, and not only in suffering; in our activities, and not only in sin. The ground for this lies in the revelation of God in Jesus Christ. He is the center of life, and he certainly did not "come" to answer our unsolved problems. From the center of life certain questions, and their answers, are seen to be wholly irrelevant (I am thinking of the judgment pronounced on Job's friends). In Christ there are no "Christian problems." — Enough of this: I have just been disturbed again.

16 July 1944

So our coming of age leads us to a true recognition of our situation before God. God would have us know that we must live as men who manage our lives without him. The God who is with us is the God who forsakes us (Mark 15.34). The God who lets us live in the world without the working hypothesis of God is the God before whom we stand continually. Before God and with God we live without God. God lets himself be pushed out of the world on to the cross. He is weak and powerless in the world, and that is precisely the way, the only way, in which he is with us and helps us. Matt. 8.17 makes it quite clear that Christ helps us, not by virtue of his omnipotence, but by virtue of his weakness and suffering.

Here is the decisive difference between Christianity and all religions. Man's religiosity makes him look in his distress to the power of God in the world: God is the deus ex machina. The Bible directs man to God's powerlessness and suffering; only the suffering God can help. To that extent we may say that the development towards the world's coming of age outlines above, which has done away with a false conception of God, opens up a way of seeing the God of the Bible, who wins power and space in the world by his weakness. This will probably be the starting-point for our "secular interpretation."

18 July 1944

He must therefore really live in the godless world, without attempting to gloss over or explain its ungodliness in some religious way or other. He must live a "secular" life, and thereby share in God's sufferings. He may live a "secular" life: i.e. he is freed (as one who has been liberated from false religious-obligation inhibitions.) To be a Christian does not mean to be religious in a particular way, to make something of oneself (a sinner, a penitent, or a saint) on the basis of some method or other, but to be a man—not a type of man, but the man that Christ creates in us. It is not the religious act that makes the Christian, but participation in the sufferings of God in the secular life.

This being caught up into the messianic suffering of God in Jesus Christ takes a variety of forms in the New Testament. It appears in the call to discipleship, in Jesus' table-fellowship with sinners, in "conversions" in the narrower sense of the word (e.g. Zacchaeus), in the act of the woman who was a sinner (Luke 7)—an act that she performed without any confession of sin, in the healing of the sick (Matt. 8.17; see above), in Jesus' acceptance of children.

Christians and pagans
Men go to God when they are sore bestead,
Pray to him for succour, for his peace, for bread,
For mercy for them sick, sinning, or dead;
All men do so, Christian and unbelieving.

Men go to God when he is sore bestead,
Find him poor and scorned, without shelter or bread,
Whelmed under weight of the wicked, the weak, the dead;
Christians stand by God in his hour of grieving.

God goeth to every man when sore bestead,
Feedeth body and spirit with his bread;

For Christians, pagans alike he hangeth dead,
And both alike forgiving.

3 August 1944

Outline for a book
Chapter 2
(b) Who is God? Not in the first place an abstract belief in God, in his omnipotence, etc. That is not a genuine experience of God, but a partial extension of the world. Encounter with Jesus Christ. The experience that a transformation of all human life is given in the fact that "Jesus is there only for others." His "being there for others" is the experience of transcendence. It is only this "being there for others," maintained till death, that is the ground of his omnipotence, omniscience, and omnipresence. Faith is participation in this being of Jesus (incarnation, cross, and resurrection). Our relation to God is not a "religious" relationship to the highest, most powerful, and best Being imaginable—this is not authentic transcendence—but our relation to God is a new life in "existence for others," through participation in being of Jesus. The transcendental is not infinite and unattainable tasks, but the neighbor who is within reach in any given situation. God in human form—not, as in oriental religions, in animal form, monstrous, chaotic, remote, and terrifying, nor in the conceptual forms of the absolute, metaphysical, infinite, etc., nor yet in the Greek divine-human form of "man in himself," but "the man for others," and therefore the Crucified, the man who lives out of the transcendent.

From *Dietrich Bonhoeffer: Letters and Papers from Prison*, edited by Eberhard Bethge (New York: The Macmillan Company).

Questions

As Bonhoeffer's experience in prison generated new questions and new ideas about religion for him, what new questions are raised for you by these excerpts? By your study of the five great religions considered in this book? By your experience in service? What will be your memorable and challenging ideas and moments in your experience of service-learning?

ISLAM

Carool Kersten

INTRODUCTION

Currently there are an estimated 1.3 billion Muslims, making Islam the second-largest religious group in the world after Christianity (2 billion). Although it is usually associated with the Middle East and its most significant cultural centers are indeed located in that region, we find the largest concentrations of Muslims in Indonesia (175 million), Pakistan (143 million), India (125 million), and Bangladesh (110 million). The most populous Arab Muslim country is Egypt (66 million). Two other very important non-Arab Muslim countries are Turkey and Iran, with 67 million and 65 million Muslim inhabitants respectively. In Sub-Saharan Africa, Nigeria has the largest Muslim population (65 million). Significant numbers of Muslims are also found in the former Central Asian Soviet Republics and China. Islam is the fastest-growing religion worldwide.

The youngest of the monotheist religions — in fact, the youngest of all major world religions — Islam can be considered a special case from a number of perspectives. First of all, present-day Islam does not have a unified hierarchical administrative structure, and consequently has no center. It does recognize a number of holy places, namely Mecca, Medina, and Jerusalem. For the Shi'is the cities of Najaf and Karbala in Iraq hold special meaning as well. In addition to that there are a number of important centers of Islamic learning, associated with centuries-old "mosque-universities." For the Sunnis these are the al-Azhar in Cairo, the Zaytuna in Tunis, and the Qarawina in Fez, Morocco. Important Shi'i seminaries are located in the Iranian city of Qom.

Another interesting aspect is that, of all world religions, Islam is the only one with a "built-in" name. The word *"islam"* occurs in the Islamic Sacred Scripture, the Qur'an, itself, and the faithful themselves insist on that term to designate their religious system. In its barest sense, the term *"islam"* means "surrender"or "resignation," but also "commitment." In this context it specifically means commitment or obedience to live one's life in accordance with God's proclaimed purpose. It is a verbal noun, indicating an action, not an institution. This active element becomes even more evident if we survey the Qur'an further. While *"islam"* occurs eight times, its related verb is found seventy-two times in various inflexions, including the participial *"muslim"* (forty-two times).

From a historical point of view, the emergence of Islam can be considered miraculous, even paradoxical. Originating on the Arabian Peninsula at the beginning of the seventh century, it had become in less than a hundred years the dominant polity and civilization in an area that stretched from Spain to the western fringes of India. The historian Gustave von Grünebaum observed that it was "not the physical domination but the cultural power of the new teaching, not its origin in a particular geographical and intellectual zone but its immanent universality, which proved the deciding factor in its development....A sect was transformed into an empire, a universal a-political community became a determining factor in political events."[1]

Islam did not develop in a vacuum. In order to appreciate the specifics of this new religious message it is useful to start with a historical excursion. It will help us to become aware of both the historical context in which Islam first took shape and how it subsequently contributed to the further course of history. This way the significance of the religious tradition called Islam will become clearer.

ENCOUNTER WITH A WORLD: PRE-ISLAMIC ARABIA

In order to appreciate the origins of the message of Islam, we must have an understanding of the setting in which it emerged. The main problem we face in this respect is not so much the paucity of hard data as the fact that information has come to us mainly through Muslim sources, refracting the image through an Islamic lens. An important indication for this is the very term used by the Muslims to designate pre-Islamic time in Arabia: *Jahiliyya*, or "the era of ignorance." In the following survey an effort will be made to qualify, and somewhat correct, that image.

It is tempting to consider the entire pre-Islamic Arabian Peninsula, not home to any great civilization, as a cultural backwater. But although located only at the fringes of great empires, Arabia had never been entirely isolated from the surrounding world. Since antiquity, Southern Arabia (current-day Yemen and southern Oman) had supplied Egypt, Mesopotamia, Greece, and the Roman Empire with frankincense. In the northwest, the earlier trading emporiums of the Nabataeans and the Palmyrans had maintained close relations with the Romans. Throughout the centuries, several Arabs even became emperor. When Islam emerged in the beginning of the seventh century, the peninsula's extreme north was controlled by the Arab pseudo-kingdoms of the Ghassanids and Lakhmids, vassals of Byzantium and Persia respectively.

But, except for a few towns and settled oases, the interior was indeed home only to roaming nomadic tribes, the Bedouins. Their lifestyle can be characterized as a kind of anarchy barely held in check by a precarious code of conduct in which tribal allegiance was the only binding factor. What we know about it is largely based on a body of poetry celebrating the constant warfare and valiance of "the Days of the Arabs." Arab posterity has an ambivalent relationship with this heritage, characterized by a degree of embarrassment because of its barbarism on the one hand, but pride in its heroes' independence on the other.

If we look for the prevailing religious traditions in pre-Islamic Arabia, we find elements of animism, experiences of divinity associated with stone fetishism, sky cults common to other Semitic people, and an idea of fatalism related to a pantheon of deities that included a Goddess of Fate as well as a concept of the supreme divinity as a king. There is some scanty evidence of a priestly caste of soothsayers, called *kâhins* (a term that can be traced back to the same origin as the Hebrew *cohen*).

But Christianity had made inroads into the Arabian Peninsula. In the wake of Persian invasions, Nestorianism got a foothold in Northeastern Arabia, probably as early as the late fourth century. Monophysites entering via Ethiopia had tried to proselytize Yemen, but were evicted in a surge of national feelings toward the end of the sixth century. The vacuum was partly filled by Judaism, brought by Jews migrating south since the fourth and fifth centuries. From the second half of the sixth century, Monophysites had also made some efforts to convert the nomads. By and large, the Bedouins were not interested in the dogmatic intricacies of Christianity, but the hermit tradition and church processions impressed them.

There was also an indigenous tradition of what can be branded as monotheism. This was propagated by the so-called *hunafa'* (plural of *hanîf*), a term that literally means "dissenters." The sympathy that was felt for these ascetics by both contemporaries and later generations is an indication of dissatisfaction with inherited religious practice.

Finally, the proximity to the Persian empire of the Sasanians and the repeated incursions by their armies exposed the Arabs also to Persian Zoroastrianism and the teachings of Mani, known as Manichaeism.

Within this constellation, the West Arabian town of Mecca held a key position for two reasons. First, it was a center of trade between the Mediterranean and the Indian Ocean. Second, it contained a sanctuary called the *Ka'ba*—"the cubicle"—which, as the holy place of the area's supreme deity known as Allah (literally, "The God") was an object of reverence and pilgrimage, in which Christians tended to participate too. The surrounding area was considered *haram*, meaning a place giving all living things asylum from being killed. The rites involved the circumambulation of the *Ka'ba*, standing in worship, and a blood sacrifice. The pilgrimage took place annually during a period of four months during which an armistice went into effect among the tribes. For the inhabitants of Mecca these religious practices were also of economic importance. It was in Mecca that in the second half of the sixth century, Muhammad was born as the scion of a lesser branch of Mecca's leading clan, the Quraish.

THE PROPHET MUHAMMAD

There is no other founder of a world religion about whom there exists such an abundance of biographical material as there is for the Prophet Muhammad. But it should be immediately added that more recent, and more critical, scholarly research has turned a large part of assumed knowledge into questions and hypotheses—especially about the earlier life of the Prophet, where much is obscure and legend has had an easy task in filling in the gaps.

The essential significance of Muhammad's appearance is the crystallization of a new experience of the divine, breaking free from the habits and ideas that were common in his day. That does not mean that the historical figure Muhammad was not subject to certain strictures imposed by the exterior circumstances of his time, because if his own understanding of the divine had been inaccessible to his contemporaries he would have found no following. Recounting some defining moments in his life on the basis of the traditional Islamic accounts will make it possible to understand the Muslim view of history and what human life should be.

Muhammad was orphaned at a very early age. His father, Abdullah, had died even before he was born, and his mother, Amina, followed not many years later. Initially, he was left in the care of his grandfather, Abd al-Mutallib, who apparently functioned as a caretaker of Mecca's sanctuary, the *Ka'ba*. When he had passed away as well, a paternal uncle, Abu Talib, was appointed as the boy's guardian. Other details are sketchy, but it is likely that Muhammad grew up in rather poor circumstances. Later tradition has infused his early life with elements of legend; there is the story of his encounter with a Christian hermit monk who recognized the boy as a future prophet.

As a young adult, Muhammad's life took a turn for the better, when at age twenty-five he married a prosperous widow, Khadija, supposedly fifteen years his senior. The orphan boy became a successful trader in his own right. In addition to that, he gained a reputation for honesty and sincerity, acquiring the nickname *al-Amin*, "the Trustworthy."

As he grew older, Muhammad developed a distinct spiritual streak, withdrawing into the surrounding hills for extensive meditation retreats. He was also becoming increasingly disillusioned with the unfairness of his society, with its sharp contrasts between the rich and the poor, its decadence, and its perpetual state of conflict.

When Muhammad was about forty years old, he reached the watershed of his personal spiritual life. According to tradition, on the twenty-sixth night of the month of Ramadan in the year 610 C.E., Muhammad received his call. It would become known as *Laylat al-Qadr*, the "Night of Decision" or "Night of Power." During it, Muhammad experienced the first of a series of visitations by the angel Gabriel, who revealed to him the words that would constitute the first revelation:

> Recite: In the Name of thy Lord who created,
> created Man of a blood-clot.
> Recite: And thy Lord is the Most Generous,
> who taught by the Pen,
> taught man that he knew not.
>
> *(Sura al'Alaq* [96:1–5])[2]

Initially distraught by this frightening experience and a subsequent temporary cessation of visitations, he kept faith through the encouragement of his wife, who was effectively his first convert. After their resumption, the revelations would continue until Muhammad's death. During the first three years, Muhammad initiated only an intimate circle into the tidings he received. But gradually, a sense of duty to warn his people to mend their ways took hold and Muhammad went public with his message. A central theme in this early period was the certainty of a Last Judgment. It was this that determined Muhammad's ethical and emotional attitude, which he tried to instill in his followers. Believing in the message was not enough; at the end of time, man would be judged based on his faith and his actions.

The relations between Muhammad's small following and the unconverted only became antagonized after the Prophet's direct attacks on the divinities of Mecca. After two years, tensions between the Muslims and their compatriots had become so acute that Muhammad thought it wise to send his most vulnerable followers into exile in Ethiopia. Most of the Ethiopian migration occurred in the year 615. What had originally been only an ideological dispute now turned gradually into a conflict with political and socioeconomic dimensions. The small community of Muslims became the target of a boycott. Although perhaps unforeseen by him, Muhammad was seen increasingly as a powerful figure since he was the intellectual center of a "reform" movement. The personal recognition accorded the Prophet could easily be regarded as a quasi-official position by his opponents. What had become decisive was the fact that Muhammad's views drew their strength from an experience of God. It seems the Meccans had become increasingly aware of this and saw that only the physical removal of Muhammad would put a halt to these new teachings.

With the death of both Khadija and Muhammad's main protector, his former guardian Abu Talib, such a prospect became more and more likely. But an immediate violent clash was avoided, because the message that was so frightening to the Meccans seemed a means of deliverance to the inhabitants of Yathrib.

This wide-spreading oasis, consisting of a number of village-like settlements occupied by both Arab and Jewish tribes, was ravaged by internal disputes that had turned into a virtual civil war. After a bloody climax, they appealed to Muhammad to mediate. Historians have interpreted this as the first explicit indication that the prevailing tribal ethic was no longer relevant in urban relationships. The Muslim community embodied a new principle for social and political order. This incident also underscores the fact that Islam did not emerge from the desert, but originated in a city and was further developed in urban settings.

Muhammad and his followers now approached what would become the watershed event for Islam from a world-historical point of view. After about two years of negotiations, in 622 Muhammad decided to migrate with his entire community to Yathrib, which henceforth became known as *Madinat al-Nabî*—"City of the Prophet"—or Medina for short. The importance of this so-called migration, or *hijra*, is illustrated by the fact that, sixteen years later, the event was made the starting point of the Muslim era and Islamic calendar.

First of all, Muhammad's role changed. The presence of Jews meant a greater exposure to the religious tradition of Judaism. Until then, Muhammad had simply been called a messenger (*rasûl*) of God. Now there appear references to Muhammad as a *nabî*, meaning a prophet in the Old Testament sense. Apart from a prophet, Muhammad also became a statesman of sorts. There was an urgent need to forge a unity between the Muslims from Mecca, known as *muhâjirûn* (Emigrants), and the converts of Medina, the so-called *ansâr* (Helpers), because the young community was soon drawn into armed conflict with Mecca. Corresponding to this was a change in the character and content of the revelations as well. In Medina, the Prophet's teachings got their final form. There was a greater concern with the definition of ritual observances, social morality, and rules pertaining to social peace, property, marriage, and inheritance.

In the years following the *hijra*, there were three armed altercations with Mecca, and in relation to all of them Muhammad would violate one or another of the rules of conduct prevailing in ancient Arabia, a conscious breach with existing pagan customs. Parallel to this, a rift developed between Muhammad and the Jewish tribes of Medina. Sixteen months after his arrival, Muhammad changed the direction of prayer, the *qibla*, 180 degrees: instead of facing Jerusalem, the Muslims bowed henceforth toward Mecca.

The first clash with Mecca took place in 624 at Badr, when the Meccans responded to a Muslim raid on one of their caravans during one of the sacred months of truce. Though greatly outnumbered, the battle ended in a victory for the Muslims. In the aftermath, Muhammad expelled the Jewish tribe of Qaynuqa', for violating its treaty with him. A year later, the Muslims were not so lucky. In revenge for their defeat at Badr, the Meccans marched with a large army on Medina. The two parties clashed near Uhud, Muhammad was wounded in battle, and discipline in the Muslim ranks broke down. The Prophet interpreted this defeat as God's punishment for the Muslims' lack of commitment. Also, Muhammad turned on the tribe of Nadîr, which had refused to join him in battle. When the tribe withdrew into its stronghold, Muhammad violated a taboo by cutting down the tribe's date trees. Eventually, the tribe was allowed to move to the oasis of Khaibar.

The final confrontation took place in 627 and became known as "the Battle of the Ditch," after the moat dug to repel the Mecca cavalry. The battle was actually a minor event of only a few skirmishes ending with the eventual retreat of the Meccan besiegers. After that, Muhammad made a decisive move against the last remaining Jewish tribe for breaking its pact with him and siding with the Meccans before the battle. Muhammad was now the undisputed leader of a virtually homogeneous Muslim community, or *umma*, made up of Meccan Emigrants and Medinan Helpers. This first generation of Muslims would be known to posterity as the Companions of the Prophet.

Coinciding with these political developments was the conscious formulation of the finality of the Prophet's mission, the basis for a distinct Muslim view of history. Although some of the ideas and imagery in Muhammad's preaching were borrowed from Judaism and Christianity, his was a specific response to man's ultimate concerns, symbolizing an awakening of a new worldview and perception of life. In its concrete shape it was articulated as a return to the unsullied divine revelation that many Jews and Christians had abandoned.

Muhammad's role as conveyor of a divine message was presented as the last in a long prophetic lineage, including Old Testament prophets as well as Jesus. The return to the uncorrupted original divine message is most clearly symbolized by the central role accorded to Abraham as a predecessor of Muhammad, who himself is the "Seal of the Prophets." Abraham, the Friend of God (*Ibrahim al-Khalîl* in Arabic), was neither Jew nor Christian—in fact, he was identified as a *hanîf*. An element of "arabization" was introduced by declaring Mecca to be the original cult center of God's covenant with man. Later tradition further emphasized this Arab connection through Ismail, Abraham's son who in the Old Testament is recognized as the ancestor of the Arabs. The *Ka'ba* is presented as the sanctuary built by Abraham and Ismail—not Isaac—in honor of God, and it remained an object of pilgrimage, but now in an entirely Muslim context.

The following years were dedicated to achieving a reconciliation with Mecca and formed the climax of Muhammad's statesmanship. In 628, a truce was negotiated. As one of the conditions, Muhammad would be permitted to perform pilgrimage to the *Ka'ba*. This took place a year later, during which the Prophet ritually cleansed the holy place of idols. On this occasion, key figures of Meccan society embraced Islam, completing the victory of Islam over its former adversaries. A final eruption of violence between nomadic allies of Mecca and Medina was used by Muhammad as an excuse to forcefully occupy Mecca and persecute the last remnants of opposition in 630.

During the last three years of his life, Muhammad's message was also carried beyond the Arabian Peninsula. He is supposed to have sent letters to the rulers of Egypt, Ethiopia,

Persia, the Ghassanids, and Byzantium. But it would be his successors who would carry the banner of Islam across the then-known world. Muhammad died in Medina in 632, after making a final farewell pilgrimage to Mecca earlier that year.

Although there may be uncertainty or disagreement regarding details of the Prophet's life, what is not disputed is his threefold legacy. First, there is his personality: a man who recognized habitual modes of human action on which he did not turn his back, but which he tried to confine within the limits of what he thought had been ordained by God's Will. The Prophet's behavior became a captivating example for the pious to follow. Second, Muhammad bequeathed Muslim posterity a community founded on the universal principle that final authority rests with God, and held together by basic rituals of conduct, all of which have a communal aspect. But above all there is a body of revelations of the Will of God, laid down in final form in the Qur'an.

THE QUR'AN

The word *"qur'ân"* in Arabic means "what is recited," but it has become specifically the term for God's Word transmitted to mankind through the Prophet Muhammad. Although there is no dispute among the Muslims about this, as will be seen below, there has been considerable controversy about the exact status of the Qur'an as God's Word.

The Qur'an itself also contains other words for this divine message or parts of it. Sometimes it is simply called *al-kitâb*, or "the Book"; other terms that are used are *"tanzîl"* ("sending down"), *"al-dhikr"* ("the admonition") and *"al-furqân"* (usually translated as "the separation," but it is related to an Aramaic word for "salvation," *"purqân"*). In one way or another, all these words indicate that the message was to be considered as divine in origin. In this respect it must be clearly understood that, if there is any analogue with the Qur'an in Christianity, it is with the figure of Christ as "the embodiment of the Word of God" and not with the Bible.

That is not to say that the Qur'an in the form we find it today has never been touched by man. Not only is this acknowledged by Muslim tradition, but it is also indicated by the very name by which Muslims often refer to their sacred scripture in its present form: *al-mushaf*, which means literally a "collection of pages containing writings" or—more simply put—a copy or volume of the scripture. In its current form the Qur'an consists of 114 chapters called Suras. Except for the first short opening chapter, they are organized according to their length; the longest at the beginning and the shortest toward the end. The Suras are divided in verses, or Ayat (literally, "signs"). Thus, the second Sura consists of 286 verses and the last few Suras of no more than three to seven lines. Each Sura has a name or title, which has no reference to the Sura's subject matter. Usually it is taken from some prominent or unusual word, but there seems to be no general rule for that. The heading of each Sura also mentions whether it belongs to the revelations in Muhammad's Meccan or Medinan period, although this dating is not definite because some Suras are composites of Meccan and Medinan revelations.

What remains is the question of the exact history of this text that has reached us, an issue fraught with uncertainties. One is the question of whether Muhammad could read and write. Islamic tradition says that he could not, which would only add to the miraculous nature of the Qur'an. Although it is likely that as a cultured businessman Muhammad was literate, there is no conclusive evidence to what extent that has been relevant to his religious mission. That parts of the revelations were put in writing during the Prophet's lifetime seems to be quite certain, but in addition to that, it was committed to memory by his Companions. The fact that the traditions mention various efforts to come to a "collection" of the Qur'an also indicates that until then its recording had been fragmentary. Scholarly research seems to confirm as well that, although Muhammad cannot have produced a complete recension of the Qur'an, it is safe to presume that he himself brought many passages together and gave them a definite order. It also suggests the likelihood of the hypothesis that the units in which the revelations were arranged corresponded more or less to the existing Suras.

The traditional account is that fixing the Qur'an in a composed form took place under Muhammad's third successor or "caliph," Uthman ibn Affan (644-656). This establishment of a final text may be called the cardinal point in the formation of the canon of the Qur'an. In connection with this it is appropriate to add a few words on the authenticity and completeness of this Qur'an text. Careful study of the Qur'an itself and comparing it against what is known of the Prophet's life by scholars of Islam indicate a consensus regarding the authenticity of its contents. Had this been otherwise, controversy would have arisen and there is little evidence of that. Although there always remains the possibility that parts may have been lost, the preservation of certain contradictory passages and the conjunction of apparently unrelated verses at various points in the Qur'an suggest that the editors made every effort to include everything of which they had reason to believe was part of what had been revealed to the Prophet.

For those not brought up in the Islamic tradition, a first encounter with the Qur'an is often frustrating. It comes across as a chaotic torrent of words and ideas, a mass of raw, unedited material without apparent structure. As we have seen, the text is indeed neither ordered chronologically, nor is there a narrative pattern that provides continuity. In fact, there are many sudden shifts in topic or subject matter, without any apparent relation to each other. It probably takes a certain degree of familiarity with the linguistic and literary traditions of seventh-century Arabia, as well as the subsequent earliest history of Islam, to be able to appreciate the Qur'anic style. Through closer reading and more careful study it becomes possible to get some sense of the power which this text holds for the faithful; its composition and structure in defiance of literary conventions might rather be taken as a confirmation of its divine origin. It certainly accentuates the majesty and simultaneous intimacy of the language employed.

A brief survey will reveal some key features of the Islamic teachings, which have been elaborated and refined by later Islamic theology. If we try to trace the development of Islamic religious concepts, the Meccan Suras should be the starting point. There is a contrast between the revelations of the early Meccan and later Meccan period; not only are the earlier ones mostly short, but the language employed is very poetic and full of imagery. They can be characterized as hymnic, with a lyricism comparable to that of the Psalms or the Upanishads. Often they contain oath-like exclamations, a style-figure known to have been used by the pre-Islamic *kâhins* or soothsayers. The subject matter of these Suras is personal and existential. The central doctrine of Islam, the oneness of God, is already mentioned in one of these early Suras, the Sura of Sincerity (112):

> Say: "He is God, One,
> God, the Everlasting Refuge,
> who has not begotten, and has not been begotten,
> and equal to Him is not any one."
> (*Sura al-Ikhlas* [112])[3]

In the later Meccan period, the style changes. The verses and Suras grow longer, oaths disappear, and there are formal introductions like, "This is the revelation of God." Also, the subject matter becomes more intricate and complex. There are more extensive discussions of sacred history and the message is fitted into a prophetic lineage. The Qur'an mentions four prophets belonging to an indigenous Arabian tradition, eighteen from the Old Testament (most prominently are Adam, Noah, Abraham, Moses, and Joseph), and three from the Gospels (Zachary, John the Baptist, and Jesus). There is not so much a change in style between these later Meccan Suras and the revelations in Medina as there is in subject matter. Not surprisingly, now that Muhammad has become the leader of a community, there is a preoccupation with law-giving and the regulation of communal behavior. Against the background of the conflict with Mecca and the disagreement with the Jews, references to fighting, treason, corruption, heresy, and schism make their entrance as well.

Leaving behind the chronological approach guided by stylistic characteristics, it is worthwhile to focus briefly on the development of the God-concept in the Qur'an, because it is of ultimate significance for the Muslim Creed. Apart from his oneness — meaning both that He has no equals or partners and that He is internally one — God is also omnipotent; He is the creator of everything. There is a difference with the Biblical view of creation, which regards creation as initial, at the beginning of time. Most of the Qur'anic descriptions of God's creative activity instead present it as a continuous act.

Not only is God all-powerful, He is also well-disposed toward mankind. This mildness in addition to his majestic and awe-inspiring aspects is expressed by the dual attributes of "benevolence" and "compassion." The prominence of this notion is also expressed by the fact it constitutes the invocation at the opening of every Sura: "In the Name of God, the Benevolent, the Compassionate." In the Qur'an text itself, God is already in an early stage referred to as *ar-rahmân* ("the Benevolent"), the etymology of which can be traced to the Arabic word for womb ("*rahm*"). God's intimacy with man is further expressed in the often quoted passage "We are nearer to him [man] than his jugular vein" (50:16). In the later mystical traditions of Islam this intimate side of the relationship with God features very prominently.

A final illustration for the contrasting aspects of the God-image in Islam is provided by juxtaposing two very famous descriptive verses, the so-called "Throne Verse" (2:255) and the "Light Verse" (24:35)

Ayat al-Qursi ("Throne Verse")

God
there is no God but He, the
Living, the Everlasting.
Slumber seizes Him not, neither sleep;
to him belongs
all that is in the heavens and in the earth.
Who is there that shall intercede with Him
    save by His leave?
He knows what lies before them
    and what is after them,
and they comprehend not anything of His Knowledge
    save such as He wills.
His Throne comprises the heavens and earth;
the preserving of them oppresses Him not;
He is the All-high, the All-glorious.

(2:255)[4]

361

Ayat an-Nur ("Light Verse")

God is the Light of the heavens and the earth;
the likeness of His Light is as a niche
wherein is a lamp
(the lamp in a glass,
the glass as it were a glittering star)
kindled from a Blessed Tree,
an olive that is neither of the East nor of the West
whose oil wellnigh would shine, even if no fire
    touched it;
Light upon Light;
(God guides to His Light whom He will.)

(24:35)[5]

The idea of God's oneness and perfection finds its ultimate expression in the so-called "Most Beautiful Names of God," each describing a certain attribute of his all-encompassing Being. Based on the names found in the Qur'an, a list of ninety-nine names was compiled that was later used as a basis for meditation and also for mystical speculation by certain Muslim thinkers.[6] Apart from these descriptive names, the Qur'an also uses a denotative name: Allah, a contraction of the Arabic "*al-Ilah*," "the god."

Apart from the doctrine about God, the second most important doctrine in the Qur'an is the one pertaining to the Day of Judgment. This climax of history, regarding which Muhammad has been designated a "warner," is referred to in various ways: "Day of Reckoning"; "the Last Day"; "the Day of Resurrection"; "the Hour"; and a number of others. Of central significance is the gathering of all mankind before the Judge. The actual judgment is described in a variety of ways in the Qur'an, each giving prominence to different details: books with man's deeds will be opened, man will be given his account, or the relative weight of good and bad deeds will be weighed in the balance. In reference to Mecca as a commercial center, scholars have pointed out the mercantile connotations of these descriptions. The abode of those condemned will be Hell, while the destination of the Just is Paradise or "the Garden." Again, the Qur'an gives at various instances very vivid descriptions of both places.

Man's relationship with God has already partly been illustrated by God's benevolent disposition toward him and his judgment on the last day. But there are some other aspects touched upon in the Qur'an. The very complexity of the relationship is captured by the different ways in which God speaks to man. The Qur'an uses alternately not only "I" or "We," but sometimes also "Your Lord" or "He." The earlier-mentioned intimacy can also be recognized in the instances in which God made a covenant with man, the first one with Adam. But, ever since Adam, man has tended to forget about this commitment to God.

This forgetfulness is also very important for the Qur'anic concept of sin. There is no mention of primordial sin; instead, the Qur'an always speaks of this forgetfulness. Consequently, man needs to be reminded. For this reason, God has repeatedly sent messengers as "warners." Prayer is also mentioned as a way of reminding man, encouraging him to pay constant attention to more ultimate concerns. Another term used in this respect is the "straying" of men, again an image that bears a direct relation to the experiential world in which the Qur'an was sent down. Probably the clearest illustration of man's dependence on God is the presentation of this relationship in terms of Lord (*rabb*) and servant or slave (*abd*). Both the legal and mystical traditions of Islam have given detailed and divergent elaborations of this relationship.

Apart from mankind, the Qur'an also features other creatures. Angels are frequently mentioned; they are created and subordinate beings who often act as God's intermediaries. The only ones mentioned by name are Gabriel and Michael. Along with the angels, there is another mysterious being, "the spirit" (*rûh*). It is associated with three occasions in the Qur'an: the creation of Adam; the descent of the prophecy; and the Day of Reckoning.

Contrasting with the angels are the demons. They are on the side of the unbelievers and lead man astray. The demon *par excellence* is the Devil or Satan (*Shaytân*). He is identified as the fallen angel who refused to worship, and is also called *Iblis*. An intermediate category is formed by the jinn (genies). These shadowy spirits were already part of the Arabs' pre-Islamic world of experience. Jinn are neither entirely good nor evil, and are vaguely feared. A madman (*majnûn*), for example, is assumed to be possessed by a jinn, and they are also thought to inspire poets and *kâhins*, which might explain Muhammad's hostility towards poet and his objection to being called a *kâhin*.

The Qur'an does make explicit reference to what became the dogmas of Islam and the tradition's key practices, which will be discussed in the next section. A final word needs to be said about the translation of the Qur'an. Muslim scholars hold the view that although the translation of the Qur'an into other languages than Arabic is permissible, these translations do not hold the same authority as the original. Instead they are regarded as "interpretations," helping those who have no (proper) command of Arabic to understand the teachings. This rather rigid stand is related to the Muslim view of the status of the Qur'an as God's Word that was mentioned at the beginning.

BASIC TEACHINGS AND RITUALS IN ISLAM

The basic principles on which the Islamic faith rests are encapsulated in the so-called Five Pillars of Islam. This figure of speech is derived from a saying of the Prophet transmitted through the Caliph Umar (r. 634–644). These Five Pillars are:

1. The confession of faith or Creed (*Shahada*)
2. The regular observation of the five daily prayers (*Salat*)
3. The offering of welfare alms (*Zakat*)
4. The performance of the pilgrimage to Mecca (Hajj)
5. The fasting during the month of Ramadan (Ramadan or *saum*)

It is important to notice that four out of these five tenets are actions rather than dogmas. Islam is something one does, and being a Muslim implies a certain way of life. In more technical theological terms, Islam can be qualified as an orthopraxis rather than an orthodoxy. All five pillars are regarded as both acts of worship and moral imperatives. They provide the general outline for a commitment to a faith and regulation of behavior. Although they are usually presented in the above order, the pillars do not occur in any fixed sequence in the Qur'an or Traditions of the Prophet. However, the first three are already mentioned in the early Meccan Suras.

Shahada

The Muslim Creed, or *Shahada* (Arabic for "bearing witness"), is the most succinct formulation of the Islamic faith. It is a very simple formula that consists of two statements: "I witness that there is no god but God, and I witness that Muhammad is the messenger of God." Pronouncing it twice in the presence of two Muslims is generally considered sufficient to convert to Islam. The first statement, originally directed against Arabian polytheism, affirms the oneness of God. The second acknowledges the prophethood of Muhammad and testifies that his revelation (the Qur'an) is divine in origin—a belief that set the new community apart from the Jews and Christians. Nowhere in the Qur'an does the *Shahada* occur in its exact composite form, but the first part of it can be found in Sura 37:35. Nearest to the full Creed comes an exhortation in Sura 7:158, "Believe then in God, and in His Messenger." The importance of the notions expressed by this Creed is further underscored by the fact that it is part of the official call to prayer.

Salat

The regular observance of prayer or *Salat* was the first practice to be instituted. The Qur'an spoke initially of only two daily prayers; at dawn and after sunset. Later it was increased to five, to be performed at dawn, noon, mid-afternoon, sunset, and evening. Muhammad himself is credited with finally fixing the ritual. The prayer must be performed in a clean place—the best being a designated place of worship or so-called mosque (the English corruption of the Arabic word "*masjid*"). A suitable place at home is acceptable as well, but in case one is forced to pray in an unclean place, like a street, the prayer is performed on a prayer rug. The only prayer for which the Muslim must attend a mosque is the noon prayer on Friday, the Islamic day of rest. The Muslim himself must also be in a personal state of purity before performing the prayer. For this purpose he or she is required to complete a ritual ablution. As a minimum this requires the symbolic cleaning of feet, hands, lower arms, the head, and rinsing of the mouth. This ritual cleansing is supposedly based on Zoroastrian practices of purification.

The actual prayer ritual is strictly prescribed as well, and it is assumed that in defining it Muhammad drew his inspiration from Christian choir chants. Positioning himself with his face towards Mecca, the Muslim places himself in a state of sacredness by exclaiming *"Allahu Akbar"* ("God is Great"); standing up, the hands slightly raised with the palms up, he then often recites the opening Sura of the Qur'an. Then follows a sequence of bowings, standing upright, and prostrations. Such a sequence is called a *rak'a*, and the number of *rak'as* that must be done varies depending on which of the daily prayers is being performed. The prayer ends with a final supplication and the traditional Islamic greeting: "Peace and God's benevolence be upon you."

Zakat

Of the Five Pillars of Islam, the obligation of alms-giving is clearly the one with the most explicit dimension of social justice. However, it is very important to realize that *Zakat*, although indeed a social duty, it is also considered an act of worship with a spiritual aspect, because the term means "purification" in Arabic. It is levied from those Muslims with means to spare and is paid out to those in need. It became not only a tool for the redistribution of wealth but also a means to safeguard the psychological integrity of both giver and recipient. Islam discourages begging, and through *Zakat* the poor are spared this humiliation. At the same time, it raises the affluent person's awareness of selfishness, greed, and attachment to material possessions that are inherent in human nature.

The inclusion of such a practical social duty among the fundamental religious principles of Islam is often attributed to Muhammad's personal experience of poverty in his youth. The fact that the earliest converts were all individuals from the poor and oppressed strata of Meccan society was most likely relevant as well.

Admonitions to the faithful to donate part of their wealth to the needy are already found in the Meccan revelations, but the obligation was further detailed and developed on the basis of the so-called Traditions of the Prophet. Because of the way it was later institutionalized, *Zakat* has often been described as a kind of taxation system. Although this may be the form in which it was eventually implemented, from a religious perspective it should be rather regarded as a "loan to God," which God will repay manifold. Originally, those entitled to receive the proceeds were the destitute, the needy, recently freed slaves, debtors, travelers, and those "in the way of Allah" – an expressing referring to all kinds of actions that lead to the enhancement of the religion. In the present day, many Muslim countries have incorporated instruments for the levying and disimbursement of *Zakat* into their bureaucratic systems.

Ramadan and *Saum*

The observation of one month of fasting during the ninth month of the lunar calendar, named Ramadan, is usually referred to under that term, although the actual practice of abstention is called *saum*. During this period, the Muslim must abstain from eating, drinking, and sexual intercourse from sunrise to sunset. Exempted are children, the sick and the infirm, women who have just given birth or who are breast-feeding, and travelers. The purpose of fasting is both disciplinary – namely, to increase the awareness of one's bodily needs and how to control them – and admonitory, reminding the Muslim of God's providence. By combining God-consciousness, striving for the good, practicing virtue, and demonstrating piety, it helps to underscore the importance of ethical integrity.

Although a matter of personal discipline, Ramadan also greatly enhances the Muslims' sense of community because it is performed jointly by the believers across the world. Furthermore, the breaking of the fast after sunset is done in the circle of the family or in the mosque. The pious will use this month-long period also as an opportunity to recite the entire Qur'an, which for this very purpose has been divided into thirty portions. On the evening of the last day of fasting, the Ramadan is concluded with the sacrificial slaughter of a lamb. This celebratory event is known as "the Feast of the Breaking" (*'Id al-Fitr*).

Apart from the practice of fasting, the month of Ramadan is also considered sacred by the Muslims for historical reasons. It will be recalled that the first revelation descended upon Muhammad during this very month, while he was meditating in a cave outside Mecca. The battle at Badr (624) and the final conquest of Mecca (630) also took place in the month of Ramadan.

Hajj

The final pillar is the pilgrimage to Mecca, or Hajj, which every Muslim who possesses the means has to perform at least one time in his life. In fact, there are two kinds of pilgrimages. There is the "lesser pilgrimage," or *umra*, modelled after the first time Muhammad revisited Mecca in 628, and which can be performed year-round, and there is the actual Hajj, involving much more elaborate rituals based on the Prophet's farewell pilgrimage in the year of his death.

The Hajj takes place during the twelfth month of the lunar calendar, called Dhu'l-Hijja, and consists of five days of rituals. Before commencing the actual pilgrimage, the Muslim must assume a state of ritual purity, which is called *ihrâm*. For this purpose the pilgrim dresses in specific dress. For men it consists

369

of a white loincloth and shoulder cloth of unseamed cotton, leaving the right shoulder exposed. Women cover themselves head to toe in white, leaving only the face and hands uncovered. While in the state of *ihrâm* it is also not permitted to cut one's hair or nails, have sexual intercourse, or engage in hunting.

Upon arrival in Mecca, the pilgrims first perform the *tawâf;* seven times they circumambulate the *Ka'ba,* which stands on the square of the Grand Mosque of Mecca. During this ritual, the Muslims will try to touch the black stone that is enshrined in a corner of the structure. This stone is believed to be a remnant of Abraham's altar of sacrifice. The ritual is concluded with two *rak'as.* This is followed by the *sa'y,* literally "the running." Adjacent to the square of the Grand Mosque there are two hillocks, named Marwa and Safa, and the pilgrims must briskly walk seven times between these two hills. This ritual is based on the story of Abraham. It is believed that, after having been evicted from Abraham's tent, the slave woman Hagar and her son Ismail nearly perished here from thirst. The *sa'y* symbolizes Hagar's frantic attempt to find water, scanning the horizon from the top of Marwa and Safa, only to be saved by the miraculous appearance of a well named Zamzam.

After performing these two acts, the only ones required for the *umra,* the actual Hajj rituals commence. On the seventh day of Dhu al-Hijja, a sermon is given in the Grand Mosque of Mecca and the next day the pilgrims make their way to the Plain of Mina, which lies some ten kilometers outside Mecca. Here the Muslims assemble to proceed to the Plain of Arafat, at a distance of some 25 kilometers from Mecca. Here the climax of the Hajj takes place on the ninth day. This event is called *wuqûf* ("the standing"); the Muslims jointly stand all day in prayer and meditation, continuously exclaiming the formula "*Labaika Allah*" — "Here I am standing in front of you, God." Many pilgrims try to scramble onto the Hill of Mercy. Tradition has it that from that elevation, Muhammad delivered his sermon during the Farewell Pilgrimage. For the Muslim pilgrim this is a deeply emotional event, as he experiences himself to be in the closest possible proximity to the Creator. At sunset, the participants move back in the direction of Mecca and spend the night near a place called Muzdalifa.

On the tenth day, the Muslims assemble again at Mina, where the sacrificial slaughter of sheep or goats is performed. All Muslims the world over perform this rite on this same day, which is known as "the Feast of the Sacrifice" (*'Id al-Adha*). Just prior to that, the pilgrims assemble around a location where three stone colums have been erected and pelt these colums with pebbles. This is a symbolic stoning of the Devil, by which one sheds oneself of sin. As a final act of purification, male pilgrims now shave their heads. On the eleventh day, the Muslims finally return to Mecca, where in the meantime the *Ka'ba* has been decorated with a new *kiswa*, the enormous black cloth that covers the entire structure and which is embroided in gold with texts from the Qur'an. Patches of the old one are distributed among the Muslims to be taken home as a souvenirs. Most pilgrims also take copious quantities of Zamzam water with them. Not only did it save Ismail's life, but the Muslims also ascribe it with healing qualities.

Nothing symbolizes the sense of community among Muslims more than the pilgrims' experience of performing Hajj together with—nowadays—an estimated two million other faithful from virtually every nation in the world. After completing the Hajj, numerous Muslims also make a visit to Medina where, in the Mosque of the Prophet, they pay their respects at Muhammad's grave.

Although taking place at a site that used to be the center of Arabia's pagan traditions, the various acts performed during the Hajj are now regarded as Islam's most explicit connection with the very origins of the three great monotheistic traditions of the world.

A "Sixth Pillar": Jihad

The message of Islam is intended for all mankind and as such it makes a claim of universal validity, creating an obligation to spread Islam. This missionary obligation is considered a collective duty for the Muslims rather than an individual one. That is why it is not enumerated with the other pillars of Islam, which are all obligations resting on each and every Muslim individually.

Spreading Islam is expressed in the formula to "exert oneself on the Way of Allah," also shortened to the infinitive of the pertaining Arabic verb, jihad. This spread of Islam can take place by means of the tongue, the pen, and the sword. Muslims must try to convince the unbelievers by peaceful means, but if they are unsuccessful it may be permissible to take recourse to violence. To vindicate this a reference is made to one Qur'an verse in particular: "Fight them, till there is no persecution and the religion is God's entirely" (8:39). And yet the Qu'ran also asserts, "Let there be no compulsion in religion" (2:256).

It is not absolutely clear if the Qur'an intended to allow fighting the unbelievers only as a defence against aggression. Support for this view is given by another Qur'an verse: "And fight in the way of God with those who fight with you, but aggress not: God loves not the aggressors. And slay them wherever you come upon them, and expel them from where they expelled you; persecution is more grievous than slaying." (2:190-191).

In these Qur'an texts, the word used for fighting is "*qatl*" ("killing") not "jihad" ("to exert oneself"). It is assumed that this former term is a reflection of a concept of warfare inspired by the experiences of Muhammad and his early Muslim community in their fights with the Meccans. However, the later formulation of a more clearly defined war policy was also influenced by another element. It must not be forgotten that in pre-Islamic times, war among the tribes was the normal state of affairs. An important source of income for the Bedouins was the so-called *ghazw*—a raid or lightning attack on the possessions of a neighboring tribe. For the newly formed Muslim community and its allies, such practices could no longer be condoned, but for economic reasons it was considered expedient to somehow accommodate this practice anyway.

When Islam started to expand in the course of the first century of its existence, legal scholars started working on the formulation of a jihad doctrine, taking into consideration the prescriptions of the Qur'an along with existing customary law. This doctrine dealt with behavior during hostilities, hostage taking, spoils of war, and so on, but also with what could be called international relations. Important in connection with this last aspect was the division of the world into those parts that had surrendered or had been conquered—the Abode of Islam (*Dar al-Islam*) and those still resisting—the Abode of War (*Dar al-Harb*). As history progressed, Islamic expansion stalled and eventually halted, rendering this concept of Muslim and non-Muslim relations increasingly irrelevant. However, in more recent times, the jihad doctrine has received a new interpretation and meaning, gaining again in relevance and notoriety, with some Islamists using it to justify terrorism and violence against non-Muslims.

It is worth noting, however, that for many Muslims, the concept of jihad also refers to the *inner* struggle "to exert oneself in the Way of Allah"—to fight against evil and temptation in oneself, to follow the "straight path" and do God's will. Abdullah Yusuf Ali, a twentieth-century Muslim scholar of the

Qur'an, wrote of jihad: "It may require fighting in Allah's cause, as a form of self-sacrifice. But its essence consists in (1) a true and sincere Faith, which so fixes its gaze on Allah, that all selfish or worldly motives seem paltry and fade away, and (2) in earnest and ceaseless activity, involving the sacrifice (if need be) of life, person, or property, in the service of Allah. Mere brutal fighting is opposed to the whole spirit of *Jihad*, while the sincere scholar's pen or preacher's voice or wealthy man's contributions may be the most valuable forms of *Jihad*."[7]

THE ARTICULATION OF ISLAM

With the Five Pillars, the edifice called Islam was by no means complete. The further shaping of the Islamic religious tradition would to a large extent be dictated by political events during the first century after the Prophet's death, in 632 C.E. This was a stormy period marred by crises of political legitimacy and religious authority, and its consequences influenced the development of Islamic law, theology, and sectarianism. These three areas would in turn affect each other and are therefore extremely difficult to disentangle. Before attempting a brief characterization of these domains of Islam's intellectual structure, it is necessary to give a brief historical overview of that first century of the Islamic era.

Following Muhammad's death, a still relatively small Muslim community elected a successor or *khalifa* (from which comes the English "caliph") to take over Muhammad's political responsibilities, but not his position as a Prophet. The first four successors, the so-called Righteous Caliphs, all came from Muhammad's immediate environment and belonged to his most intimate circle of close Companions. However, the fact that three out of four met with violent deaths was a foreboding of future dissent and rifts within the community. The first caliph, Abu Bakr, was Muhammad's close confidant and the father of the Prophet's favorite wife in later days, Aisha. He ruled for barely two years and was mainly occupied with bringing the Bedouins back under the sway of Islam, which they had deserted after Muhammad's death. Under the stern Umar (634–644), Islam started its expansion outside the Arabian Peninsula, the key prize being the capture of Jerusalem. Umar was murdered by a Persian slave.

Things started to unravel under the third caliph, Uthman (644-656). A member of Mecca's leading clan, the Umayya, he was murdered during an uprising amid accusations of nepotism, and a split occurred over his succession. Ali ibn Abu Talib, Muhammad's cousin and son-in-law, became the fourth caliph but was soon challenged by Uthman's relative, Mu'awiya, who was the governor of Syria. Civil war was constantly in the air, and after Ali's murder in 661, Mu'awiya proclaimed himself Caliph, shifting the capital to Damascus, which became the seat of the so-called Umayyad Caliphate (661–750).

Under the Umayyads, the character of the Islamic state changed; succession became hereditary and the caliphate started to resemble a kind of Arab kingship. As the Islamic state expanded, incorporating increasing numbers of non-Arab subjects, the emphasis on their Arabian heritage eventually became the Umayyads' undoing. A rebellion of Persian converts and disaffected Arab migrants broke out in northeastern Persia. Rallying around the descendants of Muhammad's uncle al-Abbas, they brought the Umayyads down in 750 and established the Abbasid Caliphate. The empire's power base shifted further east, and soon Baghdad was established as the new capital. Islam now entered its "golden age." Although its power would be on the wane from the eleventh century onward, the Abbasid dynasty lasted until 1258. It was during the first two centuries of its rule that core elements of Islamic civilization took shape.

ISLAMIC LAW

Unhappy with what they regarded as abuse of power and a drifting away from Muhammad's original mission under the Umayyads, a certain class of people that could be described as an intelligentsia began to ponder ways to safeguard the integrity of the Islamic teachings. It will be recalled that Islam is an orthopraxis, in which regulating behavior holds central importance. With the growing complexity of Islamic society as a result of the expansion of territory and incorporation of different peoples, this was to be a daunting task.

During the period of the Righteous Caliphs and the Umayyads, two processes had taken place. In administering the empire, rulers were taking existing customs and laws of various regions into consideration, while sincere and learned Muslims endeavored to work out an ideal system of human conduct. These two processes were not wholly different from each other, but in the early phases they remained broadly separate. With the coming of the Abbasids, that situation changed. A concerted effort was undertaken to develop a structured formulation of the Islamic teachings on the basis of its two key sources. The scholars involved in this process came to be known as *ulamâ* ("the learned").

The first and incontestable basis of authority was of course the Qur'an, but next to that another source had developed: the so-called Traditions of the Prophet or Sunna. This concept of tradition was not new; in the past, Arabia's tribes had all had their own codes of conduct also called sunnas. With the formation of the Muslim community, the sayings and practices of Muhammad and his first generation of followers, the

Companions, became the model for an Islamic Sunna. The Traditions of the Prophet found their particular shape in short stories relating illustrative episodes of Muhammad's conduct during his life. Such a story was called a Hadith and already during the Umayyad Caliphate such stories were incorporated into biographies of the Prophet. Originally transmitted orally, they were increasingly put into writing as well.

This body of Traditions became the second-most important source for what could be called legislation. Under the Abbasids, the contours of this rather fluid situation started to become more fixed. The creation of a centralized and bureaucratically ruled state demanded agreement on how the society was to be regulated. At the time, the religious experts were still holding varying views. The most influential scholar in Iraq, Abu Hanifa (699–767), allowed for a certain amount of individual reasoning (*ray'*) by the learned in addition to the Qur'an and Sunna, while the Medina-based Malik ibn Affan (715–795) insisted on the primacy of the practices of the early Muslim community.

A decisive step in defining the relations between the different bases for legal decisions was taken by another scholar, al-Shafi'i (767–820), who lived in Egypt. He considered the Qur'an and the Sunna to be equally infallible, and the two could not contradict each other. Apparent contradictions were to be reconciled or resolved by regarding later Qur'an verses or sayings as effectively abrogating earlier deviating ones. But what remained, of course, was the question of interpretation. The way to avoid error was the use of human reason within very strict limits. For this, al-Shafi'i insisted on using the method of reasoning by analogy or *qiyas*, which meant finding an element in the situation that was questioned which could be compared against a similar element in an earlier situation on which a ruling already existed. This disciplined way of interpretation would come to be known under the technical term *ijtihad*.

This whole process of scholarly thought was known as *fiqh* — jurisprudence — and the product that came out of it was ultimately called Shari'a, usually translated as "Islamic Law." Gradually, the scholars engaging in this discipline could be grouped into various "schools" of moral and legal inter-pretation. These schools became known as *madhhabs*, and by the eleventh century, there had developed four schools that would survive to the present day and which are all still regarded as authoritative in Sunni Islam. They were named after the earliest writers to which they traced their descent. Later-day historical developments made one or another dominant in the various geographical regions that constitute the Islamic world.

The Hanafi school (after Abu Hanifa) is found in Western and Central Asia, the Indian subcontinent, and Lower Egypt; the Malikis (after Malik ibn Affan) dominate in North and West Africa as well as Upper Egypt and most of the Gulf States; the Shafi'is (following al-Shafi'i) are well established in Indonesia and Malaysia, parts of Egypt, Syria and Lebanon, Iraq and Yemen; the Hanbali school (after Ahmad ibn Hanbal) is the official legal doctrine in Saudi Arabia and Qatar, and also holds a few pockets elsewhere in the Islamic world.

The differences between these schools are mainly due to the degree of flexibility in the use of *ijtihad*. Where Qur'an, Sunna or analogy-reasoning (*qiyas*) still leave loopholes, the consensus of religious scholars — called *ijma'* — may be used to close such gaps. The Hanafis tend to be the most flexible in that respect, and the Hanbalis, who accept only the *ijtihad* of the Companions of the Prophet, the most restrictive.

Gradually, the scholars of these various schools drew up codes of conduct that were supposed to cover all human acts.

These law books were most exact with regard to the acts of worship contained in the Five Pillars of Islam. The ritual obligations were minutely described on the basis of the Sunna. Next came the regulation of human interaction, with a particular focus on man's most intimate relations. Family law had already been a prime concern for Muhammad, and there are detailed guidelines with regards to marriage, divorce, inheritance, and the guardianship of children. Much less defined is what could be called commercial and public law. Relations outside the direct sphere of the family are assumed to be regulated on a contractual basis, with a few more detailed stipulations regarding the pursuit of profit and the creation of religious endowments. Contrary to what is often assumed, the Shari'a has not much to say on criminal law, with the exception of certain prescribed punishments pertaining to adultery, the drinking of wine, and theft (the notorious cutting off of the hands of thieves). The Shari'a says virtually nothing on "constitutional" or administrative law.

An often repeated maxim is that from the tenth century onwards, the "door of *ijtihad* was closed" — meaning that there could be no further exercise of individual judgment on issues on which a general consensus had been established. But there is no clear evidence that this precept was ever formulated in such exact terms and generally accepted. Up to the present day, the respective Law Schools still recognize an institution called mufti (jurisconsult), held by scholars who are known for their learning. Muftis can issues opinions, called fatwas, on issues of dispute. In the course of history such fatwas were incorporated in authoritative books of *fiqh* to provide future guidance to rulers and judges. In numerous Muslim countries, the office of mufti is still a (semi) official position within the religious bureaucracy.

THEOLOGY AND PHILOSOPHY

The Sunna was important as a source of law, but within the Islamic teaching its position was more complex than that. The Traditions also had a bearing on what could be called "theology." This led to the emergence of another religious science: Hadith criticism. It so happened that those involved in the great controversies over authority tried to find support for their positions in the Sunna, so that by the eight and ninth centuries, the body of sayings attributed to the Prophet had greatly expanded. A movement of criticism therefore emerged with the aim of distinguishing the true from the false. The main attention of scholars who took the critical scrutiny of Hadiths as their task was given to the so-called chains of witnesses. Hadiths consist namely of two parts: the actual story and a preceding list of names of persons credited with transmitting that specific story, going back to a Companion of Muhammad who had actually witnessed the event or heard the words. Such a sequence is called *isnad*.

The *isnad* became the main criteria for determining the reliability of these Hadiths and classification. The two great collections of Hadiths that eventually became authoritative were those composed by the scholars al-Bukhari (810–870) and Muslim (817–875). Because this duo only accepted those stories of whose truth they were sure, their collections became known as the *Sahih*, "The Healthy," with the highest grade of reliability.

Another important religious science was the exegesis of the sacred scripture, the Qur'an. This discipline is known under the technical term *Tafsir*, which means "explanation." As we have seen, because the Qur'an was revealed in Arabic, that language came to be regarded as an intrinsic aspect of the revelation. To correctly understand the Qur'an, a solid and detailed knowledge of the Arabic language was considered essential. Arabic grammar became not only a core part of Islamic education, but in the study and exegesis of the Qur'an the emphasis was also put on the lexical and grammatical aspects of the text. Consequently, *Tafsirs* contain detailed linguistic commentaries on the Qur'an text. Over time, a number of such *Tafsirs* became authoritative works of reference and were made part of the curriculum for the education of scholars.

But apart from these textual sciences, there were also more philosophical matters that needed to be addressed. In that same first century after the Abbasids, take-over debates took place on important questions such as: on what conditions somebody could be considered a Muslim, the issues of predestination and free will, and whether the Qur'an was eternal or created. Participating in these discussions was the same class of learned men who were involved in developing Islam's legal system, the *ulamâ*. They found themselves not only at loggerheads with each other, but often also with state authority. Over time, a plethora of movements, schools, and sects developed, but a more general divide could be detected between those who chose to stay as close as possible to the texts of the scriptures and those who wanted to employ new learning, such as that derived from Greek philosophy, to which the Muslims became exposed as their realm grew.

In the middle of the ninth century, things became very politicized when the Caliph al-Ma'mun declared the theories of a philosophical school inspired by Greek thought, called the Mu'tazila, to be the official doctrine. A key element in this doctrine was the dogma that the Qur'an was created; the Mu'tazila's rationalist approach proposed a more logical conclusion than an eternal Qur'an. The latter was namely problematic in view of the absolute oneness of God and also because man was held responsible for his actions. An eternal Qur'an predetermining everything would therefore be contradictory. Between 833 and 848, this belief resulted in the persecution of those scholars who refused to subscribe to the Mu'tazila doctrine. The most prominent of those opposed was Ahmad ibn Hanbal (780-855), eponymous founder of the Hanbali Law School. Ibn Hanbal's views appear somewhat contradictory. On the one hand he was very scrupulous in his ethics, insisting on strict adherence to the Shari'a; on the other hand, he was very reluctant to label transgressors as apostates. He also advocated a strict adherence to the literal meaning of the Qur'an and Sunna and rejected any philosophical speculations.

Although the Mu'tazila would survive well into the tenth and eleventh centuries, there was a gradual shift away from their rationalist approach. Two key figures that set the course of Islamic theology for centuries to come were al-Ash'ari (873–935) and al-Ghazâli (1058–1111). The first is credited with finding a middle road between Mu'tazila speculation and Hanbali scripturalism, although more careful historical research has shown that his reputation as one of the greatest theologians of Islam is actually the result of the appreciation accorded to him by later-day tradition. The form of theology of which he is considered the founder is called *Kalâm*, an Islamic form of scholastic philosophy. A core element of this line of thought is adherence to the text and acceptance of what is said there. If the Qur'an describes God by using human attributes, the faithful must take that at face value, in spite of the inherent tension with texts referring to God's oneness or describing God as the supreme being, "without asking how" (*bila kayf* in Arabic). Most important is not to quarrel in religion. The formulation of this theology was more likely the result of an extended process than the work of one man. Moreover, its often cramped attempts to reconcile Qur'anic teachings with reason remained for a long time suspect in the eyes of more legalistically oriented scholars.

At the close of this era of high Scholasticism stands the figure of al-Ghazâli, whose influence on Islamic learning is virtually uncontested. In his magisterial *Ihyâ' 'Ulûm al-Dîn (Revivification of the Sciences of Religion)*, he dealt with all important questions of faith and religious practices, as well as the causes of spiritual decay and salvation. The purpose of his work was to find a synthesis between religious learning and practice, including spirituality and mysticism. His other famous work, *Tâhafut al-Falâsifa (Refutation of Philosophy)*, was an attack on the continuation of rationalist philosophies and would lead to the final demise of speculative philosophical thinking in most parts of the Islamic world.

SCHISM AND SECTARIANISM

As mentioned earlier, the succession of the third caliph, Uthman, had been extremely controversial, eventually leading to the great schism in Islam between Sunnis and Shi'is. The name Sunni for the majority group does not imply that the Shi'is reject the Traditions of the Prophet out of hand. What lies at the base of the conflict are divergent views of history.

For the Sunnis, it is all important that the Muslims live together in peace and unity, implying that the historical course of events must be accepted. Consequently, they recognize all Four Righteous Caliphs as legitimate and also remained loyal to the successive Umayyad and Abbasid Caliphates. Although individual caliphs may not always have acted justly, they should be accepted as legitimate as long as they did not violate the basic commandments of God. Closely connected with this view of history is the status of the caliph. Sunnism in its developed form did not regard the caliph as a prophet or even infallible interpreter of Islam, but merely a leader responsible for safeguarding peace and justice in the community.

But others held very different opinions. The bickering over Uthman's succession led to an early secession by a group called the Kharijites—"those who depart." This was a rather amorphous group that would reoccur at various occasions in Islamic history, whenever a person whom they regarded as unworthy had taken over the leadership of the community. A more specific criticism was leveled by the group that would eventually become know as the Shi'is. These people did not accept the claims of the first three caliphs, but believed that the fourth caliph, Ali ibn Abu Talib, had been the anointed successor from the beginning. Their name is derived from Shi'a *Ali* or "the Party of Ali." Ali was to be the first in a line of successors of the Prophet designated as the sole and infallible interpreters of God's revelations. Instead of caliph they were known by the title imam.

What this entailed was not only that the first three caliphs were regarded as usurpers, but it had the much further-reaching consequence that the external, political history of the Muslims was considered to diverge from a truer, inner history, namely the preservation and transmission of the revealed truth by a line of imams. These imams had to be descendants of Ali through his wife Fatima, Muhammad's daughter. The theory of the imams' infallibility is rather esoteric—the imam is thought to possess hidden knowledge given to him through special communication with God. In addition, the imams are considered to be free of sin.

Shi'i history is not a happy one. Following the murder of Ali, his oldest son, al-Hasan, was maneuvered into renouncing his rights and it fell on his younger brother, al-Husayn, to keep up the claims of the house of Ali. In 680 C.E., Imam al-Husayn was killed in a battle near Kerbela in Iraq. His mutilated body was later buried there and his tomb has become one of the holiest shrines of Shi'i Islam, together with that of his father

Ali in nearby Najaf. Al-Husayn's severed head eventually ended up in the much-revered al-Husayn mosque in Cairo. Every year, al-Husayn's martyrdom is celebrated with a commemoration called *Ashura*, which takes place on the tenth day of Muharram, the first month of the Islamic calendar. The festivities throughout the Shi'i parts of the Islamic world feature passion plays reenacting al-Husayn's death, and acts of self-flagellation as expressions of mourning.

The Shi'is themselves are again subdivided into two major branches. The largest group recognizes a total of twelve imams, the last one of which, Muhammad al-Muntazar, is considered not to have died but to have gone into hiding. This phenomenon is called *ghayba* or "occultation." It is believed that in the fullness of time the "Hidden Imam" will return as the Mahdi—the "Guided One"—and bring about a reign of justice. Because of their recognition of twelve imams, this branch is known as the Twelvers and sometimes also as the Imamis.

A different view is held by a numerically lesser group, known as the Isma'ilis, or Seveners. According to them, the fifth imam, Ja'far al-Sadiq, had designated his son Isma'il as his lawful successor. However, Isma'il died in 760, five years before his father. While the Twelvers decided to recognize Isma'il's brother Musa al-Kazim as the next imam after the death of Imam Ja'far, the Isma'ilis claim that it was Ja'far's intention to be succeeded by Isma'il's son, Muhammad. Therefore the Isma'ilis regard Muhammad as the seventh and last visible imam of the line. To justify this belief, the Isma`ilis devised a detailed cyclical theory of history, according to which mankind had always been in need of divinely guided teachers. There would be seven cycles of such teachers, each beginning with a messenger followed by an interpreter. The latter was charged with revealing the inner meaning of the messenger's revelations. Each interpreter was in turn followed by seven imams, the last one of which would simultaneously be the messenger of the next cycle. But the messenger of the seventh and last era would be the expected Mahdi. In this Isma'ili view, the Prophet Muhammad had been the messenger of the sixth cycle and Ali the interpreter. Here the enumeration of imams by Twelvers and Isma'ilis starts to diverge: for the Twelvers, Ali was the first imam while the Isma'ilis start the line of imams with al-Hasan. In their computation, Muhammad ibn Isma`il would therefore be the seventh imam, first messenger of the seventh cycle and the much anticipated Mahdi. As such he was also considered the *Qa'im al-Qiyama* or Imam of the Day of Resurrection; his era would herald the end of time and human history, once he emerged again from "occultation."

Throughout history, the Isma'ilis have been persecuted by the Sunnis and other Shi'is. Until relatively recently, we only knew about their teachings through the writings of their opponents, who reviled them. From the late eleventh century onward, their reputation was further soiled by the encounters of the crusaders with an Isma'ili spin-off branch that had gained notoriety under the name Assassins. Members of this extremist sect were responsible for the murder of many political figures, supposedly committed while under the influence of narcotics ("assassin" is a corruption of the Arabic *"hashishi"* — someone using hashish or cannabis).

But in the last few decades, many Isma'ili writings have surfaced in Yemen, Central Asia, and India, giving evidence of highly sophisticated and philosophically inclined learning. From these it appears that in the earlier formative years there had been much more interaction with the Mu'tazila and other Greek-inspired philosophers, in particular Neo-platonists, than previously assumed. In the present day, one of the most visible branches of Isma'ili Shi'ism is that of the Nizaris, led by the Aga Khan.

Obtaining a clear picture of Shi'i thought in general has always been complicated by the fact that, in the face of persecution, both Twelvers and Isma'ilis have engaged in a practice called *taqiyya*, which means the dissimulation of one's true beliefs under adverse circumstances. The development, transmission, and spread of Shi'i doctrines therefore took place in utmost secrecy among limited numbers of the initiated. But what has been established is that, after the occultation of their imams, the Twelvers recognized the need for continued interpretation and leadership. From the thirteenth century onward, they would therefore look to men who were competent to interpret the deposit of faith through intellectual effort because of their intellect, character, and education. These men were not considered infallible interpreters and had no direct guidance from God like the imams; instead, they were called *mujtahids*, from the word for interpretation, *ijtihad*.

The same emphasis on the use of human reasoning was applied in the development of a Shi'i school of jurisprudence. Although the principles of Shi'i law are similar to do those of the Sunnis, there are significant differences because of the specific Shi'i view of religion and the world. The only Hadiths considered acceptable are those transmitted through a member of Muhammad's family; in addition to that, Hadiths of the words and deeds of the imams had the same status as those of the Prophet; the only form of consensus (*ijma'*) considered valid is that of communities gathered around the respective infallible imams; interestingly, the use of individual reasoning (called *'aql*) by those competent to do so, namely the *mujtahids*, is an important source of law.

In the Muslim world as a whole, the Shi'is are numerically in the minority, but due to historical circumstances, a few Muslim countries are overwhelmingly Shi'i, while in others they form rather significant minorities. In Iran, Twelver Shi'ism has been the official doctrine since the sixteenth century. Neighboring Iraq is also in majority Shi'i; the south of this country, where the holy cities of Najaf and Kerbela are located, can be considered the cradle of Shi'ism. Significant Shi'i communities can further be found in Lebanon, Afghanistan, India, Pakistan, Bahrain, and to a lesser extent in Syria, Yemen, and Saudi Arabia. Some other breakaway minorities that have their roots in Shi'ism are the Druzes, who have inhabited the mountainous border area between Israel, Lebanon, and Syria; and the Nusayris. A branch of this latter group, known as the Alawis, have held political power in Syria since the military coup of Hafiz al-Asad in 1971. However, this regime is thoroughly secularist in outlook.

SPIRITUAL DIMENSIONS OF ISLAM

In addition to scripturalism and legalism, Islamic religious experience also has a spiritual element to it, the origin of which can be traced back to the Prophet Muhammad himself. Both Qur'an and Traditions contain a multitude of indications that Muhammad was deeply spiritual and in close communion with God. Apart from the circumstances and the nature of the earliest Mecca revelations, there is also evidence of another explicit mystical experience. Sura 17 of the Qur'an relates the story of Muhammad's nocturnal journey to Jerusalem, the so-called *Isra'*, in which the Prophet is said to have traveled instantly from the Ka'ba to Jerusalem on a mythical mount named Buraq. From Jerusalem he then ascended to the seventh heaven to be shown signs from God.

On a more general level, instances pointing to the special relationship between God and man are provided by the earlier-mentioned expression of God being "nearer to him [man] than his jugular vein" (50.16), and the covenant made with man even before creation according to Sura 7:172: "'Am I not your Lord?' They said, 'Yes, we testify.'"

A number of Muhammad's closest Companions are credited with being predecessors of the later mystical tradition of Islam known as Sufism (*tasawwuf*), the practitioners of which are called Sufis. The name is thought have been derived from the woolen cloaks they usually wore (from the Arabic word for wool, "*suf*"). Two of such early key figures, prefiguring important aspects of future Sufism, were Abu Dharr, who rejected all wordly possessions, and Salman al-Farsi, a Persian convert who stood as a model for spiritual adoption and mystical initiation, which became a feature of later mystical orders.

By the end of the eighth century, the mystical tradition was already showing a number of possible ways in which it was to develop. The patriarch of Sufism, Hasan al-Basri (642–728), was deeply steeped in sadness and fear over man's sinful nature and dependence on God. The story of Ibrahim al-Adham (d. 790) echoes elements of the Buddha legend; he was the first to make a classification of the various stages of asceticism. Although Muhammad was against any form of monasticism in Islam, it is thought that the Christian hermitic tradition served as an important inspiration for Sufism. The first example of a deep mystical love for God, and the poetic expression thereof, is provided by the female mystic Rabi'a al-Adawiyya (d. 801).

In the early stages of the Abbasid Caliphate, Sufism showed an interesting parallel to the development of Islamic legal and theological thinking, as attempts were made to intellectualize the mystical experience. While advocating sober adherence to the Shari'a, two Sufis from Baghdad endeavored to describe man's relationship with God beyond obedience and to articulate ways to come to know God. Al-Muhasibi (786–857) was very much preoccupied with defining Sufism in psychological terms for which he developed a highly technical language that would form the basis for future Sufi vocabulary. Al-Junayd (d. 920) systematized Sufi experience further, and most initiation chains of later Sufi orders start with him.

While al-Muhasibi and al-Junayd were firmly rooted in the Sunni tradition, other Sufis took the experience of God one step further. Abu Yazid al-Bistami (803–874) stands at the beginning of ecstatic Sufism. Combining the firm belief in God's oneness with an intense commitment to surrender oneself completely to God, the practitioner can experience an extinguishing of the individual self and a sense of communion with God, called *fana'*. For the experience of God's presence, another term was later used as well, namely: *baqa'*. But the culmination of this identification with God is found in the figure of al-Hallaj (858–922), who was executed on grounds of heresy because, enraptured by his mystical experience of God, he is reported to have exclaimed, "*Ana al-Haqq*" — "I am Truth [God]."

Serious and concerned Muslims were aware of the dangers of the mystical path, and therefore it was thought to be necessary to accept the teaching of someone more advanced on the path. Those providing such guidance toward a spiritual life were called shaykhs or *murshids*. By the eleventh century, those following the same master began to identify themselves as members of one spiritual family moving along the same path, called *tariqa*. Later these groups received a more structured organization, and from the twelfth and thirteenth centuries, the emergence of Sufi orders (also called *tariqas*) can be discerned. Some of them would become very widespread, the most prominent being the Rifa'iyya, the Qadiriyya, and the Shadhiliyya. These orders differed in view regarding how to proceed on the mystical path. The more sober orders taught that even when achieving self-annihilation and mystical vision, the Sufi was still bound by the Shari'a and expected to return to the world of everyday activity, while others remained intoxicated with the perceived presence of God and henceforth chose a life in solitude.

What most orders shared was a certain process of initiation, consisting of taking an oath of allegiance to the shaykh, and receiving from him a special cloak and the communication of a secret prayer. A common ritual in most orders was the *dhikr*, the communal repetition of the word for God, "Allah." The exact performance differed in each order; while some orders opted for a silent recitation, others combined the exclamation of Allah's name with special breathing techniques (as in the Nakhsbandi order), singing, or even dance. The most famous representatives of this last practice are the so-called "whirling dervishes," or, more correctly, the Mevlevis (*Mawlawiyya*), who originate from Turkey.

Following the mystical path has not prevented the Muslim from simultaneously engaging in legal or other scholarly activities. Many theologians and jurists have been practicing Sufis and initiates of Sufi orders. While mainstream Muslims in some parts of the world remain suspicious of Sufism, in other areas of the world the practice of Islam is permeated with Sufi influences. And in recent years, as shaykhs have traveled to the West and once-secret, esoteric information has become more readily available, Sufism has taken hold in the West. Even secular culture has been exposed to Sufism: in recent years, the most widely read poet in the United States has been Jelaludin Rumi, the thirteenth-century Sufi saint who founded the Mevlevi order and wrote thousands of pages of ecstatic poetry.

In addition to its expression in Sufism, the notion of the nearness of God to man also found expression in another way. The Qur'an contains statements that would justify the possibility that certain men have the potential to become God's "friend" (*wali*). From this understanding, a notion of sainthood (*wilaya*) started to emerge. These "friends of God" had the power to intercede on behalf of others, and such signs of grace (*karama*) were regarded as proof of their sanctity. Thus developed an Islamic folk tradition of saint reveration, usually centered around the burial sites of such saints. Here a parallel may be drawn with the incorporation of the Ka'ba into Islamic tradition by giving it new meaning. Likewise, new converts brought their own commemoration cults with them; the association of certain places with the presence of gods or other superhuman entities is a practice that is as widespread as it is ancient, and would continue in an Islamic context. The tombs of some Muslim saints became the sites of great public liturgical acts that went far beyond the local — for example, the tombs of Abu Midyan in Algeria, Ahmad al-Badawi in Egypt, or Moulay Idris in Morocco. The descendants of such saints or the guardians of their tombs could also profit from the saint's reputation, giving them prestige as well as wealth, and — not infrequently — even political power.

ISLAM AND THE MODERN WORLD: RESPONSE AND REFORM

Islamic history from the thirteenth century onward is often generalized as a period of stagnation. After such giants as al-Ghazâli and philosophers like Ibn Sina (980–1037) and Ibn Rushd (1126–1198), who, as Avicenna and Averröes, were even known in medieval Christendom, truly pathbreaking thinkers would indeed be few and far between. However, two later medieval scholars stand out. The ideas of the jurist Ibn Taymiyya (1263–1328) regarding the importance of safeguarding the unity of the Muslims and righteousness of the rulers would continue to exercise influence over later generations of reformist thinkers. The statesman and historian

Ibn Khaldun (1332–1406) has been called a founding father of modern history writing and the social sciences.

In spite of the fact that intellectual progress had stalled in later Middle Ages, in subsequent centuries figures endeavoring to reinvigorate Islam would continue to emerge. One such reform attempt was made in the middle of the eighteenth century by Muhammad ibn Abd al-Wahhab (1703–1792), a *qadi* or judge from Central Arabia, who was disgusted by the sorry state of Islam on the Arabian Peninsula, the very cradle of the religion. Analyzing the situation, he concluded that this was the result of the Muslims' straying from the Righteous Path, and the remedy he prescribed was a return to the sources of Islam. Only uncompromising adherence to the literal meaning of the Qur'an and Traditions of the Prophet could save Islam. For this position he found support in the writings of Ahmad ibn Hanbal and Ibn Taymiyya.

Ibn Abd al-Wahhab succeeded in forging an alliance with a local political leader, Muhammad ibn Saud. Combining Ibn Saud's military might with ibn Abd al-Wahhab's ideological fervor, a powerful movement rose up in the deep interior of Arabia that would conquer nearly the entire peninsula within a generation from its emergence. The crowning event was the conquest of Mecca and Medina in the beginning of the nineteenth century, an incident that shocked the Ottoman sultan and his viceroy in Egypt. In 1818, an Egyptian expeditionary force defeated the armies of the Wahhabis—as the movement had been dubbed by its opponents (they prefer to call themselves *Muwahhidun*). Their capital was besieged and the ruler was taken captive, to be beheaded in Istanbul. A decade later, the Sauds started making modest attempts to restore their position, although they would only be able to reclaim their former power in the first half of the twentieth century. As a movement that was in the beginning mainly inward-looking, primarily reacting against "apostates" (who included in their view also Sufis and Shi'is), they nevertheless won the admiration of future Islamic reformists.

In an increasing measure, Islamic reformism would become a response to an outside force, the onslaught of Western imperialism. From the eighteenth and nineteenth centuries onward, large areas of the Islamic world had become colonies of Britain, France, and the Netherlands. The Ottoman Empire was on the verge of collapse and Persia was constantly under threat from Britain and Russia. A last indigenous challenge to Western colonialism was posed by the Mahdi uprising in Sudan during the 1880s. This mass movement around a charismatic Sufi leader was still entirely traditional in outlook, but descendants of the Mahdi still play an important role in contemporary Sudanese politics.

The earliest attempts to adjust to the demands of modern time by rulers of the Ottoman empire, Egypt, and in Tunis were limited to what would now be called a transfer of technology and the introduction of Western-style technical and military training. Not until the second half of the nineteenth century would there be a concerted effort to reinvigorate Islam.

In the vanguard of this were an enigmatic political activist from Persia, Jamal ad-Din al-Afghani (1838–1897), and Muhammad Abduh (1849–1905), an Egyptian scholar with impeccable Islamic credentials who held top positions at the al-Azhar Islamic university of Cairo. In the 1880s, this duo teamed up to make a first attempt to introduce a reform program that envisaged the revitalization of Islam by returning to the original sources, combined with the utilization of certain Western scientific achievements. Drawing their main inspiration from the deeds of the first-generation Muslims around Muhammad, this movement came to be called the *Salafiyya* (from the Arabic "*Salaf,*" "predecessors"). Later in his career, Abduh became a more systematic thinker and his ideas gave impetus to the first reforms of the Islamic educational system in Egypt. Although al-Afghani and Abduh were not successful in stemming the tide of Westernization, their writings and activities—in particular Abduh's—have been a source of inspiration for generations of future Muslim reformists.

Elsewhere in the Islamic world, Muslim intellectuals were also grappling with the question of how to respond to the challenges posed by imperialism and the ensuing influence of Western culture. In India, now firmly in the hands of the British, the ideas of Sir Sayyid Ahmad Khan (1817–1898) were quite different from those of the reformists in the Arab world. This was not only because multi-religious India posed a different set of questions for the Muslim minority, but because, since visiting England in the 1870s, Sir Sayyid was very much preoccupied in reconciling traditional Islamic knowledge with modern scientific theories such as Darwinism. Many of his views were regarded with suspicion by more traditional Muslims, but he would have a lasting influence on future Muslim education on the Indian subcontinent.

The legacy of Muhammad Abduh was perpetuated by his disciple Rashid Rida (1865–1935). Initially, Rida was deeply influenced by Sufism and the writings of al-Ghazâli, but after acquainting himself with the thought of Abduh he had a change of heart. In his subsequent studies, he was also captivated by the thought of Ibn Taymiyya and the Hanbali interpretation of Islam in general. Eventually, Rida even became a strong proponent of Wahhabism, which had again assumed center stage on the Arabian Peninsula. The 1925–26 reconquest of Mecca and Medina by the future king Abd al-Aziz of Saudi Arabia was greeted with enthusiasm by Rashid Rida because he regarded Wahhabi vigor as the only way to salvage Islam.

Rida's stand must be seen in the context of the crisis in which the Islamic world found itself after the 1924 abolition of the caliphate — which had been held by the Ottoman sultans since the beginning of the sixteenth century — by Turkey's new secularist ruler, Kemal Atatürk. Although the sultans had held only the nominal leadership of Sunni Islam, the symbolic importance of the caliph as a single figurehead had still been a rallying point for Muslim solidarity. Some Muslims found solace in populist movements like the Muslim Brotherhood, which was particularly influential in Egypt, while others turned to nationalism, socialism, and even fascism.

In the first few decades after the Second World War, it seemed as if secularism had given the final blow to Islam as an ideological force, as regimes of nationalist and socialist signature took over across the Islamic world. However, in the Arab world they were discredited as a result of two subsequent defeats in the wars against Israel in 1967 and 1973. In addition, most of these regimes had been extremely hostile toward Islamist movements like the Muslim Brotherhood. Following the political bankruptcy of these ideologies, Islam came back with a vengeance. By the mid-1970s, scores of disenfranchised Muslims had rediscovered Islam, and many of them turned to ideologists who took over the *Salafiyya* banner but gave it a more militant character.

In the Arab world, the writings of Sayyid Qutb started to be widely read. Repeatedly imprisoned under the Nasserist regime (1952–1970) and finally executed in 1966, this leading member of the Muslim Brotherhood was now regarded as a martyr. Sayyid Qutb's advocacy of an activist Islam, seeking not only the personal transformation of the individual Muslim but a complete overhaul of society on Islamic principles as well, served as an inspiration for many militant Islamic political movements, usually grouped together under general terms such as Islamic revivalism or fundamentalism. Elsewhere in the Islamic world, a Pakistani thinker-activist, Maulana al-Maududi, was venting similar ideas. As a leading figure of the Jamiat-I-Islami, he led this organization to political prominence, and during the 1970s his successor even served as a cabinet member in the Islamist government of Pakistan's General Zia-ul-Haq. The Soviet occupation of neighboring Afghanistan during the 1980s contributed to a further radicalization, when the resistance was dubbed a jihad and, with Pakistani, Saudi — and American — support, became a rallying point for a variety of groups prone to extremism and violence.

Of a different mode were the ideas of a Shi'i thinker from Iran, Ali Shariati. Trained as a sociologist but also drawing on the rich philosophical tradition of Shi'ism, his writings influenced scores of young Iranians, who in 1979 would participate in the overthrow of the Shah and the introduction of an Islamic republic under the leadership of the Ayatollah Khomeini.

However, since the appearance of Islamic reformism, there has also been a countercurrent of much more moderate thinkers. Ali Abd al-Raziq (1888–1966), who had studied at the al-Azhar and in Oxford, responded in 1925 to the "caliphate crisis" by writing a book in which he pleaded for a separation of political and religious authority. Not surprisingly, his ideas drew severe criticism from the religious establishment. Other influential figures who wrote extensively on the relationship of Islam and modernity, the "islamization" of knowledge, and other philosophical topics, include Muhammad Iqbal and Fazlur Rahman.

Some prominent contemporary Muslim thinkers who have proposed alternative — and sometimes controversial — ways of engaging with Islam are the Tunisian historian Muhammad Talbi, the Egyptian philosopher Hasan Hanafi, and the French-

Algerian scholar Muhammad Arkoun. Because their writings deal primarily with the study of Islam on the basis of new insights in the philosophy and history of religions, their influence is mainly limited to the circles of the highly educated. In Southeast Asia, we find intellectuals of a more activist bent who therefore often command a wider appeal. Malaysia's Anwar Ibrahim, Chandra Muzaffar, and Farish Noor are very much engaged in presenting Islamically inspired visions of social justice, gender issues, and human rights. Indonesia has given rise to its own particular kind of leading Muslims, many of whom were originally raised in the so-called *pesantren* (Islamic school) tradition. These include former president Abdurrahman Wahid, Nurcholish Majid, and Amin Rais. A rising star in Indonesia is Ulil-Abshar Abdallah.

At the beginning of the twenty-first century, Islam shows a wide and possibly confusing spectrum ranging from militant extremism to neo-Sufism, and from the traditionalist *ulamâ* establishment to Muslim scholars of religion holding Western degrees. What this proves is that Islam will remain a vibrant religious tradition for the time to come and that present generations of Muslims have found — and continue to explore — a variety of ways to express their Muslim identity.

NOTES

1. von Grünebaum, Gustav, *Classical Islam: A History 600–1258*, trans. Katherine Watson (Chicago: Aldine Publishing Co., 1970), p. 13.

2. A. J. Arberry, trans., *The Koran Interpreted* (New York: Touchstone Books of Simon & Schuster, 1996).

3. Ibid.

4. Ibid.

5. Ibid.

6. To give just a few of the divine names: *Al-Hayy* ("the Everliving One"), *Al-Haqq* ("the Truth"), *An-Nur* ("the Light"), *Al-Wadud* ("the Loving One"), *Ar-Razzaq* ("the Sustainer"), *Al-Wali* ("the Friend and Protector"), *Al-Aziz* ("the Magnificent"), *Al-Karim* ("the Generous One"), *Dhul-Jalali Wal-Ikram* ("the Lord of Majesty and Bounty"), *Al-Hadi* ("the Guide").

7. Abdullah Yusuf Ali, *The Meaning of the Holy Qur'an* (Brentwood, Maryland: Amana Corporation, 1991), note 1270 to 9:20.

ISLAM

Sacred Writings

&

Questions to Consider

The passages below have been taken from A. J. Arberry's English translation of the Qur'an, which was first published in 1955 under the title *The Koran Interpreted*. Since then, alternative translations have been produced by Muslims that employ a less flowery style in an attempt to stay closer to the Arabic original. This was partly done in response to objections raised against Arberry's choice to present his translation in verse. In spite of that, *The Koran Interpreted* can still be considered a successful attempt to make both the message and the style of the Qur'an accessible to an English-speaking audience.

It should be noted that every Sura of the Qur'an begins with the phrase "*Bismillah ir-Rahman ir-Rahim*," — "In the Name of God, the Merciful, the Compassionate."

GOOD AND EVIL

The first Sura of the Qur'an is *Sura al-Fatiha*, or "Opening Sura." According to the traditions, it was the first Sura that was revealed in its totality. Commentaries point out that it should not be taken as an introduction but rather a prayer of the believer as servant, to which God responded with the Qur'an. It encapsulates very concisely the key elements of the Muslim cosmology as well as hints at what is deemed good and evil.

In the Name of God, the Merciful, the Compassionate

Praise belongs to God, the Lord of all Being,
the all-Merciful, the All-compassionate,
the Master of the Day of Doom [Reckoning].
Thee only we serve; to Thee alone we pray for succour
Guide us in the straight path,
the path of those whom Thou hast blessed,

not of those against whom Thou art wrathful,
nor of those who are astray.

(1:1–7)

The briefest explanation of good and evil is found in verse 79 of Sura 4 — *Sura al-Nisa'* ("The Women"). The overriding theme of that Sura is guidance, and as such is an elaboration of the believer's plea uttered in the "Opening Sura," asking for divine guidance. The phrase is taken from a section addressed to mankind. It wraps up a lengthy explanation of the need to seek God's guidance towards the straight path and that failure to do so leads to degradation.

Whatever good visits thee, it is of God;
Whatever evil visits thee is of thyself [...]

(4:79)

The following passage is from *Sura al-Layl* (92), "The Night." It starts by presenting the distinction between good and evil in allegorical terms. The theme is a continuation of the preceding Sura, which is called "The Sun." Both are early Meccan revelations from the time when opposition to Muhammad was intensifying:

By the night enshrouding
and the day in splendour
and That which created the male and the female,
surely your striving is to diverse ends.

As for him who gives and is godfearing
and confirms the reward most fair,
We shall surely ease him to the Easing.
But as for him who is a miser, and self-sufficient,
and cries lies to the reward most fair,

We shall surely ease him to the Hardship;
his wealth shall not avail him when he perishes.

Surely upon Us rests the guidance,
and to Us belongs the Last and the First.

Now I have warned you of the Fire that flames,
whereat none but the most wretched shall be roasted,
even he who cried lies, and turned away;
and from which the most godfearing shall be
    removed,
even he who has wealth to purify himself
and confers no favor on any man for recompense,
only seeking the Face of his Lord the Most High;
and he shall surely be satisfied.

(92:1–21)

The first of the final two passages is from *Sura al-Araf* (7),
which has been alternatively translated as "The Heights" and
"The Battlements"; it gives an account of how evil came into
the world. It is followed by the one but last Sura of the Qur'an,
Sura al-Falaq (113) or "The Daybreak," which is, however, one
of the very first revelations received by the Prophet.

We created you, then We shaped you,
then we said to the angels: 'Bow yourselves,
to Adam'; so they bowed themselves,
save Iblis – he was not of those
    that bowed themselves.
Said He, 'What prevented thee to
bow thyself, when I commanded thee?'
Said he, 'I am better than he; Thou
createdst me of fire, and him Thou
    createdst of clay.'
Said He, 'Get thee down out of it;
it is not for thee to wax proud here,

so go thou forth; surely thou art
   among the humbled.'
Said he, 'Respite me till the day
   they shall be raised.'
Said He, 'Thou art among the ones
   that art respited.'
Said he, 'Now, for Thy perverting me,
I shall surely sit in ambush for them
   on Thy straight path;
then I shall come on them from before them
and from behind them, from their right hands
and their left hands; Thou wilt not find
   most of them thankful.'

                                              (7:11–17)

Say: 'I take refuge with the Lord of the Daybreak
from the evil of what He has created
from the evil of darkness when it gathers
from the evil of the women who blow on knots
from the evil of an envier when he envies.'

                                              (113:1–5)

Questions

What does a comparison of these four passages teach about
the respective origins of good and evil? Who bears the blame
for evil? The example from "The Night" presents good and
evil in an allegory of opposites, but also hints at how goodness
is manifested. Can you relate that to the Muslim ethos? Is there
anything that strikes you in the naming and wordings of the
"Opening Sura" and "The Daybreak," and their respective
places within the entire Qur'an?

These verses designate as good such behavior as compassion,
and as bad, behavior such as envy and pride. As you observe
the values of the agency or community where you are serving,
what qualities and behavior are seen as embodying good, and
which evil? Are your values compatible with or different from

those in the Qur'an? Are they the same or different from those in the community where you are serving? What historical conditions account for the values expressed in the Qur'an? In the community where you are serving? Your own values?

GOOD WORKS

The category of "good works" in Islam extends beyond acts of charity and righteousness, and includes also active participation in the defense and spread of Islam, often referred as "struggle [or expend] in the way of God." The Muslims are exhorted dozens of times to act accordingly. Even if we limit "good works" to the more conventional meaning of "charitable works," there is a multitude of such references. Due to the nature of the text, such phrases are scattered throughout the Qur'an rather than dealt with in a single or limited number of narrations on the topic.

The first three selections are from revelations received in times of great adversity when keeping up high moral standards was of utmost importance.

Ha, there you are; you are called upon
to expend in God's way, and some of
you are niggardly. Whoso is niggardly
is niggardly only to his own soul. God is
the All-sufficient; you are the needy ones.
If you turn away, He will substitute
another people instead of you, then they will
  not be your likes.

(*Sura Muhammad* 47:38-39)

How is it with you, that you expend not in the
way of God, and to God belongs the inheritance
of the heavens and the earth? Not equal is he
among you who spent, and who fought before the

victory; those are mightier in rank than they
who spent and fought afterwards; and unto each
God has promised the reward most fair; and God
    is aware of the things you do.
Who is he that will lend to God a good loan,
and He will multiply it for him, and his shall be
    a generous wage?

Upon the day when thou seest the believers,
men and women, their light running before them, and
on their right hands. "Good tidings for you today!
Gardens underneath which rivers flow, therein to
dwell for ever; that is indeed
    the mighty triumph.'
         (*Sura al-Hadid* ["The Iron"] 57:10–12)

Your wealth and your children are
only a trial; and with God is
    a mighty wage.
So fear God as far as you are able,
and give ear, and obey, and expend
well for yourselves. And whosoever
is guarded against the avarice
of his own soul, those — they are
    the prosperers
If you lend to God a good loan. He
will multiply it for you, and will
forgive you. God is All-thankful,
    All-clement,
Knower He of the Unseen and the Visible,
    the All-mighty, the All-wise.
        (*Sura Taghabun* ["Mutual Fraud"] 64:15–17)

A more detailed recording of what constitutes good works in Islam can be found in the following passage from the second Sura from the Qur'an; the great bulk of the section from which this quote is taken deals with practical measures. Some additional specifications regarding good works are given in a passage from *Sura al-Isra* (17), "The Night Journey." The introduction of this Sura refers to Muhammad's mystical nocturnal journey to Jerusalem, and from there to heaven where he was shown by God "the Signs."

It is not piety, that you turn your faces
    to the East and to the West.
        True piety is this:
to believe in God, and the Last Day,
the angels, the Book, and the Prophets,
to give of one's substance, however cherished,
    to kinsmen, and orphans,
the needy, the traveller, beggars,
    and to ransom the slave,
to perform the prayer, to pay the alms.
And they who fulfil their covenant
when they have engaged in a covenant,
    and endure with fortitude
    misfortune, hardship and peril,
these are they who are true in their faith,
    these are the truly godfearing.

                           (2:177)

And do not approach the property of the orphan
save in the fairest manner, until he is of age.
And fulfil the covenant; surely the covenant
    shall be questioned of.
And fill up the measure when you measure, and
weigh with the straight balance; that is better
    and fairer in issue.

                        (17:34-35)

The first part of *Sura Abasa* (80) — "He Frowned" — is a more difficult but important text in connection with righteous action. It was revealed in response to Muhammad's treatment of a blind man:

He frowned and turned away
that the blind man came to him.
And what should teach thee? Perchance he would
    cleanse him,
        or yet remember, and the Reminder profit him.
But the self-sufficient
to him thou attendest
though it is not thy concern, if he does not cleanse
    himself.
And he who comes eagerly
    and fearfully
to him thou payest no heed.

                                                    (80:1–10)

Questions

How would you explain the inclusion of potential violence
under "good works"? The "loan to God" does not necessarily
only imply giving up property; based on what you have learned
about Islam's worldview and teleology, can you imagine
another kind of sacrifice that could be termed a "loan to God"?
What is the reason for recording good works of even a mundane
level in a sacred scripture? What does the passage of Sura 80
teach about dignity and respect? What does a revelation like
this tell you about Muhammad's own sincerity?

In Sura 17, belief, charitable and righteous acts, worship, and
courage are set out as the marks of the faithful and God-fearing
person. Do you see each of these as separate or are they bound
together in a way that they become reinforcing of one another?
Which of these are characteristics valued by an individual or
the community as a whole? Describe an incident which
illustrates your point of view. What qualities are most valued
in the community where you are serving? In your agency?

THE INDIVIDUAL AND THE COMMUNITY

Solidarity and a sense of brotherhood are central concerns for the Muslim community. Apart from surrendering to God, adherence to Islam as an organized religion is also very much a matter of membership of a larger community, the *Umma*.

Thus We appointed you a midmost nation [*Umma*]
That you might be witnesses to the people.

(2:143)

O believers, fear God as He should be feared,
and see you do not die, save in surrender.
And hold you fast to God's bond [the Rope of God],
    together,
and do not scatter; remember God's blessing
upon you when you were enemies, and He brought
your hearts together, so that by His blessing
    you became brothers.
You were upon the brink of a pit of Fire,
and He delivered you from it; even so God
makes clear to you His Signs; so haply
    you will be guided.
Let there be one nation of you, calling to good
and bidding to honour, and forbidding dishonour;
those are the prosperers.

(3:102–104)

The believers indeed are brothers;
so set things right between your
two brothers, and fear God; haply so
    you will find mercy.

(49:10)

Islam takes a very distinct view of renouncing the world and asceticism. Muhammad was familiar with Christian hermits and their attitude toward the Muslims was described as friendly, but he saw no place for monasticism in Islam:

Narrated by Anas ibn Malik: Sahl ibn Abu Umamah said that he and his father (Abu Umamah) visited Anas ibn Malik at Medina during the time (rule) of Umar ibn Abdul Aziz when he (Anas ibn Malik) was the governor of Medina. He was praying a very short prayer as if it were the prayer of a traveller or near it.

When he gave a greeting, my father said: May Allah have mercy on you! Tell me about this prayer: Is it obligatory or supererogatory?

He said: It is obligatory; it is the prayer performed by the Apostle of Allah (peace be upon him). I did not make a mistake except in one thing that I forgot.

He said: The Apostle of Allah (peace be upon him) used to say: Do not impose austerities on yourselves so that austerities will be imposed on you, for people have imposed austerities on themselves and Allah imposed austerities on them. Their survivors are to be found in cells and monasteries. (Then he quoted:) "Monasticism, they invented it; we did not prescribe it for them."

(*Sunan of Abu Dawud*: Book 41, Number 4886)

...and We sent,
following, Jesus son of
Mary, and gave unto him
   the Gospel.
And We set in the hearts of those who
followed him tenderness and mercy.
And monasticism they invented — We
did not prescribe it for them — only
seeking the good pleasure of God; but

they observed it not as it should be
observed. So We gave those of them
who believed their wage; and many of
    them are ungodly.

(57:27)

Sura 9 — *Sura al-Tauba* or the "Repentance" — returns to the phenomenon of monasticism and depicts it in rather negative terms. It is relevant to know the context of this Sura: the revelation is associated with the conquest of the Arabian Peninsula by the Muslims, in particular the region around Tabuk on the frontier with the (Christian) Byzantine Empire:

They have taken their rabbis and their monks as Lords
apart from God...

(9:31)

O believers, many of the rabbis and monks indeed
consume the goods of the people in vanity
and bar from God's way.

(9:34)

In addition to instilling a sense of community into the Muslims, encouraging them to fully participate, there are also encouragements to exercise justice:

O believers, be you securers of
justice, witnesses for God, even though
it be against ourselves, or your parents
and kinsmen, whether the man be rich
or poor; God stands closest to either.
Then follow not caprice, so as to swerve;
for if you twist or turn, God is aware of
    the things you do.

(4:135)

Say: 'My Lord has commanded justice.
Set your faces in every place of worship
and call on Him, making your religion
sincerely his. As He originated you
so will you return; a part He guided,
and a part justly disposed to error—they
have taken Satans for friends instead of God,
  and think them guided. '

(7:29)

Furthermore, the ethos of this new community is also foreseen in certain social changes. For example, there is a noted change in the treatment of slaves; the Qur'an contains a number of explicit references to how they are to be treated. (Bear in mind that in the historical circumstances of the time, slavery as such was considered acceptable.)

Marry the spouseless among you, and your
slaves and handmaidens that are righteous;
if they are poor, God will enrich them
of His bounty; God is All-embracing,
  All-knowing.
And let those who find not the means to
marry be abstinent until God enriches them
of His bounty. Those your right hands own [slaves]
who seek emancipation, contract with
them accordingly, if you know some good
in them; and give them of the wealth of God
that He has given you. And constrain not
your slavegirls to prostitution, if they
desire to live in chastity, that you may
seek the chance goods of the present life.

(24:32–33)

And God has preferred some of you over others
in provision; but those that were preferred
shall not give over their possession
to that their right hands possess, so that
they may be equal therein. What, and do they
    deny God's blessing?

(16:73)

God has struck a similitude: a servant
possessed by his master, having no power
    over anything,
and one whom We have provided of Ourselves
with a provision fair, and he expends of it
    secretly and openly.
Are they equal? Praise belongs to God! Nay,
    most of them know not.
God has struck a similitude: two men,
one of them dumb, having no power over
anything, and he is a burden upon his
master—wherever he dispatches him,
    he brings no good.
Is he equal to him who bids to justice, and is
    on a straight path?

(16:76–78)

Questions

How do Muslims distinguish themselves as a community and
as members of that community? What might have been the
reason for Muhammad to reject the idea of monastic life? The
final passage of this section makes problematic the notion of
justice. What does it teach the believer? How is justice served
in the last two passages? What structural changes can you
detect?

The idea of community brings people together, but it also
divides because communities, by their very nature, include
some and exclude others. Who is included in these passages?

What unites Muslims? In the community where you are serving, what serves to unite? Who is excluded? Can you imagine a community that only embraces and excludes no one? What could be the uniting force of such a community?

RELIGIOUS BELIEFS AND GOOD WORKS

The Qur'an contains ample indications that belief and action cannot be separated. There are more than fifty instances in which believing and doing good works are mentioned in one breath. The next example is also from the earlier mentioned Sura of Repentance:

> Do you reckon the giving of water to pilgrims
> and the inhabiting of the Holy Mosque as the same
> as one who believes in God and the Last Day
> and struggles in the way of God? Not equal are they
> in God's sight; and God guides not the people
> of the evildoers.
> Those who believe, and have emigrated, and have
> struggled in the way of God with their possessions
> and their selves are mightier in rank with God; and
> those —
> they are the triumphant;
> their Lord gives them good tidings of mercy from Him
> and good pleasure; for them await gardens wherein
> is lasting bliss...
>
> (9:19–21)

The following two passages actually deal primarily with defending Islam and fighting bravely for its cause, but illustrate also in more detail that belief is not merely a confession of faith, but something to be "lived out."

The Bedouins say, 'We believe.'
Say: 'You do not believe; rather
say, "We surrender"; for belief
has not yet entered your hearts.
If you obey God and His Messenger,
He will not diminish you anything
of your works. God is All-forgiving,
    All-compassionate.'
The believers are those who believe
in God and His Messenger, then have
not doubted, and have struggled
with their possessions and their selves
in the way of God; those — they are
    the truthful ones.

(49:14–15)

Such believers as sit at home — unless
they have an injury — are not the equals
of those who struggle in the path of God
with their possessions and their selves.
God has preferred in rank those who struggle
with their possessions and their selves
over the ones who sit at home; yet to each
God has promised the reward most fair;
and God has preferred those who struggle
over the ones who sit at home for the bounty
    of a mighty wage,
in ranks standing before Him, forgiveness
and mercy; surely God is All-forgiving,
    All-compassionate.

(4:95–96)

Claiming formal allegiance to the faith but failing to act charitably is not the way of the true believer, and therefore has its consequences, as is shown from *Sura al-Ma'un* (107) — "Charity" — and a passage from *Sura al-Fajr* (89), "The Dawn":

Hast thou seen him who cries lies to the Doom?
That is he who repulses the orphan
and urges not the feeding of the needy.

So woe to those that pray
and are heedless of their prayers,
to those who make display
and refuse charity.

(107:1–7)

As for man, whenever his Lord tries him,
    and honours him, and blesses him,
then he says, 'My Lord has honoured me.'
But when he tries him and stints for him
            his provision,
then he says, 'My Lord has despised me.'

No indeed; but you honour not the orphan,
and you urge not the feeding of the needy,
and you devour the inheritance greedily,
and you love wealth with ardent love.

No indeed! When the earth is ground to powder,
and thy Lord comes, and the angels rank on rank,
and Gehenna [hell] is brought out, upon that day
man will remember; and how shall the Reminder be
            for him?

(89:15–21)

Acting in accordance with what is prescribed for true believers can be projected as a test of faith, as the following passage from *Sura al-Balad* (90) — "The Land" — shows:

> Have We not appointed to him two eyes,
> and a tongue, and two lips,
> and guided him on the two highways?
> Yet he has not assaulted the steep;
> and what shall teach thee what is the steep?
> The freeing of a slave
> or giving food upon a day of hunger
> To an orphan or near of kin
> or a needy man in misery;
> then that he become of those who believe
> and counsel each other to be steadfast,
> and counsel each other to be merciful.
>
> (90:8–18)

Questions

When you compare the passages from Suras 49 and 4 with those taken from 107 and 89, what change in tone do you detect? How might you explain or reconcile that change? How is the last passage from Sura 90 a test of faith?

Are there supervisors and/or staff members of your agency for whom their work is an expression of faith? Is it religious faith or secular humanism? Some say that action is in fact the most sincere expression of prayer. If you think of your service in this way, what characterizes your prayer? Anger at the condition of the lives of those you serve and at the way they are treated by society? Thankfulness that you are given the privilege to respond to need? Petition that you will know what to do and be of use to the community?

WORSHIP, RITUAL PRACTICES, AND GOOD WORKS

Central to Islam is the notion that the true believer is one who maintains the integrity of worship, ritual practice, and acts of compassion, made evident by the following passages from three Medinan Suras in which the two Pillars of Islam that most evidently exemplify worship and acting charitably are repeatedly mentioned in combination; in *Sura al-Baqara* (2) even four times:

> And when We took compact with the Children of
>   Israel:
> 'You shall not serve any save God;
> and to be good to parents, and the near kinsman,
> and to orphans, and to the needy;
> and speak good to men, and perform the prayer,
> and pay the alms.'...
>
> (2:83)

> And perform prayer, and pay the alms; whatever
> good you shall forward to your souls' account,
> you shall find it with God; assuredly God
>   sees the things you do.
>
> (2:110)

> Those who believe and do deeds of righteousness,
> and perform the prayer, and pay the alms —
> their wage awaits them with the Lord,
> and no fear shall be on them, neither shall they sorrow.
>
> (2:277)

> Hast thou not regarded those to whom it was said,
> 'Restrain your hands, and perform the prayer,
> and pay the alms'?...
>
> (4:77)

Yet if they repent, and perform the prayer,
and pay the alms, then they are your brothers
in religion....

(9:11)

Only he shall inhabit God's places of worship
who believes in God and in the Last Day, and
performs the prayer, and pays the alms, and fears
none but God alone; it may be that those will
    be among the guided.

(9:18)

In another revelation from the same period, namely the
end of *Sura al-Fath* (48) or the "Sura of Victory," once again an
explicit link is made between worship, ritual prayer, and acting
righteously. The historical perspective is probably relevant: the
Sura was revealed after the signing of a truce with Mecca; one
of the conditions of this so-called Treaty of Hudaybiyya was
that Muhammad would be permitted to make the pilgrimage
to the Ka'ba.

Muhammad is the Messenger of God
and those who are with him are hard
against the unbelievers, merciful
one to another. Thou seest them
bowing, prostrating, seeking bounty
from God and good pleasure. Their
mark is on their faces, the trace of
prostration. That is their likeness
in the Torah; and their likeness
in the Gospel; as a seed that
puts forth its shoot, and strengthens it,
and it grows stout and rises straight
upon its stalk, pleasing the sowers,
that through them He may enrage
the unbelievers. God has promised

those of them who believe and do deeds
of righteousness forgiveness and
    a mighty wage.

(48:29)

    Sura al-Ma'ida (5) — "The Table" — gives detailed pre-scriptions of the dietary rules that the Muslims must observe. But the following passage is an example of how worship, ritual, and acts of compassion are intertwined in the Islamic concept of a righteous life:

O believers, slay not the game while you
are in pilgrim sanctity; whosoever of you
slays it wilfully, there shall be recompense —
the like of what he has slain, in flocks
as shall be judged by two men of equity [justice]
among you, an offering to reach the Kaaba;
or expiation — food for poor persons
or the equivalent of that in fasting, so that
He may taste the mischief of his actions.

(5:95)

Questions

What is the reasoning behind the notion that faith, worship, adherence to ritual practice, and performance of "good works" should be an integrated whole? Which other two rituals instill a sense of community in Muslims?

Does your agency have any rituals that reinforce the beliefs, values, and actions of the community? These may be religious, national, or simply the customs and ceremonies created by and for the agency and the community it serves. Who participates and with what degree of involvement? Do these rituals and ceremonies appear to have a strong influence on the clients and staff? Is the wedding of ritual and action reinforced in these rituals? Could you suggest a ceremony that embodies the values and actions of the agency?

PROSELYTIZING AND GOOD WORKS

Much has always been made of the role of jihad in bringing people under the sway of Islam. Looking at the scriptures, however, it appears that proselytizing is a matter of qualification in Islam. The whole of *Sura al-Kafirun* (109), "The Unbelievers," as well as parts of verses 2:256 and 2:271, might even suggest a "hands-off" approach:

> Say: 'O unbelievers,
> I serve not what you serve
> and you are not serving what I serve,
> nor am I serving what you have served,
> neither are you serving what I serve.
>
> To you your religion, and to me my religion!'
> (109:1–6)

> No compulsion is there in religion.
> Rectitude has become clear from error.
> So whosoever disbelieves in idols
> and believes in God, has laid hold of
> the most firm handle, unbreaking; God is
>   All-hearing, All-knowing.
> (2:256)

> Thou art not responsible for guiding them;
> But God guides whomsoever He will.
> (2:272)

However, other instances clearly indicate that the messenger must warn and admonish people to heed the teachings of the Lord, although actually entering the faith is entirely in God's hands. The first two passages are from one of the very first revelations. The opening line refers to the traditional accounts that Muhammad hid under a blanket or his mantle after the frightening experience of the first revelation:

O thou shrouded in thy mantle,
arise and warn!...

(74:1–2)

...So God leads astray whomsoever He will,
and He guides whomsoever He will; and
none knows the hosts of thy Lord but He.
And it is naught but Reminder to mortals.

(74:31)

Say: 'Obey God, and obey the Messenger;
then, if you turn away, only upon
him rests what is laid on him, and
upon you rests what is laid on you.
If you obey him, you will be guided.
It is only for the Messenger to deliver
    the manifest Message.

(24:54)

Now there has come to you a Messenger from among
yourselves; grievous to him is your suffering;
anxious is he over you, gentle to the believers,
    compassionate.
So if they turn their backs, say: 'God is enough for me.
There is no God but He. In Him I have put my trust.
    He is the Lord of the Mighty Throne.'

(9:128–129)

Apart from carrying the message to people, Muslims are also presented as an example to those who have not yet converted. Furthermore, they are also to act in an examplary manner themselves. The passages here are taken from *Sura al-Qasas* (28), "The Story," *Sura al-Zukhruf* (43), "The Ornaments," and *Sura al-Tahrim* (66), "The Forbidding." To illustrate the point they try to make, the stories of Noah, Lot, Moses, and Jesus are used for inspiration:

> God has struck a similitude
> for the unbelievers—the wife of
> Noah, and the wife of Lot; for
> they were under two of Our
> righteous servants, but they
> betrayed them, so they availed
> them nothing whatsoever
> against God; so it was said,
> 'Enter, you two, the Fire with
> those who enter.'
>
> (66:10)

> Yet We desired to be gracious to those that were
> abased in the land, and to make them leaders, and to
> make them the inheritors...
>
> (28:5)

> And when the son of Mary is
> cited as an example, behold,
> thy people turn away from it
> and say, 'What, are our gods
> better, or he?' They cite not
> him to thee, save to dispute;
> nay, but they are a people
> contentious. He is only a
> servant We blessed, and We

made him to be an example
to the Children of Israel.

(43:57)

Questions

The passages suggesting a "hands-off" approach might be interpreted as giving in to fatalism; however, a closer reading in connection with the other passages regarding the Prophet's duty to warn people could also suggest accountability. On whose part? Can you detect any similarities with other religious traditions? If so, which one(s)? Given the above, would you say it is a Muslim's duty to proselytize? And if so, what role is he or she to play?

Does your agency have religious and/or secular beliefs and values that it tries to instill in the clients? Does it do so directly or indirectly? Are there differing opinions on this issue within the staff of the agency? Have you encountered a difference between your beliefs and values and those of your agency, and if so, how have you dealt with this difference?

DUTY TO THOSE IN SPECIAL NEED

In pre-Islamic Arabia, the old codes of customs offered little security against abuse to those who were without strong protectors. A first admonition to counteract this is found in an early Meccan revelation, *Sura al-Duha* (93) or "the Forenoon."

Did He not find thee an orphan, and shelter thee?
Did He not find thee erring, and guide thee?
Did He not find thee needy, and suffice thee?

As for the orphan, do not oppress him,
and as for the beggar, scold him not;
and as for thy Lord's blessing, declare it.

(93:6-11)

Before Islam, women in the Arab world were regarded almost as commodities. Orphans and the destitute faced material and other hardships in a world constantly balanced on the verge of anarchy. In Sura 4, aptly called *Sura al-Nisa* or "The Women," a more detailed elaboration is given of a new set of ethics for dealing with the weaker members of society. Following the passage quoted here, the Sura continues with detailed instructions regarding the distribution of inheritance and permissible and nonpermissible marriages. Further on, there is another listing of those deserving charity.

> Give the orphans their property, and do not
> exchange the corrupt for the good; and devour
> not their property with your property; surely
>   that is a great crime.
> If you fear that you will not act justly
> towards the orphans, marry such women
> as seem good to you, two, three, or four;
> but if you fear you will not be equitable,
> then only one, or what your right hands own;
> so it is likelier you will not be partial.
> And give women their dowries as a gift
> spontaneous; but if they are pleased
> to offer you any of it, consume it
>   with wholesome appetite.
> But do not give to fools their property
> that God has assigned to you to manage;
> provide for them and clothe them out of it,
> and speak to them honourable words.
> Test well the orphans, until they reach
> the age of marrying; then, if you perceive
> in them right judgment, deliver to them
> their property; consume it not wastefully and hastily
> ere they are grown. If any man is rich
> let him be abstinent; if poor, let him
>   consume in reason.

And when you deliver to them their property,
take witnesses over them; God suffices
    for a reckoner.
To the men a share of what parents and kinsmen
leave, and to the women a share of what
parents and kinsmen leave, whether it be
little or much, a share apportioned;
and when the division is attended by
kinsmen and orphans and the poor,
make provision for them out of it,
and speak to them honourable words.

                         (4:2–8)

Be kind to parents, and the near kinsman,
and to orphans, and to the needy,
and to the neighbour who is of kin,
and to the neighbour who is a stranger,
and to the companion on your side,
and to the traveller, and to that your
right hands own. Surely God loves not
    the proud and boastful
such as are niggardly, and themselves conceal
the bounty that God has given them....

                        (4:36–37)

The next passage is taken from *Sura al-Isra* (17), "the Night Journey." Bearing witness of a direct experience of God gives additional power and importance to this revelation on how to deal with the elderly and less fortunate:

Set not up with God
another God, or thou
wilt sit condemned
    and forsaken.
Thy Lord has decreed
you shall not serve
    any but Him,

and to be good to parents,
whether one or both of them
attains old age with thee;
    say not to them 'Fie'
    neither chide them, but
speak unto them words
    respectful,
and lower to them
the wing of humbleness
out of mercy and say,
    'My Lord,
have mercy upon them,
as they raised me up
when I was little.'
Your Lord knows very well what is in your hearts
    if you are righteous,
for He is All-forgiving to those who are penitent.
And give the kinsman his right,
and the needy, and the traveller;
and never squander....

                               (17:23–26)

Questions

How can you relate the passage of the treatment of women and orphans to Muhammad's own experience and the position of the early Muslim community in Mecca? What are implications of these admonitions for the social structure?

Is the mission of your agency directed toward those of special need? To what extent are the problems of the clients of your agency created or fostered by social circumstances? Would there be a need for your agency if society were organized differently and/or held different values? Are there people with special needs that are not being served by any agency in your community? What is the status of women and their children in your community? Are they seen as dependents who must be provided for, or are they seen to have equal status and resources? Do you see examples of abuse of persons with special needs, and is your agency trying to address these? By meeting their needs, advocating for change on their behalf, or both?

THE TREATMENT OF STRANGERS

The relationship of the believers with the outside world is very complex. Not only are there a variety of possibilities described in the Qur'an, but later history seems sometimes strangely at odds with the teachings. The first passage below is from *Sura al-Hujarat* (49), "The Chambers," and follows a condemnation of national and racial distinction saying that these distinctions are important factors in filling the world with injustice and tyranny. In a brief verse, Allah has cut at the root of this evil by stating that all men are descendants of the same one:

> O Mankind, We have created you
> male and female, and appointed you
> races and tribes, that you may know
> one another. Surely the noblest
> among you in the sight of God is
> the most godfearing of you. God is
>   All-knowing, All-aware.
>
> (49:13)

Other passages, however, shift away from that and focus instead on the differences that emerge between people:

> The people were one nation; then God sent forth
> the Prophets, good tidings to bear
> and warning, and He sent down with them
> the Book with the truth, that He might
> decide between the people touching their differences;

and only those who had been given it [the scripture]
were at variance upon it, after the
clear signs had come to them, being insolent
one to another; then God guided those
who believed to the truth, touching which
they were at variance, by His leave;
and God guides whomsoever He will
    to a straight path.

(2:213)

You are the best nation ever brought forth
to men, bidding to honour, and forbidding
dishonour, and believing in God. Had the People
of the Book [Jews and Christians] believed, it were
    better for them;
some of them are believers, but the most of
    them are ungodly.

(3:110)

If God had willed, He would have made you
one nation: but that He may try you
in what has come to you. So be you forward
in good works; unto God shall you
return, all together; and He will tell you
of that whereon you were at variance.

(5:48)

So respite the unbelievers; delay with them awhile.

(86:17)

Other instances are much sterner in tone and the
unbelievers are clearly set apart as the "out group," becoming
even subject to outright rejection:

Let not the believers take the unbelievers
for friends, rather than the believers —
for whoso does that belongs not to God in
anything — unless you have a fear of them.

(3:28)

Thou didst not hope that the Book should be
cast unto thee, except it be as a mercy
from thy Lord; so be thou not a partisan
of the unbelievers. Let them not bar thee
from the signs of God, after that they have been
sent down to thee. And call upon thy Lord,
and be thou not of the idolaters.

(28:86–87)

And fight in the way of God with those
who fight with you, but aggress not: God loves
    not the aggressors.

(2:190)

Questions

The name of *Sura al-Hujarat* refers to the women's quarters in Muhammad's compound. What allegorical explanation can be derived from that for the moral imperatives regarding dealing with others? This verse is often quoted to illustrate that Islam recognizes pluralism. Can you explain how? If you take the first passage in conjunction with the other ones, on what basis can distinctions between people be made? On what grounds can others be judged?

Who are considered strangers in the community where you are serving? Does your agency welcome them? Ignore them? Is it waging a war against them and their values? Is it possible to be welcoming and accepting of the strangers even if you oppose their beliefs?

MOTIVATION TO SERVE

While Islam does recognize the ancient Arabian virtue of generosity, it is the motivation behind that generosity that is questioned. Islam demands from the believer a new ethos.

> If you publish your freewill offerings, it is
> excellent; but if you conceal them, and give them
> to the poor, that is better for you, and will
> acquit you of your evil deeds; God is aware of
> the things you do.
>
> (2:271)

> ...We have prepared for the unbelievers
>   a humbling chastisement,
> and such as expend of their substance
> to show off to men, and believe not
> in God and the Last Day. Whosoever
> has Satan for a comrade, an evil
>   comrade is he.
> Why, what would it harm them, if they
> believed in God and the Last Day, and
> expended of that God has provided them?
>
> (4:37–39)

Questions

How has the new ethos changed the regard in which generosity was held by the pre-Islamic Arabs?

According to this passage, motivation is important to God. How does your agency ask for funding? To what qualities in potential donors does the fund-raising campaign appeal? Does it publish the names of donors and otherwise give them public recognition? Have you learned of any instances in which a donation has been rejected because the motivation, beliefs, or example of the donor is at odds with the values of the agency?

Alec Dickson, the founder of Voluntary Service Overseas and a proponent of community service for juvenile offenders, once said, "You do not need to be good to do good." Do you agree with that philosophy? Do you see examples of your agency encouraging service by all, even those who seem least likely of use?

THE REWARDS OF SERVICE

There are many instances in the Qur'an where the rewards for those who believe and perform good works are described.

So fight in God's way, and know that God is
    All-hearing, All-knowing.
Who is he that will lend to God a good loan,
And he will multiply it for him manifold?

(2:245)

And whosoever does deeds of righteousness,
be it male or female, believing—
they shall enter Paradise, and not be wronged
    a single date-spot.

(4:124)

And God said, 'I am with you.
Surely, if you perform prayer, and pay
the alms, and believe in My Messengers
and succour them, and lend to God
a good loan, I will acquit you of
your evil deeds, and I will admit you
to gardens underneath which rivers flow."

(5:12)

And give the kinsman his right,
and the needy, and the traveller;
that is better for those who desire
God's Face; those—they are
    the prosperers.
And what you give in usury,
that it may increase upon
people's wealth, increases not
with God; but what you give in
alms, desiring God's Face,
those—they receive recompense
    manifold.

                                            (30:39)

And whosoever does a righteous deed,
be it male or female, believing, We
shall assuredly give him to live a
goodly life; and We shall recompense them
their wage, according to the best
    of what they did.

                                            (16:97)

The most elaborate and at the same time powerful description of the rewards that await the believers and punishments destined for unbelievers is in *Sura al-Insan* (76), "Man":

Has there come on man a while of time
when he was a thing unremembered?

We created man of a sperm-drop, a mingling, trying
    him;
and We made him hearing, seeing.
Surely We guided him upon the way
whether he be thankful or unthankful.
Surely We have prepared for the unbelievers
chains, fetters, and a Blaze.

Surely the pious shall drink of a cup
whose mixture is camphor,
a fountain whereat drink the servants of God,
making it to gush forth plenteously.
They fulfil their vows, and fear a day whose evil is
    upon the wing;
they give food, for the love of Him, to the needy,
the orphan, the captive:
'We feed you only for the Face of God;
we desire no recompense from you, no
    thankfulness;
for we fear from our Lord a frowning day,
    inauspicious.'
So God has guarded them from the evil of
that day, and has procured them radiancy
    and gladness,
and recompensed them for their patience
    with a Garden, and silk;
therein they shall recline upon couches,
therein they shall see neither sun nor
    bitter cold;
near them shall be its shades, and its clusters hung
    meekly down,
and there shall be passed around them vessels of
silver, and goblets of crystal,
crystal of silver that they have measured
    very exactly.
And therein they shall be given to drink a cup whose
    mixture is ginger,
there is a fountain whose name is called Salsabil.
Immortal youths shall go about them;
when thou seest them, thou supposest them
    scattered pearls,
when thou seest them then thou seest bliss
    and a great kingdom.
Upon them shall be green garments of silk
and brocade; they are adorned with
bracelets of silver, and their Lord shall

give them to drink a pure draught.
'Behold, this is recompense for you, and
your striving is thanked.'

(76:1–22)

Questions

The Sura entitled "Man" not only vividly describes heaven and hell, but also summarizes the message of Islam. Based on the other readings from the scripture and the background information provided, write a brief characterization of Islam's view of man and his position and role in creation.

Sura 76 describes the rewards of service to include "radiancy and gladness." Among the people who make up the staff of your agency — paid and volunteer — are there those who exhibit "radiancy and gladness?" How do they describe the rewards of service? Have you had any similar feelings? Has the experience of service changed your ideas about what constitutes a satisfying and happy life? Have you, in any way large or small, changed your ideas about your future direction as a result?

Suggested Further Reading

Hinduism

This very lucid introduction to early Hindu philosophy is highly recommended:

Dasgupta, S. N. *History of Indian Philosophy*. Vol. 1. Cambridge, U.K.: Cambridge University Press, 1973.

The following books on India, Hinduism, and Hindu sacred texts are also recommended:

Basham, A.L. *The Wonder That Was India*. New York: Grove Press, 1959.

Easwaran, Eknath, trans. *The Upanishads*. New Delhi: Penguin Books India, 1996.

Gandhi, Mahatma. *Collected Works*. Delhi: Publications Division, Ministry of Information and Broadcasting, Govt. of India, 1958.

Keith, A. B. *Religion and Philosophy of the Veda and Upanishads* (2 vols.). Cambridge, Mass.: Harvard University Press; and London: H. Milford, Oxford U. Press, 1925.

Mascaro, Juan, trans. *The Upanishads*. Harmondsworth, U.K.: Penguin Books, 1965.

O'Flaherty, Wendy Doniger, trans. *The Rig Veda*. Harmondsworth, U.K.: Penguin Books, 1981.

Ramanujan, A. K., complier and trans. *Speaking of Siva*. New York: Penguin Books, 1973.

Richman, Paula, ed. *Many Ramayanas: The Diversity of a Narrative Tradition in South Asia.* Berkeley: University of California Press, 1991.

Rolland, Romain, *Life of Ramakrishna.* Trans. by E. F. Malcolm-Smith. Calcutta: Advaita Ashrama, 1984.

Stoller, Barbara. *Bhagavad Gita.* Trans. with an intro by Barbara Stoller Miller. New York: Bantam, 1986.

Swami Nikhilananda. *Gospel of Sri Ramakrishna.* New York: Ramakrishna-Vivekananda Center, 1988.

Zaehner, R. C. *Hinduism.* London and New York: Oxford University Press, 1962.

Buddhism

The number of books and articles about Buddhist religion that are now available in English is enormous. This is truly astonishing when one considers that only about 200 years ago almost no accurate information about this religious community and its traditions was available to Western readers in their own languages.

One searches in vain, for example, in the fourth edition of the *Encyclopaedia Britannica* (published in 1810) for any article on the Buddhist community and its traditions. In discussing Chinese religion, there is passing mention of a sect of the idol "Fo." This is a reference to the Chinese Buddhist religion, but the beliefs and practices of the sect are described as a "pernicious superstition" introduced from India that contaminated and perverted the purity of ancient Chinese religion. There is also a brief separate entry with the heading "Fo," in which the Buddha is simply defined as "an idol of the Chinese." Not until the seventh edition of the Encyclopaedia (published in 1875) is there an entry on "Buddhism." See Notes for Chapter Three, footnote 36 in Wilfred Cantwell Smith, *The Meaning and End of Religion: A New Approach to the Religious Traditions of Mankind* (New York: A Mentor Book Published by the New American Library, 1963), p. 245.

Today, almost any library and most bookstores will have a section devoted to Buddhist religion. Many of the books provide excellent information and interpretations about the beliefs and practices of the various Buddhist communities as well as perceptive insights into the religious faith of Buddhists. Indeed, many of the volumes are written by Buddhists themselves or by Western scholars who respect and understand the traditions and faith of the Buddhist community.

The books listed below are intended to give students an idea of the scope of materials on Buddhist religion now available and to give suggestions about where they might begin their further reading and study. Several of the following books have their own lists of recommended readings and most have extensive bibliographies that students should also consult.

General Introductions and Surveys

There are several surveys of major world religions with one or more chapters devoted to Buddhism. Some of these are available in more recent editions or publications. Among the best are:

Hutchison, John A. *Paths of Faith*. 4th ed. New York: McGraw-Hill, Inc., 1991.

Smart, Ninian. *The Religious Experience of Mankind*. New York: Charles Scribner's Sons, 1969.

Smith, Huston. *The Religions of Man*. New York: Perennial Library, Harper & Row, 1989.

Smith, Wilfred Cantwell. *The Faith of Other Men*. New York: A Mentor Book Published by the New American Library, 1963.

Zaehner, R. C., ed. *The Concise Encyclopaedia of Living Faiths*. London: Hutchinson & Co. Ltd., 1971.

The following general surveys focusing specifically on the Buddhist religion and its various branches are recommended:

Bechert, Heinz, and Richard Gombrich, eds. *The World of Buddhism: Buddhist Monks and Nuns in Society and Culture.* London: Thames and Hudson, 1984.

Ch'en, Kenneth K. S. *Buddhism: The Light of Asia.* Woodbury, N.Y.: Barron's Eucational Series, Inc., 1968.

Conze, Edward. *Buddhism: Its Essence and Development.* New York: Harper Torchbooks, Harper & Brothers, 1959.

Eckel, Malcolm David. *Buddhism: Origins, Beliefs, Practices, Holy Texts, Sacred Places.* Oxford: Oxford University Press, 2003.

Harvey, Peter. *An Introduction to Buddhism: Teachings, History, and Practices.* Cambridge: Cambridge University Press, 1990.

Robinson, Richard H., and Willard L. Johnson. *The Buddhist Religion: A Historical Introduction.* 4th Ed. Encino, Calif. and Belmont, Calif.: Wadsworth Publishing Company, 1997.

Trainor, Kevin, ed. *Buddhism: The Illustrated Guide.* London: Duncan Baird Publishers, 2001.

Among those books dealing specifically with one particular branch of Buddhist religion, the following are recommended for the Theravada tradition:

Buddhadasa Bhikkhu. *Handbook for Mankind.* Bangkok: Thammasapa Publishing, n.d. (Original date of lectures 1956.) Portions of this book together with other writings of Buddhadasa Bhikkhu can be found in a volume edited by Donald K. Swearer entitled *Toward the Truth.*

Gombrich, Richard. *Theravada Buddhism: A Social History from Ancient Benares to Modern Colombo*. London and New York: Routledge & Kegan Paul, 1988.

Lester, Robert C. *Theravada Buddhism in Southeast Asia*. Ann Arbor: Ann Arbor Paperbacks, The University of Michigan Press, 1973.

Rahula, Walpola. *What the Buddha Taught*. Evergreen Original. New York: Grove Press, Inc., 1962.

Swearer, Donald K. *The Buddhist World of Southeast Asia*. SUNY Series in Religion. Albany: State University of New York Press, 1995.

For additional readings focusing on other branches of Buddhist religion students should consult the Select Bibiliography in the Robinson and Johnson volume mentioned above. Also, on Japanese Buddhist religion, see the excellent volume by H. Bryon Earhart, *Japanese Religion: Unity and Diversity*, 3d Ed. On Chinese Buddhist religion, a good beginning is Arthur Wright's *Buddhism in Chinese History* (New York: Atheneum, 1965). For Tibetan Buddhist religion see any of the writings of the Dalai Lama. Also see the writings of Robert Thurmond.

Judaism

On Judaism Generally

Jacobs, Louis. *The Book of Jewish Belief.* West Orange, N.J.: Behrman House, 1984.

Jacobs, Louis. *The Book of Jewish Practice.* West Orange, N.J.: Behrman House, 1987.

Kushner, Harold. *To Life! A Celebration of Jewish Being and Thinking.* Boston: Little Brown, 1993.

On Judaism and Service

Abrahams, Israel. *Jewish Life in the Middle Ages.* New York: Atheneum, and Philadelphia: Jewish Publication Society of America, 1969. See especially Chapters 17 and 18.

Brooks, Roger. "Support for the Poor in the Mishnaic Law of Agriculture: Tractate Peah." *Brown Judaic Studies,* 43. Chico, Calif.: Scholars Press, 1983.

Dorff, Elliot N. *To Do the Right and the Good: A Jewish Approach to Modern Social Ethics.* Philadelphia: Jewish Publication Society, 2002. See especially Chapter 6.

Goitein, S. D. *A Mediterranean Society: The Jewish Communities of the Arab World as Portrayed in the Documents of the Cairo Geniza.* 3 vols. Berkeley, Calif.: University of California Press, 1971. See especially Vol II, pp. 91–143.

Katz, Mordecai. *Protection of the Weak in the Talmud.* New York: Columbia University Press, 1925.

Kimelman, Reuven. *Tsedakah and Us.* New York: National Jewish Resource Center, 1983.

Neusner, Jacob. *Tzedakah: Can Jewish Philanthropy Buy Jewish Survival?* Chappaqua, N.Y.: Rossel Books, 1982.

Rubenstein, Richard L. *The Age of Triage: Fear and Hope in an Overcrowded World.* Boston: Beacon Press, 1983. See especially Chapters 1, 9, and 10.

Rubin, Gary, ed. *The Poor Among Us: Jewish Tradition and Social Policy.* New York: American Jewish Committee, 1986.

Shapiro, Aharon. "The Poverty Program of Judaism." *Review of Social Economy,* 9:2 (September, 1971), pp. 200–206.

Siegel, Danny. *Gym Shoes and Irises: Personalized Tzedakah.* Spring Valley, N.Y.: Town House Press, 1982.

Christianity

Bethge, Eberhard. *Prayer and Righteous Action in the Life of Dietrich Bonhoeffer*. Belfast: Christian Journals, 1979.

Boff, Leonardo, and Clodovis Boff. *Introducing Liberation Theology*. Tunbridge Wells, Kent, U.K.: Burns and Oats, 1987.

Brown, Robert McAfee. *Spirituality and Liberation: Overcoming the Great Fallacy*. Philadelphia: Westminster Press, 1988.

Brown, Robert McAfee. *Unexpected News: Reading the Bible with Third World Eyes*. Philadelphia: Westminster Press, 1984.

Carson, Clayborne, and Shepart Kris, eds. *A Call to Conscience: The Landmark Speeches of Dr. Martin Luther King, Jr.* New York: IPM (Intellectual Properties Management), in association with Warner Books, 2001.

Crossan, John Cominic. *The Historical Jesus: The Life of a Mediterranean Jewish Peasant*. San Francisco: Harper San Francisco, 1991.

Curt, Cadorette, et al. *Liberation Theology: An Introductory Reader*. Maryknoll, N.Y.: Orbis Books, 1992.

Ehrenreich, Barbara, and Deirdre English. *Witches, Midwives and Nurses: A History of Women Healers*. London: Compendium, 1974.

Fabella, Virginia. "Christology from an Asian Woman's Perspective," in *We Dare to Dream: Doing Theology as Asian Women*. Hong Kong: AWCCT, 1989.

Frank, Isnard Wilhelm, *A Concise History of the Medieval Church.* New York: Continuum Publishing Group, 1995.

Marty, Martin. *A Short History of Christianity.* Minneapolis: Fortress Press, 1987.

Pelikan, Jaroslav. *The Illustrated Jesus Through the Ages.* New Haven: Yale Univerity Press, 1997.

Song, C. S. *Jesus, the Crucified People.* Minneapolis: Fortress Press, 1990.

Sugirtharajah, R. S., ed. *Asian Faces of Jesus.* Maryknoll: Orbis Books, 1993.

Tamez, Elsa. *The Scandalous Message of James.* New York: Crossroad Publishing Co., 1990.

Islam

General Introductions

Denny, Frederick Mathewson. *An Introduction to Islam*. 2nd ed. New York: MacMillan, 1994.

Gibb, Sir Hamilton. *Mohammedanism: A Historical Survey*. Oxford: Oxford University Press, 1969.

The Qur'an

Arberry, Arthur J. *The Koran Interpreted*. New York: Touchstone, 1996 (reprint).

Sells, Michael. *Approaching the Qur'an: The Early Revelations*. Ashland, Oregon: White Cloud Press, 1999.

Watt, William Montgomery. *Bell's Introduction to the Qur'an*. Edinburgh: Edinburgh University Press Paperbacks, 1977.

The Prophet Muhammad

Guilleaume, A. *The Life of Muhammad: A Translation of Ibn Ishaq's Sirat Rasul Allah*. Oxford: Oxford University Press, 1978.

Rodinson, Maxime. *Muhammad: An Introduction to the Life and Message of the Prophet*. Trans. Ann Carter. New York: The New Press, 2000.

Islamic History and Civilization

Hodgson, Marshall. *The Venture of Islam*: Conscience and History in a World Civilization. 3 Vols. Chicago: Chicago University Press, 1974.

Leaman, Oliver. *A Brief Introduction to Islamic Philosophy.* Cambridge, U.K.: Polity Press, 2000.

Rosenthal, Franz. *The Classical Heritage of Islam.* London: Routledge, 1992.

von Grünebaum, Gustav. *Classical Islam: A History 600-1258.* Trans. Katherine Watson. Chicago: Aldine Publishing Co., 1970.

Sufism

Ernst, Carl W. *The Shambala Guide to Sufism.* Boston: Shambala Publications, 1997.

Fadiman, James, and Robert Frager, eds. *Essential Sufism.* San Francisco: Harper San Francisco, 1997.

Schimmel, Annemarie. *Mystical Dimensions of Islam.* Chapel Hill: University of North Carolina Press, 1975.

Current Trends

Cooper, John, Ronald L. Nettler, and Mohamed Mahmoud, eds. *Islam and Modernity: Muslim Intellectuals Respond.* London and New York: I.B. Tauris, 2000.

Esposito, John, and John O. Voll, eds. *Makers of Contemporary Islam.* Oxford and New York: Oxford University Press, 2001.

Kepel, Gilles, *Jihad: The Trail of Political Islam.* Trans. Anthony F. Roberts. Cambridge, Mass.: The Belknap Press of Harvard University Press, 2002.

Kurzman, Charles, ed. *Liberal Islam: A Sourcebook.* Oxford and New York: Oxford University Press, 1998.

Ruthven, Marlise. *A Fury for God: The Islamist Attack on America.* London and New York: Granta, 2002.

General

Armstrong, Karen. *A History of God: The 4,000-Year Quest of Judaism, Christianity and Islam.* New York: Gramercy Books, 2004.

Eck, Diana. *On Common Ground: World Religions in America.* New York: Columbia University Press, 2001.

Küng, Hans. *Tracing the Way: Spiritual Dimensions of the World Religions.* U.K. and U.S.A.: Continuum, 2001.

About the Authors

John Butt

Buddhism

John W. Butt is currently the director of the Institute for the Study of Religion and Culture at Payap University in Chiang Mai, Thailand. He holds a B.A. from Rhodes College (Southwestern at Memphis), an S.T.B. (M.Div.) and an S.T.M. from Harvard University, where he also completed course work for a Th.D. in the Comparative Study of Religion.

Previously, Professor Butt served as a teaching fellow at Harvard University, a member of the faculty at Macalester College, and as visiting professor at Waseda University, Tokyo, where he was the resident director of the Associated Colleges of the Midwest and the Great Lakes Colleges Association's Japan Studies Program.

John Butt is an ordained minister of the Presbyterian Church (U.S.A.) and serves as a co-worker in the Mission of the Presbyterian Church (U.S.A.) assigned to work with the main Protestant Christian Church in Thailand (The Church of Christ in Thailand).

His published writings include: "Thai Kingship and Religious Reform," in *Religion and Legitimation of Power in Thailand, Laos, and Burma*; "The Challenge of Interreligious Understanding for Asian Christian Colleges and Universities: The Payap University Example," in *Quest: An Interdisciplinary Journal for Asian Christian Scholars*; and "The Role of the Christian Missionary," in *Socially Engaged Spirituality: Essays in Honor of Sulaksivaraksa on His 70th Birthday*. He currently serves as a member of the editorial board of *Quest*.

Linda A. Chisholm

Editor

Linda Armstrong Chisholm is the founder, with Howard Berry, of The International Partnership for Service-Learning and Leadership. She served first as co-director, then executive vice president, and upon Howard Berry's death in 2002, became the president of the International Partnership. She attended Vassar College, earned a B.A. and M.A. in history from the University of Tulsa, and the Ph.D. in Higher Education Research from Columbia University. She also served as president of the Association of Episcopal Colleges from 1985 to 2001, during which years she founded and served as first general secretary of Colleges and Universities of the Anglican Communion. She is the author of *Charting a Hero's Journey* (2000) and, with Howard Berry, *Understanding the Education – And Through It the Culture – in Education Abroad* (2002); *Service-Learning in Higher Education Around the World: An Initial Look* (1999); and *How to Serve and Learn Effectively: Students Tell Students* (1992). Dr. Chisholm has been awarded the D.D. (hon.) from the General Theological Seminary, in New York City; the D.H.L. (hon.) by Cuttington University College, Suacoco, Liberia; and a University Fellowship (hon.) by the University of Surrey Roehampton, London. She was a trustee, vice chair and chair of the United Board for Christian Higher Education in Asia, and served as a trustee of the Harvard-Yenching Institute.

Elliot N. Dorff
Judaism

Elliot Dorff was ordained a Conservative rabbi by the Jewish Theological Seminary of America in 1970 and earned his Ph.D. in philosophy from Columbia University in 1971 with a dissertation in moral theory. Since then he has directed the rabbinical and Masters programs at the University of Judaism, where he currently is rector and distinguished professor of Philosophy. He also teaches a course on Jewish law at U.C.L.A. School of Law as a Visiting Professor.

Rabbi Dorff is a member of the Conservative Movement's Committee on Jewish Law and Standards and the editorial committee of the new Torah commentary for the Conservative Movement. His papers have formulated the validated stance of the Conservative Movement on infertility treatments and on end-of-life issues, and his Rabbinic Letters on human sexuality and on poverty have become the voice of the Conservative Movement on those topics. He has chaired two scholarly organizations, the Academy of Jewish Philosophy and the Jewish Law Association. In spring, 1993, he served on the Ethics Committee of Hillary Rodham Clinton's Health Care Task Force; in March, 1997, and May, 1999, he testified on behalf of the Jewish tradition on the subjects of human cloning and stem-cell research before the President's National Bioethics Advisory Commission; in 1999 and 2000, he was part of the Surgeon General's commission to draft a Call to Action for Responsible Sexual Behavior; and from 2000 to 2002, he served on a commission charged with reviewing and revising the federal guidelines for protecting human subjects in research projects.

In Los Angeles, he is a member of the Board of Jewish Family Service, and he is a member of the Ethics committees at the Jewish Homes for the Aging and U.C.L.A. Medical Center. He serves as co-chair of the Priest-Rabbi Dialogue sponsored by the Los Angeles Archdiocese and the Board of Rabbis of Southern California, and he is a vice-president of the Academy for Jewish, Christian, and Muslim Studies.

Rabbi Dorff's publications include over 150 articles on Jewish thought, law, and ethics, together with ten books, including: *Jewish Law and Modern Ideology* (1970); *Conservative Judaism: Our Ancestors to Our Descendants* (1977; second, revised edition: 1996); *A Living Tree: The Roots and Growth of Jewish Law* (1988) (with Arthur Rosett); *Mitzvah Means Commandment* (1989); *Knowing God: Jewish Journeys to the Unknowable* (1992); *Contemporary Jewish Ethics and Morality: A Reader* (1995) (edited with Louis E. Newman); *Matters of Life and Death: A Jewish Approach to Modern Medical Ethics* (1998); *Contemporary Jewish Theology: A Reader* (1999) (edited with Louis E. Newman); *To Do the Right and the Good: A Jewish Approach to Modern Social Ethics* (2002); and *Love Your Neighbor and Yourself: A Jewish Approach to Modern Personal Ethics* (2003).

Rabbi Dorff is married and has four children and two grandchildren—may their number increase!

Carool Kersten

Islam

Carool Kersten directs a study-abroad program, teaches history, and occasionally lectures on things Islamic at Payap University in Chiang Mai, Thailand. A native of the Netherlands, he holds the equivalent of a Master's Degree (*cum laude*) in Arabic Language and Culture, with a specialization in Islamic Studies, from the University of Nijmegen (1987), and a Certificate in Southeast Asian Studies from Payap University (2001). In addition, he is a sworn translator accredited with the Dutch District Courts (1988). During a sabbatical year (1995–1996) he did advanced work in philosophy.

While in university he served as secretary of the Middle East Committee of a Dutch political youth organization, co-authoring a booklet on the Arab–Israeli conflict, drafting a conference resolution, and representing the organization on two occasions in official delegations visiting Cairo, Tunis, and the Polisario refugee camps in Southern Algeria.

Following his graduation, he spent four months studying colloquial Arabic in Egypt, before embarking on a career in business. He worked for more than ten years in Saudi Arabia with an international contractor as a professional translator, personnel officer, and, finally, human resources manager for the company's Middle East operations. He has also acted as a freelance translator and consultant on cross-cultural and Middle Eastern affairs.

Returning to the academic world in early 2001, he focused his research interests on Islamic thought and intellectual history, Islam in Southeast Asia, and the European expansion in Southeast Asia. He is the author of *Strange Events in the Kingdoms of Cambodia and Laos (1635-1644),* an account of early Dutch activities in mainland Southeast Asia. Other writings on topics pertaining to the Middle East, Islam, and Southeast Asia have appeared in both English- and Dutch-language periodicals and journals.

He and his wife Nida, daughter Melanie, and son Christopher currently live in Chiang Mai.

Kalyan Ray

Hinduism

Kalyan Ray, a native of India, was educated at Presidency College, Calcutta, and at Delhi University, after which he taught at St. Stephen's College in Delhi and selected post-graduate courses at Delhi University. In the U.S., where he earned a Ph.D. at the University of Rochester, he has taught at Queens College of the City University of New York, William Paterson College (now University) of New Jersey, and is currently ranked professor at the County College of Morris in Western New Jersey; he has also taught courses in World Religions at Centenary College, New Jersey. As an invited scholar, Dr. Ray has spoken before academic bodies in Greece, the Czech Republic, Jamaica, Ecuador, Mexico, and Thailand. He has been a visiting professor of Comparative Theology at a multi-national seminar funded by the Henry Luce Foundation at Trinity College in the Philippines, where he has also addressed several college convocations.

Dr. Ray has served on several occasions as advisor to the New Jersey Council for the Humanities. From 2002 to 2004, he gave a series of lectures on Sacred Writings of the World at the Bernards Library in New Jersey.

In addition to his publications in literary criticism journals, Kalyan Ray is a published poet. His English poems have appeared in publications including the *Beloit Poetry Journal*; his Bengali poems and short stories have appeared in such prestigious journals as *Sananda*, *Desh*, and the annual autumn anthology *Sharadiya Desh*.

Kalyan Ray's list of publications include books of translated poetry, most notably Sankha Ghosh's *Emperor Babur's Prayer and Other Poems* (with a critical introduction by Dr. Ray), published by Sahitya Akademi, the National Academy of Letters of the Government of India; Sunil Gangopadhyay's *City of Memories* (published by Viking Penguin), which includes a preface by Allen Ginsberg and a critical introduction by Kalyan Ray; *The Grey Manuscript: Selected Poems of Jibanananda Das*, who was the most important Indian poet in the post-Tagore period. He has given numerous readings of his translations in many academic institutions, including Harvard University.

Kalyan Ray recently completed a novel, *EastWords*, which is slated for publication by Penguin India in December 2004, in time for the biannual International Shakespeare Conference, where it will be a featured book for discussion at a half-day special session, since the post-colonial novel deals with several Shakespearean themes.

For the past sixteen years, Dr. Kalyan Ray has directed the India Program of the International Partnership for Service-Learning and Leadership based in Kolkata, where he also serves as an honorary faculty member and advisor of the Tagore-Gandhi Institute for Culture Studies and Service-Learning.

Kalyan Ray is married to Aparna Sen, the distinguished film director; between them they have three very opinionated daughters and an autistic son.

David Kwang-sun Suh

Christianity

Dr. David Kwang-sun Suh is the founding executive director of the Asian Christian Higher Education Institute, established in 2001 as a new initiative of the United Board for Christian Higher Education in Asia. The Institute's mission is to identify, support, and coordinate programs to strengthen a Christian presence in the academic communities of Asia by facilitating institutional cooperation in developing leadership training for administrators, networks for Christian faculty, student exchange programs, interfaith dialogue, reflection on the varieties of Asian Christian identities, women's studies, service-learning programs, curricula, and degree programs.

Before becoming the Institute's executive director, Dr. Suh served as professor of philosophy and theology and as dean of the chapel and the graduate school at Ewha Womans University in Seoul, Korea. In 1996, after retiring from Ewha Womans University, Dr. Suh was the Henry Luce Visiting Professor of World Christianity at Union Theological Seminary in New York. He then served on the faculty of Drew University Theological School in New Jersey before returning to Asia.

Ordained as a minister of the Presbyterian Church of Korea in 1982, Dr. Suh's career also includes service as the president of the World Alliance of YMCAs, membership on the Commission of Theological Education of the World Council of Churches, chair of the Korean Student Christian Federation, and commission member of the National Council of Churches in Korea.

Dr. Suh has written more than ten books, including the widely-acclaimed *Korean Minjung in Christ,* and published hundreds of articles. He received his Master of Divinity degree from Union Theological Seminary in New York and a Ph.D. from Vanderbilt University in Nashville, Tennessee, U.S.

Also available from the IPSL Press:

Charting a Hero's Journey
by Linda A. Chisholm

Based on the work of Joseph Campbell and using excerpts from the journals of such people as Jane Addams, Langston Hughes, Octavio Paz, Samuel Johnson, Mary Kingsley, and Kathleen Norris, *Charting a Hero's Journey* is a guide to the writing of a journal for college students engaged in study abroad, off-campus study, and/or service-learning. 2000.

Understanding the Education— and through It the culture— in Education Abroad
by Linda A. Chisholm and Howard A. Berry

Based on the premise that an educational system both reflects and shapes a culture, this book is a guide for students going abroad to study. It leads them step-by-step through an in-depth investigation of the university they attend overseas and higher education in their host country. The study will help them both to be a successful student and to come to a deeper knowledge of their host culture. 2002.

How to Serve & Learn Abroad Effectively: Students Tell Students
by Howard A. Berry and Linda A. Chisholm

Based on the experiences and reflections of over 1,000 students who served and learned through The International Partnership for Service-Learning, the authors have organized the students' advice into a lively and readable book that helps current students to choose a study abroad and/or volunteer program that is right for them and then give and get the most through their community service at home or abroad. It is also useful to those who advise, orient, and re-enter study abroad students. 1992.

Service-Learning in Higher Education Around the World: An Initial Look
a report by Howard A. Berry and Linda A. Chisholm

This report, supported by the Ford Foundation, is the first international survey of service-learning. In addition to describing models of service-learning programs, it gives examples of service-learning from over 100 institutions in 33 countries. 1999.

Leadership and Democracy
by Adel Safty

How do leadership and democracy intersect, and what are the qualities of leadership in a world of democratic empowerment? Professor Adel Safty, Permanent UNESCO Chair in International Leadership and a superb observer of the world political scene, offers a panoramic view of the state of democracy across the world. 2004.

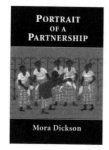

Portrait of a Partnership
by Mora Dickson

This book, the last of many written by Mora Dickson, documents her life with Alec Dickson, founder of Voluntary Service Overseas, the British organization upon which John F. Kennedy modeled the U.S. Peace Corps. 2004.

Knowing and Doing
edited by Linda A. Chisholm

This book is a collection of the papers and speeches of Howard A. Berry, the founder and first president of the International Partnership for Service-Learning, and papers about international service-learning in honor of his memory. 2005.

For more information about IPSL publications, visit www.ipsl.org or e-mail publications@ipsl.org.